ENCYCLOPEDIA OF THE U.S. AIR FORCE

Alan Axelrod

Checkmark Books
An imprint of Infobase Publishing

Encyclopedia of the U.S. Air Force

Checkmark Books
An imprint of Infobase Publishing
132 West 31st Street
New York NY 10001

Library of Congress Cataloging-in-Publication Data

Axelrod, Alan, 1952–
Encyclopedia of the U.S. Air Force / Alan Axelrod.
p. cm.
Includes index.
ISBN 0-8160-4713-8 (pb:alk. paper)
1. United States. Air Force—Encyclopedias—Juvenile literature.
2. United States. Air Force—Biography—Juvenile literature. I. Title.

UF633.A94 2006
358.400973'03—dc22   2005027688

Checkmark Books are available at special discounts when purchased in bulk quantities for businesses, associations, institutions, or sales promotions. Please call our Special Sales Department in New York at (212) 967-8800 or (800) 322-8755.

You can find Facts On File on the World Wide Web at http://www.factsonfile.com

Text design by Joan M. Toro
Text design adapted by Erika K. Arroyo
Cover design by Dorothy Preston

Printed in the United States of America

VB FOF 10 9 8 7 6 5 4 3 2 1

This book is printed on acid-free paper.

Contents

List of Entries
UNITED STATES AIR FORCE

★ ────────────────────────────────

Aerial Achievement Medal   See DECORA-
TIONS AND MEDALS.

Aeronautical Division, U.S. Army Signal Corps

Established on August 1, 1907, the Aeronautical Division of the U.S. Army Signal Corps was the earliest antecedent organization of the USAF. The commanding officer was Captain CHARLES DEFOR-EST CHANDLER, who was assigned two enlisted men—one of whom deserted.

The Aeronautical Division was primarily concerned with balloon operations (see BALLOONS AND DIRIGIBLES) until 1911. In July 1914, it was replaced by the AVIATION SECTION, U.S. ARMY SIGNAL CORPS.

Aerospace Defense Command (ADC)

Originally designated the Air Defense Command when it was established in 1946, the ADC was replaced during 1948–51 by CONTINENTAL AIR COMMAND (CONAC), then reestablished in 1951 as a MAJCOM. Its redesignation as the Aerospace Defense Command (ADC) came in 1965. ADC was responsible for the air defense of the continental United States, and, when NORAD was activated in 1957, integrating U.S. defense with that of Canada, ADC became a part of this command.

Over the years, the role of ADC was increasingly transferred to the AIR NATIONAL GUARD and the AIR FORCE RESERVE, and ADC was inactivated in 1980.

African Americans in the U.S. Air Force

African Americans have served in every war fought by the United States since the American Revolution. Typically, however, much of that service was performed in segregated units, and African Americans were afforded little opportunity to attain officer status or, indeed, to progress very far in a military career. Some 900,000 African Americans served during WORLD WAR II, mainly in the army. The exigencies of the war, however, together with a desire to demonstrate opposition to Nazi racist ideology, motivated the U.S. Coast Guard and, to a lesser extent, the U.S. Navy to integrate shipboard service. The marines and the army, including the U.S. ARMY AIR FORCES, remained segregated.

In 1940, President Franklin D. Roosevelt promoted Colonel BENJAMIN O. DAVIS, Sr., to brigadier general—the first African American of this rank—and opened the U.S. ARMY AIR CORPS to black pilots. One of these men, Davis's son, Benjamin O. Davis, Jr., was among the first of the TUSKEGEE AIRMEN, a segregated unit of African-American fighter pilots trained at an airfield established at the Tuskegee Institute in Alabama. The Tuskegee Airmen served with distinction in the North African and Italian theaters, but they remained segregated throughout the war.

In 1948, President Harry S. Truman issued Executive Order 9981, which mandated an end to segregation in the military and a universal policy of equal treatment and opportunity regardless of race. Among the services, the USAF (an independent service as of 1947) stood at the forefront of implementing the integration policy. The army and the marines continued to maintain all-black units until 1951, during the KOREAN WAR—although the officer corps remained overwhelmingly white. As of 2005, African Americans make up about 15 percent of the total USAF population. Six percent of USAF officer are African American.

In 1975 Daniel "Chappie" James, Jr., one of the Tuskegee Airmen of World War II, became the first African-American four-star general in the USAF. In 1973, Thomas N. Barnes became the USAF's first African American CHIEF MASTER SERGEANT OF THE AIR FORCE, the highest noncommissioned rank in the service.

Air Combat Command (ACC)

ACC is a MAJCOM responsible for fighters, bombers, and reconnaissance aircraft based in the continental United States (CONUS) and for CONUS command, control, communications, and intelligence platforms. ACC also controls some theater AIRLIFT and tanker/refueling operations. ACC provides forces to unified commands and augments theater forces already deployed.

ACC was created in 1992 from elements of STRATEGIC AIR COMMAND (SAC), TACTICAL AIR COMMAND (TAC), and MILITARY AIRLIFT COMMAND

Gunners of the U.S. Fifth Air Force in Korea, September 1952   *(National Archives and Records Administration)*

A KC-135R Stratotanker has just refueled an F-16 Fighting Falcon. Three more F-16s wait their turn, as does an F-15C Eagle (the plane with the twin vertical stabilizers). *(U.S. Air Force)*

(MAC). It is headquartered at Langley AFB, Virginia.

Air Corps Act of 1926

On the recommendation of the President's Advisory Board, the Air Corps Act of 1926 raised the U.S. ARMY AIR SERVICE to a corps and renamed it the U.S. ARMY AIR CORPS. The act created the post of assistant secretary of war (for air), provided for air sections on the general staff, and authorized the addition of two general officers as assistant chiefs of the air corps. Rank, promotion, and pay status were raised for USAAC officers and enlisted men, and a five-year program was introduced to expand the USAAC from 919 to 1,650 officers, from 8,725 to 15,000 enlisted men, and from 1,254 aircraft to 1,800.

The approach and onset of the Great Depression reduced the funding authorized by the Air Corps Act by 55 percent, which meant that the goals of the five-year program were not realized by 1931; however, the quality, if not the quantity, of USAAC aircraft was substantially improved under the act.

Air Corps Training Center, San Antonio

Pursuant to the AIR CORPS ACT OF 1926, Brigadier General FRANK P. LAHM was put in command of U.S. ARMY AIR CORPS training. He wanted to concentrate training at a single airfield, and, in 1929, construction began on Randolph Field outside of San Antonio, Texas. The base became headquarters of the Air Corps Training Center in 1931 and, dubbed the "West Point of the Air," handled all primary flight training. Advanced flight training remained at Kelly Field, Texas. With the expansion of the USAAC in 1938 and later, training was extended to other facilities, and the mission of Randolph Field became mainly the training of instructor pilots. Further expansion of the USAAC in 1940 brought extensive reorganization of training under a new Training and Operations Division of the Office, Chief of Air Corps, and three Air Corps Training Centers were established, at Maxwell Field, Alabama, at Moffett Field, California, and at Randolph.

aircraft, cold war and after

The cold war spanned roughly 1948 through the collapse of the Soviet Union in 1991. This period encompasses the KOREAN WAR and the VIETNAM WAR (see AIRCRAFT, KOREAN WAR and AIRCRAFT, VIETNAM WAR), and some of the aircraft described in this article were used in those conflicts; however, most of the aircraft included here were intended primarily for strategic roles or other roles directly related to cold war conflicts.

Attack (designated "A") Aircraft

A-10 Thunderbolt II: Korea, Vietnam, and various "brushfire" conflicts of the cold war period pointed up the need for the strategically oriented USAF to add specially designed tactical aircraft to its inventory. The A/OA-10 Thunderbolt II was the first USAF aircraft specially designed for CLOSE AIR SUPPORT of ground forces. The aircraft has excellent maneuverability at low air speeds and altitude and serves as a highly accurate weapons-delivery platform. Advanced electronics give A-10s night-vision capability, and redundant primary structural sections endow it with the kind of survivability necessary in close air support. Armament includes a 30-mm GAU-8/A Gatling gun, which can fire 3,900 rounds a minute, and AGM-65 Maverick and AIM-9 Sidewinder missiles (see MISSILES, TACTICAL).

Fairchild Republic delivered the first production A-10A in October 1975. The aircraft saw extensive service in the PERSIAN GULF WAR, launching 90 percent of the AGM-65 Maverick missiles used in the conflict. Top speed is 420 mph, ceiling is 45,000 feet, and range is 800 miles. The aircraft can carry up to 16,000 pounds of mixed ordnance on eight underwing and three under-fuselage pylon stations,

The XB-70 Valkyrie lands on the main, 15,000-foot runway of Edwards AFB, California, during the 1960s. *(U.S. Air Force)*

including 500 pounds of Mk-82 and 2,000 pounds of Mk-84 series low/high drag bombs, incendiary cluster bombs, combined effects munitions, mine dispensing munitions, AGM-65 Maverick missiles, and laser-guided/electro-optically guided bombs, infrared countermeasure flares, electronic counter-measure chaff, jammer pods, 2.75-inch (6.99-centimeter) rockets, illumination flares, and AIM-9 Sidewinder missiles.

Bomber (designated "B") Aircraft

B-52 Stratofortress (see AIRCRAFT, VIETNAM WAR)

B-57 Canberra: The Martin Company derived, under licenses, the B-57 from a British design, English Electric's Canberra B.Mk.2, and it was thus the only non-U.S. design used in the USAF after WORLD WAR II. The B-57A first flew in 1953 and entered service the following year. Sixteen B-57Bs were later converted for night intruder operations and 11 aircraft saw Vietnam service. Most extensively used in operations directly relating to the cold war was the reconnaissance version, the RB-57D, which was the principal USAF "spy" plane before the U-2. Other Canberras were converted into EB-57Es, for aerospace electronic warfare. The last Canberras left service (with the AIR NATIONAL GUARD) in 1982. Top speed was 598 mph, service ceiling was 40,100 feet, and range was 2,300 miles. The Canberra could carry 9,200 pounds of bombs, including nuclear weapons.

B-70 Valkyrie: Conceived in the 1950s, the B-70 was intended for use by the STRATEGIC AIR COMMAND (SAC) as its principal high-altitude bomber, which could fly at Mach 3, and would replace the subsonic B-52 as a nuclear weapons delivery platform. Funding cutbacks aborted production, however, and only two were built, with XB-70 designations, indicating their status as research aircraft for the advanced study of aerodynamics, propulsion, and other issues related to large supersonic aircraft. The Valkyrie was built largely of stainless-steel honeycomb sandwich panels and titanium. The Number 1 XB-70 made its initial flight on September 21, 1964, and achieved Mach 3 flight on October 14, 1965. The Number 2 airplane first flew on July 17, 1965, but crashed on June 8,

1966, following a mid-air collision. Number 1 was retired on February 4, 1969.

This beautiful aircraft has a delta-wing span of 105 feet and a fuselage length of almost 186 feet. Its six jet engines propel it to a top speed of 2,056 mph (Mach 3.1). Range is 4,288 miles and service ceiling is 77,350 feet.

B-1 Lancer: The B-1, now the backbone of the USAF's long-range bomber force, had a difficult birth. The original B-1A model never went into production, although the USAF acquired four prototype flight test models in the 1970s and continued tests through 1981. In that year, President Ronald Reagan approved production of the improved variant B-1B, and the first production model flew in October 1984, with the first delivery made in June 1985. The final B-1B was delivered on May 2, 1988.

The B-1B is of an advanced blended wing/body configuration, and it features variable-geometry design to maximize performance at sub- and supersonic speeds. The aircraft was first used in combat against Iraq during Operation Desert Fox in December 1998. The aircraft have been used in Operation Allied Force and in the campaign in Afghanistan in response to the September 11, 2001, terrorist attacks on the United States. Built by Boeing, the B-1B has a top speed in excess of 900 mph and an intercontinental range. Its service ceiling is in excess of 30,000 feet. Three internal weapons bays can accommodate up to 84 Mk-82 general purpose bombs or Mk-62 naval mines, 30 CBU-87/89 cluster munitions or CBU-97 sensor-fused weapons and up to 24 GBU-31 JDAM GPS guided bombs or Mk-84 general purpose bombs. The USAF has acquired more than 70 of the aircraft.

B-2 Spirit: One of two radar-foiling "stealth" aircraft in the USAF inventory (see F-117 Nighthawk), the B-2 Spirit is a multirole bomber capable of delivering both conventional and nuclear munitions. The bomber's stealth characteristics (reduced infrared, acoustic, electromagnetic, visual, and radar signatures) make it ideal for penetrating deep into enemy airspace.

The aircraft was developed in deep secrecy, and the first B-2 was publicly displayed on November

22, 1988. Its first flight came on July 17, 1989, and the first operational aircraft was delivered on December 17, 1993. The principal contractor is Northrop Grumman Integrated Systems Sector, with Boeing Military Airplanes Company, Hughes Radar Systems Group, General Electric Aircraft Engine Group, and Vought Aircraft Industries, Inc. Capable of reaching high subsonic speeds, with a service ceiling of 50,000 feet, the B-2 carries a 40,000-pound payload of conventional or nuclear weapons. The USAF inventory includes 21 operational aircraft, in addition to one test aircraft.

Cargo and Transport (designated "C") Aircraft

C-10A Extender: This modification of the McDonnell Douglas DC-10 commercial transport for military tanker and cargo use first flew in 1980, with active service beginning the next year; 59 were built. The three-engine jet aircraft can carry a 169,000-pound payload over 4,370 miles at about 600 mph and to a service ceiling of 42,000 feet.

C-17A Globemaster: The Boeing C-17 is capable of rapid strategic delivery of troops and all types of cargo to main operating bases or directly to forward bases in the deployment area. In addition, the aircraft can perform tactical airlift and airdrop missions. Measuring 174 feet long with a wingspan of 169 feet, 10 inches, the aircraft is powered by four jet engines. Cargo is loaded through a large aft door that accommodates military vehicles and palletized cargo, to a maximum payload of 170,900 pounds. Unrefueled range is 2,400 nautical miles; cruise speed is approximately 450 knots (.74 Mach). Despite its size, the aircraft can operate through short, poorly improved airfields.

First flight was on September 15, 1991, and the first production model was delivered on June 14, 1993.

C-18: This designation was applied to eight Boeing 707-323Cs acquired by the USAF from American Airlines for training and support missions. They were subsequently modified as EC-18B Advanced Range Instrumentation Aircraft, for use in the U.S. space program as telemetry platforms. Two were further modified to

EC-18C Joint STAR aircraft (see E-8A Joint STARS, below).

C-25: These two aircraft are military variants of the Boeing 747-200 "jumbo jet" commercial transports. Further modified as VC-25A in 1990, they are used for presidential airlift as AIR FORCE ONE. The aircraft are capable of in-air refueling.

C-47 Skytrain (see AIRCRAFT, WORLD WAR II)

C-54 Skymaster (see AIRCRAFT, WORLD WAR II)

C-121 Constellation (see AIRCRAFT, KOREAN WAR)

C-135 Stratolifter: The Boeing C-135 Stratolifter was the first USAF strategic jet transport. It went into service in 1961. Although originally designed as a cargo transport, 732 of 820 actually built were tankers. Others were converted for use in a variety of roles: In 1961, the Strategic Air Command (SAC) used an EC-135 conversion as the "Looking Glass" electronic warfare aircraft, an airborne command and control post to be used in the event that the SAC underground command center and other alternates were lost. Although the last plane was delivered in 1965, special reconnaissance missions still use RC-135s, and another modification, the NKC-135A, is flown in test programs for AIR FORCE SYSTEMS COMMAND (AFSC). AIR COMBAT COMMAND (ACC) operates the OC-135s as an observation platform in compliance with the Open Skies Treaty. Top speed is 600 mph, service ceiling, 45,000 feet, and range, 4,625. The aircraft can carry 126 troops or 44 litter patients and 48 ambulatory, with six attendants.

C-137 and VC-137: Based on the Boeing 707-153, the C-137 is a military passenger transport. In 1959, a VC-137 became the first jet aircraft to be used for presidential airlift as Air Force One. Modified as EC-137Ds, the aircraft became the backbone of the AWACS system. See E-3 Sentry (AWACS), next.

Electronic Warfare (designated "E") Aircraft

E-3 Sentry (AWACS): The E-3 Sentry is an airborne warning and control system (AWACS) aircraft that provides all-weather surveillance, command, control, and communications needed by commanders of U.S., NATO, and other allied air defense forces. The E-3 Sentry is a modified Boeing 707/320 commercial airframe equipped most conspicuously with a large rotating radar dome housing a radar subsystem that permits surveillance from the earth's surface up into the stratosphere, over land or water. The E-3 fleet is continuously upgraded with cutting-edge electronics to gather and present broad and detailed battlefield information in real time.

Engineering, test, and evaluation began on the first E-3 Sentry in October 1975; first deliveries came in March 1977. The USAF has 33 E-3s in its inventory. The aircraft's optimum cruising speed is 360 mph with a ceiling above 29,000 feet. Unrefueled endurance is in excess of eight hours.

E-4: This modification of the Boeing 747-200 commercial transport was selected for service as the Advanced Airborne National Command Post (AANCP), the communications link between the U.S. National Command Authority and the armed forces. The latest iteration is the E-4B. Like the C-25 and VC-25, these aircraft can be refueled in flight for unlimited endurance.

E-8A Joint STARS: A modification of ED-18D aircraft (also see *C-137 and VC-137*), two aircraft serve in the Joint Surveillance and Target Attack Radar System (Joint STARS) mission. The E-8A first flew in 1988. A joint undertaking of the USAF and U.S. Army, JSTARS directs attacks by ground forces with extreme precision. The aircraft performed extraordinary service in the Persian Gulf War, and, as of 2002, a program was under way to build at least 22 E-8As.

Fighter (designated "F") Aircraft

F-106 Delta Dart: This all-weather interceptor was developed by Convair from its F-102 "Delta Dagger" and was originally designated the F-102B. The first flight was December 26, 1956, and deliveries to the USAF began in July 1959. Production ended in late 1960, after 277 F-106As and 63 F-106Bs had been built. Top speed was 1,525 mph, range, 1,500 miles, and service ceiling, 53,000 feet.

F-15 Eagle: This all-weather air-superiority fighter was built by McDonnell during the early 1970s and first flew in July 1972. Deliveries began in November 1974. The single-seat F-15C and two-seat F-15D models entered the USAF inventory beginning in 1979. The aircraft have been continuously upgraded with an improved central computer; a programmable armament control set, allowing for advanced versions of the AIM-7, AIM-9, and AIM-120A missiles; and an expanded tactical electronic warfare system, which provides improvements to the ALR-56C radar warning receiver and ALQ-135 countermeasure set; and a highly advanced radar system. F-15C, D, and E models were deployed during the Persian Gulf War and achieved a confirmed 26:0 kill ratio, accounting for 36 of the 39 USAF air-to-air victories. Top speed of the F-15 is 1,875 mph, ceiling is 65,000 feet, and range is 3,450 with conformal fuel tanks and three external fuel tanks. The aircraft is typically armed with one internally mounted M-61A1 20-mm six-barrel cannon with 940 rounds of ammunition; four AIM-9L/M Sidewinder and four AIM-7F/M Sparrow air-to-air missiles, or eight AIM-120 AMRAAMs, carried externally.

F-16 Fighting Falcon: The sleek, compact, highly agile F-16 is a multirole fighter used in air-to-air combat and air-to-surface attack. The F-16A first flew in December 1976, and the first operational F-16A was delivered in January 1979. The F-16B is a two-seat model with tandem cockpits. Many iterations have kept the F-16 at the cutting edge of avionics and weapons delivery. In the Persian Gulf War, F-16s flew more sorties than any other aircraft and were used to attack airfields, military production facilities, Scud missiles sites, and a variety of other targets. Produced by Lockheed Martin, the F-16 reaches 1,500 mph and has a ceiling above 50,000 feet. Its ferry range exceeds 2,000 miles. Typically, the aircraft is armed with one M-61A1 20-mm multibarrel cannon with 500 rounds; external stations can carry up to six air-to-air missiles, conventional air-to-air and air-to-surface munitions, and electronic countermeasure pods.

F-111 Aardvark: Development of the F-111 took place amid much controversy over effectiveness and cost. Its principal feature is its variable-

An F-16C Fighting Falcon banks right, revealing the dome of its ordnance load.   *(U.S. Air Force)*

sweep wings, which allow the pilot to fly from slow approach speeds to supersonic velocity at sea level and more than twice the speed of sound at higher altitudes. Using internal fuel only, the plane has a range of more than 2,500 nautical miles and can carry conventional as well as nuclear weapons. The aircraft first flew in December 1964 and delivery began in October 1967. Some aircraft were used in Vietnam. F-111F models were deployed during the Persian Gulf War. The last F model was delivered to the USAF in November 1976.

The F-111F reaches Mach 2.5 at its ceiling of 60,000 feet and has a range of 3,565 miles with external fuel tanks. It can carry up to four nuclear bombs on four pivoting wing pylons, and two in an internal weapons bay. Wing pylons carry a total external load of 25,000 pounds of bombs, rockets, missiles, or fuel tanks. After 30 years of service, the F-111 was retired in 1997.

F-117A Nighthawk: The F-117A Nighthawk was the world's first "stealth" aircraft, designed to be virtually invisible to radar, infrared, and other detection technologies. A single-seat, twin-engine fighter, the F-117A was first delivered in 1982 by Lockheed. The last delivery was in the summer of 1990. Its exact speed is classified, but known to be in the high subsonic range. It was used with great success in the Persian Gulf War and in subsequent conflicts.

YF-22 Raptor: In conjunction with Lockheed Martin (now Lockheed-Boeing-General Dynamics) and Pratt and Whitney, Boeing developed the F-22 Raptor as a replacement for the F-15C. As of the end of 2001, USAF plans were to procure 339 F-22s, and production was scheduled to run through 2013. Budget constraints for F-Y2006 may limit acquisition to 180 aircraft at a staggering cost of $330 million each.

The stealthy air superiority fighter began delivery in November 2001. It first flew in May 1998. Maximum speed is in excess of Mach 1.8, and ceiling is above 50,000 feet.

Reconnaissance and Surveillance (designated "U" and "SR") Aircraft

U-2: The most famous "spy" plane in history, the peculiar designation of this Lockheed craft, "U," for "utility," was used to *disguise,* not to express, its

U-2 "Dragon Lady"   *(National Archives)*

purpose: high-altitude surveillance deep in enemy (primarily Soviet) airspace. The aircraft was a fixture of the cold war (made most famous when one, piloted by Francis Gary Powers, was shot down over the USSR in 1960), played a central role in the Cuban missile crisis of 1962, and served in Vietnam and the Persian Gulf War as well as other conflicts. The "Skunk Works" team of famed Lockheed designer Kelly Johnson began work on the U-2 in 1954, first flight was 1955, and delivery began soon

afterward. The U-2R, a major redesign, was executed in 1966.

The U-2 has a single jet and is relatively slow—top speed 528 mph—but capable of reaching very high altitude—70,000 feet. Its range is also great at 4,600 miles.

SR-71 "Blackbird": This "strategic reconnaissance" aircraft is one of aviation's truly spectacular achievements. With a maximum speed in excess of 2,000 mph, it is the fastest jet aircraft ever built. Its

The SR-71 Blackbird aircraft   *(National Archives)*

range is 2,900 miles, and its service ceiling is 85,000 feet, higher than any other conventional jct and at the very edge of what an air-breathing engine is capable of operating in. The first flight took place on December 22, 1964, and the first SR-71 entered service in January 1966. The fleet was retired on January 26, 1990, but some aircraft were returned to service in 1995 and began flying operational missions in January 1997. Recently, the SR-71 was permanently retired by the USAF, although NASA still uses one for experimental purposes.

From 80,000 feet, the SR-71 could survey 100,000 square miles of the earth's surface each hour. The jet is unarmed.

Helicopter (designated "H")

HH-60G Pave Hawk: The Sikorsky HH-60G Pave Hawk is designed to conduct day or night operations into hostile environments to recover downed aircrew or other isolated personnel during war. The helicopter also performs civil search and rescue, emergency aeromedical evacuation (MEDEVAC), disaster relief, international aid, counterdrug activities, and NASA space shuttle support. It is a highly modified version of the U.S. Army Black Hawk helicopter, with upgraded communications and navigation equipment, automatic flight control system, night vision goggles, and a forward looking infrared (FLIR) system. It can be refueled in flight and is armed with two crew-served 7.62-mm machine guns. The twin-engine helicopter achieves a 184 mph top speed and has a range of 445 miles (with in-air refueling, unlimited). It was first deployed in 1982. USAF inventory currently includes 64, with 18 in the Air National Guard, and 23 in the Air Force Reserve.

aircraft, interwar period (1919–1940)

Even after WORLD WAR I demonstrated the importance of the airplane in combat, the United States was slow to develop military aviation. The aircraft included in this entry are planes developed and *used* after World War I but before World War II. A number of famous planes were developed before World War II but were manufactured and used primarily during that war; these are treated in AIRCRAFT, WORLD WAR II.

Attack (designated "A") Aircraft

A-12 Shrike: Attack aircraft are primarily intended for the CLOSE AIR SUPPORT role. The A-12 entered service in 1932 as an all-metal monoplane built by Curtiss. It served into the early months of World War II—until 1942—and was capable of a 177 mph top speed with a 15,150-foot service ceiling. Its bomb load was 400 pounds.

A-17: The Northrup A-17 became the principal attack plane of the U.S. ARMY AIR CORPS during the interwar years. It entered service in 1935 and could hit 220 mph with a service ceiling of 19,400 feet. It carried 400 pounds in bombs.

Bomber (designated "B") Aircraft

Martin bombers: The series of bombers designed by Glenn Martin of the Glenn L. Martin Company immediately following World War I came in response to a U.S. ARMY AIR SERVICE order for a bomber superior to Britain's famed Handley Page. The MB-1 first flew in 1918, but it was never used as a bomber; a few were used as observation planes and at least one as a transport. The MB-2, derived from the MB-1, went into production in 1920. It was MB-2s that WILLIAM MITCHELL used in 1921 to demonstrate the effectiveness of aerial bombardment against large naval vessels. The aircraft carried a 2,000-pound bomb load at 99 mph to a ceiling of 8,500 feet.

Keystone Bomber: Used by the USAAS and then the U.S. ARMY AIR CORPS from 1923 to 1933, the Keystone Bomber (manufactured by the Keystone Aircraft Corporation) replaced the MB-2 and was produced in several versions. The LB-6 ("Light Bomber") achieved 114 mph and had a service ceiling of 11,650 feet. It carried a bomb load of 2,000 pounds and was especially significant as the vehicle the USAAC used to develop its early doctrine of strategic bombing (see BOMBING, STRATEGIC).

B-9: This Boeing design was the first all-metal monoplane bomber used by the USAAC. It was based on the design of the company's Model 200 Monomail commercial transport and first flew in

1931. The twin-engine craft had a top speed of 188 mph and a service ceiling of 20,750 feet. Bomb load was 2,260 pounds.

B-10: Built by the Glenn L. Martin Company, the twin-engine B-10 (followed by the B-12 and B-14) was the first *mass-produced* all-metal bomber used by the USAAC. The aircraft entered production in 1934 and was capable of 213 mph and could reach a service ceiling of 24,200 feet with a bomb load of 2,260 pounds.

B-15: Boeing built the four-engine B-15 in response to a USAAC order for a bomber that could hit targets as far away as Alaska and Hawaii. It first flew in 1937 and had a range of 5,130 miles, a top speed of 200 mph, and a service ceiling of 18,900 feet. Underpowered, it was not used as a bomber in World War II but did serve as a transport. Lessons learned in designing the aircraft were incorporated into the famed B-17 Flying Fortress, which is discussed in AIRCRAFT, WORLD WAR II.

B-18 Bolo: This Douglas Aircraft Company twin-engine design was intended to replace the B-10 by doubling its bomb load and range. Capable of flying at 215 mph, with a service ceiling of 10,000 feet, the B-18 could carry a 6,500-pound bomb load over a range of 1,150 miles. The USAAC ordered 217, making the B-18 the most common bomber in the service during the mid-1930s. Production stopped just before World War II, in 1940, but some were converted to transport use (as the C-58) during the war.

B-19: The Douglas B-19 never entered production, but, designed in 1935 and first flown in 1941, it was an important experiment in long-range bomber design and prefigured the B-29 of World War II and the B-36 of the KOREAN WAR and Cold War eras. The four-engine B-19 had a spectacular 212-foot wingspan, could hit 224 mph, reach 39,000 feet, and carry a 37,100-pound bomb load over 7,710 miles.

Fighter (designated "FM" for fighter, multiplace) and Pursuit (designated "P") Aircraft

FM-1 Airacuda: Bell Aircraft Corporation built only a dozen twin-engine Airacudas during the 1930s as long-range interceptors. The design was unique, with the props mounted as pushers rather than tractors and a gunner armed with a 37-mm and .30-caliber gun forward of each engine. In the fuselage, there were .50-caliber and .30-caliber guns as well. The Airacuda carried a small bomb load. Although faster (270 mph) than the bombers of the day, the Airacuda was not as fast as most single-engine pursuit and fighter craft.

P-1, P-3, P-5, P-6, P-23: These aircraft, all built by Curtiss, were the principal USAAC fighters (then designated "pursuit" planes) of the 1920s. The P-6 was the most advanced of this series (the P-23 was simply a modification of the P-6) and emerged in 1927. With a top speed of 193 mph, the P-6 had a service ceiling of 23,900 feet and a range of 244 miles. The Curtiss company called the series the "Hawks," but this never became an official USAAC designation.

P-12: This Boeing design first flew in 1929 and would be the last of the biplane fighters. The U.S. Navy also adopted the aircraft, as the F4B. The P-12 had a top speed of 189 mph and a service ceiling of 29,300 feet.

P-26: As the P-12 was the last biplane fighter in the USAAC inventory, so the P-26 was the first monoplane fighter produced for the service. Built by Boeing, it first flew in 1932 and was produced in a total quantity of 184. Top speed was 234 mph, with a service ceiling of 27,400 feet, and a range of 360 miles.

P-35: Designed by Seversky Aircraft Corporation (subsequently renamed Republic Aircraft Corporation), the P-35 was accepted by the USAAC in 1937; 77 were ordered before production ended in 1940. Forty-eight of these aircraft were lost when the Japanese attacked the Philippines in 1941. Capable of a 290 mph top speed and a 31,400-foot service ceiling, the P-35 had a range of 950 miles.

P-36: Curtiss-Wright received a USAAC contract for 210 P-36s, to that time, the largest order the service had ever placed. The all-aluminum aircraft was the USAAC's frontline fighter through the first months of World War II. It could reach 323 mph and attain a service ceiling of 32,700 feet. Range was 650 miles.

Observation (designated "O") Aircraft

O-1 Falcon: A Curtiss Aeroplane and Motor Company update of the kind of observation planes common in World War I, the O-1 Falcon was accepted by the USAAC in 1925 and was produced in relatively small numbers, but in several variations. Top speed was 140 mph; service ceiling, 15,300 feet.

O-47: A single-engine, canopied monoplane, this observation aircraft accommodated three crewmembers: pilot, observer, and gunner. General Aviation Company, renamed North American Aviation, began production in 1937, the first model flew the following year, and the plane became the standard observation craft for the USAAC. By the time World War II began, the O-47 was already obsolete. The plane could reach 221 mph and had a service ceiling of 23,200 feet.

Trainer (designated "PT," primary trainer) Aircraft

PT-1: Consolidated Aircraft Corporation built 171 PT-1s for USAAS and USAAC during the 1920s and into the 1930s. The aircraft design went through many iterations, finally becoming the BT-7, a basic trainer. The most typical version, PT-3A, flew at 102 mph to a ceiling of 14,000 feet.

PT-13 Kaydet: Built by Stearman Aircraft Company, the PT-13 Kaydet was one of the most successful trainers ever built. It was first ordered by the USAAC in 1936 and was used throughout World War II. Some 5,000 were built for the USAAC and USAAF; the U.S. Navy also ordered many, as did foreign air forces. After the war, the Kaydets, more familiarly called Stearmans, were frequently used as crop dusters and for aerobatics in air shows. Top speed was 135 mph, and the service ceiling was 13,200 feet.

aircraft, Korean War

While many of the aircraft flown during this war had also been used in WORLD WAR II (see AIRCRAFT, WORLD WAR II), the KOREAN WAR saw the transition from piston power to jet propulsion, especially in the realm of the fighter.

Bomber (designated "B") Aircraft

B-26 Invader (see AIRCRAFT, WORLD WAR II)

B-35: Developed on the eve of the Korean War era, this "flying wing," designed by Jack Northrup of Northrup Aviation, was intended as the new wave of bomber design. Stability problems caused cancellation of production; however, the concept of a plane without a traditional fuselage and tail section, or with the fuselage incorporated into the wing as a "lifting body," concepts pioneered in this aircraft and in the B-49, would emerge again in the B-2 and F-117 stealth aircraft of the late cold war era (see AIRCRAFT, COLD WAR AND AFTER).

B-49: The B-49, converted from the B-35, addressed stability problems with the "flying wing" design—but not satisfactorily enough to warrant full production. The USAF opted for the far more conservative and conventional B-36 Peacemaker.

The B-49 was powered by six turbojets and could achieve a top speed of 520 mph.

B-36 Peacemaker: The B-36 was a hybrid transition between the age of piston power and the age of the jet. Built by Consolidated-Vultee, it was intended to replace the B-29 as the platform from which nuclear weapons could be deployed. Design work began as early as 1941, and the plane first flew in 1946. Operational during the Korean War, it was never used in combat. Its main purpose was as a bomber for the STRATEGIC AIR COMMAND (SAC), capable of carrying nuclear weapons to the Soviet Union.

The B-36 was enormous, heavy, and ungainly in appearance. It had a 230-foot wingspan and a fuselage 162 feet long. Gross weight was 410,000 pounds. While its six pusher piston engines and four turbojets allowed it to carry five tons of bombs over 6,800 miles, it was slow at 411 mph and had a limited service ceiling of 36,400 feet, making it very vulnerable to Soviet fighters, which could fly faster and higher. A total of 385 of the aircraft were built.

B-45 Tornado: Built by North American, the Tornado was the first U.S. production jet bomber. It was also the first aircraft to combine a tactical role with the ability to carry nuclear weapons. Design work had begun in 1945, before World War

II ended, and the plane made its first flight in 1947. It served for 10 years, between 1948 and 1958, and 143 were delivered. In addition to the bomber configuration, a reconnaissance version, RB-45, was also built. The B-45 was used in Korea, but not in areas controlled by MiGs. The B-45 was the first aircraft to demonstrate the feasibility of in-air refueling, in 1950.

Capable of making 589 mph and with a service ceiling of 43,200 feet, the B-45 could carry 22,000 pounds of bombs over 1,910 miles.

B-47 Stratojet: This medium-range jet bomber prefigured the great strategic warhorse, the B-52 Stratofortress (see AIRCRAFT, VIETNAM WAR). With a three-man crew, and powered by six turbojets, it could carry 20,000 pounds of bombs (including nuclear weapons) at 606 mph over a 4,000-mile range. Service ceiling was 40,500 feet.

The B-47 first flew in 1947 and was produced by Douglas and, under license, by Lockheed in large numbers: 2,040 planes. An RB-47 variant was used for photo reconnaissance. By 1965, the Stratojet was withdrawn from Strategic Air Command service as nuclear deterrence became increasingly invested in missiles (see MISSILES, STRATEGIC).

B-50 Superfortress: The B-50, a piston-driven bomber (some variants added two turbojets), resembled the B-29, but with greater power. It was intended as an interim bomber until the B-47 could be made fully operational. Between 1945 and 1953, 370 were produced. Although fully operational during the Korean War, the B-50 was not used in combat. It did appear briefly during the VIETNAM WAR, in 1964–65, just as it was being retired.

The B-50's top speed was 380 mph, its service ceiling 36,700 feet, range 4,900 miles, and bomb capacity 20,000 pounds.

Cargo and Transport (designated "C") Aircraft

C-46 Commando (see AIRCRAFT, WORLD WAR II)

C-47 Skytrain (see AIRCRAFT, WORLD WAR II)

C-82 Packet: The Fairchild Packet was designed in 1941 and first flew in 1944. The 100 ordered arrived too late for service in World War II, but they were used in Korea for tactical airlift. Between 1945 and 1948, 220 were built. The principal feature of this two-engine freighter was its large cargo hold, which gave direct access for ground-level loading. Top speed was 248 mph, service ceiling was 21,200 feet, and range 1,920 miles.

C-119 Flying Boxcar: This Fairchild design was developed from the C-82 Packet and produced by Fairchild and, under license, by the Kaiser Manufacturing Corporation. It made its first flight it 1947 and, by the time production ceased in 1955, more than 1,100 had been built. The C-119 was used extensively in Korea in paratroop drops as well as in aerial resupply. In the Vietnam War, the C-119 was used as a gunship, the AC-119, in two variants, the AC-119G (with four 7.62-mm Gatling guns) and the AC-119K (with two M-61s and two turbojets for added thrust).

The standard C-119 had a top speed of 281 mph, a service ceiling of 21,580, a range of 1,630 miles, and a payload of 62 troops, with equipment.

C-121 Constellation: The Constellation was a highly successful passenger transport, which the USAAF commandeered from Lockheed production lines for military service. In World War II, the aircraft began service in 1943 as the C-69. An improved design appeared after the war and, in addition to the extensive civilian production, it was used as a military passenger transport, designated C-121A and VC-121A. The latter configuration was used to transport VIPs, including Dwight Eisenhower, first as NATO commander and then as U.S. president, and Douglas MacArthur. In 1953, a larger version, the C-121C, was modified as the RC-121C, the TC-121C, and the EC-121C, all reconnaissance aircraft. The EC-121C was equipped with advanced electronics and served during the Vietnam War as the "College Eye" surveillance aircraft.

The C-121G (corresponding to the civilian Super-G Constellation) had four engines, a distinctive tailplane with three vertical stabilizers, and a 123-foot wingspan. Its top speed was 368 mph with a service ceiling of 22,300 feet and a range of 2,100 miles.

C-124 Globemaster II: Designed in 1949 as a larger improvement on the C-74 Globemaster, the Globemaster II was the first of the USAF's "heavy lifters." It first flew in 1949 and deliveries began in 1950. Built by Douglas, it had a double-decker cargo hold, equipped with ramps and elevators to accommodate vehicles and cargo on both decks. Two hundred troops, with equipment, could be accommodated—a total payload of 26,375 pounds. Top speed was 271 mph, service ceiling 18,400 feet, and range 4,030 miles.

Fighter (designated "F") Aircraft

F-80 Shooting Star: The USAF's first operational jet fighter, the F-80 was also modified as the T-33 trainer and the F-94 Starfire interceptor. The first Shooting Star flew in January 1944, but it saw no combat in World War II. It came into its own during the Korean War and engaged in the first dogfight between jets, on November 15, 1950, when an F-80 shot down a MiG-15. The F-94 Starfire, the last of the F-80 line, was retired in 1959.

With a top speed of 543 mph, the F-80 had a service ceiling of 47,500 feet.

F-84 Thunderjet, Thunderstreak, and Thunderflash: The Republic Aviation Corporation began design work on the F-84 in 1944, essentially modifying a piston-driven design to accommodate a jet engine. The first flight of the F-84 took place in 1946 and service began two years later. F-84s served in the Korean War as B-29 escorts, but they soon proved too vulnerable to the superior MiG-15. F-84 use was restricted to an attack role. Republic built 4,457 Thunderjets, but also worked on a redesign with swept wings. This resulted in the F-84F Thunderstreak, which began service in 1954; 2,711 were built. Another variant was the F-84F Thunderflash, built by General Motors. Yet another variant, the RF-84F Thunderflash, was modified

A formation of four Shooting Stars in their training configuration, as T-33As   *(U.S. Air Force)*

with a retractable hook, so that it could be launched and retrieved from a trapeze device on the B-36. These "parasite fighters" were intended to defend the slow and vulnerable B-36 from fighter attack.

The F-84G Thunderflash, the last version of the aircraft, could make 622 mph and reach 40,500 feet. Its range was 2,000 miles, and it carried an ordnance load of 2,000 pounds.

F-86 Sabre: The poor performance of the F-80 and F-84 against the Russian MiG-15 in the Korean War quickly persuaded USAF planners of the need for a high-performance swept wing aircraft. They turned to North American's F-86 Sabre, which had first flown in 1947 and was based on advanced Luftwaffe wing designs, captured at the end of World War II. In 1948, a Sabre exceeded Mach I, becoming the USAF's first supersonic fighter. It entered active service the following year, and, in 1950, the F-86E was rushed into Korean War service. At low altitudes, the F-86E had the edge over the MiG-15, but, at higher altitudes, the MiG-15 was superior. Armament also proved a problem, as the range of the F-86E's six Browning machine guns was inadequate to jet-age speeds. Nevertheless, in the hands of more highly skilled U.S. pilots, the Sabre performed very well against the MiG: 792 MiG-15s were shot down, with the loss of 78 F-86s. North American produced 5,893 F-86s before production ended in 1956. Top speed was 690 mph with a service ceiling of 50,000 feet and a range of 1,270 miles carrying 2,000 pounds of ordnance.

F-89 Scorpion: Northrup designed this, the USAF's first multiseat jet interceptor. The first flight took place in 1948, and it entered active service in 1951. The plane was relegated to the AIR NATIONAL GUARD in 1960. The plane was never entirely satisfactory and was replaced by the F-102 Delta Dagger (see AIRCRAFT, VIETNAM WAR). Top speed was 636 mph, service ceiling 49,200 feet, and range was 1,370 miles.

F-94 Starfire (see *F-80 Shooting Star*)

F-100 Super Sabre: North American commenced design of a successor to the F-86 Sabre in 1951, and, before the year was out, the USAF ordered production. In 1953, a Super Sabre set a

The F-86 Sabre was the USAF's first swept-wing jet fighter.   *(U.S. Air Force)*

world speed record of 755 mph and was the first USAF fighter to break the sound barrier in *level* flight (an F-86 had gone supersonic in a dive). The F-100 became well-known around the nation and the world as the show plane of the THUNDERBIRDS exhibition team. Flown late in the Korean War, it was also used in Vietnam, beginning in 1965. It was withdrawn from USAF service in 1972 and flew with Air National Guard units until 1978. The Super Sabre had a top speed of 864 mph and a service ceiling of 39,600 feet. Its range was limited to 530 miles, but it bristled with ordnance—7,040 pounds of it.

Helicopters (designated "H")

H-19 Chickasaw: Sikorsky designed the Chickasaw in 1948, it first flew in 1949, and it entered active service in 1951, mainly as a rescue aircraft, extensively used in the Korean War. It was retired in 1967. With a top speed of 112 mph, the H-19 had a 360-mile range and could haul 10 troops.

H-21 Workhorse: The tandem-rotor H-21 was built by Piasecki Helicopter Corporation. In naval service, it was used mostly for rescue work, whereas the USAF used it for tactical airlift—as did the U.S. Army. Nicknamed the Flying Banana, because of its distinctive shape, the last H-21 was retired from the USAF in 1970. It served in Korea and in the Vietnam War.

Trainer (designated "T") Aircraft

T-28 Trojan: A piston-powered trainer, the Trojan first flew in 1949 and entered USAF service in 1950. It quickly proved a disappointment and was replaced by the T-37A jet-powered trainer. A version designated AT-28D was modified for close air support, but it was seriously vulnerable to ground fire. Top speed was 283 mph, service ceiling was 24,000 feet, and range, 1,000 miles.

T-29: The Consolidated-Vultee T-29 was used as a navigator trainer. It entered service in 1950 and also appeared in staff transport (VT-29) and electronic warfare variants (ET-29). Two major variants were designated the C-131A, a transport, and the MC-131A Samaritan, an aeromedical evacuation aircraft. The Air National Guard flew some C-131s as late as the 1990s. With a top speed of 296 mph and a service ceiling of 23,500 feet, the twin-engine T-29/C-131 had a range of 1,500 miles.

T-33 (see F-80 Shooting Star)

aircraft, Vietnam War

After the end of WORLD WAR II, which ushered in the nuclear and thermonuclear age, the thrust of USAF planning was mainly toward strategic weaponry. Vietnam, however, was an intensively tactical war, and the USAF found itself scrambling to adopt strategic aircraft (especially the B-52) to tactical roles.

Attack (designated "A") Aircraft and Gunships (designated "AC")

A-1 Skyraider: This was primarily designed as a carrier-based naval aircraft in 1944 and was in production through 1957. However, in 1963, a number of A-1 Skyraiders were assigned to the USAF Special Warfare Center at Eglin AFB and were used as attack (CLOSE AIR SUPPORT) aircraft in Vietnam. A huge single-engine piston plane (wingspan 51 feet, length 39 feet, weight 24,872 pounds), the A-1 made 365 mph and had a service ceiling of 25,000 feet over an impressive 2,700-mile range.

A-7 Corsair II: Vought built the A-7 Corsair II as a naval carrier attack plane in 1963, and the exi-gencies of the Vietnam War, which called for more tactical aircraft than the USAF had in its inventory, prompted the air force to order A-7s. Although the aircraft entered USAF service in 1970, it did not see action in Vietnam until 1972. It proved highly effective in the close air support role. With a top speed of 698 mph, it had a long range (2,871 miles) and could carry a full 15,000 pounds of ordnance.

A-26/B-26 Invader (see AIRCRAFT, WORLD WAR II)

AC-47 (see C-47 in AIRCRAFT, WORLD WAR II)

AC-119 (see C-119 in AIRCRAFT, KOREAN WAR)

Bomber (designated "B") Aircraft

B-52 Stratofortress: This remarkable aircraft first flew in 1954, and the B-52B model entered service in 1955. A total of 744 B-52s were built; the last, a B-52H, was delivered in October 1962. Only the H model is still in the USAF inventory; however, continually updated with modern technology, the B-52 is projected to continue service *beyond* 2045—a service life approaching a century.

The B-52 Stratofortress was built as the USAF's principal manned strategic bomber; however, in Vietnam, it was pressed into service in a tactical role and is indeed capable of dropping or launching the widest array of weapons in the U.S. inventory. In addition to its intended strategic role, the B-52 performs air interdiction and offensive counter-air and maritime operations. It delivered huge quantities of ordnance in tactical operations in Vietnam and was used again during the PERSIAN GULF WAR and in operations in Afghanistan following the September 11, 2001, terrorist attacks against the United States.

Aerial refueling has given the B-52 a range limited only by crew endurance. Unrefueled, its combat range exceeds 8,800 miles. The B-52 is 159 feet long with a wingspan of 185 feet. Its top speed is 650 mph with a service ceiling of 50,000 feet. A crew of five—aircraft commander, pilot, radar navigator, navigator, and electronic warfare officer—flies the plane.

B-57 Canberra (see AIRCRAFT, COLD WAR AND AFTER)

A B-52H Stratofortress in flight   (U.S. Air Force)

mobile scissors bridge, and it can do so from the United States to any point in the world.

Lockheed-Georgia delivered the first operational Galaxy to the 437th Airlift Wing, Charleston AFB, in June l970. With maintenance and modernization programs, the C-5 is expected to remain operational far into the 21st century. Top speed is 518 mph, and range is 6,320 nautical miles.

C-7 Caribou: Built by DeHavilland Aircraft of Canada, the C-7 is a twin-engine, short takeoff and landing (STOL) utility transport used primarily for tactical airlift missions in forward battle areas with short, unimproved airstrips. It can carry 26 fully equipped paratroops or 20 wounded personnel on litters. In a cargo configuration, the C-7 carries more than three tons. The aircraft first flew in

B-66 Destroyer: The USAF commissioned Douglas to develop the B-66 from the navy A3D Skywarrior as a tactical light bomber and photo reconnaissance aircraft. It was a reconnaissance version (designated RB-66A) that first flew in 1954. The B-66s became operational in 1956, and production ended in 1958 after 294 had been built. It was the last tactical bomber built for the USAF. For service in Vietnam, some B-66s were modified as electronic countermeasures aircraft to confuse enemy radar defenses.

The plane's top speed was 585 mph, service ceiling was 43,000 feet, and range was 1,800 miles.

Cargo and Transport (designated "C") Aircraft

C-5 Galaxy: Lockheed's C-5 is one of the largest aircraft in the world, developed in the 1960s to carry outsize and oversize cargo over intercontinental distances. Despite its size—wingspan: 222.9 feet; length: 247.1 feet; height: 65.1 feet; cargo capacity: 270,000 pounds; maximum takeoff weight: 769,000 pounds—the C-5 can take off and land in relatively short distances. Moreover, ground crews can load and off-load the C-5 simultaneously at the front and rear cargo openings. The C-5 Galaxy carries nearly all of the U.S. Army's combat equipment, even such items as its 74-ton

A C-5A Galaxy prepares to unload   (U.S. Air Force)

1958, and, in 1961, 22 were delivered to the U.S. Army. In January 1967, responsibility for all fixed-wing tactical transports was transferred to the USAF—along with the Caribous. The aircraft's STOL capability gave it great utility in Vietnam. Capable of reaching 216 mph and with a range of 1,175 miles, the Caribou has a service ceiling of 24,800 feet.

C-9 Nightingale: A modified version of the Douglas (now Boeing) DC-9 commercial transport, the C-9A is the only USAF aircraft specifically designed to move litter and ambulatory patients. Another configuration, the C-9C, is used to transport high-ranking government and Department of Defense officials for special air missions. A C-9C is often used to transport the vice president or the first lady. The C-9A carries 40 litter patients or 40 ambulatory and four litter patients, or other combinations. It flies at 525 mph over a range of 2,500 miles.

C-46 Commando (see AIRCRAFT, WORLD WAR II)

C-47 Skytrain (see AIRCRAFT, WORLD WAR II)

C-123 Provider: The C-123 is a short-range assault transport used to airlift troops and cargo onto short runways and unprepared airstrips. The Chase Aircraft Company designed the C-123 on the basis of earlier designs for large assault gliders. The first prototype flew on October 14, 1949. Chase began manufacture in 1953, but production was subsequently transferred to Fairchild, which built more than 300 C-123Bs. These began entering service in 1955. Between 1966 and 1969, 184 C-123Bs were converted to C-123Ks with the addition of two J85 jet engines for improved performance. In Vietnam, Providers not only flew troops and cargo but also were used to spray defoliant and insecticide. The C-123B has a top speed of 240 mph, a range of 1,825 miles, and a service ceiling of 28,000 feet.

C-130 Hercules: One of the greatest workhorse cargo aircraft ever built, the C-130 Hercules primarily performs tactical airlift functions. Capable of operating from unimproved airstrips, it is the prime transport for air dropping troops and equipment into hostile areas. The basic C-130 has been modified for various specialized roles, including airlift support, Antarctic ice resupply, aeromedical missions, weather reconnaissance, aerial spray missions, fire-fighting duties for the U.S. Forest Service, and natural disaster relief missions. An attack version, the AC-130, was used extensively in Vietnam as a close air support gunship.

The first C-130 was delivered by Lockheed in 1956 and has gone through several versions. It is still in production. The latest C-130, the C-130J, was introduced in February 1999. It has an advanced six-bladed composite propeller coupled to a Rolls-Royce turboprop engine and, in a stretch version (C-130J-30), it will replace retiring C-130Es.

The C-130E could hit 345 mph, whereas the C-130J achieves 417 mph with a ceiling of 33,000 feet carrying a 45,000-pound payload. Range of the C-130E is 1,838 miles versus 2,897 miles for the stretch C-130J-30. The USAF has 186 C-130s in active service, the AIR NATIONAL GUARD, 217, and the AIR FORCE RESERVE, 107.

C-133 Cargomaster: The Douglas C-133 Cargomaster was a four-engine, turboprop transport, which first flew in 1956. It could fly the equivalent of 22 loaded railroad boxcars nonstop between Los Angeles and New York and was used to carry fully assembled tanks as well as the Thor IRBM (INTERMEDIATE RANGE BALLISTIC MISSILE). The plane went out of production in 1961, after 50 had been delivered to the USAF. Top speed was 359 mph, service ceiling, 19,000 feet, range, 3,975 miles. The C-133 could carry 10 crew and 200 passengers or 80,000 pounds of cargo.

C-135 Stratolifter (see AIRCRAFT, COLD WAR AND AFTER)

KC-135 Stratotanker: A specially modified version of the Boeing 707 commercial transport, the KC-135 Stratotanker is the USAF's principal air-refueling aircraft. It also provides aerial refueling support to navy and Marine Corps aircraft, as well as aircraft of allied nations. In Vietnam, midair refueling was extensively used, bringing even the most distant targets within reach of virtually all attack aircraft.

The first 29 KC-135s were purchased in 1954. The first aircraft flew in 1956, and first deliveries were made in 1957. The last was delivered in 1965. Various updates will keep the KC-135 flying for many more years. The aircraft has also been modified for other applications, ranging from flying command post missions to reconnaissance. The EC-135C is U.S. Strategic Command's flying command post, RC-135s are used for special reconnaissance missions, and NKC-135As are flown in test programs. An OC-135 is used as an observation platform in compliance with the Open Skies Treaty.

Top speed is 530 mph, service ceiling is 50,000 feet, and range, 1,500 miles with 150,000 pounds of transfer fuel. About 732 KC-135s are in the USAF inventory.

C-141 Starlifter: The C-141B, a stretched version of the original C-141A, airlifts combat forces over long distances, resupplies forces, and transports casualties. Lockheed delivered the first C-141A in 1964, and the first C-141B in 1979. It was the first jet transport from which U.S. Army paratroopers jumped, and the first to land in the Antarctic. Top speed is 500 mph, service ceiling, 41,000 feet; with in-flight refueling, range is unlimited. Maximum payload is 200 troops, 155 paratroops, 103 litters, and 14 seats, or 68,725 pounds

of cargo. The USAF has 74 C-141Bs on active duty, the Air National Guard, 28, and the Air Force Reserve, 68.

EC-121C (see C-121 Constellation in AIRCRAFT, KOREAN WAR)

Fighter (designated "F") Aircraft

F-4 Phantom II: First flown in 1958, the Phantom II was developed for the U.S. Navy and entered service in 1961. The following year, the USAF approved a version for close air support, interdiction, and counter-air operations. The USAF version was designated F-4C and made its first flight on May 27, 1963, with first deliveries arriving in November 1963. The F-4 can carry twice the normal bomb load of a World War II B-17 and can also fly in a reconnaissance role and on "Wild Weasel" antiaircraft missile suppression missions. Production ended in 1979, after more than 5,000 had been built, including some 2,600 for the USAF. The first USAF Phantom IIs were sent to Vietnam in 1965.

The Phantom II can carry up to 16,000 pounds of externally carried nuclear or conventional bombs, rockets, missiles, or 20-mm cannon pods in various combinations. Its two General Electric

F-4 Phantom   *(U.S. Air Force)*

J-79-GE-15s engine push it to an afterburner top speed of 1,400 mph. Service ceiling is 59,600 feet, range is 1,750 miles without aerial refueling.

F-5 Freedom Fighter: Northrop began development of the F-5 in 1954 in response to the company's evaluation of the defense needs of NATO and SEATO countries. The conclusion was that a lightweight supersonic fighter was called for, one that was relatively inexpensive and easy to maintain, and capable of operating out of short runways. Initially, the USAF saw no need for a lightweight fighter, but it ordered the trainer version of the F-5, the T-38 Talon. The F-5 was used extensively by the U.S. Military Assistance Program to supply NATO and SEATO allies. In October 1965, the USAF decided to test a dozen combat-ready F-5As in Vietnam combat operational service trials. The program was code named Skoshi Tiger (Little Tiger), and, as a result, the F-5 was often called "Tiger." Top speed is 925 mph, range, 1,100 miles, and service ceiling, 50,700 feet.

F-100 Super Sabre (see AIRCRAFT, KOREAN WAR)

F-101 Voodoo: The F-101 was designed as a long-range bomber escort for the STRATEGIC AIR COMMAND, but when high-speed, high-altitude jet bombers such as the B-52 were introduced, escort fighters were no longer needed. Before production began, therefore, the F-101 was redesigned as a tactical and air defense fighter. The prototype first flew on September 29, 1954, and the first production F-101A became operational in May 1957, followed by the F-101C in 1957 and the F-101B in 1959. When production ended in March 1961, McDonnell had built 785 Voodoos, including the two-seat interceptor version and the reconnaissance versions—the world's first supersonic photo reconnaissance aircraft. Capable of a maximum speed of 1,095 mph and a range of 1,754 miles, the Voodoo can reach a service ceiling of 52,100 feet.

F-102 Delta Dagger: The F-102 was the world's first supersonic all-weather jet interceptor—and the first operational delta-wing aircraft in the USAF inventory. The first F-102 flew on October 24, 1953, and became operational in 1956. Convair built 1,101 F-102s, including 975 F-102As and 111

TF-102s as combat trainers with side-by-side seating. The interceptor could carry 24 unguided 2.75 inch rockets and six guided missiles. Maximum speed was 810 mph, range 1,000 miles, and service ceiling 55,000 feet.

F-104 Starfighter: The F-104, a supersonic air superiority fighter, was produced in two major versions. Armed with a six-barrel M-61 20-mm Vulcan cannon, it served as a tactical fighter; equipped additionally with heat-seeking Sidewinder missiles, it was a day-night interceptor. Development at Lockheed began in 1952 and the prototype first flew in 1954. On May 18, 1958, an F-104A set a world speed record of 1,404.19 mph, and, on December 14, 1959, an F-104C set a world altitude record of 103,395 feet. The Starfighter became the first aircraft to hold simultaneous official world records for speed, altitude, and time-to-climb.

About 300 Starfighters in one- and two-seat versions were delivered to the USAF, and more than 1,700 F-104s were built for various allies. Top speed was 1,320 mph, range, 1,250 miles, and service ceiling, 58,000 feet.

F-105 Thunderchief: The F-105 (nicknamed "Thud") began development in 1951 at Republic Aviation. The prototype flew on October 22, 1955, but the first production aircraft, an F-105B, was not delivered to the USAF until 1958. The F-105D version was an all-weather strike fighter, and the two-place F-105F was a dual-purpose trainer-fighter. All F-105 production—833 aircraft—ended in 1964. The F-105 was extensively used in Vietnam, flying more sorties and suffering more losses than any other USAF aircraft there. Although the F-105 scored 137 MiG victories, it was a heavy and hard-to-maneuver plane (carrying as much ordnance as a World War II B-17) and was vulnerable to air superiority fighters and to flak. It was, however, less vulnerable to surface-to-air missiles. Top speed was 831 mph, range, 1,500 miles, and service ceiling, 50,000 feet.

Observation (designated "O") Aircraft
O-1 Bird Dog: The O-1, a two-place observation and liaison aircraft, was developed from the com-

mercial Cessna Model 170 as early as 1949. The USAF, army, and marines used Bird Dogs for artillery spotting, frontline communications, medical evacuation, and pilot training. In Vietnam, USAF Bird Dogs were used by forward air controllers (FACS) for reconnaissance—an extremely hazardous mission in these light planes, which were vulnerable to ground fire of all kinds, including that from small arms. More that 3,200 Bird Dogs were ordered by the USAF, most of which were built between 1950 and 1959. Maximum speed was 150 mph, range was 530 miles, and service ceiling, 20,300 feet.

O-2 Super Skymaster: This military version of the Cessna Model 337 Super Skymaster has twin tail booms and tandem-mounted engines, one forward, one aft, in a tractor-pusher propeller arrangement. The Model 337 went into civilian production in 1965 and was selected by the USAF the following year as a supplement to the O-1 Bird Dog forward air controller (FAC) aircraft then operating in Vietnam. The twin engines made the O-2 more survivable. Deliveries began in March 1967 and ended in June 1970, after 532 had been built for the USAF. Top speed was 199 mph, range, 1,060 miles, service ceiling, 19,300 feet.

OV-10 Bronco: This twin-turboprop short take-off and landing (STOL) aircraft was designed by North American Aviation in response to a Marine Corps order, but it was developed under a USAF, navy, and Marine Corps tri-service program. The first production OV-10A was ordered in 1966 and the first flight took place in August 1967. The OV-10 was designed to perform observation, forward air control, helicopter escort, armed reconnaissance, gunfire spotting, and utility and limited ground attack. The USAF used it primarily for forward air control, especially in Vietnam. The OV-10 also has limited (3,200-pound) cargo capacity and can accommodate five combat-equipped troops or two litter patients and a medical attendant. OV-10s began Vietnam service in July 1968; 157 were delivered to the USAF before production ended in April 1969. Top speed is 281 mph. Cruising speed: 223

mph, range, 1,240 miles, and service ceiling is 26,000 feet.

Utility (designated "U") Aircraft

U-16 Albatross: This venerable (first flew in 1947) Grumman design was used widely in the Vietnam era and earlier for air-sea rescue. It was also designated SA-16 (and nicknamed "Slobbering Albert"). The USAF bought 302 U-16s, and the aircraft saw service for more than a quarter century. An amphibious design, the U-16 had twin engines that propelled it to 236 mph over a range of 3,220 miles.

Training (designated "T") Aircraft

T-37 Tweet: The T-37 Tweet is a twin-engine jet used for training in the fundamentals of aircraft handling and instrument, formation, and night flying. It was developed by Cessna, first flown in 1954, and entered service in 1957. An attack variant, the A-37, was used in the Vietnam War and is now designated as the OA-37B Dragonfly. This configuration is used for forward air control and for rescue work. But it is as a trainer that the T-37 is still most extensively employed. It is designed to give student pilots a feel for handling the larger, faster T-38 Talon or T-1A Jayhawk, which are used in a later training phase. The instructor and student sit side by side. More than 1,000 T-37s were built, and 419 remain in the USAF inventory. Top speed is 360 mph, ceiling 35,000, and range 460 miles.

T-38 Talon: This twin-engine, high-altitude, supersonic jet trainer was built by Northrop as a vehicle to prepare pilots for a variety of advanced fighters. The T-38 is ideal for aerobatics, formation, night, instrument, and cross-country navigation training. The T-38 is also frequently used as a test bed for such experimental equipment as electronics and weapon systems, and NASA uses the aircraft to train astronauts and to serve as chase planes on programs such as the space shuttle.

The Talon first flew in 1959, and more than 1,100 were delivered to the USAF between 1961 and 1972 when production ended. However, through maintenance and upgrade programs, it is

This T-37 Tweet from the 85th Fighter Training Squadron, Laughlin AFB, Texas, flies over Lake Amistad, Texas, during a training mission. After mastering the Tweet, student pilots move up to the faster, more sophisticated T-38 Talon.   *(U.S. Air Force)*

expected that the Talon will continue to serve at least until 2020. Top speed is 812 mph, service ceiling exceeds 55,000 feet, and range is 1,093 miles. Currently, 509 are in the USAF inventory.

T-39 Sabreliner: This twin-jet, multipurpose aircraft was built by North American for the USAF and U.S. Navy, both of which designate it T-39. Capable of cruising at 500 mph at 40,000 feet, it resembles the F-86 Sabre Jet and the F-100 Super Sabre, but it is capable of carrying a crew of two, with four passengers. Highly modifiable, the T-39 was used as a radar and navigational trainer and as a test bed for various instruments, as well as a small cargo (2,300-pound capacity) and passenger carrier. Active service began in 1960, and the aircraft was retired in 1984.

Helicopters (designated "H")

H-3 Jolly Green Giant: The USAF version of the H-3, the Sikorsky S-61 amphibious transport helicopter originally developed for the U.S. Navy, is

the CH-3E. After operating six Navy HSS-2 (SH-3A) versions in 1962, the USAF ordered 75 H-3s, which were modified with a new rear fuselage design incorporating a ramp for vehicles and other cargo. The first USAF CH-3C was flown on June 17, 1963; 41 were updated with more powerful engines in 1966 and were redesignated CH-3Es. Later, 50 CH-3Es were modified for combat rescue missions with armor, defensive armament, self-sealing fuel tanks, a rescue hoist, and in-flight refueling capability. Redesignated HH-3Es, they were used extensively in Vietnam; it was this configuration that was nicknamed the "Jolly Green Giant." Maximum speed was 177 mph, range 779 miles (with external fuel tanks), and service ceiling 21,000 feet.

H-21 Workhorse (see AIRCRAFT, KOREAN WAR)

H-53 Super Jolly: As the Vietnam War continued, the USAF determined a need for a better combat rescue helicopter than the H-3. The Marine Corps already had the Sikorsky H-53 Sea

Stallion, which the USAF ordered modified as the H-53 Super Jolly. It entered service in 1967, a twin-engine helicopter capable of lifting seven tons and equipped with modern avionics and ejection seats. In addition to rescue, H-53s were used for heavy-lift operations, military transport, vertical replenishment, vertical onboard delivery, airborne mine countermeasures, advanced early warning, minesweeping, humanitarian aid, and disaster relief. The helicopters were extensively used for astronaut rescue and space capsule and satellite recovery. Updated in 1987 with Pave Low III Enhanced equipment, including forward-looking infrared (FLIR) and terrain-following and terrain-avoidance radar, the H-53s (designated MH-53J) continue to be used extensively and are the largest and most powerful helicopters in the USAF inventory and the most technologically advanced helicopters in the world. Top speed is 186 mph, service ceiling is 18,550 feet, range is 540 miles. The HH-53C configuration can lift 20,000 pounds.

aircraft, World War I

Although powered flight by heavier-than-air aircraft was born in the United States with the Wright brothers' *Flyer I* of 1903, the nation's military had little interest in aviation as a weapon, and, as a result, the U.S. aircraft industry lagged far behind that of Europe when the nation entered WORLD WAR I in 1917.

U.S. manufacturers began turning out De Haviland DH-4 aircraft under license from the British manufacturer in August 1918, but, before this, the U.S. ARMY AIR SERVICE chiefly flew two French-made aircraft for observation and bombing.

Breguet 14: The aircraft came in two configurations, the 14A for observation and the 14B for bombing. The planes were capable of a top speed of 129 miles per hour. The USAAS used 229 14As, 47 14Bs, and 100 "14E" trainers.

Salmson 2A-2: 705 of these French-built observation planes were used by the USAAS. It was in all respects similar to the Breuget 14.

De Haviland DH-4: Built in the United States under British license by Standard Aircraft Company, Dayton-Wright Company, and General Motors, with a U.S.-designed and built "Liberty Engine," the DH-4, a 1916 design, was, in fact, obsolescent by the time it began rolling off U.S. assembly lines in 1918. A staggering 4,846 were built, but they proved defective in design and so prone to catch fire that the aircraft were nicknamed "Flaming Coffins." A DH-4B version corrected these faults, but the version arrived too late to be flown in combat. The USAAS and U.S. ARMY AIR CORPS flew DH-4Bs until 1931. The aircraft had a top speed of 118 mph and a service ceiling of 12,800 feet. It carried 1,200 pounds of bombs.

Nieuport 28: This French-built fighter was obsolete by the time the United States purchased it for use in combat. Nevertheless, it flew with the 94th and 95th Aero Squadrons and Lieutenant Alan Winslow scored the first U.S. aerial victory of the war in one. In this aircraft, Lieutenant Douglas Campbell became the first U.S.-trained ace of the war.

Spad XIII: This aircraft replaced the obsolete Nieuport 28 and was the favorite fighter of USAAS pilots. The Spad XIII was made especially famous in the United States by the exploits of Captain EDWARD V. RICKENBACKER, the nation's dashing top ace. Capable of making 138 mph (200 mph in a dive), the Spad XIII had an impressive service ceiling of 22,300 feet. The United States purchased 893 of the aircraft.

JN Jenny: Manufactured by the Curtiss Aeroplane and Motor Company, the Jenny was ordered by the AVIATION SECTION, U.S. ARMY SIGNAL CORPS in 1916 and was used (without much success) in the PUNITIVE EXPEDITION against Pancho Villa that year. Although it was not used overseas in World War I—and was hopelessly obsolete as a combat aircraft—it served as the primary trainer for 90 percent of U.S. World War I pilots. More than 8,000 were manufactured. A slow plane, with a top speed of 75 mph as driven by its standard 90-horsepower Curtiss OX-5 engine, it had a service ceiling of 8,000 feet.

Two Army Service Curtiss JN-4 Jennys   *(San Diego Aerospace Museum)*

aircraft, World War II

Listed here are the principal U.S. ARMY AIR CORPS and U.S. ARMY AIR FORCES aircraft used in WORLD WAR II. Some were developed during the interwar period, some during the war itself. Some aircraft developed before the war saw very limited service during the war; these are covered in AIRCRAFT, INTERWAR PERIOD (1919–1940).

Attack (designated "A") Aircraft

A-20 Havoc: This was the principal USAAC and USAAF attack (close ground support) aircraft of World War II. The air arm received 7,230 of them from the Douglas Aircraft Company. The plane went into production at the close of the 1930s and was the first USAAF aircraft type to see action in Europe, arriving there in 1942. The twin-engine craft was nicknamed the "Flying Pike" and had a top speed of 329 mph, a service ceiling of 28,250, and a range of 1,060 miles. Production ended in 1944.

Bomber (designated "B") Aircraft

B-17 Flying Fortress: One of the most celebrated airplanes of World War II, the B-17 was the first U.S. bomber built for strategic operations and was the first U.S. four-engine monoplane bomber. Designed by Boeing, a total of 12,731 of these planes were produced by Boeing and, under license, by Douglas and by Vega, a Lockheed subsidiary. The most successful version, the B-17G, was powered by four 1,200-horsepower Wright R-1820-97 engines that drove the 65,500-pound Fortress at 287 mph and to a service ceiling of 35,600 feet. The aircraft could deliver up to 8,000 pounds of bombs and had a range of 2,000 miles. It bristled with defensive guns and was renowned for its ability to withstand massive damage from enemy fighters and antiaircraft fire.

B-24 Liberator: Less celebrated that the B-17 Flying Fortress, Consolidated Aircraft's B-24 Liberator was nevertheless built in significantly greater numbers—18,482 produced by five manufacturers; no combat aircraft, save the German Bf 109 (a single-engine fighter of World War II), has ever been built in greater quantity.

The B-24 was a notoriously difficult plane to fly, especially in the close formations required for strategic bombing (see BOMBING, STRATEGIC) missions; however, it had two performance edges on the much better loved B-17: top speed was 300 mph (vs. 287 mph for the B-17) and range was 2,100 miles (vs. 2,000). However, the B-17 was capable of greater altitude: 35,600 feet versus 28,000 feet.

B-17 Flying Fortress   *(U.S. Air Force)*

B-25 Mitchell: Design work at North American Aviation began in 1938 on this twin-engine medium bomber named in honor of controversial military aviation advocate WILLIAM MITCHELL. It first flew in 1939, and, by the time the war was over, more than 11,000 had been built, 9,815 for the USAAC and USAAF. Considered one of the great bombers of the war, the Mitchell was made spectacularly famous by JAMES HAROLD DOOLITTLE's breathtaking, morale-boosting carrier-launched 1942 raid on Tokyo.

The Mitchell flew at 272 mph with a service ceiling of 24,200 feet and a range of 1,350 miles with a 3,000-pound bomb load. In addition to bombing work, modified B-25s were used as transports and as reconnaissance aircraft, and from 1943 to 1959, they also served as pilot trainers.

B-26 Invader: The Douglas B-26 entered service in World War II in 1944 and proved so successful that it was used in the KOREAN WAR and even in the early phases (1961–64) of the VIETNAM WAR. It was a very fast twin-engine bomber, with a top speed of 372 mph and a service ceiling of 20,450 feet. Carrying a 4,000-pound bomb load, it had a range of 892 miles. Total production of this aircraft was 2,446.

B-26 Marauder: In contrast to the Invader, which bore the same B-26 designation, the Martin Marauder was a difficult plane to master and was soon branded "The Widow Maker," because of the high rate of loss in the hands of inexperienced pilots. Once the aircraft entered full-time service in the war, however, it amply proved itself, and, by the time production stopped in 1945, the USAAF had

B-25C Mitchell   *(San Diego Aerospace Museum)*

accepted 5,157 Marauders. The twin-engine medium bomber flew at 283 mph and had a service ceiling of 19,800 feet. Range was 1,100 miles with 4,000 pounds of bombs.

B-29 Superfortress: The most advanced bomber of its time, the B-29 outclassed everything else in the sky and was the only USAAF aircraft capable of delivering atomic weapons, the bomb dropped on Hiroshima on August 6, 1945, and the bomb dropped on Nagasaki on August 9. In effect, then, the B-29 ended World War II.

Design work began at Boeing in 1940, the first flight took place in 1942, and the aircraft was put into service exclusively in the Pacific theater beginning in the last two months of 1944. The TWENTI-ETH AIR FORCE and the TWENTY-FIRST AIR FORCE were established exclusively to fly the new bomber, whose four engines drove it at 364 mph to a service ceiling of 32,000 feet. Carrying a 20,000-pound bomb load, its range was 4,200 miles, and with a 141-foot wingspan and 99-foot fuselage, it was by far the biggest bomber of the era.

B-32 Dominator: Consolidated Aircraft Company was commissioned to build this four-engine bomber as a kind of hedge against the possible failure of the B-29. However, the B-29 proved a spectacular success, while the B-32 was criticized for basic design and production flaws. Of the 115 built, only 15 saw action, in the Pacific. Most of the scheduled production of 1,588 was canceled before the war ended.

Capable of 357 mph, the B-32 had a service ceiling of 30,700 feet and could carry 10 tons of bombs over 2,400 miles.

Cargo and Military Transport (designated "C") Aircraft

C-46 Commando: Curtiss-Wright designed this aircraft in 1937 as a two-engine commercial passenger plane. On the eve of World War II, the USAAC ordered a model converted for military transport. The aircraft, of which 3,144 were built, was a workhorse that served famously "flying the Hump"—the treacherous Burma-China airlift—and was used after World War II in the Korean War. Although officially retired in 1960, the C-46 was used in the

Vietnam War and in Southeast Asia generally through 1969. With a top speed of 269 mph and a service ceiling of 27,600 feet, the C-46 could carry a payload of 10,000 pounds over 1,200 miles.

C-47 Skytrain: Dwight D. Eisenhower observed that, without the bazooka, the Jeep, the atom bomb, and the C-47, the Allies could not have won World War II. The military variant of the Douglas DC-3, a spectacularly successful and long-lived commercial passenger transport first flown in 1935, the C-47 (in many configurations) was built for the USAAC and USAAF in a quantity of more than 10,000.

The C-47 was used throughout World War II to carry personnel and cargo, to tow gliders, and to drop paratroopers. During the Normandy ("D-day") invasion of June 6, 1944, C-47s dropped 60,000 paratroopers and towed thousands of CG-4 gliders. After the war, the aircraft saw spectacular service in the BERLIN AIRLIFT, in the Korean War, and in the Vietnam War, where it was used not only as a transport but also as an attack gunship (AC-47), nicknamed "Puff the Magic Dragon." The last C-47 was not retired from the USAF until 1975. Commercially, a fair number are still in service.

The twin-engine C-47 flew at 230 mph with a service ceiling of 24,000 feet, a range of 1,600 miles, and a payload of 10,000 pounds.

C-54 Skymaster: Like the C-47, the C-54 was originally developed in the 1930s as a commercial airliner, the four-engine DC-4. The first run of DC-4s was commandeered off the Douglas assembly line by the USAAF in 1942 and redesignated C-54. Before the end of the war, the service bought 1,163 C-54s. This long-range transport was the primary airlifter across the Atlantic and Pacific. By the end of the war, C-54s had made 79,642 crossings of the North Atlantic with the loss of only three aircraft. It was a specially modified C-54 (designated VC-54C), nicknamed *The Sacred Cow,* which became the first aircraft assigned to presidential airlift. It took President Franklin D. Roosevelt to the Yalta Conference. After the war, C-54s were extensively used in the Berlin Airlift and in the Korean War. The aircraft remained in USAF service until 1972.

The C-54 had a top speed of 265 mph, a service ceiling of 22,000 feet, a range of 3,900 miles, and could carry 50 troops with equipment.

C-69: See C-121 Constellation in AIRCRAFT, KOREAN WAR.

Fighter (designated "F" or "P," for pursuit) Aircraft

P-38 Lightning: Lockheed designed this twin-engine fighter with distinctive twin booms (German Luftwaffe pilots called it *Der Gabelschwanz Teufel,* the "Fork-Tailed Devil") and produced a prototype in 1939. By the end of World War II, 9,923 had been delivered to the USAAC and USAAF. The P-38 was more successful flying against Japanese fighters in the Pacific than against German fighters in the European theater. In the Pacific, the top-scoring USAF ace of all time, RICHARD I. BONG, flew a P-38. Its twin engines drove the aircraft at 414 mph, and it could attain a service ceiling of 44,000 feet. Range was 450 miles.

P-39 Airacobra: Bell Aircraft Corporation flew the first prototype Airacobra in 1939, and it was used by the British and the Soviets as well as by the USAAF. In Europe, the P-39 was used mainly in an attack (close air support) role. Early in the war, P-39s also saw action in the Pacific. The fighter was replaced by the F-47 Thunderbolt early in 1944. Capable of a top speed of 399 mph, the P-39 had a service ceiling of 38,500 feet and a range of 750 miles.

P-40 Warhawk: This Curtiss-Wright fighter gained its greatest fame in service with the AMERICAN VOLUNTEER GROUP, the famed "Flying Tigers" serving with the Nationalist Chinese air force against Japan. The distinctive shark-like profile formed by the plane's air scoop was emphasized by the Flying Tigers with a row of tiger teeth. The P-40 was hardly a cutting-edge fighter by the time the war began, but it was ready for production and, in the hands of a capable pilot, held its own against German and Japanese rivals. Some 13,700 were built for the USAAF before production ended in 1944. With a top speed of 378 mph and a service ceiling of 38,000 feet, the P-40 had a limited range of 240 miles.

P-38 Lightning   *(U.S. Air Force)*

P-43 Lancer: Republic Aviation (originally Seversky) produced a small number of this aircraft, which did not perform well against Axis rivals. Speed was 349 mph, service ceiling 38,000 feet, and range 800 miles.

P-59 Airacomet: Bell Aircraft Corporation developed this, the first U.S. jet aircraft, during 1941–42. Thirty were built before production was stopped when the F-80 Shooting Star was introduced just before the end of the war. No U.S. jets saw combat in World War II. P-59 performance was disappointing—inferior to the best piston-powered fighters—and the aircraft was inherently unstable. Top speed was 413 mph, service ceiling 46,200 feet, and range 525 miles.

P-61 Black Widow: The Northrup company built the Black Widow as the USAAF's first night interceptor and the first aircraft specially designed to be equipped with radar. The plane was painted all black for night operations. It first flew in 1942, 732 were built, and it remained in service—as a reconnaissance aircraft—until 1952. The twin-engine P-61 was capable of 366 mph and had a service ceiling of 31,000 feet. Maximum range was 3,000 miles.

P-63 Kingcobra: This Bell Aircraft design was an update of the P-39 Airacobra and first flew in 1942. Although 3,303 were built, the USAAF

Affectionately nicknamed "Jug," the P-47 was one of the most famous AAF fighter planes of World War II. Although originally conceived as a lightweight interceptor, the P-47 developed as a heavyweight fighter.   *(U.S. Air Force)*

North American P-51 Mustang fighter plane over France. Mustangs served in nearly every combat zone. P-51s destroyed 4,950 enemy aircraft in the air, more than any other fighter in Europe. *(U.S. Air Force)*

received relatively few; most were given to the Soviet Union and to France. Top speed was 408 mph with a service ceiling of 43,000 feet and a range of 390 miles.

F-47 Thunderbolt (P-47): More F-47s were built than any other USAAF fighter—15,579 before the end of the war. This Republic design entered service in 1942 and began combat the following year, operating with the Eighth Air Force out of England, then with units in the Pacific, and also with the Fifteenth Air Force in Italy. Britain and the USSR used many as well. The F-47 was an air-superiority fighter, dominating the skies with a victory rate of 4.6 to 1 (F-47s shot down 3,752 enemy aircraft). The airplane was also well suited to ground attack. After World War II, the Air National Guard acquired some F-47s, which were returned to the USAF for service in the Korean War, until they were replaced by jets.

A massive single-engine plane, the powerful F-47 could reach 467 mph and had a service ceiling of 43,000 feet. Its range was 800 miles carrying 2,000 pounds in bombs and other ordnance.

F-51 Mustang (P-51): Arguably the finest fighter of World War II, the F-51 was produced by North American and made its first flight in May

1943. Not only was its performance outstanding—437 mph and a service ceiling of 41,900 feet—it had sufficient range (950 miles) to escort bombers deep into enemy territory. A total of 14,490 were produced.

F-82 Twin Mustang: North American developed the Twin Mustang as a very long range (2,240 miles) fighter escort, intended for the great distances of the Pacific theater. The plane was essentially a mating of two P-51s joined by a center wing section and tailplane. Each otherwise independent fuselage had its own engine and pilot. The aircraft did not see action before the end of the war, but did fly after it and, with an order of 250, it was the last piston fighter the USAAF acquired.

Glider (designated "G") Aircraft

G-4: The Waco Aircraft Company built almost 14,000 G-4s, which were made mostly of wood and carried 15 fully equipped troops (or four soldiers and a jeep, or a 75-mm howitzer and crew). It was replaced late in the war by the G-15 Hadrian.

G-15 Hadrian: The G-15 was an improved, more airworthy and sturdier, version of the G-4. Capable of carrying 7,500 pounds, it glided at about 120 mph.

Trainer (designated "PT," primary trainer; "BT," basic trainer; and "T," trainer) Aircraft

PT-16: This version of the Ryan Model S-T was the first monoplane the USAAC used for training. It was ordered in 1940 and was produced in several variants, PT-20, PT-21, and PT-22. Production ended in 1942. The single-engine PT-16 flew at 128 mph to a service ceiling of 15,000 feet over 350 miles.

PT-19: Fairchild (and other manufacturers under license) produced the PT-19 for the USAAC in 1940. There were a number of variants; however, the PT-19 was generally replaced by the more capable PT-13 Kaydet (see AIRCRAFT, INTERWAR PERIOD [1919–1940]). Top speed was 132 mph, service ceiling 15,300 feet, range 400 miles.

BT-13: Basic training was the next step up from primary training. The BT-13, manufactured by Vultee Aircraft, Inc., was the most popular basic trainer. It made 180 mph and had a service ceiling of 21,650 feet over a range of 725 miles.

BT-15 Valiant: This later version of the BT-13 was quite similar to the earlier plane in performance.

T-6 Texan: This North American Aviation design first flew in 1938 and became the USAAF's advanced trainer during World War II. More than 8,000 were acquired. In addition to training, the T-6 was used for forward air control during the Korean War. The plane was and is much loved, with many still flying in the civilian community. Its top speed was 210 mph, its service ceiling 24,200 feet, and its range 629 miles.

Aircraft Identification Codes (AIC)

USAF uses alphabetical prefixes to designate different types of aircraft. The most common prefixes are B, for bomber (e.g., B-52); C, for cargo (e.g., C-5), F, for fighter (e.g., F-16), and T, for trainer (e.g., T-38). Occasionally, two letters are combined for special designations, as in the SR-71 (for "strategic reconnaissance") and the TR-1 (for "tactical reconnaissance").

Air Defense Command   See AEROSPACE DEFENSE COMMAND.

Air Education and Training Command (AETC)

AETC is a MAJCOM responsible for recruiting, accessing, commissioning, and training USAF

A 25th Flying Training Squadron instructor pilot and student walk toward a T-38 Talon at Vance AFB, Oklahoma.   *(Department of Defense)*

enlisted and officer personnel. AETC responsibility encompasses basic military training, initial and advanced technical training, and flight training.

AETC integrates a large array of educational operations, including the AIR FORCE RESERVE OFFICER TRAINING CORPS (AFROTC), COMMUNITY COLLEGE OF THE AIR FORCE, and the many operations and responsibilities of the AIR UNIVERSITY. It is headquartered at Randolph AFB, Texas.

Air Force 2000

Air Force 2000 was an important study released in 1982, which envisioned the expansion of the USAF air superiority doctrine into space. With regard to air combat against surface forces, the study advocated development of an advanced tactical fighter (ATF), a conclusion that stood in direct opposition to an army study, *AirLand Battle,* released earlier in the year. The army document foresaw at least partial replacement of manned aircraft by smart weapons and remotely piloted vehicles.

Air Force Achievement Medal   See DECORATIONS AND MEDALS.

Air Force Aero-Propulsion Laboratory

See AIR FORCE RESEARCH LABORATORY.

Air Force Agency for Modeling and Simulation (AFAMS)

AFAMS is a FIELD OPERATING AGENCY created in June 1996 to coordinate the USAF's growing requirement for modeling and simulation. The agency's mission is to support implementation and use of the Joint Synthetic Battlespace, a Department of Defense modeling and simulation initiative that is used as a planning and training tool by all of the services. The agency also implements USAF, joint, and Department of Defense policy and standards, it supports corporate USAF modeling and simulation operations, and it coordinates and manages selected modeling and simulation initiatives. AFAMS reports to the director of command and control in the Pentagon, but it is located in Orlando's Central Florida Research Park.

Modeling and simulation have long been used by the USAF to support training, analysis, and operations, but, more recently, the USAF has expanded modeling and simulation activities as a practical solution to improve readiness and lower costs. Modeling and simulation also aid the USAF in improving its warfighting capabilities by allowing real people to conduct operations in a synthetic world.

Air Force Association (AFA)

The AFA was founded on February 4, 1946, and operates today as an international nonprofit organization dedicated to the application of aerospace technology for the betterment of humankind. With 200,000 members and patrons in all 50 states, in Europe, and in the Far East, it publishes *Air Force Magazine,* conducts educational programs, works with industry, sponsors nationwide symposia featuring USAF and Department of Defense leaders, and sponsors the annual Outstanding Airman of the Air Force Program. Its leading mission is to promote public understanding and support of aerospace power in the United States.

The AFA was founded by General of the Air Force HENRY HARLEY ARNOLD and was organized by Major General Edward P. "Ted" Curtis, with Lieutenant General JAMES HAROLD DOOLITTLE as the organization's first president.

Air Force Audit Agency (AFAA)

The AFAA evaluates operations, support, and financial responsibilities for the USAF and is headquartered at Norton AFB, California. Administered by the auditor general of the air force reporting directly to the SECRETARY OF THE AIR FORCE, AFAA consists of three directorates: Acquisitions and Logistics Audit, Financial and Support Audit, and Field Activities.

Air Force bands

Air Force bands provide military and patriotic music for official military and government activities such as ceremonies, formations, and parades, and they provide an essential element for maintaining troop morale, for cultivating positive relations with many communities interacting with USAF units, and for enhancing general public relations.

Air Force bands are classified as either premier bands or regional bands. There are two premier bands: the United States Air Force Band in Washington, D.C., and the United States Air Force Band of the Rockies in Colorado Springs, Colorado. Ten regional bands are found at eight locations in the continental United States and operate from four locations overseas (Germany, Japan, Alaska, and Hawaii). In addition, there are 11 AIR NATIONAL GUARD bands throughout the United States.

Air Force bands are typically organized so that they may be subdivided into several smaller musical units capable of performing autonomously. For example, band members may function as a concert band, a marching or ceremonial band, a jazz or show band, a popular music ensemble, a chamber ensemble, or a "protocol combo" (providing background, dinner, and dance music for official military social functions). Individual musicians, such as buglers, solo vocalists, pianists, and other instrumentalists, may also perform for official functions or ceremonies.

The first known "air force" band, 14 strong, landed in France in September 1917 during WORLD WAR I, their instruments having been purchased from their lieutenant's personal funds. In WORLD WAR II, bands of the U.S. ARMY AIR CORPS and U.S. ARMY AIR FORCES were very active, and, since then, bands have been important adjuncts to USAF morale and presence.

Premier USAF bands:

United States Air Force Band (Bolling AFB)
United States Air Force Band of the Rockies (Peterson AFB)

Regional USAF bands:

For Connecticut, Massachusetts, Maine, New Hampshire, New York, Rhode Island, Vermont: United States Air Force Band of Liberty (Hanscom AFB)

For Louisiana, New Mexico, Oklahoma, Texas: United States Air Force Band of the West (Lackland AFB)

For Delaware, eastern Maryland, eastern Pennsylvania, North Carolina, New Jersey, South Carolina, Virginia: United States Air Force Heritage of America Band (Langley AFB)

For Iowa, Kansas, Minnesota, Montana, North Dakota, Nebraska, South Dakota, Wyoming: United States Air Force Heartland of America Band (Offutt AFB)

For Alabama, Florida, Georgia, Mississippi, Tennessee: Band of the United States Air Force Reserve (Robins AFB)

For Arkansas, Illinois, Missouri, Wisconsin: United States Air Force Band of Mid-America (Scott AFB)

For California, Oregon, Washington: United States Air Force Band of the Golden West (Travis AFB)

For Indiana, Kentucky, Michigan, Ohio, western Maryland, western Pennsylvania, West Virginia: United States Air Force Band of Flight (Wright-Patterson AFB)

For Europe, North Africa, and the Middle East: United States Air Forces in Europe Band (Unit 3315, APO AE 09136-5000)

For Alaska, PACIFIC AIR FORCES, as appropriate: United States Air Force Band of the Pacific (Elmendorf AFB)

For Japan, Pacific Air Forces, as appropriate: United States Air Force Band of the Pacific-Asia, Det 1 (Unit 5075, APO AP 96328-5000)

For Hawaii, Pacific Air Forces, as appropriate: United States Air Force Band of the Pacific-Hawaii (OL-A) (Hickam AFB)

Air Force Base Conversion Agency (AFBCA)

AFBCA is a FIELD OPERATING AGENCY headquartered in Washington, D.C., and serves as the federal real property disposal agent and managing agency for USAF bases as they are closed under the Base Closure and Realignment Act of 1988 and the Defense Base Closure and Realignment Act of 1990. AFBCA works with state and local authorities and communities to help develop reuse opportunities to minimize adverse economic impacts on communities affected by base closings.

Air Force bases

All major USAF installations in the United States and its territories are called Air Force bases, abbreviated AFB. Bases located in foreign countries are called air bases (AB). Two USAF units based in the United Kingdom are known by the name of the host country's base: RAF [Royal Air Force] Lakenheath and RAF Mildenhall.

Altus AFB, Oklahoma

Altus was established as Altus Army Air Field in 1942, was inactivated after WORLD WAR II, then reactivated on August 1, 1953. Currently an AIR EDUCATION AND TRAINING COMMAND (AETC) base and home of the 97th Air Mobility Wing, it operates strategic airlift and aerial flying training schools and maintains and supports C-5, KC-135, C-141, and C-17 aircraft. Approximately 3,500 military personnel are stationed here.

Further reading: Altus AFB Web site, www. altus.af.mil.

Andersen AFB, Guam

Andersen was established as North Field in 1944, during WORLD WAR II and was instrumental in bomber operations against Japan. Today it is a PACIFIC AIR FORCES base and headquarters of the THIRTEENTH AIR FORCE. It is the Pacific center for power projection, regional cooperation, and multinational training, and it serves as a logistics sup-

port and staging base for aircraft operating in the Pacific and Indian Oceans. The base is home to 2,163 military personnel and has a USAF clinic and a navy hospital. It was named for General James Roy Andersen, lost at sea on February 26, 1946.

Further reading: Andersen AFB Web site, www. andersen.af.mil.

Andrews AFB, Maryland

Andrews is most famous as the home of AIR FORCE ONE and is the home of the 89th Airlift Wing, which provides mission support to the nation's leaders, including the president. Naval and marine installations are also hosted by the base.

Andrews was established in 1942 as Camp Springs Army Air Field. Located just 12 miles east of Washington, D.C., it served principally as a base for air defense of the capital. It was named for Lieutenant General FRANK MAXWELL ANDREWS, military air power advocate, killed in an aircraft crash on May 3, 1943, in Iceland. The large base is home to 7,400 military personnel and more than 3,000 civilian employees. The base also includes a large hospital.

Further reading: Andrews AFB Web site, www. dcmilitary.com/baseguides/airforce/andrews.

Arnold AFB, Tennessee

This AIR FORCE MATERIEL COMMAND (AFMC) base houses the ARNOLD ENGINEERING DEVELOPMENT CENTER (AEDC), the world's largest test facility for advanced aerodynamics and propulsion systems. The center conducts research, development, and evaluation testing for the USAF and the Department of Defense. Only 123 military personnel work at the base, which is staffed mainly by some 3,000 civilian contract employees.

Dedicated June 25, 1951, the base is named for HENRY HARLEY ARNOLD, WORLD WAR II chief of the U.S. ARMY AIR FORCES.

Further reading: Arnold AFB Web site, www. arnold.af.mil.

This A-10 Thunderbolt from the 81st Fighter Squadron, Spangdahlem AB, Germany, takes off from Aviano AB, Italy. *(U.S. Air Force)*

Aviano AB, Italy

Located 50 miles north of Venice, Aviano AB is a UNITED STATES AIR FORCES IN EUROPE (USAFE) base, headquarters of the SIXTEENTH AIR FORCE, and host to the 31st Fighter Wing—the only permanent NATO fighter WING in southern Europe.

Aviano has served as an Italian air base since 1911; USAF operations began here in 1954. It is home to 3,163 military personnel.

Further reading: Aviano AB Web site, www. aviano.af.mil.

Barksdale AFB, Louisiana

Located in Bossier City, Louisiana, Barksdale was activated in 1933, principally to provide air defense of the Gulf Coast. It was named for Lieutenant Eugene H. Barksdale, an aviator who died in a crash near Wright Field, Ohio, in 1926. In 1949, Barksdale became a STRATEGIC AIR COMMAND (SAC) base and headquarters for the SECOND AIR FORCE. In 1990, it became the headquarters base for the EIGHTH AIR FORCE and the 2nd Bomb Wing and has continued to serve in these capacities after SAC was disbanded in 1992. The base is also the site of the fine Eighth Air Force Museum.

A very large facility handling mainly B-52 and A-10 operations and the 1307th Civil Engineering (Red Horse) Squadron, Barksdale is home to 5,799 military personnel and 649 civilian employees. Facilities include a 40-bed base hospital.

Further reading: Barksdale AFB Web site, www.barksdale.af.mil.

Beale AFB, California

Home of the 9th Reconnaissance Wing and the 7th Space Warning Squadron, Beale operates U-2 reconnaissance aircraft and T-38 Talon trainers.

Formerly the U.S. Army's Camp Beale (named for Army Brigadier General Edward F. Beale), the facility was acquired by the USAF in 1951 and was first used as a STRATEGIC AIR COMMAND (SAC) base, operating heavy bombers and tankers. More than 3,000 military personnel are assigned to the base.

Further reading: Beale AFB Web site, www. beale.af.mil.

Bolling AFB, Washington, D.C.

Named for Colonel Raynal C. Bolling, first high-ranking U.S. aviator killed in WORLD WAR I, the airfield was established in October 1917. In 1940, part of the base was transferred to the navy as the Anacostia Naval Air Station.

Bolling is now home to the 11th Wing, the USAF Honor Guard, the U.S. Air Force Band, the AIR FORCE OFFICE OF SCIENTIFIC RESEARCH (AFOSR), the Air Force Chief of Chaplains, and the Air Force Surgeon General. It is headquarters of the AIR FORCE HISTORY SUPPORT OFFICE (AFHSO) and headquarters of the AIR FORCE OFFICE OF SPECIAL INVESTIGATIONS (AFOSI), and also houses the AIR FORCE REAL ESTATE AGENCY (AFREA), AIR FORCE MEDICAL OPERATIONS AGENCY (AFMOA), Defense Intelligence Agency, and the AIR FORCE LEGAL SERVICES AGENCY (AFLSA).

Further reading: Bolling AFB Web site, www. bolling.af.mil.

Brooks AFB, Texas

Located in San Antonio, Brooks is an AIR FORCE MATERIEL COMMAND (AFMC) base, which houses the Human Systems Center, the UNITED STATES AIR FORCE SCHOOL OF AEROSPACE MEDICINE, and the Armstrong Laboratory of the Human Systems Program Office. Other units on base are the Systems Acquisition School, AIR FORCE MEDICAL SUPPORT AGENCY (AFMSA), 68th Intelligence Squadron, AIR FORCE CENTER FOR ENVIRONMENTAL EXCELLENCE (AFCEE), and the Medical Systems Implementation and Training Element.

Activated in 1917, the base was named for Cadet Sidney J. Brooks, Jr., who was killed on November 13, 1917, during his commissioning flight. From 1919 to 1923, the field served as a balloon and airship school, and from 1922 to 1931 it was a primary flight training school. The School of Aviation Medicine was established here in 1926. Flight operations ceased at Brooks in 1960.

Further reading: Brooks AFB Web site, www.brooks.af.mil.

Cannon AFB, New Mexico

An AIR COMBAT COMMAND (ACC) base, Cannon is home to the 27th Fighter Wing, with F-16 operations. Activated in August 1942, the base was named for General John K. Cannon, WORLD WAR II Mediterranean theater commander. Cannon was the last USAF base to operate the F-111 "Aardvark," which was retired after 30 years of service in 1996.

Located near Clovis, New Mexico, Cannon is home to almost 5,000 military personnel.

Further reading: Cannon AFB Web site, www.cannon.af.mil.

Carswell AFB

Carswell was activated in 1942 near Fort Worth, Texas, as Tarant Field. Later named Griffiss AFB, it was, in 1948, renamed in honor of Major Horace S. Carswell, Jr., a Fort Worth winner of the Medal of Honor, killed in a B-24 crash landing in China in 1944.

As a STRATEGIC AIR COMMAND (SAC) base, Carswell, home of the 7th Bomb Group, operated B-36 bombers and then B-52s and B-58s. The base was closed in 1991.

Further reading: Carswell AFB information, Global Security.Org, "Carswell AFB," www.globalsecurity.org/wmd/facility/carswell.htm.

Castle AFB

Activated in 1941 at Merced, California, the Castle predecessor installation operated throughout WORLD WAR II as a basic flight training field. In 1946, it was named after Brigadier General Frederick W. Castle, Medal of Honor winner killed in action in 1944, and was inactivated shortly afterward. Reactivated in 1955, as a STRATEGIC AIR COMMAND (SAC) base, it was one of the first installations to operate B-52s. Castle AFB was closed in 1991.

Further reading: Castle AFB information, Global Security.Org, "Castle AFB," at www.globalsecurity.org/wmd/facility/castle.htm.

Chanute AFB, Illinois

Established in 1917 as Rantoul Aviation Field in Rantoul, Illinois, the facility was renamed for aviation pioneer Octave Chanute before the close of the year. During WORLD WAR I, it served as a flight training facility, and, after the war, three military aviation-related training schools were established here, collectively forming the Air Service Technical School. With the advent of WORLD WAR II, Chanute became a major training center for technicians as well as pilots; some 200,000 students passed through schools here.

Renamed Chanute Technical Training Center in 1990, the entire installation was closed in 1993.

Further reading: Chanute AFB information, Octave Chanute Aerospace Museum, "From Swords to Plowshares: The Closure of Chanute," at www.aeromuseum.org/History/plough.html.

Charleston AFB, South Carolina

An AIR FORCE MATERIEL COMMAND (AFMC) base, Charleston is home to the 437th Airlift Wing and other organizations. Activated in October 1942, the base was inactivated in March 1946, then reactivated in August 1953. Charleston AFB is located just outside of Charleston, S.C., and is staffed by 7,352 military personnel and 1,295 civilian employees.

Further reading: Charleston AFB Web site, www.charleston.af.mil.

Clark AB

Located 50 miles north of Manila in the Philippines, Clark was established as Fort Stotsenberg, an army installation, in 1903. In March 1912, Lieutenant FRANK P. LAHM was named to command the Philippine Air School here, with a single aircraft, and in 1919 the installation officially became Clark Field, named in honor of Captain Harold M. Clark, a U.S. Army pilot killed in a crash in Panama. It was in the summer of 1941, on the eve of America's entry into WORLD WAR II, that the 19th Bombardment Group, with B-17s and B-18s, arrived. When the Japanese attacked Clark Field on December 8, 1941, most of the aircraft were destroyed on the ground. Most of the personnel stationed at Clark who survived the initial attack participated in the defense of Bataan, surrendered with the U.S. and Philippine troops under command of Lieutenant General Jonathan Wainwright, and endured the infamous "Bataan Death March" to distant POW camps. U.S. forces began to retake Clark Field late in 1944, forcing the Japanese out by January 1945.

The THIRTEENTH AIR FORCE became resident at Clark AB in 1947, and the base was a central logistics hub during both the KOREAN WAR and the VIETNAM WAR. It was also the first stop for returning U.S. POWs from Vietnam in 1973. During the 1986 revolution against the Philippine's dictatorial president Ferdinand Marcos, Marcos was evacuated through Clark AB, and, in 1989, USAF F-4s, flying from the base, supported Philippine president Corazon Aquino's successful defense in the sixth coup attempt against her.

In 1991, the Philippine Senate rejected an extension of the U.S.-Philippines Military Bases Agreement, which expired on September 16, effectively terminating the American military's lease for Clark AB. The USAF formally transferred Clark AB to the Philippines on November 26, 1991.

Further reading: Clark AB information, Clark Air Base (CAB) home pages, at www.clarkab.org.

Columbus AFB, Mississippi

Activated in 1941 for pilot training, the base is home to the 14th Flying Training Wing and is a location for undergraduate pilot training and an Introduction to Fighter Fundamentals course.

Further reading: Columbus AFB Web site, www.columbus.af.mil.

Davis-Monthan AFB, Arizona

Located within the city limits of Tucson, Davis-Monthan is an AIR COMBAT COMMAND (ACC) base, which houses the 355th Wing and is headquarters of the TWELFTH AIR FORCE. The base is a center for electronic combat training and operations and also hosts a Montana ANG F-16 fighter wing. The base is also the site of the AIR FORCE MATERIEL COMMAND (AFMC) Aerospace Maintenance and Regeneration Center, a storage facility for excess USAF and Department of Defense aerospace vehicles. Almost 6,000 military personnel are stationed here, and the base includes a large military hospital.

Activated in 1927, the base is named for two Tucson-area aviators killed in accidents, Lieutenant Samuel H. Davis (killed December 28, 1921) and Second Lieutenant Oscar Monthan (killed March 27, 1924).

Further reading: Davis-Monthan AFB Web site, www.dm.af.mil.

Dover AFB, Delaware

The largest AIRLIFT aerial post on the East Coast, Dover AFB, an AIR MOBILITY COMMAND (AMC) base, is home to the 436th Airlift Wing. Activated in December 1941, just 10 days after the Japanese attack on Pearl Harbor, the base was inactivated in 1946, then reactivated early in 1951. It was the first airbase to receive the giant C-5 Galaxy transport. More than 7,000 military personnel are stationed here.

Further reading: Dover AFB Web site, www. dover.af.mil.

Dyess AFB, Texas

An AIR COMBAT COMMAND (ACC) base, Dyess is home to the 7th Wing and operates two B-1B bomber squadrons and two C-130 squadrons. All B-1B training is conducted here.

It is named for Lieutenant Colonel William E. Dyess, who escaped from a Japanese POW camp in WORLD WAR II and was subsequently killed in a P-38 crash in December 1943. Almost 5,000 military personnel are stationed here, just outside of Abilene.

Further reading: Dyess AFB Web site, www. dyess.af.mil.

Edwards AFB, California

This AIR FORCE MATERIEL COMMAND (AFMC) base is best known to the public as an advanced aircraft and aerospace vehicle test site and as the secondary landing site for the Space Shuttle. It is home to the AIR FORCE FLIGHT TEST CENTER (AFFTC) and the UNITED STATES AIR FORCE TEST PILOT SCHOOL. Also housed here are the Astronautics Directorate of the Phillips Laboratory and NASA's Ames Dryden Flight Research Facility.

Base activities began here in September 1933 when the site was known as Muroc Army Air Field. It was renamed for Captain Glen W. Edwards, killed on June 5, 1948, while testing the revolutionary YB-49 "Flying Wing." More than 4,200 military personnel are stationed on the base, and government and contract civilian personnel number about 7,400.

Further reading: Edwards AFB Web site, www. edwards.af.mil.

Eglin AFB, Florida

Covering 463,452 acres—two-thirds the size of Rhode Island—Eglin is the nation's largest USAF base. Its host unit is the AIR FORCE DEVELOPMENT TEST CENTER (AFDTC) with an associate unit, the Aeronautical Systems Center. Also located here is the Armament Directorate of the Wright Laboratory. Operational units include 33rd Fighter Wing, 53rd Wing (ACC), 96th Air Base Wing, 46th Test Wing, 9191th Special Operations Wing, 20th Space Surveillance Squadron, 9th Special Operations Squadron, 728th Tactical Control Squadron, a U.S. Army Ranger Training Battalion, a U.S. Navy Explosive Ordnance Disposal School, and the Air Force Armament Museum. Almost 8,500 military personnel are stationed here, and the base also employs 4,303 civilians.

Activated in 1935, the base was subsequently named for Lieutenant Colonel Frederick I. Eglin, a WORLD WAR I pilot killed in an accident on January 1, 1937.

Further reading: Eglin AFB Web site, www. eglin.af.mil.

Eielson AFB, Alaska

A PACIFIC AIR FORCES (PACAF) base, Eielson hosts the 354th Fighter Wing with F-16, A-10, and OA-10 operations. Also operating from Eielson are the Arctic Survival School and the 168th Air Refueling Wing (ANG) as well as a detachment of the AIR FORCE TECHNICAL APPLICATIONS CENTER (AFTAC).

Activated in 1944, the base was named for Carl Ben Eielson, an Arctic aviation pioneer who died on an Arctic rescue mission in November 1929. More than 2,700 military personnel are stationed here.

Further reading: Eielson AFB Web site, www. eielson.af.mil.

Ellsworth AFB, South Dakota

The base is home to the 28th Bomb Wing, with one B1-B squadron, and the South Dakota Air and Space Museum.

Activated in July 1942 as the Rapid City AAB, it was renamed in 1953 for Brigadier General

Richard E. Ellsworth, killed March 18, 1953, in the crash of an RB-36 in Newfoundland. There are 3,724 military personnel stationed here.

Further reading: Ellsworth AFB Web site, www. ellsworth.af.mil.

Elmendorf AFB, Alaska

Located just outside Anchorage, Elmendorf is a PACIFIC AIR FORCES (PACAF) base and a hub for all traffic to and from the Far East. It houses headquarters for the following: ALASKAN AIR COMMAND; ELEVENTH AIR FORCE; and Alaska NORAD Region. The base host unit is the 3rd Wing, with F-15 fighter and C-130 and C-12 airlift operations, as well as E-3 airborne air control operations, and 3rd Medical Group. Associated units also operate from the base, which also hosts various U.S. Army, U.S. Navy, and U.S. Marine activities. More than 6,500 military personnel are stationed at Elmendorf. Facilities include a 60-bed hospital.

Activated in July 1940, the installation was named for Captain Hugh Elmendorf, killed January 13, 1933, at Wright Field, Ohio, while testing a new pursuit aircraft.

Further reading: Elmendorf AFB Web site, www. elmendorf.af.mil.

England AFB, Louisiana

This base was activated near Alexandria, Louisiana, in 1941 and was known as Alexandria AAB until 1955, when it was named for Lieutenant Colonel John B. England, a WORLD WAR II fighter ace killed in a 1954 F-86 accident. He had formerly commanded a bomber unit stationed at Alexandria AAB.

The base was used during World War II for B-17 and B-29 training, was inactivated from 1946 to 1950, then was used by the AIR NATIONAL GUARD until 1953, when the USAF took it over. At the time of its closure in 1992, England AFB was home to the 23rd Tactical Fighter Wing, flying A-10s.

Fairchild AFB, Washington

An AIR FORCE MATERIEL COMMAND (AFMC) base, Fairchild is the air refueling hub to the western

United States. Its host unit is the 92nd Air Refueling Wing, with KC-135 aircraft, and the base also houses tenant units, most notably the 366th Crew Training Group, which operates the AIR EDUCATION AND TRAINING COMMAND (AETC) Survival School. The base is home to 4,316 military personnel.

Activated in 1942 as Galena Field, then renamed Spokane AFB, it was finally named in 1950 after General Muir S. Fairchild, USAF vice chief of staff.

Further reading: Fairchild AFB Web site, www. fairchild.af.mil.

Falcon AFB

Listed under Schriever AFB.

Francis E. Warren AFB, Wyoming

Located just outside of Cheyenne, the base is home to the 90th Missile Wing, with 50 Peacekeeper and 150 Minuteman III missiles. The 37th Air Rescue Flight also operates out of the base. The Air Force ICBM Museum is located on the base.

Activated on July 4, 1867, by the U.S. Army as Fort D. A. Russell, the base was assigned to the USAF in 1947. It had been renamed after the first state governor of Wyoming, Francis Emory Warren, in 1930. The base has no runway; 3,655 military personnel serve here.

Further reading: Francis E. Warren AFB Web site, www.warren.af.mil.

Goodfellow AFB, Texas

This AIR EDUCATION AND TRAINING COMMAND (AETC) base is home to the 17th Training Wing, which provides technical training in intelligence areas, serving not only USAF personnel but members of other services as well as civilian intelligence agencies and members of foreign military services. The wing also trains USAF, U.S. Army, and U.S. Marine Corps personnel in fire protection and fire rescue and conducts USAF special instruments training.

Activated in January 1941, the base was named for Lieutenant John J. Goodfellow, Jr., a WORLD

WAR I pilot killed in action on September 14, 1918. More than 3,000 military personnel are stationed here. The base has no runway.

Further reading: Goodfellow AFB Web site, www.goodfellow.af.mil.

Grand Forks AFB, North Dakota

An AIR FORCE MATERIEL COMMAND (AFMC) base, Grand Forks is home to the 319th Air Refueling Wing and the 321st Missile Group (150 Minuteman III ICBMs). Until the STRATEGIC AIR COMMAND (SAC) was disbanded in 1992, Grand Forks was a SAC base. The base was also home to 319 Bomb Group, which flew B-1 bombers until it was inactivated in May 1994.

Activated in 1956 on land donated to the USAF by the citizens of Grand Forks, the base itself covers 5,418 acres and the missile complex an additional 7,500 square miles. More than 5,000 military personnel are stationed here.

Further reading: Grand Forks AFB Web site, www.grandforks.af.mil.

Griffiss AFB, New York

This longtime STRATEGIC AIR COMMAND (SAC) base was located near Rome, New York, until its phaseout and closure during 1995–98. Activated in 1942 as Rome AAF, it was named in honor of Lieutenant Colonel Townsend E. Griffiss, whose aircraft was shot down by friendly fire during WORLD WAR II in 1942. Its principal unit at the time of its phaseout and closure was the 416th Wing with B-52 bombers and KC-135 tankers.

Further reading: Griffiss AFB information, GlobalSecurity.Org, "Griffiss AFB," at www.globalsecurity.org/military/facility/griffiss.htm.

Grissom AFB, Indiana

Originally a U.S. Navy base near Kokomo, Indiana, then a USAF storage branch from 1951 to 1954, when it became Bunker Hill AFB, it was renamed in honor of Virgil I. "Gus" Grissom, one of America's original seven astronauts, who was killed dur-

ing an Apollo spacecraft test in 1967. The base served both as a STRATEGIC AIR COMMAND (SAC) facility and as a TACTICAL AIR COMMAND (TAC) base, with B-47s and B-58s. At the time of its closure in 1994, it was primarily used by the 305th Air Refueling Wing, flying EC-135s and KC-135s.

Gunter AFB (Gunter Annex)

Listed under Maxwell AFB, Gunter Annex.

Hanscom AFB, Massachusetts

This AIR FORCE MATERIEL COMMAND (AFMC) base is headquarters of the Electronic Systems Center and is responsible for acquisition of C^4I (command, control, communications, and intelligence) systems for the USAF and for other services and government agencies. The base is the site for much advanced electronic warfare research and development.

In 1943, the base was named Hanscom Field in honor of Laurence G. Hanscom, an aviation advocate and pioneer killed in a civilian aircraft accident in 1941. More than 2,000 military personnel serve on the base, together with almost 2,000 civilian employees.

Further reading: Hanscom AFB Web site, www.hanscom.af.mil.

Hickam AFB, Hawaii

Located just west of Honolulu, the base was named Hickam Field in 1935 to honor Lieutenant Colonel Horace M. Hickam, killed in an aircraft accident in Texas the year before. Hickam Field was heavily damaged in the December 7, 1941, Japanese attack on Pearl Harbor (157 of 231 planes destroyed or damaged on the ground), but quickly recovered to become a major staging area for WORLD WAR II operations in the Pacific.

In 1957, PACIFIC AIR FORCES (PACAF) headquarters was established at Hickam AFB, which also hosts the 15th Air Base Wing and major tenant units, including 154th Wing (ANG), 201st Combat Communications Group, and 615th Air Mobility Support Group. There are 3,657 military personnel at Hickam AFB and 1,280 civilian employees.

Further reading: Hickam AFB Web site, www2. hickam.af.mil.

Hill AFB, Utah

An AIR FORCE MATERIEL COMMAND (AFMC) base, Hill is headquarters of the Ogden Air Logistics Center, which provides support for silo-based ICBM (INTERCONTINENTAL BALLISTIC MISSILE) weapons—Minutemen and Peacekeepers—and for F-16 and C-130 aircraft, conventional munitions, and other aerospace components, including software and photonics. Other units on base include the 412th Test Wing, which manages the Utah Test and Training Range, the 388th Fighter Wing, the 419th Fighter Wing, and the Defense Megacenter Ogden. The Hill Aerospace Museum is also on base. More than 4,600 military personnel are stationed at Hill, which also employs a large number (9,532) of civilians.

Activated in November 1940, the base was named for Major Ployer P. Hill, killed on October 30, 1935, while testing the first B-17 bomber.

Further reading: Hill AFB Web site, www.hill. af.mil.

Holloman AFB, New Mexico

This AIR COMBAT COMMAND (ACC) base is home to the 49th Fighter Wing, with F-117 Stealth fighter operations. Also on base are F-4E aircrew training (20th Fighter Squadron and 1st German Air Force Training Squadron), AT-38B training, and the 48th Rescue Squadron. Twelve German Tornado aircraft, with 350 German personnel, are permanently assigned to the WING. The base is also home to a number of associated units.

Activated in 1942 as the Alamogordo Bombing and Gunnery Range, the base was named in 1948 in honor of Colonel George Holloman, an instrument flying and missile pioneer who died in a B-17 accident in Formosa in 1946. More than 4,000 military personnel are stationed here.

Further reading: Holloman AFB Web site, www.holloman.af.mil.

Howard AFB, Panama

The 24th Wing, an AIR COMBAT COMMAND (ACC) unit, is headquartered here as the USAF presence throughout Latin America. Also on base are the 640th Air Mobility Support Squadron and the 33rd Intelligence Squadron. Sixteen hundred military personnel are stationed at Howard, which was established in 1928 as Bruja Point Military Reservation, then named for Major Charles H. Howard.

Further reading: Howard AFB information, GlobalSecurity.Org, "Howard AFB," www.globalsecurity.org/military/facility/howard.htm.

Hurlburt Field, Florida

This base is headquarters of the AIR FORCE SPECIAL OPERATIONS COMMAND (AFSOC) and is home to the 16th Special Operations Wing. Also on base are the 505th Command and Control Evaluation Group, which includes the USAF Air Ground Operations School, the USAF Battle Staff Training School (Blue Flag), the 720th Special Tactics Group, the 23rd Special Tactics Squadron, the Joint Warfare Center, the USAF Special Operations School, the 18th Flight Test Squadron, the 823rd Civil Engineering Squadron (Red Horse), a detachment of the 11335th Technical Training Squadron, and a detachment of the AIR WEATHER SERVICE (AWS). More than 7,000 military personnel are stationed at Hurlburt.

Hurlburt was activated in 1941 as an auxiliary field of Eglin AAF (see Eglin AFB) and in 1944 was named in honor of Lieutenant Donald W. Hurlburt, killed while flying from Eglin in 1943.

Further reading: Hurlburt Field Web site, www. hurlburt.af.mil.

Incirlik AB, Turkey

A UNITED STATES AIR FORCES IN EUROPE (USAFE) base, Incirlik, near Ankara, is home to the 39th Wing and operates Combined Task Force assets, including Turkish, British, French, and U.S. combat and tanker aircraft. The base is also home to the 628th Air Mobility Support Squadron, which provides a full aerial port operation.

Activated in May 1954 in what was once a fig orchard (*incirlik* is the Turkish word for fig orchard), the base now has almost 2,500 U.S. military personnel and almost 3,000 civilian employees. It incorporates a medium-sized regional military hospital.

Further reading: Incirlik AB information, GlobalSecurity.Org, "Sixteenth Air Force," at www.globalsecurity.org/military/agency/usaf/16af.htm.

Kadena AB, Japan

A PACIFIC AIR FORCES (PACAF) base, Kadena, is home to the 18th Wing (F-15 operations) and the 909th Air Refueling Squadron (KC-135 operations), the 961st Airborne Air Control Squadron (E-3 operations), and the 33rd Rescue Squadron (HH-60 operations), in addition to associated units.

Kadena was a Japanese airfield during WORLD WAR II when it was taken by U.S. forces invading Okinawa. The USAAF used it as a base from which bombing raids against the Japanese homeland were launched. Kadena was headquarters of the TWENTIETH AIR FORCE during the KOREAN WAR. The base is named for the nearest city. There are some 7,300 military personnel at Kadena and more than 4,000 civilian employees, U.S. nationals, and locals.

Further reading: Kadena AB Web site, www.kadena.af.mil.

Keesler AFB, Mississippi

Located in Biloxi on the Gulf of Mexico, Keesler is an AIR EDUCATION AND TRAINING COMMAND (AETC) base and headquarters of the SECOND AIR FORCE. Housed here is the 81st Training Wing, which specializes in avionics, communications, electronics, and related technical areas, and the Keesler Medical Center (with a 250-bed hospital). The base is also home to the AETC NCO Academy. About 8,300 military personnel are stationed at Keesler, together with more than 4,000 civilian employees.

The base, activated on June 12, 1941, is named for Second Lieutenant Samuel R. Keesler, Jr., a Mississippi native killed in action as an aerial observer during WORLD WAR I, on October 9, 1918.

Further reading: Keesler AFB Web site, www.keesler.af.mil.

Kelly AFB, Texas

Located outside of San Antonio, Kelly AFB, inactivated in 2001, was an AIR FORCE MATERIEL COMMAND (AFMC) base and the headquarters of the San Antonio Air Logistics Center, which provided logistics management, procurement, and systems support for an array of aircraft, including the C-5 Galaxy. The center managed more than 75 percent of the USAF engine inventory, the fuel and lubricants used by USAF and NASA, and nuclear weapons. The base also housed the headquarters of the AIR INTELLIGENCE AGENCY (AIA) and was home to the AIR FORCE INFORMATION WARFARE CENTER (AFIWC), the Joint Command and Control Warfare Center, the Air Force News Agency, the Defense Commissary Agency, and other agencies and offices. In all, 4,581 military and 14,397 civilian personnel work at Kelly AFB.

Established on November 21, 1916, as Aviation Camp, Fort Houston, Kelly was the oldest continuously active air force base in the United States. It was named for Lieutenant George E. M. Kelly, the first U.S. Army pilot to lose his life flying a military aircraft, killed May 10, 1911.

Further reading: Kelly AFB information, Global Security.Org, "Kelly AFB," at www.globalsecurity.org/military/facility/kelly.htm.

Kirtland AFB, New Mexico

Located in Albuquerque, Kirtland is an AIR FORCE MATERIEL COMMAND (AFMC) base and headquarters of the 377th Air Base Wing. An array of agencies and units are housed here, including 58th Special Operations Wing; AIR FORCE OPERATIONAL TEST AND EVALUATION CENTER (AFOTEC); Philips Laboratory; 150th Fighter Wing (ANG); Field Command's Defense Nuclear Agency; Sandia National Laboratories; Department of Energy's Albuquerque Operations Office; Kirtland NCO

Academy; 898th Munitions Squadron; Air Force Security Police Agency (AFSPA); Defense Nuclear Weapons School; Air Force Inspection Agency; and Air Force Safety Center.

The base is staffed by almost 6,000 military personnel and almost 14,000 civilian employees. It was established in January 1941 as the Albuquerque Army Air Base and was renamed in honor of Colonel Roy C. Kirtland, an air pioneer who died on May 2, 1941.

Further reading: Kirtland AFB Web site, www. kirtland.af.mil.

Kunsan AB, Republic of Korea

A PACIFIC AIR FORCES (PACAF) base, Kunsan is home to the 8th Fighter Wing F-16 operations and also hosts several U.S. Army units. About 2,300 military personnel are stationed at Kunsan, which was built by the Japanese in 1938 and taken over and expanded by the USAF in 1951.

Further reading: Kunsan AB Web site, www. kunsan.af.mil.

Lackland AFB, Texas

This AIR EDUCATION AND TRAINING COMMAND (AETC) base is home to the 37th Training Wing, largest training wing in the USAF, graduating 65,000 students each year. The 737th Training Group provides basic military training. The 37th Training Group conducts more than 250 technical training courses. The Defense Language Institute English Language Center conducts English language training for international and U.S. military students. The INTER-AMERICAN AIR FORCES ACADEMY (IAAFA) offers professional, technical, and management training in Spanish to military forces and government agencies from Latin American and Caribbean nations. Some 6,300 military personnel serve at Lackland, in addition to 6,200 civilian employees, and approximately 8,700 students.

Lackland is also the home of the USAF's largest medical organization, the 59th Medical Wing (Wilford Hall USAF Medical Center), which runs a 592-bed hospital on base.

Activated in 1941 as part of Kelly Field (see Kelly AFB), it was detached in 1942 and, in 1948, was named for Brigadier General Frank D. Lackland, early commandant of Kelly Field, who died in 1943.

Further reading: Lackland AFB Web site, www. lackland.af.mil.

Langley AFB, Virginia

Langley is headquarters of AIR COMBAT COMMAND (ACC) and houses the 1st Fighter Wing F-15 operations. Associate units include Air Operations Squadron, Training Support Squadron, Computer Systems Squadron, the ACC Heritage of America Band, a U.S. Army TRADOC Flight Detachment, the Army/USAF Center for Low-Intensity Conflict, and the AIR FORCE DOCTRINE CENTER (AFDC). NASA's Langley Research Center is adjacent to the base. Almost 8,000 military personnel are stationed at Langley, together with about 1,100 civilian employees.

Activated on December 30, 1916, as an "Aviation Experimental Station and Proving Grounds," the facility was named to honor Samuel P. Langley, aviation pioneer and scientist, who died in 1906.

Further reading: Langley AFB Web site, www. langley.af.mil.

Laughlin AFB, Texas

This AIR EDUCATION AND TRAINING COMMAND (AETC) base is home to the 47th Flying Training Wing, which provides specialized undergraduate pilot training. About 1,200 military personnel are stationed here, along with approximately 1,000 civilian employees. The base was activated in July 1942 and named for First Lieutenant Jack Thomas Laughlin, a native of Del Rio (location of the base), a B-17 pilot killed over Java, January 29, 1942.

Further reading: Laughlin AFB Web site, www. laughlin.af.mil.

Little Rock AFB, Arkansas

An AIR COMBAT COMMAND (ACC) base, Little Rock, is home to the 314th Airlift Wing, the only C-130 training base in the Department of Defense. The base trains USAF crews as well as crews from all service branches and some foreign countries. Tenant organizations include 189th Airlift Wing (ANG); 96th Mobile Aerial Port Squadron; 348th USAF Recruiting Squadron; a detachment of the AIR FORCE OFFICE OF SPECIAL INVESTIGATIONS (AFPSI); a detachment of the 373rd Field Training Squadron; a detachment of the AIR FORCE AUDIT AGENCY (AFAA); and the Combat Aerial Delivery School (ACC). The base is also headquarters for the Arkansas AIR NATIONAL GUARD.

Activated in 1955, the base has 4,450 military personnel and includes a 25-bed hospital.

Further reading: Little Rock AFB Web site, www. littlerock.af.mil.

Los Angeles AFB, California

Located in El Segundo, just outside of Los Angeles, this AIR FORCE MATERIEL COMMAND (AFMC) base is headquarters for AFMC's Space and Missile Systems Center, which is responsible for research, development, acquisition, in-orbit testing, and sustainment of military space and missile systems. The on-base support unit is the 61st Air Base Group. The base has no runway. About 1,500 military personnel are stationed here, together with more than 1,000 civilian employees.

Further reading: Los Angeles AFB Web site, www.losangeles.af.mil.

Malmstrom AFB, Montana

An AIR FORCE SPACE COMMAND (AFSPC) base, Malmstrom's host unit is the 341st Missile Wing, operating Minuteman III missiles. The base tenant unit is the 43rd Air Refueling Group, operating KC-135 tankers. There are 4,350 military personnel stationed at Malmstrom, which was activated on December 15, 1942, as Great Falls AAF and, in 1955, was named for Colonel Einar A. Malmstrom, a WORLD WAR II fighter commander killed in an air accident on August 21, 1954. Malmstrom was the first Minuteman wing of the STRATEGIC AIR COMMAND (SAC).

Further reading: Malmstrom AFB Web site, www.malmstrom.af.mil.

Maxwell AFB, Alabama

An AIR EDUCATION AND TRAINING COMMAND (AETC) base, Maxwell is home to the 42nd Air Base Wing and is the headquarters of AIR UNIVERSITY (AU) as well as home to AIR WAR COLLEGE (AWC), Air Command and Staff College (ACSC), AIR FORCE QUALITY INSTITUTE (AFQI), Air University Library; COLLEGE OF AEROSPACE DOCTRINE, RESEARCH AND EDUCATION; AIR FORCE RESERVE OFFICERS TRAINING CORPS (AFROTC), Officer Training School, and the Ira C. Eaker College for Professional Development. The base is headquarters for the COMMUNITY COLLEGE OF THE AIR FORCE (CCAF) and the CIVIL AIR PATROL (CAP). Also resident here are the Squadron Officer School and the AIR FORCE INSTITUTE OF TECHNOLOGY (AFIT). Associate units base here include 908th Airlift Wing (AIR FORCE RESERVE) and the AIR FORCE HISTORICAL RESEARCH AGENCY (AFHRA). There are 3,729 military personnel stationed at Maxwell, together with 2,986 civilian employees. The base has a 30-bed hospital.

The site of Maxwell AFB, near Montgomery, was a civilian flying school opened by the Wright brothers in 1910. It was activated as a military base in 1918 and was subsequently named for Second Lieutenant William C. Maxwell, killed in air accident on August 12, 1920, in the Philippines. Also see Maxwell AFB, Gunter Annex.

Further reading: Maxwell AFB Web site, www. au.af.mil.

Maxwell AFB, Gunter Annex, Alabama

This AIR EDUCATION AND TRAINING COMMAND (AETC) base is operated under the headquarters of AIR UNIVERSITY (AU). Gunter Annex includes the College for Enlisted Professional Military Education (includes USAF Senior NCO Academy); Extension Course Institute; Standard Systems Group; and AIR FORCE LOGISTICS MANAGEMENT AGENCY (AFLMA). See Maxwell AFB for numbers of personnel on base.

Gunter Annex was activated on August 27, 1940, and was named for William A. Gunter, long-time mayor of Montgomery, Alabama, and a champion of air power, who died in 1940.

Further reading: Maxwell AFB Web site, www. au.af.mil.

McChord AFB, Washington

An AIR MOBILITY COMMAND (AMC) base, McChord's host unit is the 62nd Airlift Wing, and its major tenants include 446th Airlift Wing (AIR FORCE RESERVE) and Western Air Defense Sector (AIR NATIONAL GUARD). The base is responsible for strategic AIRLIFT of personnel and cargo worldwide, on short notice, in support of national objectives. Its primary customer is the U.S. Army's Fort Lewis. There are more than 4,100 military personnel stationed here, together with about 1,300 civilian employees.

Activated on May 5, 1938, the base is named for Colonel William C. McChord, killed August 18, 1937, while attempting a forced landing at Maidens, Virginia.

Further reading: McChord AFB Web site, http:// public.mcchord.amc.af.mil.

McClellan AFB, California

Before it was closed in July 2001, this AIR FORCE MATERIEL COMMAND (AFMC) base, located near Sacramento, California, was the headquarters of the Sacramento Air Logistics Center, which provided logistics management, procurement, maintenance, and distribution support for F/EF-111 and A-10 aircraft and, as a second source, for the F-15 and KC-135 weapon systems. The center was program manager for the F-117A stealth fighter and the support center for the F-22. The center supported more than 200 electronic systems and programs as well as eight space systems. It also specialized in very-high-speed integrated circuits, fiber optics, and advanced composites. The center had facilities for robotic nondestructive inspection using X-ray and neutron radiography of F-111-size aircraft. With closure of the base, the USAF contracted many of the center's functions to private industry.

Other major units on base included Defense Depot-McClellan; Defense Information Systems Organization-McClellan; 938th Engineering Installation Squadron; Technical Operations Division, AIR FORCE TECHNICAL APPLICATIONS CENTER (AFTAC); FOURTH AIR FORCE (AIR FORCE RESERVE); and U.S. Coast Guard Air Station, Sacramento.

The base was named for Major Hezekiah McClellan, a pioneer in Arctic aeronautical experiments, who was killed in a crash on May 25, 1936.

Further reading: McClellan AFB information, GlobalSecurity.Org, "McClellan AFB," at www. globalsecurity.org/military/facility/mcclellan.htm.

McConnell AFB, Kansas

An AIR MOBILITY COMMAND (AMC) base, McConnell is home to the 22nd Air Refueling Wing; 931st Air Refueling Group (AIR FORCE RESERVE), and the 184th Bomb Wing (AIR NATIONAL GUARD). Almost 3,000 military personnel are assigned here.

Activated on June 5, 1951, the base is named for Captain Fred J. McConnell, a WORLD WAR II B-24 pilot who died in a crash of a private plane on October 25, 1945, and for his brother, Second Lieutenant Thomas L. McConnell, also a World War II B-24 pilot, who was killed on July 10, 1943, in the Pacific, during an attack on Bougainville.

Further reading: McConnell AFB Web site, www.mcconnell.af.mil.

McGuire AFB, New Jersey

This AIR MOBILITY COMMAND (AMC) base, located near Trenton, is home to the 305th Air Mobility Wing and is headquarters of the TWENTY-FIRST AIR FORCE. Also in residence are the 621st Air Mobility Operations Group, the Air Mobility Warfare Center (at Fort Dix, N.J.), the New Jersey AIR NATIONAL GUARD, the New Jersey CIVIL AIR PATROL, 108th Air Refueling Wing (ANG), 514th Air Mobility Wing (AIR FORCE RESERVE), and the McGuire NCO Academy. Including AFR and ANG units, 10,512 military personnel are assigned to McGuire, along with 1,604 civilian employees.

Activated in 1937 as Fort Dix AFB and adjoining Fort Dix, the installation was renamed in 1948 for Major Thomas B. McGuire, Jr., P-38 pilot, second leading U.S. ace of WORLD WAR II, and recipient of the Medal of Honor, who was killed in action on January 7, 1945, in the Philippines.

Further reading: McGuire AFB Web site, www.mcguire.af.mil.

Minot AFB, North Dakota
An AIR COMBAT COMMAND (ACC) base, Minot is home to the 5th Bomb Wing, operating B-52s, as well as the 91st Missile Wing, with Minuteman III ICBM operations. Other units include the 23rd Bomb Squadron and the 54th Rescue Flight. On base are 3,768 military personnel.

The base was activated in January 1957 and is named after the city of Minot, whose citizens donated $50,000 toward purchase of the land for the USAF. There is a 45-bed hospital on base.

Further reading: Minot AFB Web site, www.minot.af.mil.

Misawa AB, Japan
A PACIFIC AIR FORCES (PACAF) and joint-service base located within the city of Misawa, the base is home to the 35th Fighter Wing, F-16 operations, and includes the 3rd Space Surveillance Squadron, 301st Intelligence Squadron, a Naval Air Facility, a Naval Security Group, a U.S. Army field station, and Company E, U.S. Marine Support Battalion.

The Japanese army built an airfield at Misawa in 1938, and the base was occupied by U.S. forces in September 1945. Currently, more than 4,600 military personnel (USAF, navy, army, marines) are stationed here.

Further reading: Misawa AB Web site, www.misawa.af.mil.

Moody AFB, Georgia
Located in southern Georgia, near Valdosta, this AIR COMBAT COMMAND (ACC) base is home to the 347th Wing, operating F-16 LANTIRN-equipped

night fighters, as well as C-130E and A/OA-10 aircraft, and the 71st Air Control Squadron. Tenant units include 336th USAF Recruiting Squadron, a detachment of AIR FORCE OFFICE OF SPECIAL INVESTIGATIONS (AFOSI), and the 332nd Training Detachment. Military personnel on base number 3,752.

The base was activated in June 1941 and named for Major George P. Moody, who had been killed on May 5, 1941, while test-flying a Beech AT-l0.

Further reading: Moody AFB Web site, www.moody.af.mil.

Mountain Home AFB, Idaho
This AIR COMBAT COMMAND (ACC) base is home to the 366th Wing, the first and only air-intervention composite WING in the USAF, with F-l6C attack, F-15E interdiction, F-l5C air superiority, and KC-135R air refueling aircraft prepared to deploy rapidly worldwide for composite air-intervention operations. There are 3,635 military personnel assigned to the base, which was activated in August 1943. A 50-bed hospital is on base.

Further reading: Mountain Home AFB Web site, www.mountainhome.af.mil.

Nellis AFB, Nevada
Located outside of Las Vegas, this AIR COMBAT COMMAND (ACC) base is home to the AIR WARFARE CENTER (AWC) and also has three operational elements: 57th Wing; 99th Air Base Wing; and 53rd Wing (Eglin AFB, Florida). Within 57th Wing are the USAF Weapons School, USAF Air Demonstration Squadron (THUNDERBIRDS), 57th Operations Group, 57th Test Group (including 422nd Test and Evaluation Squadron), and 57th Logistics Group. A-l0, F-15E, F-16, and HH-60G aircraft operate out of the base.

A large facility, Nellis is also home to the 414th Combat Training Squadron (Red Flag), 549th Combat Training Squadron (Air Warrior), 547th Intelligence Squadron, 99th Range Group, 820th Civil Engineering Squadron (Red Horse), 896th Munitions Squadron, 11th Reconnaissance Squadron, and 66th Rescue Squadron. More than 7,000 military personnel and almost 1,000 civilians are assigned to the base.

Activated in July 1941 as the AAF Flexible Gunnery School, the base was closed in 1947, then reopened in 1949 and named for First Lieutenant William H. Nellis, a WORLD WAR II P-47 fighter pilot, killed December 27, 1944, in Europe. The main base sprawls over 11,000 acres with a range restricted area of 3.5 million acres, plus 12,000 square miles of airspace over the range and the military operating area. The 119-bed Nellis Federal Hospital is on base, a joint Air Force-Veterans Administration venture assigned to the 99th Medical Group.

Further reading: Nellis AFB Web site, www. nellis.af.mil.

Newark AFB, Ohio

Located at Newark, Ohio, and operated by the AIR FORCE MATERIEL COMMAND (AFMC), the base was closed on September 30, 1996. It was home to the Aerospace Guidance and Metrology Center, which repaired inertial guidance and navigation systems for most USAF missiles and aircraft as well as a variety of inertial systems for other branches of the armed forces. The center also managed the USAF's worldwide measurement and calibration program, providing a link between the National Institutes of Science and Technology and the USAF's 180 precision measurement equipment laboratories at bases around the world.

Activated as a USAF station on November 7, 1962, the facility had no runway.

Further reading: Newark AFB information, Global Security.Org, "Newark AFB," at www.globalsecurity. org/military/facility/newark.htm.

Offutt AFB, Nebraska

Located outside of Omaha, Offut was a major STRATEGIC AIR COMMAND (SAC) base and is now an AIR COMBAT COMMAND (ACC) base and headquarters of the U.S. Strategic Command. It is home to the 55th Wing; Strategic Joint Intelligence Center;

the headquarters of Strategic Communications–Computer Center; Air Force Global Weather Central; 6th Space Operations Squadron; National Airborne Operations Center (NAOC); and the Air Combat Command Heartland of America Band. A very large installation, Offut is staffed by 9,340 military and 1,592 civilian personnel. A 60-bed hospital is on base.

The base was originally activated by the U.S. Army in 1896 as Fort Crook and was first used for balloons in 1918 and for aircraft in 1924. In that year, it was named for First Lieutenant Jarvis J. Offutt, a WORLD WAR I pilot who died on August 13, 1918, in France.

Further reading: Offutt AFB Web site, www. offutt.af.mil.

Osan AB, Republic of Korea

This PACIFIC AIR FORCES base is the headquarters of SEVENTH AIR FORCE. Its host unit is the 51st Fighter Wing, F-16, C-12, A-10, and OA-10 operations, with tenant units including the 303rd Intelligence Squadron, 631st Air Mobility Support Squadron, 5th Reconnaissance Squadron, 31st Special Operations Squadron, and a detachment of the 4th Space Surveillance Squadron. There are 5,538 military personnel stationed at Osan.

The facility was originally designated simply K-55 when its runway was opened in December 1952 during the KOREAN WAR. It was renamed Osan AB in 1956 for the nearby town that was the scene of the first fighting between U.S. and North Korean forces in July 1950.

Further reading: Osan AB Web site, www.osan. af.mil.

Patrick AFB, Florida

Located near Cocoa Beach and the Kennedy Space Center at Cape Canaveral, this AIR FORCE SPACE COMMAND (AFSPC) base is operated by the 45th Space Wing in support of Department of Defense, NASA, and other agency and commercial missile and space programs. Its major tenants include the Defense Equal Opportunity Management Institute; Air Force Technical Applications Center (AFTAC); 1st Rescue Group, 41st Rescue Squadron; 71st Rescue Squadron; and the 301st Rescue Squadron (Air Force Reserve); 741st Consolidated Aircraft Maintenance Squadron; and the Joint Task Force for Joint STARS at Melbourne Regional Airport, Florida. Besides host responsibilities for Patrick AFB and Cape Canaveral AS, the 45th Space Wing also oversees operations at tracking stations on Antigua and Ascension islands. There are 2,700 military and 1,900 civilian personnel at Patrick.

Patrick AFB has supported more than 3,000 space launches from Cape Canaveral since 1950. It was activated in 1940 and named for Major General Mason M. Patrick, chief of the U.S. Army Air Service in World War I and chief of the USAAC and U.S. Army Air Corps from 1921 to 1927.

Further reading: Patrick AFB Web site, www. patrick.af.mil.

Peterson AFB, Colorado

Located near Colorado Springs, Peterson is headquarters of the Air Force Space Command (AFSPC). Its host unit is the 21st Space Wing, which supports the headquarters of North American Aerospace Defense Command, U.S. Space Command, and Army Space Command. Also on base is the 302nd Airlift Wing (Air Force Reserve) and the Edward J. Peterson Air and Space Museum. Active-duty military personnel number 4,299; reserves, 1,260; and civilians 3,065.

The base was activated in 1942 and was soon after named for First Lieutenant Edward J. Peterson, who was killed on August 8, 1942, in an aircraft crash at the base.

Further reading: Peterson AFB Web site, www. peterson.af.mil.

Pope AFB, North Carolina

This Air Combat Command (ACC) base is home to the 23rd Wing; 624th Air Mobility Support Group; 23rd Aeromedical Evacuation Squadron; 23rd Combat Control Squadron; 3rd Aerial Port Squad-

ron; a detachment of MACOS (Combat Control School); 18th Air Support Operations Group; and 24th Special Tactics Squadron. The base adjoins the U.S. Army's Fort Bragg and provides intratheater airlift and close air support for airborne forces and other personnel, equipment, and supplies. More than 4,000 military personnel are stationed at Pope.

Pope was activated in 1919 and named after First Lieutenant Harley H. Pope, a World War I pilot killed on January 7, 1917, near Fayetteville, North Carolina.

Further reading: Pope AFB Web site, http:// public.pope.amc.af.mil.

RAF Lakenheath, United Kingdom

This Royal Air Force (RAF) base hosts the 48th Fighter Wing (United States Air Forces in Europe [USAFE]), which flies the F-15E and the F-15C and trains for and conducts air operations in support of NATO. On base are 5,200 U.S. personnel.

RAF Lakenheath was activated in 1941 and is named after a nearby village.

Further reading: RAF Lakenheath Web site, www.lakenheath.af.mil.

RAF Mildenhall, United Kingdom

This Royal Air Force (RAF) base hosts the headquarters of the Third Air Force (United States Air Forces in Europe [USAFE]). It is home to 100th Air Refueling Wing, KC-135R and European Tanker Task Force operations, with regional logistics support. Associate units on base include 352nd Special Operations Group; 627th Air Mobility Support Squadron; 95th Reconnaissance Squadron; 488th Intelligence Squadron; and a naval air facility. U.S. military personnel here number 4,765.

The base was activated by the RAF in 1934, with a U.S. presence beginning in July 1950. It is named after the nearby town.

Further reading: RAF Mildenhall Web site, www.mildenhall.af.mil.

Ramstein AB, Germany

Ramstein is headquarters of UNITED STATES AIR FORCES IN EUROPE (USAFE) and headquarters of Allied Air Forces Central Europe (NATO). Its host unit is the 86th Airlift Wing, whose 37th Airlift Squadron flies the C-130E Hercules, the 75th Airlift Squadron, the C-9 Nightingale, and the 76th Airlift squadron, the C-20 Gulfstream, C-21 Learjet, and CT-43. Ramstein provides inter- and intratheater operational AIRLIFT, intratheater aeromedical evacuation, and continental U.S. staging and aeromedical evacuation. The wing commander also serves as commander of the Kaiserslautern Military Community, the largest concentration of U.S. citizens (49,300) outside of the United States. KMC encompasses more than 1,000 square miles and 12 USAF and army military installations.

Ramstein was activated with the beginning of the U.S. presence in 1953.

Further reading: Ramstein AB Web site, "AFPC—Ramstein AB," www.afpc.randolph.af.mil/medical/Dental/Maps/ramstein.htm.

Randolph AFB, Texas

Located outside of San Antonio, Randolph is headquarters of the AIR EDUCATION AND TRAINING COMMAND (AEDTC) as well as of the NINETEENTH AIR FORCE. On base is the 12th Flying Training Wing, with T-37, T-38, and T-1A pilot instructor training, and, at Hondo, Texas, T-43 undergraduate navigator training and C-21A AIRLIFT, and T-3 flight screening. Other headquarters located here include AIR FORCE PERSONNEL CENTER (AFPC), AIR FORCE MANAGEMENT ENGINEERING AGENCY (AFMEA), AIR FORCE SERVICES AGENCY (AFSA), and AIR FORCE RECRUITING SERVICE (AFRS). The USAF Occupational Measurement Squadron is also based at Randolph. More than 5,600 military personnel staff the base, along with almost 4,000 civilian employees.

The base was activated in June 1930 and named for Captain William M. Randolph, killed February 17, 1928, when his AF-4 crashed on takeoff.

Further reading: Randolph AFB Web site, www.randolph.af.mil.

Reese AFB, Texas

Located adjacent to Lubbock, this AIR EDUCATION AND TRAINING COMMAND (AETC) base was, until its deactivation in 1997, home to the 64th Flying Training Wing, which provided specialized undergraduate pilot training. More than 1,300 military personnel were active here, along with 1,166 civilian employees and contractors.

Activated in 1942, the base was subsequently named for First Lieutenant Augustus F. Reese, Jr., a P-38 fighter pilot killed during a train-strafing mission at Cagliari, Sardinia, on May 14, 1943.

Further reading: Reese AFB information, Bruce Richardson, "Reese Air Force Base," www.w9fz.com/reeseafb.

Rhein-Main AB, Germany

Located near Frankfurt-am-Rhein, Germany, Rhein-Main AB has been one of the most historically important of U.S. air bases in the postwar world and during the cold war.

The site of Rhein-Mein AB was used for aerial operations as early as 1909, when Count von Zeppelin employed it as a landing area for his great dirigible Z-II. It became a commercial airport in 1936 and the home port of the famed dirigibles *Graf Zeppelin* and *Hindenburg*. On May 6, 1940, the base was converted for military use by the Luftwaffe and was used during WORLD WAR II as a fighter base and as an experimental station for early jet aircraft. Allied bombers heavily damaged the base during late 1944 and early 1945.

In April 1945, the U.S. 826th Engineering Aviation Battalion began clearing rubble and reconstructing major buildings on the base. Army engineers built new runways and extended and widened the existing runways. A passenger terminal was completed in 1946. It was planned to make Rhein-Main a base for NINTH AIR FORCE bombers, but, instead, Rhein-Main became a principal European air transport terminal from 1947 to 1959. Most famously, Rhein-Main served as the main western base for the BERLIN AIRLIFT from June 1948 to September 1949. In April 1959, UNITED STATES AIR FORCES IN EUROPE (USAFE) turned over the northern part of the base to the German government for use as a civilian airport, the *Flughafen.* The rest of the base, under USAFE control, became the principal aerial port for U.S. forces in Germany.

On July 1, 1975, Rhein-Main AB was assigned to MILITARY AIRLIFT COMMAND (MAC), and, by agreement with the German government, only transport aircraft have been stationed at Rhein-Main since May 1975. On April 1, 1992, the base was reassigned to USAFE and functioned as a major hub for U.S. forces deploying and redeploying during the PERSIAN GULF WAR and subsequent international operations. On December 20, 1993, plans were announced to draw down Rhein-Mein AB to half the size and reduce the active duty force by more than two-thirds. This drawdown was completed on April 1, 1995, and Rhein-Mein AB now consists of 2,600 personnel and 30 tenant units. No aircraft are permanently assigned to the base.

Further reading: Rhein-Main AB Web site, www. rheinmain.af.mil.

Robins AFB, Georgia

Located outside of Macon at Warner Robins, this AIR FORCE MATERIEL COMMAND (AFMC) base is the headquarters of Warner Robins Air Logistics Center, which provides worldwide logistics management for the F-15 air-superiority fighter, and for C-130 and C-l41 cargo aircraft, helicopters, missiles, and remotely piloted vehicles. Other management responsibilities include many avionics and most USAF airborne ELECTRONIC WARFARE equipment, airborne communications equipment, airborne bomb- and gun-directing systems, firefighting equipment, general-purpose vehicles, and the Worldwide Military Command and Control System. The base is also home to the 93rd Air Control Wing. Other major units, including AIR FORCE RESERVE headquarters, operate out of Robins AFB.

The base was activated in March 1942 and was named for Brigadier General Augustine Warner Robins, an early chief of the Materiel Division of the U.S. ARMY AIR CORPS, who died on June 16,

1940. Some 4,000 military personnel are stationed at the base, which employs 12,409 civilians.

Further reading: Robins AFB Web site, www. robins.af.mil/fsc.

Schriever AFB, Colorado

Activated in 1985 as Falcon AFB and later renamed, Schriever AFB is located about 10 miles east of Peterson AFB and 12 miles east of Colorado Springs, Colorado. The base is the home of the 50th Space Wing and has tenant units that include the 76th Space Operations Squadron, National Test Facility, and the Space Warfare Center (SWC). Work on the STRATEGIC DEFENSE INITIATIVE (SDI, "Star Wars") project is conducted here. The base has no runway, and it is staffed by more than 4,600 military and civilian personnel.

The 50th Space Wing provides command and control for Department of Defense warning, navigational, and communications satellites. Also housed at Schriever AFB is the Space Warfare Center and the Ballistic Missile Defense Organization, which supports strategic space systems and missile defense programs.

Further reading: Schriever AFB Web site, www. schriever.af.mil.

Scott AFB, Illinois

An AIR MOBILITY COMMAND (AMC) base, Scott is home to the 375th Airlift Wing and is the headquarters of Air Mobility Command as well as of the Air Force C^4 Agency, the U.S. Transportation Command, and the AIR WEATHER SERVICE (AWS), which maintains the Combat Climatology Center here. Also on base is the 932nd Airlift Wing (AIR FORCE RESERVE). Military personnel number about 6,100, civilian employees, 3,550.

Activated on June 14, 1917, the facility was named for Corporal Frank S. Scott, the first enlisted man to die in an aircraft accident, killed September 28, 1912, in a Wright B Flyer at College Park, Maryland.

Further reading: Scott AFB Web site, http:// public.scott.af.mil.

Sembach AB, Germany

Located nine miles from Kaiserslautern, Germany, Sembach is a UNITED STATES AIR FORCES IN EUROPE (USAFE) base. Its origins date back to 1919, when French occupation troops after WORLD WAR I used the area as a landing ground and erected some provisional buildings. The French withdrew in 1930, and Sembach reverted to farmland. In 1951, the French began to build Sembach as an air base, and, on September 1, 1951, U.S. authorities took over construction and named it Sembach Air Auxiliary Field. In 1953, the installation was renamed Sembach AB and became home to reconnaissance and air rescue units. In 1956, the first Matador missile squadron arrived. On September 1, 1959, Sembach became USAFE's primary missile base.

In 1973, Sembach AB became headquarters for the SEVENTEENTH AIR FORCE and served as a base for ELECTRONIC WARFARE operations. On September 30, 1996, the 17AF was inactivated, and most of the base was returned to German control, except for a portion designated the Sembach Annex, which remains under USAFE control.

Further reading: Sembach AB information, "A Brief History of Sembach AB," www.jomo.net/sembach/sabhistory.htm.

Seymour Johnson AFB, North Carolina

Located in Goldsboro, this AIR COMBAT COMMAND (ACC) base is home to the 4th Fighter Wing, F-15E operations and 916th Air Refueling Wing (AIR FORCE RESERVE), KC-135 operations. About 4,600 military personnel are stationed at Seymour Johnson.

The base was activated on June 12, 1942, and named for Lieutenant Seymour A. Johnson, USN, a Goldsboro native killed March 5, 1941, in an aircraft accident in Maryland.

Further reading: Seymour Johnson AFB Web site, www.seymourjohnson.af.mil.

Shaw AFB, South Carolina

Located south of Sumter, this AIR COMBAT COMMAND (ACC) base is home to the 20th Fighter Wing, F-16 fighter operations and A/OA-10 close air support/forward air control operations. It is also the headquarters base of the NINTH AIR FORCE. There are 5,462 military personnel assigned to the base.

Shaw was activated on August 30, 1941, and named for Second Lieutenant Ervin D. Shaw, one of the first Americans to see air action in WORLD WAR I; he was killed in France on July 9, 1918.

Further reading: Shaw AFB Web site, www.shaw.af.mil.

Shemya AFB, Alaska

Today designated Eareckson Air Station, Shemya AFB is located on the island of Shemya, Alaska, and it constitutes the most westerly of the ELEVENTH AIR FORCE bases, approximately 1,500 miles from Anchorage, near the tip of the Aleutian chain. Uninhabited before occupation by U.S. military forces on May 28, 1943, during the Aleutian campaign of WORLD WAR II, the Shemya Island facility was planned as a B-29 base for the bombing of Japan. However, the Joint Chiefs of Staff decided to deploy B-29s from China and the Mariana Islands in the central Pacific, and Shemya was assigned to the 28th Bomber Group, who flew B-24 missions against the northern Kurile Islands and B-25 attacks on Japanese shipping in the North Pacific.

USAF activities at Shemya AB were reduced after World War II, but the base served as a refueling stop on the Great Circle Route, particularly during the KOREAN WAR. The 5021st Air Base Squadron (AAC) provided base support. After the Korean War, Shemya AFB was deactivated on July 1, 1954. In 1958, the USAF resumed operations on Shemya to support strategic intelligence collection activities and to resume support for the Great Circle Route. During the 1970s, the Cobra Dane AN/FPS-108 Phased Array Radar facility was constructed and operated under the AEROSPACE DEFENSE COMMAND (ADC), then the STRATEGIC AIR COMMAND (SAC), and finally the AIR FORCE SPACE COMMAND (AFSPC). Shemya AFB was renamed Eareckson Air Station on April 6, 1993.

Further reading: Shaw AFB information, U.S. Air Force, "Eareckson Air Station History," www.elmendorf.af.mil/units/eareckson/history.htm.

Sheppard AFB, Texas

Located outside of Wichita Falls, Sheppard is an AIR EDUCATION AND TRAINING COMMAND (AEDTC) base and home to the 82nd Training Wing and the 82nd and 782nd Training Groups. These conduct courses in financial management, communications, electronics, aircraft maintenance, munitions, aerospace ground equipment, transportation, civil engineering skills, and education/training career fields. The 882nd Training Group provides training in biomedical sciences, dentistry, health service administration, medical readiness, medicine, nursing, and the Physician Assistant Training program. The 982nd Training Group provides weapon system training at training detachments and operating locations worldwide. Also on base are the 82nd Support Group; 82nd Medical Group, and 82nd Logistics Group.

The 80th Flying Training Wing (AETC), also on base, conducts T-37 and T-38 undergraduate pilot training and instructor pilot training in the Euro-NATO Joint Jet Pilot Training program. The wing also conducts the Introduction to Fighter Fundamentals course with AT-38 aircraft. This large installation has almost 9,000 military personnel on base, together with almost 4,000 civilian employees. A 90-bed hospital is located on base.

The base was activated on June 14, 1941, and named for U.S. senator Morris E. Sheppard of Texas, who died on April 9, 1941.

Further reading: Sheppard AFB Web site, www.sheppard.af.mil.

Soesterberg AB, Netherlands

This Royal Netherlands AB is located 26 miles outside of Amsterdam and has hosted USAF operations since 1954 in a section of the installation called Camp New Amsterdam.

Spangdahlem AB, Germany

A UNITED STATES AIR FORCES IN EUROPE (USAFE) base, Spangdahlem is home to the 52nd Fighter Wing, flying A/OA-lOs, F-15s, and F-16s. The base is manned by almost 6,000 military personnel.

Activated in 1953, the U.S. presence began then as well. It is named after the local town.

Further reading: Spangdahlem AB information, GlobalSecurity.Org, "Spangdahlem AB," www.globalsecurity.org/military/facility/spangdahlem.htm.

Tinker AFB, Oklahoma

Located outside of Oklahoma City, this AIR FORCE MATERIEL COMMAND (AFMC) base is the headquarters of the Oklahoma City Air Logistics Center, which manages and provides logistics support and depot maintenance for more than 850 aircraft, including the B-1B, B-2, B-52, and KC-135. Tinker is home to the 552nd Air Control Wing; 507th Air Refueling Wing (AIR FORCE RESERVE); and Navy Strategic Communications Wing One. Also located here are the Defense Logistics Agency's Defense Distribution Depot Oklahoma City; the 3rd Combat Communications Group; Air Force Electronic Systems Center's 38th Engineering Installation Wing; and the Oklahoma City Megacenter, which manages Tinker's computer systems and services 110 other bases in 46 states. Stationed here are 8,425 military personnel and 12,858 civilian employees. There is a 22-bed hospital on base.

Activated in March 1942, the base was named for Major General Clarence L. Tinker, whose LB-30 (an early model B-24) went down at sea southwest of Midway Island on June 7, 1942.

Further reading: Tinker AFB Web site, http://www-ext.tinker.af.mil.

Travis AFB, California

An AIR MOBILITY COMMAND (AMC) base, Travis is the headquarters of the FIFTEENTH AIR FORCE and home to 60th Air Mobility Wing; 615th Air Mobility Operations Group; 349th Air Mobility Wing (AIR FORCE RESERVE); David Grant Medical Center (with 298-bed hospital); America's Band of the Golden West; and the Air Museum. Well over 12,000 military personnel are stationed at this major base, along with about 2,000 civilian employees.

The base was activated on May 17, 1943, as Fairfield-Suison Army Air Base and was renamed for Brigadier General Robert F. Travis, killed on August 5, 1950, in a B-29 accident.

Further reading: Travis AFB Web site, http://public.travis.amc.af.mil.

Tyndall AFB, Florida

An AIR EDUCATION AND TRAINING COMMAND (AETC) base, Tyndall is home to the 325th Fighter Wing, F-15 operations. The wing provides training for all USAF F-15 air-to-air pilots and maintains readiness for 77 aircraft and assigned operations and support personnel for combat units worldwide. Associate units at Tyndall include the headquarters of the FIRST AIR FORCE; Southeast Air Defense Sector (AIR NATIONAL GUARD); 475th Weapons Evaluation Group; Air Force Civil Engineer Support Agency; and 325th Training Squadron. Military personnel on the base number 5,237, civilians 1,109. There is a 35-bed hospital.

Activated on December 7, 1941, the base was named for First Lieutenant Frank B. Tyndall, a WORLD WAR I fighter pilot killed on July 15, 1930, in a P-1 crash.

Further reading: Tyndall AFB Web site, www.tyndall.af.mil.

Vance AFB, Oklahoma

An AIR EDUCATION AND TRAINING COMMAND (AETC) base located near Enid, Vance is home to the 71st Flying Training Wing, which provides undergraduate pilot training. There are 854 military personnel at Vance, in addition to 1,410 civilian employees.

The base was activated in November 1941 as Enid Army Air Field and was renamed for Lieutenant Colonel Leon R. Vance, Jr., an Enid native and Medal of Honor recipient, who was killed on July 26, 1944, when an air evacuation plane returning to the United States went down in the Atlantic near Iceland.

Further reading: Vance AFB Web site, www.vance.af.mil.

Vandenberg AFB, California

This AIR FORCE SPACE COMMAND (AFSPC) base is the headquarters of the FOURTEENTH AIR FORCE and its host unit, the 30th Space Wing, which conducts polar-orbiting space launches and supports research and development tests for Department of Defense, USAF, and NASA space, ballistic missile, and aeronautical systems. There are 3,255 military personnel on base, together with 1,387 civilians. There is a 45-bed hospital on base.

Originally the U.S. Army's Camp Cooke, activated in October 1941, the base was taken over by the USAF on June 7, 1957, and renamed for General Hoyt S. Vandenberg, second CHIEF OF STAFF, USAF.

Further reading: Vandenberg AFB Web site, www.vandenberg.af.mil.

Whiteman AFB, Missouri

This AIR COMBAT COMMAND (ACC) base, located outside Sedalia, is home to the 509th Bomb Wing, operating B-2 bombers, and the 442nd Fighter Wing (AIR FORCE RESERVE). More than 3,000 military personnel are stationed here. There is a 30-bed hospital on base.

The base was activated in 1942 and named for Sedalia resident Second Lieutenant George A. Whiteman, the first pilot to die in aerial combat during the attack on Pearl Harbor, December 7, 1941.

Further reading: Whiteman AFB Web site, www.whiteman.af.mil.

Wright-Patterson AFB, Ohio

Located outside of Dayton, this is the headquarters of AIR FORCE MATERIEL COMMAND (AFMC) as well as of the Aeronautical Systems Center. Also at

Wright-Patterson are the Wright Laboratory; AIR FORCE INSTITUTE OF TECHNOLOGY (AFIT); Wright-Patterson Medical Center (a 301-bed hospital); 88th Air Base Wing; 445th Airlift Wing (AIR FORCE RESERVE); and some 70 other Department of Defense activities and government agencies. Military personnel here number 8,505; civilians, 14,628.

Originally, Wright Field and Patterson Field were separate facilities. They were merged on January 13, 1948, and named for aviation pioneers Orville and Wilbur Wright and for First Lieutenant Frank S. Patterson, killed on June 19, 1918, in the crash of a DeHaviland DH-4. The base encompasses the site (Huffman Prairie) of much of the Wright brothers' early flying. Now designated Area C of the present base, Huffman Prairie is part of the Dayton Aviation Heritage National Historical Park and is open to the public.

Further reading: Wright-Patterson AFB Web site, www.wpafb.af.mil.

Yokota AB, Japan

This PACIFIC AIR FORCES (PACAF) base is headquarters of U.S. Forces, Japan, as well as of the FIFTH AIR FORCE, 630th Air Mobility Support Squadron. The host unit is the 374th Airlift Wing, with C-130, UH-1N, C-9, and C-21 operations. Yokota is the primary aerial port in Japan. More than 4,000 U.S. military personnel are stationed here, together with 2,563 U.S. civilian employees, and 1,359 local nationals. There is a 30-bed hospital on the base.

The base was opened as Tama Field by the Japanese in 1939.

Further reading: Yokota AB Web site, www.yokota.af.mil.

Air Force Basic Military Training Instructor Ribbon See DECORATIONS AND MEDALS.

USAF structural maintenance technicians work on parts for a C-130 Hercules at the 374th Maintenance Squadron, Yokota AB, Japan. *(U.S. Air Force)*

Air Force Center for Environmental Excellence (AFCEE)

AFCEE, headquartered at Brooks AFB, is a FIELD OPERATING AGENCY of the Office of the Air Force Civil Engineer. The center provides USAF leaders with the expertise they need to protect, preserve, restore, develop, and sustain our nation's environmental and installation resources. The center provides commanders a full range of technical and professional services in the areas of environmental restoration, pollution prevention, natural and cultural resources conservation, design and construction management, and comprehensive planning. Of the agency's 448 personnel, only 58 are military members; the rest are civilians with degrees in engineering and the sciences, including such fields as architecture, hydrogeology, wildlife biology, and chemistry. AFCEE also relies on contractor employees for technical assistance in computer operations and other areas.

A civilian director heads the center, and an executive director, a USAF colonel (who also serves as the commander of the center's military personnel), assists the director.

In addition to the headquarters-based organizations, the center also has three Regional Environmental Offices located in Dallas (Central Region), Atlanta (Eastern Region), and San Francisco (Western Region). These offices are responsible for keeping USAF commanders advised of all applicable environmental laws and advocate USAF needs to state and federal regulators. They also serve as regional environmental coordinators with the responsibility of coordinating environmental matters among all Department of Defense components within their regions.

The center was created in 1991 as a centralized office to which commanders could go for assistance with their installation's environmental programs.

Air Force Center for Quality and Management Innovation (AFCQMI)

AFCQMI was activated at Randolph AFB, Texas, on December 19, 1996, as a FIELD OPERATING AGENCY merging the Air Force Quality Institute (formerly headquartered at Maxwell AFB, Alabama), with the AIR FORCE MANAGEMENT ENGINEERING AGENCY (at Randolph). AFCQMI focuses on strategic planning, process improvement, applying modern business practices, and analyzing opportunities to outsource and privatize various USAF activities.

Air Force Civil Engineer Support Agency (AFCESA)

Headquartered at Tyndall AFB, AFCESA is a FIELD OPERATING AGENCY that reports to the Office of the Civil Engineer of the Air Force at Headquarters U.S. Air Force, Washington, D.C. The agency provides tools, practices, and professional support to

maximize USAF civil engineer capabilities in base and contingency operations. The staff includes specialists in engineering, readiness, training, management analysis, fire protection, systems engineering, computer automation, and equipment and supply management—approximately 215 civilian and military members in all. There are five directorates: Contingency Support, Technical Support, Field Support, Operations Support, and Executive Support. AFCESA also has geographically separated units at Dover AFB, Delaware, and Travis AFB, California.

Contingency Support Directorate (CEX) is responsible for ensuring USAF active-duty and AIR FORCE RESERVE engineer personnel are trained and equipped to deploy anywhere in the world during wartime or peacetime emergencies. The directorate also manages the Air Force Contract Augmentation Program, which allows the USAF to contract a wide-range of noncombatant civil engineer services during disaster response and humanitarian efforts.

The Technical Support Directorate (CES) is responsible for establishing standards and criteria for life-cycle planning, programming, design, construction, operation, maintenance, repair, and revitalization of base infrastructure. It assists MAJCOMs and installations in assessing the condition of infrastructure systems and developing strategies and plans for their upgrade. CES is also home to the Airfield Pavements Evaluation Team and the Utility Rates Management Team.

The Field Support Directorate (CEM) supports base civil engineering units throughout the air force. It provides intermediate- and depot-level repair support on power generation, electrical distribution, heating, ventilating, air conditioning systems, and aircraft arresting systems.

The Operations Support Directorate (CEO) helps increase the capabilities of the base-level civil engineer by enhancing management and logistics practices, systems automation, and training systems. It also provides contracting consultation and manages the Department of Defense–mandated Utilities Privatization Program, which requires the

USAF to turn over most of its water, wastewater, gas, and electric utility systems to private industry by 2003.

The Executive Support Staff (ES) provides internal support to the AFCESA commander and agency staff. The ES staff is made up of diverse career fields including historian, public affairs, graphic support, communications, information management, logistics support, computer support, individual mobilization augmentee support, and financial management. ES also publishes the civil engineer flagship publication *The CE Magazine*.

Air Force Combat Climatology Center (AFCCC)

AFCCC collects, maintains, and applies worldwide weather data, creating climatological analyses to strengthen the combat capability of America's warfighters in all service branches. Operating under the control of the AIR FORCE WEATHER AGENCY (AFWA), AFCCC is located in Asheville, North Carolina.

Air Force Combat Command (AFCC)

AFCC was established under the U.S. ARMY AIR FORCES on June 20, 1941, to take over combat readiness duties from GENERAL HEADQUARTERS (GHQ) AIR FORCE. It was abolished on March 2, 1942, and the groups assigned to it were distributed to other commands.

Air Force Command, Control, Communications, and Computer Agency (AFCCCA)

AFCCCA is headquartered at Scott AFB, Illinois, and develops and validates C^4 architectures, technical standards, requirements, policies, procedures, and solutions. AFCCCA also ensures full integration of all USAF C^4 systems. AFCCCA headquarters consists of four major functional areas: Plans and Analysis, Systems and Procedures, Interoperability and Technology, and Resources.

Air Force Commendation Medal   See DE-

CORATIONS AND MEDALS.

Air Force Commissary Service (AFCOMS)

AFCOMS supplies food to the USAF and was established in 1976 as a SEPARATE OPERATING AGENCY. It is headquartered at Kelly AFB, Texas. AFCOMS supplies food to USAF dining facilities and to commissary resale stores.

Air Force Communications Command (AFCC)

AFCC has its origin in the 1938 establishment of the Army Airways Communication System (AACS), which, starting with three officers, 300 enlisted men, and 33 stations, was tasked with providing communication between ground stations and fliers along the airways, disseminating weather information and providing air traffic control. By 1945, AACS had grown to a worldwide organization and had become a MAJCOM—a status soon lost to peacetime budget cutbacks. The organization was restored to MAJCOM status in 1961 as the Air Force Communications Service (AFCS) and in 1979 was renamed the Air Force Communications Command.

Headquartered at Scott AFB, Illinois, its tasks include all aspects of communications and computer support. The command has 700 units at 430 locations throughout the United States and in 26 foreign countries.

Air Force Communications Service   See AIR FORCE COMMUNICATIONS COMMAND.

Air Force Computer Emergency Response Team (AFCERT)

AFCERT was established by the AIR FORCE INFORMATION WARFARE CENTER (AFIWC), AIR INTELLIGENCE AGENCY (AIA), as the single point of contact in the USAF for reporting and handling computer security incidents and vulnerabilities. AFCERT coordinates the technical resources of AFIWC to assess, analyze, and provide countermeasures for computer security incidents and vulnerabilities reported by USAF computer users, security managers, and system managers.

Air Force Cost Analysis Agency (AFCAA)

AFCAA is based in Arlington, Virginia, and is responsible for developing cost-analysis tools, methods, databases, models, and automated systems. AFCAA products serve the entire USAF.

Air Force Cost Center (AFCSTC)

AFCSTC is a Direct Reporting Unit established in 1985 to apply standard and state-of-the-art cost and economic analysis to estimate costs of acquisitions, operation, and support of weapons systems.

Air Force Council (AFC)

Established in 1951, the Air Force Council serves the CHIEF OF STAFF, USAF, by recommending actions and policies. The AFC also furnishes policy guidance to the AIR STAFF and monitors on an ongoing basis the ability of the USAF to fulfill its mission. The vice chief of staff serves as chair of the AFC.

Air Force: creation as separate service

Well before WORLD WAR II, such U.S. military aviation pioneers as WILLIAM MITCHELL and HENRY

President Truman signs, on September 19, 1951, HR1726, an act "to provide for the organization of the Air Force and the Department of the Air Force," a technicality in the unification plans to make the Air Force Department official. Left to right: Chief of Staff of the Air Force general Hoyt S. Vandenberg, Representative Overton Brooks (D-La.), and Secretary of the Air Force Thomas K. Finletter   *(U.S. Air Force)*

HARLEY ARNOLD advocated the creation of an air force independent from the U.S. Army. These men and those of like mind reasoned that air power required a doctrine distinctly different and separate from the doctrines that governed warfare on land and on the sea; the most thorough and efficient way of creating that doctrine would be in the context of an independent air arm. But it was only after the U.S. ARMY AIR FORCES actually functioned as virtually an independent service in World War II that plans went forward for the creation of an independent USAF.

The process of independence was tied to President Harry S. Truman's 1946 order that the army and navy draft a legislative proposal for the unification of the armed forces. This led, ultimately, to enactment of the NATIONAL SECURITY ACT OF 1947, which created the Department of Defense and much of the structure of the modern defense establishment. The act also called for the creation of an independent air force, which, like the army and navy, would have a civilian-controlled executive department, the DEPARTMENT OF THE AIR FORCE, led by a SECRETARY OF THE AIR FORCE.

The National Security Act was signed into law (PL 253) on July 26, 1947, by President Truman. At the time of signing, he also signed EXECUTIVE ORDER 9877, which completed the administrative actions necessary to implement PL 253, unify the armed forces, and create the USAF. The USAF officially came into existence on September 18, 1947.

Air Force Cross   See DECORATIONS AND MEDALS.

Air Force Development Test Center (AFDTC)

AFDTC is located at Eglin AFB, Florida, and provides a water and land range for weapons testing and firing. On land, the center covers 724 square miles; it also includes the Gulf Test Range, covering an area of 86,500 square miles, encompassing most of the Gulf of Mexico. At AFDTC, testing is carried out for the army, navy, USAF, and Marine Corps as well as for other government, commercial, and international customers. The center is capable of climatic testing, dynamic ground testing, electromagnetic testing, guided projectile testing, gun system testing, inertial guidance testing, radio frequency environment testing, and security system testing.

Air Force Doctrine Center (AFDC)

Headquartered at Maxwell AFB, AFDC is a Direct Reporting Unit to the CHIEF OF STAFF, USAF. It was established on February 24, 1997, as is the "single voice" for all doctrinal matters within the USAF and to the joint community. Its mission is to research, develop, and produce USAF basic and operational doctrine, as well as joint and multinational doctrine, coordinating with the MAJCOMs on their development of tactical doctrine, and assisting the doctrinal development efforts of other services.

AFDC is responsible for reviewing the application of doctrine education for all USAF personnel and is an advocate for the doctrinally correct representation of aerospace power in key USAF, other service, and joint campaign models and exercise scenarios. The center participates in war games and key exercises, and it examines, explores, and advocates methods to better use modeling and simulation to support realistic training, exercises, and studies. AFDC provides research assistance to doctrine development and education and collects and maintains inputs for USAF "Lessons Learned," which arise from exercises and operations.

A major general reporting directly to the Chief of Staff of the Air Force commands the AFDC, which is staffed by 97 active-duty members and civilians. There are three directorates at headquarters, as well as a directorate at Langley AFB, responsible for joint doctrine; an air staff liaison at the Pentagon; five operating locations at major U.S. Army training centers; and an operating location at Nellis AFB. At headquarters, the Doctrine Development Directorate researches, develops, and produces USAF basic and operational doctrine as well as joint and multinational doctrine. The Doctrine Applications Directorate is responsible for effecting the accurate representation of aerospace power in service, joint, and multinational events of doctrinal significance. The Doctrine Deployment Directorate advocates and deploys timely and focused aerospace doctrine, developing and implementing doctrine-specific instruction for USAF senior officers and senior mentors, and providing doctrinal instruction to selected USAF warfighters in preparation for their participation in war games and exercises.

The Joint Integration Directorate at Langley AFB represents the center and provides USAF doctrinal advocacy in the joint arena. The operating locations at Nellis and at army training centers provide USAF representation on matters of aerospace power doctrine, organization, mission, equipment capabilities, tactics, and procedures. Operating Locations include U.S. Army Air Defense Artillery School, Fort Bliss, Texas; U.S. Army Armor Center and School, Fort Knox, Kentucky; U.S. Combined Arms Center, Fort Leavenworth, Kansas; U.S. Army Aviation Center, Fort Rucker, Alabama; U.S. Army Field Artillery School, Fort Sill, Oklahoma; and Nellis AFB, Nevada.

The Joint and Air Staff Liaison Directorate is the liaison between the center, the Joint Staff, Air Staff and the Office of the Secretary of Defense on doctrinal and related issues. It advocates the doctrinally correct representation of aerospace power in publications, models, and exercises, and it oversees the Air and Joint Staff doctrine review processes. It is the conduit with congressional staff offices for the correct representation of aerospace power in national security matters.

Air Force Engineering and Services Center (AFESC)

AFESC was established in 1977 (and was originally called the Air Force Engineering and Services Agency) as a SEPARATE OPERATING AGENCY tasked with assisting MAJCOMs and other USAF installations to operate and maintain their facilities. The center is based at Tyndall AFB, Florida.

Air Force Flight Standards Agency (AFFSA)

AFFSA manages the interoperability of civil and military airspace and air traffic control systems. The agency is based in Washington, D.C.

Air Force Flight Test Center (AFFTC)

AFFTC is located at Edwards AFB, California, on the western edge of the Mojave Desert. Also under the control of AFFTC is the Utah Test and Training Range (UTTR), located in northwestern Utah and northeastern Nevada, about 70 miles west of Salt Lake City, with mission control facilities located off-range at Hill AFB, Utah. In all, AFFTC controls 8,800 square miles of airspace and shares control of 23,800 square miles of airspace with other agencies. Edwards AFB occupies more than 470 square miles, while UTTR covers 2,700 square miles, including the 1,315-square-mile Dugway Proving Ground (DPG).

AFFTC is responsible for flight testing aircraft and aircraft avionics systems for the USAF and other services as well as private and international customers.

Air Force Frequency Management Agency (AFFMA)

AFFMA represents the USAF in all national and international forums concerning the use of the radio frequency electromagnetic spectrum. The agency is based in the Pentagon.

Air Force Global Weather Center   See AIR FORCE WEATHER AGENCY.

Air Force Good Conduct Medal   See DECORATIONS AND MEDALS.

Air Force Historical Foundation

AFHF was founded in 1953 at Maxwell AFB as a nonprofit corporation, which, since its founding, has enjoyed the endorsement of the CHIEF OF STAFF, USAF. The organization is devoted to recording, writing, and publishing the history of American air power and has done so through the journal *Airpower Historian,* begun in 1954, renamed *Aerospace Historian* in 1965, and renamed again *Air Power History* in 1989. In the 1980s, AFHF also began sponsorship of a series of book-length historical studies of the USAF and its antecedents.

Air Force Historical Research Agency (AFHRA)

Based at Maxwell AFB, Alabama, AFHRA provides facilities for research into USAF history. The agency maintains USAF archives and is the principal repository for all USAF historical materials— at present about 3 million documents. Other AFHRA functions include determining USAF lineage and honors and the creation of books and other historical works on the USAF and on military aviation history. AFHRA also serves as adviser regarding declassification of USAF records held at the National Archives and Records Administration.

Air Force History Support Office (AFHSO)

Headquartered in Washington, D.C., AFHSO researches, writes, and publishes books and other materials on the history of the USAF. AFHSO provides historical support through the Air Force historian to USAF headquarters. The agency also publishes books intended to help the USAF in creating strategy, doctrine, and other plans, and to assist in the education of USAF students at professional military schools. AFHSO also provides civilian scholars with research and teaching materials and serves a public-outreach function, to educate and inform the general public about the role of the USAF in national security.

Air Force Information Warfare Center (AFIWC)

The AFIWC is collocated with the AIR INTELLIGENCE AGENCY (AIA) to conduct offensive and defensive counterinformation and information operations. AFIWC was originally activated as the 6901st Special Communication Center in July 1953, then redesignated in August of that year as the Air Force Special Communications Center. It became the Air Force Electronic Warfare Center (AFEWC) in 1975 and the AFIWC on September 10, 1993, combining assets from the former AFEWC, the Air Force Cryptologic Support Center's Securities Directorate, and the former AIR FORCE INTELLIGENCE AGENCY. AFIWC consists of about 1,000 military and civilian specialists in the areas of operations, engineering, operations research, intelligence, radar technology, communications, and computer applications.

AFIWC is divided into eight directorates:

Advanced Programs
Communications-Computer Systems
C^2W Information
Engineering Analysis
Mission Support
Systems Analysis
Operations Support
Information Warfare Battlelab (which identifies innovative and superior ways to plan and employ information warfare capabilities)

Air Force Inspection Agency (AFIA)

The AFIA is headquartered at Kirtland AFB and is a FIELD OPERATING AGENCY that reports to the Secretary of the Air Force Inspector General. Its mission is to provide USAF senior leaders independent assessments of mission capability, health care, and resource management. AFIA recommends improvements to existing USAF processes, policies, and programs for fulfilling peacetime, contingency, and wartime missions. AFIA is staffed by 115 military and 19 civilian personnel and is organized into three inspection directorates, a mission support directorate, and an operations support division.

The Acquisition and Logistics Directorate conducts "Eagle Looks" management reviews of USAF acquisition and logistics processes and programs. The Field Operations Directorate conducts Eagle Looks of a broad range of USAF programs and policies encompassing operations, services, personnel, communications, security, financial management, and civil engineering. The Medical Operations Directorate performs health services inspections of all active duty, AIR FORCE RESERVE, and AIR NATIONAL GUARD medical units. The Mission Support Directorate administers the infrastructure for AFIA and manages the personnel, financial, information systems, logistics, and internal resources to ensure inspectors have the knowledge and equipment to conduct assessments. The Operations Support Division is the single Eagle Look support function for AFIA inspectors, who provide administrative support to inspection teams throughout the Eagle Look process.

AFIA's antecedents include the Inspection Division, established in 1927 under the chief of the U.S. ARMY AIR CORPS. By the end of WORLD WAR II, division functions were aligned under the Office of the Air Inspector, and, in 1948, after USAF independence, the CHIEF OF STAFF, USAF, designated the Office of the Inspector General to oversee all inspection and safety functions. On December 31, 1971, the Air Force Inspection and Safety Center was activated, divided into the Air Force Inspection Agency and the Air Force Safety Agency in August 1991. Both agencies moved to Kirtland AFB in July 1993 after the closure of Norton AFB.

Air Force Inspection and Safety Center (AFISC)

AFISC is a SEPARATE OPERATING AGENCY charged with evaluating the fighting and management effectiveness of the USAF. The center was created in 1971 from the former Office of the Inspector General, which had been established in 1948. Headquartered at Norton AFB, the center has four directorates: one evaluates operational readiness and management; one manages USAF non-nuclear safety programs; one exclusively manages nuclear-related USAF safety programs; and a fourth directorate inspects USAF medical facilities.

Air Force Institute of Technology (AFIT)

AFIT meets USAF needs in graduate education. Located at Wright-Patterson AFB, Ohio, AFIT grants masters and doctoral degrees at its two resident graduate schools and supervises students enrolled in its civilian institutions program. AFIT's Graduate School of Engineering is among the nation's top engineering schools and provides advanced education and research focused on aerospace technology. AFIT's Graduate School of Logistics and Acquisition Management provides officers the advanced expertise they need to manage the life cycles of complex weapons systems. AFIT's Civilian Institutions Program places students in more than 400 civilian universities, research centers, hospitals, and industrial organizations throughout the United States and in several other countries.

AFIT graduates about 800 degree students annually and also operates two resident schools dedicated to short, specialized courses in professional continuing education. These schools also provide expert consultation services to USAF commanders and their staffs. The Civil Engineer and Services School provides engineering, environmental, services, and management courses throughout the Department of Defense and other federal agencies, and the School of Systems and Logistics is responsible for the Air Technology Network, which offers distance-learning courses via satellite. More than 30,000 students graduate from the two short-course schools and Air Technology Network programs each year.

Air Force Intelligence Agency (AFIA)

AFIA, headquartered in Washington, D.C., was established in 1972 as the Air Force Intelligence Service (AFIS). It provides AIR STAFF and USAF units with assistance in the use of intelligence and generally collects, processes, analyzes, and disseminates information.

Air Force Legal Services Agency (AFLSA)

This SEPARATE OPERATING AGENCY was established in 1978 to provide specialized legal service to the USAF, both in military and civil contexts. The AFLSA is commanded by the judge advocate general and is headquartered in Washington, D.C. The range of its civil law specialties is suggested by its staff units: Claims and Tort Litigation Staff, General Litigation Division, Contract Law Division, Environmental Law Division, Patents Division, and Preventive Law and Legal Assistance Office. Its military justice divisions include: Court of Military Review, Military Justice Division, Defense Services Division, Trial Judiciary Division, Government Trial and Appellate Counsel Division, and the Clemency, Corrections, and Officer Review Division. Prior to May 1, 1991, AFLSA was called Air Force Legal Services Center (AFLSC).

Air Force Logistics Command (AFLC)

Created in 1921 as the USAAS Property, Maintenance and Cost Compilation Office, AFLC was the Air Service Command (ASC) during WORLD WAR II, was renamed the Air Materiel Command after the war, became the AFLC in 1982, and merged with AIR FORCE SYSTEMS COMMAND in 1992 as the AIR FORCE MATERIEL COMMAND. The mission of the AFLC, now subsumed by the AFMC, was the logistical support of the USAF through buying, supplying, transporting, and maintaining equipment.

Air Force Logistics Management Agency (AFLMA)

AFLMA is located at Gunter Annex to Maxwell AFB, Alabama. Its mission is to enhance USAF readiness and combat capability by conducting studies and developing, testing, analyzing, and recommending concepts, methods, systems, and procedures to improve logistics efficiency and effectiveness.

Air Force Longevity Service Ribbon   See DECORATIONS AND MEDALS.

Air Force Management Engineering Agency (AFMEA)

Now merged with the Air Force Quality Institute as the AIR FORCE CENTER FOR QUALITY AND MANAGEMENT INNOVATION (AFCQMI), AFMEA develops and maintains USAF manpower standards with the object of improving manpower utilization. The entire AFCQMI is headquartered at Randolph AFB, Texas. Within this organization, AFMEA is responsible for sending and supervising Management Engineering Teams (METs), which use process-analysis and work-measurement techniques to generate recommendations for improving USAF productivity.

Air Force Manpower and Innovation Agency (AFMIA)

Headquartered at Randolph AFB, Texas, AFMIA is tasked with improving USAF mission performance, effectiveness, and resource efficiency by making determinations of current and future peacetime and wartime resource requirements. The principal activity of the agency is to create "objective and innovative" manpower studies and to assists MAJCOMs with competitive sourcing.

Air Force Materiel Command (AFMC)

AFMC is a MAJCOM that researches, develops, tests, acquires, delivers, and logistically supports all USAF weapons systems. The command was created in 1992 as a result of the integration of AIR FORCE LOGISTICS COMMAND and AIR FORCE SYSTEMS COMMAND. AFMC operates logistics centers, test centers, and laboratories and is headquartered at Wright-Patterson AFB, Ohio.

Air Force Medical Operations Agency (AFMOA)

AFMOA is headquartered at Bolling AFB, Washington, D.C., and functions to support the Air Force Surgeon General in creating plans, policies, and programs for all aspects of USAF medicine, including research and clinical areas. In addition to supporting such functions as clinical investigations, aerospace medicine, health promotion, bioenvironmental engineering, family advocacy, and military public health, AFMOA advises on the safe management of radioactive materials.

Air Force Medical Support Agency (AFMSA)

AFMSA assists the Air Force Surgeon General in developing programs, policies, and practices relating to USAF health care. AFMSA divisions include Patient Administration, Health Facilities, Medical Information Systems, and Medical Logistics. The agency is headquartered at Brooks AFB, Texas.

Air Force National Security Emergency Preparedness (AFNSEP)

With facilities in the Pentagon, at Fort McPherson, Atlanta, and at Hickam AFB, Hawaii, AFNSEP oversees—and assists commanders in implementing—the USAF's National Security Emergency Preparedness program, including Domestic Support Operations (DSO) and Continuity of Government (COG) programs. The purpose of these programs is to provide sufficient capabilities at all levels of the USAF to meet essential defense and civilian needs during any national security emergency, in peacetime as well as wartime.

AFNSEP serves as USAF office of primary responsibility for all military support to civil authorities and national security emergency preparedness issues. This includes military support to civilian authorities and military support to civilian law enforcement agencies. In addition to serving as the principal and regional planning agent for military support to civil authorities, AFNSEP approves and coordinates USAF auxiliary activities of the CIVIL AIR PATROL.

Air Force News Agency (AFNEWS)

AFNEWS is headquartered in San Antonio and is a FIELD OPERATING AGENCY of the Office of Public Affairs (SAF/PA) of the SECRETARY OF THE AIR FORCE. Its mission is to gather, package, and disseminate printed and electronic news and information. The agency manages the Air Force Broadcasting Service and its outlets, Army and Air Force Hometown News Service, and Air Force News Service. AFNEWS has approximately 489 air force, army, navy, and marine military and civilian personnel assigned at more than 26 locations worldwide.

The mission of the Air Force Broadcasting Service is to inform and entertain Department of Defense personnel and their families in Central and Southern Europe, Southwest Asia, Turkey, the United Kingdom, the Azores, and the Pacific Rim. The Army and Air Force Hometown News Service reports on the individual accomplishments of active-duty, guard, reserve members, and Department of Defense civilians. The news service sends news releases to media outlets serving their hometowns. More than 14,000 newspapers, radio, and television stations subscribe to the hometown news service. The Air Force News Service provides USAF and Department of Defense news and information to the USAF community and the public through print, electronic, and Internet-based media.

Air Force News Service creates and distributes the following:

Air Force Link: The USAF official home page on the World Wide Web.
Air Force Link Plus: A multimedia version of the USAF story to a growing Internet audience.
AFNEWS Home Page: Information and links to news service products through the Internet at http://www.afnews.af.mil.
Airman (AFRP 35-1): A nationally recognized monthly feature and information magazine,

Airman reports on events and issues affecting Air Force people.

Air Force Art: A collection of USAF-related artwork created especially for use in base newspapers, briefings, etc.

Air Force Biographies: Accurate, approved biographical information on USAF active-duty general officers, senior civilians, and the chief master sergeant of the air force.

Air Force Fact Sheets: Timely information on USAF aircraft, missiles, major commands, and selected high-interest subjects.

Air Force Policy Letter Digest: A six-page monthly newsletter that is the primary medium for communicating unclassified USAF, DOD, and national policy.

Air Force Print News: USAF and DOD news every weekday. Once each weekday a compilation of the day's news is sent electronically to thousands of subscribers using the e-mail subscription service and is available by FTP.

Air Force Public Affairs Staff Directory: Information about the rank or grade, location, and duties of key public affairs people at USAF.

Air Force Radio News: A five-minute weekday program offering instant access to news and information for and about the USAF community.

Air Force Satellite News: Video news releases produced biweekly on current USAF and DOD issues.

Air Force Speech Series: Original speeches about national days of recognition and special topics.

Air Force Television News: Thirty-minute biweekly television program covering USAF and DOD news and policy issues.

Commander's Call Topics: A monthly publication for use in commander's calls that provides current information on items of interest or importance to USAF military and civilian members and their families.

Internal Talk: Provides USAF base newspaper staffs with tips on journalism and communications technology techniques and ways to improve the communication effectiveness of base newspapers.

Air Force Lithographs: Color reproductions of photographs of USAF subjects. Used for display in buildings, hallways, and common-use areas to promote esprit de corps.

Air Force Nuclear Weapons and Counterproliferation Agency (AFNWCA)

Located at Kirtland Air Force Base, New Mexico, the Air Force Nuclear Weapons and Counterproliferation Agency (AFNWCA) designs and builds systems to enable the air force to operate across the full spectrum of chemical, biological, radiological, nuclear, and explosive (CBRNE) environments. Staffed by scientists, engineers, and program managers, the agency provides air force warfighters with advanced weapons and technical assessments to counter CBRNE threats. In addition, AFNWCA assures the military effectiveness of the air force portion of the nation's nuclear weapon stockpile and oversees stewardship of this stockpile.

AFNWCA is the air force liaison with the National Nuclear Security Administration, and it manages all air force nuclear weapons activities as well as coordinates mission requirements, analyses, and assessments in the areas of counterforce weaponry, passive and active defense, passive and remote detection, target characterization intelligence, and technical issues associated with treaty compliance. AFNWCA also provides technical assessments to support air force warfighting operations and advanced weapons concepts, and it supports requirements for countering chemical, biological, radiological, nuclear, and explosive (CBRNE) weapons of mass destruction.

Air Force Office of Medical Support (AFOMS)

Headquartered at Brooks AFB, Texas, AFOMS is a SEPARATE OPERATING AGENCY that assists the Air Force Surgeon General by preparing plans, programs, studies, policies, and practices for health care in the USAF.

Air Force Office of Scientific Research (AFOSR)

The mission of AFOSR, a technology directorate of the Air Force Research Laboratory (AFRL), is to manage all basic research conducted by the USAF. AFOSR solicits proposals for research in numerous broad areas, including:

- Physics
- Solid Mechanics and Structures
- Chemistry
- Mathematics and Computer Sciences
- Electronics
- Structural Materials
- Fluid Mechanics
- Propulsion
- Atmospheric Sciences
- Space Sciences
- Biological Sciences
- Human Performance
- Science and Engineering Education Programs

The directorate manages a number of researcher assistance programs, including the United States Air Force/National Research Council–Resident Research Associateship Program, the University Resident Research Program, and the National Defense Science and Engineering Graduate Fellowship Program, and others. AFOSR is headquartered at Arlington Virginia.

The predecessor organization of AFOSR was created in October 1951 in the headquarters of the Air Research and Development Command. Before this time, USAF had sponsored some basic research under the auspices of the Office of Air Research at the old Air Material Command headquartered at Wright-Patterson AFB and, later, under the Directorate of Research at the newly created Air Research and Development Command (ARDC). The new office was designated AFOSR in August 1955, charged with planning, formulating, initiating, and managing a basic research program. It was

the Russians' successful orbit of *Sputnik I* in 1957 that prompted a major budget for AFOSR, and, in the 1950s, the directorate contributed to such notable scientific advancements as providing support to Nobel laureates Richard Hofstadter (for his work on the structure of nuclei and nucleons) and C. H. Townes (for his role in developing microwave amplification by stimulated emission of radiation [MASER]).

Reorganization within the Department of Defense led to the creation of the short-lived Air Force Research Division (AFRD), which, in 1961, became Air Force Systems Command (AFSC), concentrating on applied research, while AFOSR became part of the Office of Aerospace Research (OAR) and continued to manage research in basic science. However, AFOSR-sponsored basic research typically paid off in applications, such as laser weapons. AFOSR played a central role in managing research for the Strategic Defense Initiative (SDI) program in the 1980s.

Air Force Office of Security Police (AFOSP)

AFOSP is a Separate Operating Agency that sets USAF policy for security, police law enforcement, air base ground defense, information security, and training in small arms. Established in 1979, AFOSP in headquartered at Kirtland AFB, New Mexico.

Air Force Office of Special Investigations (AFOSI)

The USAF's major investigative service since August 1, 1948, AFOSI is a Field Operating Agency with headquarters at Andrews AFB. Reporting to the Inspector General, Office of the Secretary of the Air Force, AFOSI provides professional investigative service to commanders of all USAF activities. Primary responsibilities include criminal investigative and counterintelligence services: to identify, investigate, and neutralize espionage, terrorism, fraud, and other major criminal activities that may threaten USAF and Department of Defense resources.

AFOSI has 2,274 active-duty officer and enlisted, civilian, and AIR FORCE RESERVE personnel. Of this number, 1,672 are federally credentialed special agents.

In addition to the command's headquarters and U.S. Air Force Special Investigations Academy at Andrews AFB, AFOSI has eight field investigations regions (two of which are overseas), seven field investigations squadrons (six of which are overseas), and more than 160 detachments and operating locations worldwide.

Air Force Officer Training School (OTS)

OTS, located at Maxwell AFB, Alabama, provides a 12-week basic officer training course, designed (as of 2002) to commission 1,700 officers annually, and a four-week commissioned officer training program, which each year provides training for 1,500 new judge advocates, chaplains, and medical officers.

Basic officer training (BOT) is designed for college graduates who seek a USAF commission. Commissioned officer training (COT) is designed for professionals who have received a direct-com-

missioned appointment as a lawyer, chaplain, or medical practitioner. In addition to the regular COT, OTS offers the Reserve COT course, a two-week intensive program designed for AIR FORCE RESERVE and AIR NATIONAL GUARD medical service officers.

Air Force One

Any aircraft that carries the president of the United States is designated by the radio call sign "Air Force One" when the president is onboard. At present, two VC-25A aircraft, military modifications of the Boeing 747-200B civilian plane, are regularly used for presidential airlift and, when carrying the president, are designated Air Force One. The aircraft is a flying office, living quarters, and command post, which accommodates an aircrew of 23 and 75 passengers. It is equipped with advanced communication equipment (including 85 telephones) and 19 television receivers. The aircraft operate out of Andrews AFB, home of the 89th Airlift Wing.

The routine aerial transport of the president began in 1943, from Miami, Florida, to Morocco for the Casablanca Conference, on board a Navy-operated Boeing 314 flying boat called the *Dixie*

A USAF VC-25A, a modified Boeing 747-200B, serves as the primary aircraft for presidential airlift. It is designated *Air Force One* only when the president is on board.   *(U.S. Air Force)*

Clipper. This led to Project 51, the building of a U.S. ARMY AIR FORCES C-54 Skymaster transport especially for use as a presidential transport. Officially named *The Flying White House,* the aircraft was better known by its nickname, *The Sacred Cow,* and it incorporated special modifications to accommodate President Franklin D. Roosevelt's paraplegic condition.

The Sacred Cow was retired in 1947 and replaced by a Douglas DC-6, designated by the USAF as a C-118, and named the *Independence,* after the Missouri hometown of President Harry S. Truman. In 1948, a Lockheed Constellation (USAF designation C-121) was prepared for Thomas Dewey, who was expected to win election over Truman, and was christened the *Dewdrop.* When, in an upset, Truman won, he continued to use the *Independence,* and it wasn't until President Dwight D. Eisenhower assumed office in 1953 that a C-121, which Eisenhower named the *Columbine II,* was used for presidential airlift. In 1954, the Constellation was replaced by a Super-Constellation, which was designated *Columbine III* and served until President John F. Kennedy chose a Douglas DC-6A (USAF designation VC-118A) as his presidential transport. Kennedy did not name the aircraft. He also used several Boeing 707-153 jet aircraft (USAF designation VC-137A). The jets had been used on occasion for presidential airlift as early as 1959.

The VC-137A aircraft would continue to serve as "Air Force One" through 1990, when they were replaced by the Boeing 747-200B (VC-25A) aircraft.

Air Force Operational Test and Evaluation Center (AFOTEC)

AFOTEC manages USAF operational test and evaluation and may be involved with a weapon system from inception and design through deployment on the flight line.

AFOTEC was established in 1974 at the Air Force Test and Evaluation Center; the word "Operational" was added in 1983. The center's mission is to test and evaluate weapons and other systems independently and under the most realistic conditions possible. AFOTEC's antecedent organization was the Air Proving Ground Command, which existed in various forms from 1941 to 1957, and which emphasized the validation of production and the meeting of specifications rather than rigorous field testing with an eye toward improvement and modification. The disappointing performance and outright failure of certain systems during the VIETNAM WAR motivated creation of AFOTEC, with a far broader mission.

Air Force Operations Group (AFOG)

AFOG monitors on a 24/7 basis all current USAF operations and handles emergencies through the Air Force Operations Center. Headquartered in Washington, D.C., AFOG coordinates action among USAF MAJCOMs, other Field Operating Agencies, and Direct Reporting Units in response to taskings from the Joint Chiefs of Staff National Military Command Center. In addition, AFOG manages the USAF portion of the Worldwide Military Command and Control System Intercomputer Network, the USAF resources and training system database, and the Joint Uniform Lessons Learned database.

Air Force Organization Act of 1951

The NATIONAL SECURITY ACT OF 1947, which authorized the creation of the USAF as an independent air arm, failed to provide a statutory basis for the composition and organization of the USAF. The 1951 act redressed this omission, specifying not only the internal organization of the USAF but also the responsibilities and authority of the SECRETARY OF THE AIR FORCE.

Air Force Organizational Excellence Award   See DECORATIONS AND MEDALS.

Air Force Outstanding Unit Award   See DECORATIONS AND MEDALS.

Air Force Overseas Ribbon–Long Tour
See DECORATIONS AND MEDALS.

Air Force Pentagon Communications Agency (AFPCA)
AFPCA provides C^4 (Command, Control, Communications, and Computer) systems and services for the Office of the Secretary of Defense, the Joint Chiefs of Staff, the National Military Command Center, the SECRETARY OF THE AIR FORCE, HQ USAF, and other Washington, D.C.-based command centers. Among its other functions, AFPCA maintains secure and nonsecure telecommunications switches, 8,000 telephones, and a network of pagers and cellular telephones. The agency is headquartered in Washington, D.C.

Air Force Personnel Center (AFPC)
Headquartered at Randolph AFB, Texas, AFPC implements personnel programs affecting the nearly 400,000 USAF active-duty members and 185,000 civilian employees through major commands (see MAJCOM) and a worldwide network of military and civilian personnel flights. AFPC also manages some personnel matters affecting more than 109,000 Air National Guardsmen and 78,000 Air Force Reservists.

AFPC began operations on July 25, 1963, and, in 1971, became a Separate Operating Agency. It was renamed the Air Force Manpower and Personnel Center in 1978, then, in October 1985, when the manpower function was separated from personnel, the center was renamed the Air Force Military Personnel Center, effective January 1, 1986. The center became a Field Operating Agency on February 5, 1991.

Air Force Personnel Operations Agency (AFPOA)
AFPOA develops and operates officer, enlisted, and civilian models and databases for management information. The agency manages the Air Force Employee Development Program and the Air Force Relocation, Employee, and Labor Relations Program.

Air Force Program Executive Office (AFPEO)
The Pentagon-based AFPEO consists of six senior USAF officials who manage major and selected USAF acquisition programs in the following areas: Bombers, Missiles, and Trainers; Conventional Strike Systems; Tactical and Airlift Systems; Information Systems; Space Systems; and Command, Control, and Communications Systems.

Air Force Quality Institute
See AIR FORCE CENTER FOR QUALITY AND MANAGEMENT INNOVATION.

Air Force Real Estate Agency (AFREA)
AFREA works with the Office of the Deputy Assistant Secretary for Installations to acquire, manage, and dispose of real property for the USAF. The agency is located at Bolling AFB, Washington, D.C.

Air Force Recognition Ribbon
See DECORATIONS AND MEDALS.

Air Force Recruiter Ribbon
See DECORATIONS AND MEDALS.

Air Force Recruiting Service (AFRS)
Headquartered at Randolph AFB, AFRS is a major component of AIR EDUCATION AND TRAINING COMMAND (AETC), tasked with the mission of recruiting a high-quality volunteer force from a cross-section of America responsive to the personnel needs of the USAF. AFRS is also responsible for recruiting chaplains, physicians, dentists, nurses, health care administrators, and Biomedical Science Corps officers in various specialties, and for obtaining officer candidates for the AIR FORCE RESERVE OFFICER TRAINING CORPS (AFROTC) and AIR FORCE OFFICER TRAINING SCHOOL (OTS).

Headquarters directs four groups and 28 squadrons with approximately 3,350 active-duty and 360 civilian personnel. Every USAF recruiter is a volunteer or is nominated and selected from among the best in his or her career field. Recruiters are trained at the Recruiting School at Lackland AFB, and they staff more than 1,100 recruiting offices around the country and overseas.

When the USAF became an independent service in 1947, it conducted a joint recruiting program with the U.S. Army through the army's recruiting organization. The USAF assumed responsibility for its own recruiting in 1954, assigning the mission to the 3500th USAF Recruiting Wing at Wright-Patterson AFB. This became the U.S. Air Force Recruiting Service in 1959.

Air Force Research Laboratory (AFRL)

The mission of AFRL is to lead the discovery, development, and integration of affordable warfighting technologies for U.S. aerospace forces. AFRL consists of nine technology directorates located throughout the United States, in addition to the AIR FORCE OFFICE OF SCIENTIFIC RESEARCH, and a central staff. However, AFRL also works collaboratively with universities and industry, who receive nearly 80 percent of the AFRL budget.

AFRL staff numbers 5,700 to 5,900 people, responsible for planning and executing the USAF's entire science and technology budget, including basic research, applied research, and advanced technology development. AFRL research sites follow:

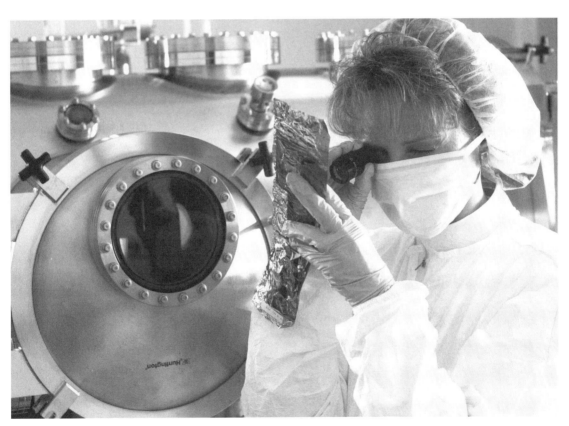

A researcher analyzes an experiment in the Air Force Research Laboratory at Wright-Patterson AFB, Ohio. *(U.S. Air Force)*

- Air Force Office of Scientific Research, head-quartered in Arlington, Virginia
- Wright-Patterson AFB facilities, including research in air vehicles, materials and manufacturing, propulsion, sensors, and human effectiveness
- Tyndall AFB facility for research in materials and manufacturing
- Eglin AFB facility for research in munitions
- Brooks AFB facility for research in human effectiveness
- Williams AFB facility for research in human effectiveness
- Kirtland AFB facilities for research in space vehicles and in directed energy
- Edwards AFB facility for propulsion research
- Rome AFB (New York) facilities for information and sensors research
- Hanscom AFB facilities for research in space vehicles and sensors

Air Force Reserve (AFR)

For a discussion of the basic organization and mission of the AFR, see AIR FORCE RESERVE COMMAND.

Air Force reservists are categorized as Ready Reserve, Standby Reserve, or Retired Reserve.

The *Ready Reserve* is made up of 193,042 trained reservists who may be recalled to active duty to augment active forces in time of war or national emergency. Of this number, 72,195 are members of the Selected Reserve, who train regularly and are paid for their participation in unit or individual programs. These reservists are combat ready and can deploy to anywhere in the world in 72 hours. Additionally, 48,981 are part of the Individual Ready Reserve. IRR members continue to have a service obligation, but they do not train and are not paid. They are subject to recall if needed. The president may recall Ready Reserve personnel from all Department of Defense components for up to 270 days if necessary. Some 24,000 USAF reservists from 220 units were called to active duty during the PERSIAN GULF WAR to work side-by-side with their active-duty counterparts.

Standby Reserve includes reservists whose civilian jobs are considered vital to national defense, or who have temporary disability or personal hardship. Most standby reservists do not train and are not assigned to units. There are 16,858 reservists in this category. *Retired Reserve* includes officers and enlisted personnel—52,057 men and women—who receive pay after retiring from active duty or from the reserve, or are reservists awaiting retirement pay at age 60.

Selected reservists train to active-duty standards, and mission readiness is verified periodically, using active-force inspection criteria. More than 60,000 reservists are assigned to specific AFR units. These are the people who are obligated to report for duty one weekend each month and two weeks of annual training a year. Most work many additional days. Reserve aircrews, for example, average more than 100 duty days a year, often flying in support of national objectives at home and around the world.

Air reserve technicians (ART) are a special group of reservists who work as civil service employees during the week in the same jobs they hold as reservists on drill weekends. ARTs are the full-time backbone of the unit training program, providing day-to-day leadership, administrative, and logistical support, as well as operational continuity for their units. More than 9,500 reservists (in excess of 15 percent of the force) are ARTs. The IMA training program is made up of approximately 13,144 "individual mobilization augmentees." IMAs are assigned to active-duty units in specific wartime positions and train on an individual basis. Their mission is to augment active-duty manning by filling wartime surge requirements.

The AFRC Associate Program provides trained crews and maintenance personnel for active-duty aircraft and space operations. The program pairs an AFR unit with an active-duty unit to share a single set of aircraft. The result is a more cost-effective way to meet increasing mission requirements. Associate aircrews fly C-5 Galaxies, C-141 Starlifters, C-17 Globemaster IIIs, C-9 Nightingales,

KC-10 Extenders, KC-135 Stratotankers, T-1 Jay-hawks, T-37 Tweets, T-38 Talons, F-16 Fighting Falcons, MC-130P Combat Shadows and MC-130 Talon I (Reserve Associate Unit), and E-3 Sentry Airborne Warning and Control System (AWACS) aircraft. Space operations associate units operate Defense Meteorological, Defense Support Program, and Global Positioning System satellites.

USAF reservists are on duty around the world, carrying out the USAF vision of "global engagement." In addition to combat roles, AFR is often engaged in humanitarian relief missions. At the request of local, state, or federal agencies, AFR conducts aerial spray missions using specially equipped C-130s. These missions range from spraying pesticides to control insects to spraying compounds used in the control of oil spills. Other specially equipped C-130s check the spread of forest fires by dropping fire-retardant chemicals. Additional real-world missions include weather reconnaissance, rescue, international missions in support of U.S. Southern Command, and aeromedical evacuation. Recently, AFR has taken an active role in the national counternarcotics effort.

Air Force Reserve Command (AFRC)

AFRC, headquartered at Robins AFB, became a MAJCOM on February 17, 1997, pursuant to the National Defense Authorization Act of Fiscal Year 1997. It supports the USAF mission to defend the United States through control and exploitation of air and space by supporting global engagement. AFRC serves day to day in this mission and is not a force merely held in reserve for possible war or contingency operations.

AFRC consists of 35 flying wings equipped with their own aircraft and nine associate units that share aircraft with an active-duty unit. Four space operations squadrons share satellite control mission with the active force. There also are more than 620 mission support units in the AFRC, equipped and trained to provide a wide range of services, including medical and aeromedical evacuation, aerial port, civil engineer, security force, intelli-

gence, communications, mobility support, logistics and transportation operations, among others. The 447 aircraft assigned to AFRC include the F-16, O/A-10, C-5, C-130, MC-130, HC-130, WC-130, KC-135, B-52, and HH-60. On any given day, 99 percent of these aircraft are mission-ready and able to deploy within 72 hours.

The Office of Air Force Reserve, in the Pentagon, is headed by the Chief of Air Force Reserve, an AIR FORCE RESERVE lieutenant general, who is the principal adviser to the CHIEF OF STAFF of the Air Force for all AFR matters. The Chief of Air Force Reserve establishes AFR policy and initiates plans and programs. In addition to being a senior member of the AIR STAFF, he is also commander of the AFRC. Headquarters AFRC supervises the unit training program, provides logistics support, reviews unit training, and ensures combat readiness. FOURTH AIR FORCE at March Air Reserve Base, California, TENTH AIR FORCE at Carswell Air Reserve Station, Texas, and TWENTY-SECOND AIR FORCE at Dobbins Air Reserve Base, Georgia, report to Headquarters AFRC. They act as operational headquarters for their subordinate units, providing training, operational, logistical and safety support, and regional support for geographically separated units.

The Air Reserve Personnel Center, a Direct Reporting Unit located in Denver, Colorado, provides personnel services to all members of the AFRC and AIR NATIONAL GUARD.

Air Force Reserve Officer Training Corps (AFROTC)

AFROTC, headquartered at Maxwell AFB and administered by the AIR UNIVERSITY, is the largest and oldest source of commissioned officers for the USAF. AFROTC's mission is to produce leaders for the USAF while building better citizens for America. AFROTC is active on more than 144 college and university campuses, and an additional 750 schools offer the AFROTC program under crosstown agreements that allow their students to attend AFROTC classes at an area host school. The program commissions about 1,900 second lieutenants each year and also administers the Air Force Junior ROTC program, which provides citizenship training and an aerospace science program for high school youth. Air Force Junior ROTC programs are offered in 609 high school campuses throughout the nation, as well as in Guam, Puerto Rico, and selected U.S. dependent schools overseas. About 91,000 students are enrolled.

Air Force Review Boards Agency (AFRBA)

AFRBA is based in the Pentagon and manages military and civilian appellate processes for the SECRETARY OF THE AIR FORCE. AFRBA consists of the Air Force Board for Correction of Military Records; the Air Force Civilian Appellate Review Agency; and the Air Force Personnel Council. The council has special authority in examining discharges, decorations, and cases of physical disability.

air forces (organizational units)

Until the USAF underwent a major organizational restructuring in 1993, air forces were organizational units that equated to an army in the U.S. Army. They were subordinate to operational and support commands but superior to a division. There have been numbered air forces and named air forces—as many as 23 numbered air forces and 13 named air forces. After 1993, only the numbered air forces (NAFs) were retained, and these were restructured for strictly warfighting and operational roles; all support functions were allocated elsewhere. Today, a NAF is typically commanded by a major general or lieutenant general, and its staff (about half the pre-1993 strength) is dedicated to operational planning and employment of forces for several wings within the NAF.

In the U.S. ARMY AIR FORCES, before the USAF became an independent service arm (1947), the NAFS were the equivalent of today's Major Commands (MAJCOMs).

Air Force Safety Center (AFSC)

AFSC is a Field Operating Agency with headquarters at Kirtland AFB. The center develops and manages USAF mishap prevention programs and the Nuclear Surety Program. It develops regulatory guidance, provides technical assistance in the flight, ground, and weapons and space safety disciplines, and maintains the USAF database for all safety mishaps. The center oversees all major command mishap investigations and evaluates corrective actions for applicability and implementation USAF-wide. It also develops and directs safety education programs for all safety disciplines.

About 130 people are assigned to AFSC, equally divided between military and civilians. The center is composed of nine divisions, including an AIR STAFF liaison division at the Pentagon.

The Aviation Safety Division manages USAF flight mishap prevention programs for all manned aircraft. The Ground Safety Division develops ground safety programs and procedures to provide a safe work environment for all personnel. The Weapons, Space and Nuclear Safety Division establishes and executes mishap prevention programs for all weapons, reactor, space, and nuclear systems. The division provides nuclear systems design certification, explosive safety standards development, space and weapon safety consultation, as well as system inspection, oversight, education and staff assistance in its areas of responsibility. The Policy, Plans and Programs Division ensures proactive and effective mishap guidance for all safety disciplines. The Computer Operations and Programming Division provides AFSC with the communications and computer infrastructure and expertise. It also maintains the USAF database of all safety mishaps. The Education and Media Division publishes three USAF special publications: *Flying Safety, Road and Rec,* and *Nuclear Surety and Weapons Safety Journal.* The Media Branch is responsible for producing videotape presentations on relevant safety issues to support mishap prevention programs. The Safety Education Branch manages, administers, and sponsors educational courses that encompass the safety disciplines: aviation, ground, weapons, space, and missiles. The branch also manages the USAF Crash Laboratory used as a hands-on training facility with aviation safety courses. The Resource Management, Manpower, and Career Programs Division establishes policy and manages USAF civilian and enlisted safety personnel. The Issues Division, a detachment in the Pentagon, provides a direct interface with members of the Air Staff to facilitate responses to questions on safety-related issues raised by the CHIEF OF STAFF and members of the staff. The Office of the Staff Judge Advocate provides legal advice and general counsel on all aspects of mishap prevention programs and safety investigations.

After the USAF became an independent service, the Office of the Inspector General oversaw all inspection and safety functions. On December 31, 1971, the Air Force Inspection and Safety Center was activated, divided into the AIR FORCE INSPECTION AGENCY and the Air Force Safety Agency in August 1991. Both agencies moved to Kirtland AFB in July 1993 after the closure of Norton AFB. On January 1, 1996, the Air Force Safety Center was activated when the air force chief of safety and staff moved from Washington, D.C., to consolidate all safety functions at Kirtland.

Air Force Scientific Advisory Board (SAB)

Located near the Pentagon in Arlington, Virginia, the SAB is charged with providing independent wisdom and insight to USAF senior leadership on science and technology for continued air and space dominance. The SAB functions as a link between the USAF and the civilian scientific and engineering communities. The board continually reviews and evaluates USAF research and development plans, recommending applications that can be derived from promising scientific and technological developments and discoveries. The board also conducts a variety of studies at the request of senior USAF leadership to assess scientific and engineering aspects of particular operational or acquisition problems or issues. SAB members are selected on the basis of eminence in scientific fields of interest to the USAF.

Air Force Security Forces Center (AFSFC)

Headquartered at Lackland Air Force Base, Texas, AFSFC was known as the Air Force Security Police Agency before 1991. The AFSFC consists of four major divisions:

> Air Force Corrections Division
> Operations Division
> Force Protection Division
> Training and Combat Arms Division

The Corrections Division is responsible for the transfer and management of Air Force court-martialed members from worldwide confinement facilities for continued confinement in Regional Correctional Facilities (RCFs) operated by the air force, army, navy, and marines. The division maintains court-martial, personnel, and financial data of inmates confined in the Air Force Corrections System as well as for members released on parole or appellate leave.

The Operations Division consists of a Police Services Branch, DoD Canine, an Operations Center, Requirements Branch, Nuclear Security Branch, and an Installation Security Branch.

Police Services administers basic police functions on air force bases and other installations. DoD Canine is responsible for the care, training, management, and deployment of working police dogs. The Operations Center is tasked with maintaining functional management over all USAF Security Forces personnel and equipment to support wartime and peacetime contingencies. The branch is the executive agent responsible for tasking Security Forces through each Major Command (MAJCOM) Security Forces functional manager. Branch personnel also collect, process, analyze and communicate force protection information to assist air force leaders in making informed decisions. During contingencies, crises, and wartime operations, the branch provides force protection recommendations to the Air Force Directory of Security Forces.

Air Force Security Police Agency personnel train in airbase defense and antiterrorism. This security forces airman fires an M-249 during a training exercise at Indian Springs Air Force Auxiliary Field, Nevada.   *(U.S. Air Force)*

The Requirements Branch manages current and future requirements, based on operational deficiencies and provides requirement oversight in the development, review and validation, of emerging technology to fulfill operational capabilities. The Nuclear Security Branch develops guidance and policy for the physical security of air force weapons systems worldwide. The Installation Security Branch has primary responsibility for creating systems and policies to ensure the security of air force bases and other facilities.

The Force Protection Division of the Air Force Security Forces Center provides policy, resource advocacy, and guidance in the areas of doctrine, antiterrorism, and training, and also conducts vulnerability assessments.

The Training and Combat Arms Division consist of a Training Branch and a Combat Arms Branch. The Training Branch provides high-quality, cost-effective training to security personnel. The branch also develops policy and guidance for security forces, combat arms, and security aware-

ness and education training programs. The branch also provides professional career development programs for Security Force officers, airmen, and civilians.

The Combat Arms Branch implements policies and procedures for the Air Force Combat Arms Training Program, including ground weapons and munitions. The branch develops ground-weapons training and qualifications programs and establishes qualification standards. It implements field and organizational-level maintenance and repair policies for ground weapons, and implements maintenance policies and procedures and range safety criteria for new types of group weapons.

Air Force Services Agency (AFSVA)

AFSVA, headquartered in San Antonio, Texas, was formed during the reorganization of Morale, Welfare and Recreation and Services functions in 1993 and is tasked with supporting the bases, MAJCOMs, and AIR STAFF by providing technical assistance, fielding new initiatives, developing procedures, and managing selected central support functions to ensure successful services programs. The agency manages USAF central nonappropriated funds and operates central systems for field support such as banking, investments, purchasing, data flow, insurance and benefits programs, and the personnel system. HQ AFSVA supports the Air Force Morale, Welfare, and Recreation Advisory Board. About 400 USAF military and civilian personnel are assigned to AFSVA.

Air Forces Iceland

The smallest of the named air forces, Air Forces Iceland was established in 1952 as the Iceland Air Defense Force under MILITARY AIR TRANSPORT SERVICE (MATS) command and became Air Forces Iceland in 1960 under the AIR DEFENSE COMMAND (ADC). In 1979, it was assigned to TACTICAL AIR COMMAND (TAC) and was reassigned to the FIRST AIR FORCE in 1990.

Air Forces Iceland is important to the defense of the hemisphere because of the strategically critical position Iceland occupies in relation to North Atlantic air and sea routes.

Air Force Space Command (AFSPACECOM)

AFSPACECOM is a USAF MAJCOM as well as a component of the United States Space Command, a unified command of the U.S. armed forces. AFSPACECOM plans, manages, and operates such space assets as ballistic missile warning and offensive attack and spacelift/launch and ground control for Department of Defense satellite operations. AFSPACECOM also serves to coordinate research and development among operational users of USAF space programs. The command is headquartered at Peterson AFB, Colorado.

Air Force Special Operations Command (AFSOC)

AFSOC organizes, trains, and equips USAF special operations forces for worldwide deployment as well as for assignment to regional unified commands. Special operations conducts unconventional warfare, direct action, special reconnaissance, counterterrorism, foreign international defense, humanitarian assistance, psychological operations, personnel recovery, and counternarcotics missions. This MAJCOM is headquartered at Hurlburt Field, Florida.

Air Force Specialty Codes (AFSC)

The USAF developed the AFSC system to identify the duties for all enlisted positions essential to accomplishing the mission of the USAF. Every USAF job—and every USAF member's job qualifications—can be identified by a five-digit code.

- The first character of the AFSC identifies the career grouping.
- The second character identifies the career field.
- The third character identifies a career field subdivision.
- The fourth character identifies the airman's level of qualification (1: helper; 3: apprentice; 5: journeyman; 7: craftsman; 9: superintendent; 0: chief enlisted manager).
- The fifth character denotes the airman's specialty.

Air Force Studies and Analyses Agency (AFSAA)

The Pentagon-based AFSAA assists the SECRETARY OF THE AIR FORCE, the CHIEF OF STAFF, USAF, and other senior staff concerning such issues as force structure, resource allocation, weapons system acquisition and employment, and arms reduction proposals, all in relation to national security policy.

Air Force Systems Command (AFSC)

Since 1992 combined with AIR FORCE LOGISTICS COMMAND as the AIR FORCE MATERIEL COMMAND, AFSC was established in 1950 as the Research and Development Command (RDC). The mission of AFSC, now subsumed by AFMC, is to advise USAF leadership on scientific and technical options available for aerospace equipment needs.

AFSC's antecedent, RDC, was born of the revolutionary technological developments that had burgeoned during WORLD WAR II. U.S. commanders were concerned because a great many of the truly innovative weapons and weapons systems—such as radar, jets, ballistic missiles, and (in its theoretical aspects) even nuclear weaponry—had originated abroad. The mission of the RDC and its successor organizations was, in effect, to get the jump on technology and bring weapons innovations home.

AFSC was especially active during the VIETNAM WAR, when it was called on to develop "instant" solutions for some of the needs of large-scale unconventional warfare. During the Vietnam period, AFSC advanced the development of electronic warfare systems, of gunships, of "smart" (precision-guided) munitions, and of FLIR (forward-looking infrared) sensor technology. AFSC also developed a defense meteorological satellite program during this period.

Air Force Technical Applications Center (AFTAC)

AFTAC is a Direct Reporting Unit originally established in 1959 as the USAF Field Activities Group and redesignated AFTAC in 1980. AFTAC is tasked with the detection of nuclear events, principally the detection of nuclear test detonations in violation of any of several international treaty agreements. One of AFTAC's most vital missions was the detection and tracking of radioactive matter that resulted from the 1986 accident at the Chernobyl nuclear power plant in the former Soviet Union.

AFTAC is headquartered at Patrick AFB, Florida.

Air Force Training Ribbon   See DECORATIONS AND MEDALS.

Air Force Weather Agency (AFWA)

This Field Operating Agency was formed October 15, 1997, and is located at Offutt AFB. Its mission is to enhance our nation's combat capability by arming our forces with quality weather and space products, training, equipment, and communications—anytime, anywhere. AFWA fields well-equipped, well-trained USAF weather units and ensures that USAF weather procedures, practices, and equipment are standardized while leaving units with sufficient flexibility to support their missions. AFWA staff provides specialized training, primarily relating to meteorology, and provides technical assistance as required.

AFWA personnel gather over 140,000 weather reports each day from conventional meteorological sources throughout the world and relay them to AFWA via the Automated Weather Network (AWN). By combining these data with information available from military and civilian meteorological satellites, AFWA constructs a real-time, integrated environmental database. A series of scientific computer programs model the existing atmosphere and project changes. These meteorological tools are made available to technicians for application to specific aerospace environmental problems encountered by operational personnel. AFWA supports the warfighter, the base or post weather station, national programs, command and control agencies and systems, and other operational and planning functions. AFWA exchanges data with the National Weather Service and the Naval Oceanography Command and is the backup agency for two National Weather Service centers.

AFWA is organized into a headquarters element with two subordinate centers. Nearly 574 of the agency's 729 members are located at Offutt AFB.

Air Intelligence Agency (AIA)

Headquartered at Kelly AFB, AIA was activated on October 1, 1993, to gain, exploit, defend, and attack information to ensure superiority in the air, space, and information domains. Approximately 16,000 AIA personnel are stationed worldwide. The agency is organized as follows:

National Air Intelligence Center: Headquartered at Wright-Patterson AFB, the NAIC is the primary Department of Defense producer of foreign aerospace intelligence. The center analyzes all available data on foreign aerospace forces and weapons systems to determine performance characteristics, capabilities, vulnerabilities, and intentions. Its antecedent was the Air Force Systems Command's Foreign Technology Division, organized in 1961.

Air Force Information Warfare Center: Headquartered at Kelly AFB, the AFIWC develops, maintains, and deploys information warfare and command and control warfare capabilities in support of operations, campaign planning, acquisition, and testing. The center is a focal point for intelligence data and provides technical expertise for computer and communications security and for tactical deception and operations security training. Activated on September 10, 1993, the AFIWC combined the Air Force Electronic Warfare Center and elements of the Air Force Cryptologic Support Center's securities directorate.

497th Intelligence Group: Headquartered at Bolling AFB, the group provides worldwide intelligence infrastructure support, physical and personal security, threat support to weapon systems acquisition, and employment and automation support. The group also serves as the Washington, D.C.-area focal point for USAF intelligence planning, logistics, and readiness issues, communications/computer system support, and all military and civilian personnel actions and programs. Formerly the Air Force Intelligence Support Agency, the group was renamed the 497th IG on October 1, 1993.

543rd Intelligence Group: Headquartered at Kelly AFB, the group is a major component of the 67th Intelligence Wing and is headquarters for two Intelligence Squadrons, the 31st IS at Fort Gordon, Georgia, and the 93rd IS, at Lackland AFB.

544th Intelligence Group: Headquartered at Peterson AFB, the group directs, manages,

and supports units worldwide in the collection, refinement, and delivery of intelligence.

67th Intelligence Wing: Headquartered at Kelly AFB, the wing manages the agency's global mission and is the only intelligence wing in the USAF. It assists USAF components in the development of concepts, exercises, and employment of AIA forces to support contingency, low-intensity conflict, counterdrug, and special operations. Subordinate to the wing are five intelligence groups located in the continental United States, Hawaii, and Germany. With more than 9,600 personnel assigned, the 67th IW is one of the largest wings in USAF.

Joint Information Operations Center: This is a Joint Chiefs of Staff organization for coordination of joint-service intelligence operations, activities, and needs.

airlift

One of the most important USAF missions, airlift uses large transport aircraft or helicopters to move people, equipment, and supplies. Large-scale strategic airlift supports strategic operations, and smaller-scale tactical airlift supports tactical operations. Formerly, the MILITARY AIRLIFT COMMAND (MAC) managed airlift for the USAF and the Department of Defense. In June 1992, MAC was subsumed by the newly formed AIR MOBILITY COMMAND (AMC), which now manages all Department of Defense airlift.

See also BERLIN AIRLIFT.

Air Materiel Force, European Area

Established as Air Materiel Force, Europe, in 1954 under the UNITED STATES AIR FORCES IN EUROPE (USAFE), this named air force was headquartered at Wiesbaden, Germany, then redesignated Air Materiel Force, European Area, under the AIR MATERIEL COMMAND (AMC) in 1956 and, two years later, moved to Châteauroux Air Station, France. In

The airborne combat team from 1st Battalion, 508th Infantry, jumps from a USAF C-130 Hercules in an exercise over Maniago, Italy.   *(U.S. Air Force)*

1962, it was inactivated because improved distribution systems made this organization's huge supply depots unnecessary.

Air Materiel Force, Pacific Area

The Air Materiel Force, Pacific Area was established in 1944 as the Far East Air Service Command, with headquarters at Brisbane, Australia, and functioning as a named air force under the FAR EAST AIR FORCES (FEAF). In 1946, it was renamed Pacific Air Service Command, U.S. Army, then Far East Air Materiel Command the following year. In 1952, it was redesignated the Far East Air Logistics Forces, and, in 1955, the Air Materiel Force, Pacific Area, under the AIR MATERIEL COMMAND (AMC). Its headquarters changed location several times, and, at the time of its inactivation in 1962, it was headquartered at Tachikawa AB, with another principal location at Clark AB, Philippines. As with the AIR MATERIEL FORCE, EUROPEAN AREA, also inactivated in 1962, improved distribution systems rendered large remote depots unnecessary.

Air Medal   See DECORATIONS AND MEDALS.

airman   See RANKS AND GRADES.

airman basic   See RANKS AND GRADES.

airman first class   See RANKS AND GRADES.

Airman's Medal   See DECORATIONS AND MEDALS.

Airmen Memorial Museum

Located outside of Washington, D.C., in Suitland, Maryland, the Airmen Memorial Museum was founded in 1988 by the Air Force Sergeants Association and is meant to record and commemorate the service and sacrifices of enlisted airmen from the Signal Corps (1907–18), the U.S. ARMY AIR SERVICE (1918–26), the U.S. ARMY AIR CORPS (1926–41), the U.S. ARMY AIR FORCES (1941–47), and the USAF (1947–present). The museum collects and exhibits artifacts, photographs, diaries, personnel records, letters, books, and other items pertaining to the service of enlisted airmen. Exhibit galleries present text and artifacts that illustrate the history of enlisted airmen from 1907 to the present day.

Airmen Memorial Museum is located at 5211 Auth Road, Suitland, MD 20746; phone: 1-800-638-0594. Web site: www.afsahq.org.

Air Mobility Command (AMC)

Formed in June 1992 from elements of STRATEGIC AIR COMMAND (SAC) and MILITARY AIRLIFT COMMAND (MAC), AMC is a MAJCOM responsible for intertheater AIRLIFT and for most tanker and airlift forces. The rationale behind integrating airlift and tanker operations is to provide truly global mobility and reach, to enhance rapid response, and to enable other services and foreign nations to operate more efficiently with USAF assets. AMC is headquartered at Scott AFB, Illinois.

This C-17 Globemaster III is from the 437th Air Wing, Charleston AFB. The photo was taken from a KC-10 Extender, just after it refueled the Globemaster. *(U.S. Air Force)*

Air National Guard (ANG)

The Air National Guard was established as a separate reserve component of the USAF on September 18, 1947, although National Guard aviators were active in all of America's wars and most of its major contingencies since the era of WORLD WAR I.

Currently, the ANG is administered by the National Guard Bureau, a joint bureau of the departments of the Army and Air Force, located in the Pentagon, Washington, D.C. The ANG is one of the seven reserve components of the U.S. armed forces and has a federal as well as a state mission. In accordance with the U.S. Constitution and federal law, each guardsman holds membership in the National Guard of his or her state as well as the National Guard of the United States.

The ANG's federal mission is to maintain well-trained, well-equipped units available for prompt mobilization during war and to provide assistance during national emergencies, such as natural disasters or civil disturbances. During peacetime, the combat-ready units and support units are assigned to most USAF major commands to carry out missions compatible with training, mobilization readiness, and contingency operations. The ANG provides almost half of the USAF's tactical airlift support, combat communications functions, aeromedical evacuations, and aerial refueling. The ANG has total responsibility for air defense of the entire United States.

When ANG units are not mobilized or under federal control, they report to the governor of their respective state or territory, or, in the case of the District of Columbia, to the commanding general of the District of Columbia National Guard. Each of the 54 ANG organizations is supervised by the adjutant general of the state or territory. Operating under state law, the ANG provides protection of life and property and preserves peace, order, and public safety. State-level missions include emergency relief support during natural disasters such as floods, earthquakes, and forest fires; search and rescue operations; support to civil defense authorities; maintenance of vital public services and antinarcotics operations.

Besides providing 100 percent of the United States air defense interceptor force, the ANG provides:

- air traffic control
- tactical airlift
- air refueling KC-135 tankers
- general purpose fighter force
- rescue and recovery capability
- tactical air support
- weather flights
- bomber force
- strategic airlift forces
- special operations capability

As of 2005, the ANG has more than 107,000 officers and enlisted people who serve in 88 flying units and 280 independent support units.

Air Reserve Personnel Center (ARPC)

ARPC is a Special Operating Agency that was established in 1956 as the Air Reserve Records Center and was redesignated ARPC in 1965. Headquartered in Denver, ARPC handles personnel support functions for the mobilization and demobilization of the AIR NATIONAL GUARD, AIR FORCE RESERVE, and retired members of the ANG and AFR.

Air Reserves Forces Meritorious Service Medal   See DECORATIONS AND MEDALS.

Air Staff

Air Staff is a headquarters group that advises and assists the top USAF leadership, in addition to the SECRETARY OF THE AIR FORCE, undersecretary and assistant secretaries, and the CHIEF OF STAFF, USAF. The Air Staff is made up of the chief of staff, vice chief of staff, assistant vice chief of staff, and as many as four deputy chiefs of staff, in addition to other members who might be assigned from time to time. The Air Staff antedates the establishment of the independent USAF and was created with the U.S. ARMY AIR FORCES in 1941, becoming active the following year.

Air Superiority Doctrine

The USAF created an air superiority doctrine in 1984, making air superiority the number one priority of the USAF in any conflict, regardless of its nature. The objective of air superiority is to deny the enemy the use of its own air space while allowing U.S. aircraft to accomplish their tasks and missions. The PERSIAN GULF WAR was an extraordinarily dramatic demonstration of the doctrine in action.

Air Transport Command (ATC)   See AIR MOBILITY COMMAND; MILITARY AIRLIFT COMMAND.

Air University (AU)

Headquartered at Maxwell AFB, Alabama, Air University is a component of the AIR EDUCATION AND TRAINING COMMAND (AETC), which also includes the Air Training Command (ATC), and functions as the USAF's center for professional military education. AU conducts professional military education, graduate education, and professional continuing education for officers, enlisted personnel, and civilians to prepare them for command, staff, leadership, and management responsibilities. AU offers specialized as well as degree-granting programs to serve USAF needs in scientific, technological, managerial, and other areas. AU is also responsible for research in aerospace education, leadership, and management, and it provides precommissioning training and offers courses for enlisted personnel leading to the awarding of select USAF specialty credentials. Finally, AU is also instrumental in the development and testing of USAF doctrine, concepts, and strategy.

The reach of AU extends beyond the active and reserve USAF through such Air University programs as Air Force Junior Reserve Officer Training Corps, AIR FORCE RESERVE OFFICER TRAINING CORPS (AFROTC), and the CIVIL AIR PATROL (CAP).

The AIR FORCE OFFICER TRAINING SCHOOL (OTS), located at Maxwell AFB, provides two officer training programs: Basic Officer Training and Commissioned Officer Training. Basic Officer Training is an intensive thirteen-and-a-half-week program that prepares officer candidates for the technical, physical, and professional requirements of commissioned service. In wartime, OTS may produce as many as 7,000 new second lieutenants in one year. Commissioned officer training, located at Gunter Annex, provides initial officer training for nearly 2,700 USAF judge advocates, chaplains, medical service officers (doctors, nurses, pharmacists, bioenvironmental engineers, and hospital administrators), and medical scholarship recipients each year.

Professional military education for USAF officers begins with Squadron Officer School, where captains study officership, air and space power, leadership tools, and applications. The Air Command and Staff College, the next level of officer professional military education, offers a 40-week curriculum devoted to educating students in the profession of arms, the requisites of command, the nature of war, and the application of air and space power at the theater warfare level. The emphasis is on warfare at the operational and strategic levels. The AIR WAR COLLEGE, senior school in the USAF professional military education system, is treated in a separate entry.

The College for Enlisted Professional Military Education, headquartered at Maxwell's Gunter Annex, is responsible for designing the curriculum taught at Airman Leadership Schools, noncommissioned officer academies, and the Air Force Senior Noncommissioned Officer Academy. The college directly operates the two advanced phases of enlisted professional military education, the stateside NCO academies and the Senior NCO Academy. Major commands operate their own Airman Leadership Schools using curriculum designed by the college. Airman Leadership Schools prepare senior airmen to be noncommissioned officers, and NCO academies prepare technical sergeants to be senior NCOs.

The USAF Senior Noncommissioned Officer Academy is the capstone of enlisted professional military education. Located at Maxwell's Gunter Annex, the school prepares senior enlisted leaders to be chiefs with a curriculum focused on leadership and management, communication skills, and military studies.

In addition to military education, AU administers programs of academic education, including the COMMUNITY COLLEGE OF THE AIR FORCE and the AIR FORCE INSTITUTE OF TECHNOLOGY, both treated in separate entries. Continuing professional education is offered at the Ira C. Eaker College for Professional Development, Air University's largest resident college. The college provides courses for chaplains, commanders, personnel and manpower managers, comptrollers, family support center mangers, judge advocates, first sergeants, and historians. The COLLEGE OF AEROSPACE DOCTRINE, RESEARCH AND EDUCATION (CADRE), another continuing education facility, offers a Contingency Wartime Planning Course and a Joint Doctrine Air Campaign Course, as well as a Joint Flag Officer

Warfighting Course and a Joint Forces Air Component Commanders Course. These two courses prepare general officers from all military services for leadership positions in the joint warfighting environment. CADRE is also a research organization. CADRE doctrine analysts examine both existing and proposed concepts and strategies and deliver the results directly to the AIR FORCE DOCTRINE CENTER. CADRE's Air Force Wargaming Institute conducts numerous games each year to enhance the warfighting skills of both U.S. and international military officers.

Other AU entities are administered through its Office of Academic Support, which directs the Air University Library, the Academic Instructor School, and the International Officer School, tasked with preparing international officers to enter schools and courses. Other organizations under the OAS include: Air University Television, which supports resident and distance learning instruction; the Extension Course Institute, which publishes approximately 330 correspondence courses in specialized, career development, and professional military education; Air University Press, which acquires, edits, and publishes books, monographs, and journals on airpower topics; and Educational Technology.

Air War College (AWC)

The senior school in the USAF professional military education system, the Air War College is part of the AIR UNIVERSITY (AU) system and prepares selected senior officers for key staff and command assignments, in which they will manage and employ aerospace power as a major component of national security.

Air War College curriculum focuses on warfighting and national security issues, with emphasis on the effective employment of aerospace forces in joint and combined combat operations. Each class lasts 44 weeks and enrolls officers from all branches of the armed forces, international officers, and civilians of equivalent rank from U.S. government agencies.

The Air War College operates the National Security Forum, which brings students into contact with business, civic, and professional leaders from throughout the United States to discuss issues affecting national security. The forum is the culmination of the 10-month Air War College course of study.

Air Warfare Center (AWFC)

Located at Nellis AFB, Nevada, the Air Warfare Center manages USAF advanced pilot training and integrates many USAF test and evaluation requirements. The center's first predecessor organization, the USAF Tactical Fighter Weapons Center, was established in 1966. In 1991, the center became the USAF Fighter Weapons Center, and then the USAF Weapons and Tactics Center in 1992. AWFC was created in October 1995.

AWFC uses the Nellis Air Force Range Complex, some 3 million acres, together with another 5-million-acre military operating area, which is shared with civilian aircraft. AWFC also operates at the Eglin AFB range in Florida, which provides over-water and additional electronic expertise.

AWFC oversees operations of four WINGS, the 57th Wing, the 98th Range Wing, and 99th Air Base Wing at Nellis, and the 53rd Wing at Eglin.

The 57th Wing is responsible for such activities as Red Flag, which provides training in a combined air, ground, and electronic threat environment; the USAF Weapons School, which provides USAF graduate-level training for A-10, B-1, B-52, EC-130, F-15, F-15E, F-16, HH-60, RC-135, command and control operations, and intelligence and space weapons. The wing also plans and executes CLOSE AIR SUPPORT missions in support of U.S. Army exercises. In addition, the wing oversees the USAF air demonstration team, the THUNDERBIRDS, and manages the operation and deployment of the Predator, an unmanned reconnaissance aircraft.

The 53rd Wing (Eglin AFB) is the focal point for the combat air forces in electronic combat, armament and avionics, chemical defense, reconnaissance, command and control, and aircrew training devices.

The 99th Air Base Wing is the host wing at Nellis, and the 98th Range Wing manages the operations of the Nellis Air Force Range Complex, including two emergency airfields.

Air Weather Service (AWS)

AWS furnishes technical advice, procedures, and systems for weather support systems. Through various subordinate units, AWS provides weather, climatological, and space support to the USAF. The service is headquartered at Scott AFB, Illinois.

Alaskan Air Command (AAC)

The earliest AAC antecedent was the Alaskan Air Force, activated at Elmendorf Field, Alaska, in January 1942 and redesignated the ELEVENTH AIR FORCE the following month. The organization served in the offensive that liberated the Aleutian Islands from the Japanese, then served in the defense of Alaska. In December 1945, 11AF became the AAC. Somewhat confusingly, a new Eleventh Air Force was formed as part of the Air Defense Command (ADC) and assigned to AAC during 1946–48. In 1990, the AAC became 11AF.

During the cold war period, AAC provided (according to its motto) "Top Cover for America" under NORAD. The command controlled three bases in Alaska, Elmendorf AFB, Eielson AFB, and Shemya AFB, with fighters stationed in forward positions at King Salmon and Galena airports—Galena being the closest U.S. airfield to what was then the Soviet Union. AAC aircraft routinely intercepted Soviet bombers probing U.S. airspace.

Altus AFB, Altus, Oklahoma   See AIR FORCE BASES.

American Volunteer Group (AVG)

In 1940–41, President Franklin D. Roosevelt authorized the creation of a covert U.S. air force to fight for China in the Sino-Japanese War, the con-

flict that began in 1937 and that ultimately merged with WORLD WAR II. This American Volunteer Group (AVG) was planned to consist of two fighter groups and one medium bomber group. To equip the first of the fighter groups, 100 Tomahawk II-B fighters—equivalent to the Curtiss P-40C pursuit craft—were diverted from British order, and 100 U.S. military pilots and 200 technicians officially resigned from the military to accept private employment as civilian mercenaries with the AVG. The unit, now designated the First American Volunteer Group, was put under the command of a retired U.S. ARMY AIR CORPS captain, CLAIRE L. CHENNAULT, and trained in Burma, then a British colony.

The 1st AVG was not committed to combat until after Pearl Harbor and the U.S. entry into the war in December 1941. America's entry into the war brought the cancellation of the planned second

One of the redoubtable "Flying Tigers" ready to take off in a Curtiss P-40 (Warhawk) fighter plane
(National Archives)

fighter group and the bomber group, but the 1st AVG continued to fly, under Chennault, as what the public came to call the "Flying Tigers." AVG pilots painted a vivid tigerlike mouth and row of jagged teeth on either side of the P-40's distinctive air scoop, and journalists came up with the moniker, which conveyed the aggressive spirit that was in short supply among the Allies during the early days of the Pacific war.

The Flying Tigers played a major role in defending Burma until the Japanese routed the Allies in May 1942. Later in the year, the 1st AVG was instrumental in holding western China until reinforcements reached the Nationalist government. Formally disbanded on July 4, 1942, the AVG was instantly merged into the 23rd Pursuit Group of the U.S. ARMY AIR FORCES. Only five AVG pilots accepted induction in China, but many subsequently rejoined the U.S. military. AVG fliers are credited with having shot down 297 Japanese aircraft; 23 pilots were killed or captured.

Recent historians have concluded that the record of Flying Tiger victories was inflated, but it is beyond dispute that the AVG was highly effective against Japanese air and ground forces during the winter of 1941–42, a period in which all other Allied news in Asia and the Pacific was bleak indeed.

Andersen AFB, Guam   See AIR FORCE BASES.

Andrews, Frank Maxwell (1884–1943) *Air Force general*

A founding father of the USAF, Andrews was born in Nashville, Tennessee, and graduated from the U.S. Military Academy at West Point in 1906, with a commission as a cavalry officer. He entered the U.S. ARMY AIR SERVICE in 1917, received pilot training, and remained in the United States during WORLD WAR I, serving as a training officer. While serving in a series of routine postings during the 1920s, he attended and graduated from both the Air Corps Tactical School (ACTS) and the Com-

mand and General Staff College. During the 1930s, he served a staff tour in Washington, D.C., then attended the Army War College, graduating in 1933. He was assigned to command the 1st Pursuit Group at Selfridge Field, Michigan, but he was recalled to Washington in 1934 to participate in planning the new GENERAL HEADQUARTERS AIR FORCE (GHQ Air Force). In 1935, Andrews was temporarily promoted to brigadier general and took command of the newly created GHQ Air Force, which was the only independent combat unit of the U.S. ARMY AIR CORPS.

As GHQ Air Force commander, Andrews was in a key position to mount a campaign for the establishment of the air force as an independent service arm. He believed that the USAAC had to prove itself by deeds, not theory, in order to achieve independence. Under his command, USAAC personnel staged a number of spectacular exercises to demonstrate the potential of air power. Andrews also focused on developing the B-17 Flying Fortress heavy bomber as the weapon that would transform the air force into an indispensable and highly potent strategic operations force. He laid his career on the line to promote the four-engine bomber over the cheaper B-18, and was passed over for promotion to chief of the USAAC. By 1939, he was returned to his permanent grade of colonel and posted in San Antonio, Texas. However, General George C. Marshall, newly appointed army chief of staff, ended Andrews's exile and brought him to Washington, D.C., as assistant chief of staff for operations and training. In this post, Andrews directed the vital prewar expansion and training of both ground and air forces.

He left this post at the outbreak of WORLD WAR II and served successively as commander of the Panama Canal Air Force, the Caribbean Defense Command, and in Europe. In 1943, his career was cut short when he was killed in a plane crash. Andrews AFB is named in his honor.

Andrews AFB, Maryland   See AIR FORCE BASES.

Appropriations Act of July 24, 1917

This legislative milestone funded U.S. air power in WORLD WAR I to the sum of $640 million, the largest amount of money ever appropriated by Congress for a single purpose up to that time. Funding authorized by the act was used to develop flying fields in the United States and for the manufacture of aircraft intended to equip as many as 345 combat squadrons. Production fell very far short of this goal. By the time of the armistice in November 1918, only 45 U.S. combat squadrons had been committed to action, and these were equipped exclusively with foreign-built planes.

Army Air Forces Antisubmarine Command (AAFAC)

The AAFAC was established at New York City in October 1942 and tasked with countering the German U-boat threat in United States continental waters and elsewhere. AAFAC headquarters was in New York and training facilities were at Langley Field (see Langley AFB), Virginia, but the command operated from three continents in addition to North America and was responsible for the following areas of operation: the north and middle Atlantic, from Newfoundland to Trinidad; the Bay of Biscay; and the approaches to North Africa. AAFAC pilots flew A-20, A-29, B-17, B-18, B-25, and B-34 aircraft, but they relied most heavily on the B-24. Newly developed radar technologies were extensively pioneered by the command.

The AAFAC was active only until August 1943, when its mission was taken over by the U.S. Navy. During its 10 months of operation, U-boats sunk by air action rose from a paltry 10 percent to an impressive 50 percent. Officially, AAFAC pilots were credited with 10 U-boat sinkings.

As of 1986, antisubmarine work once again became a USAF mission, although the navy continues to take primary responsibility for antisubmarine operations. The USAF now uses B-52G bombers equipped with AGM-84 air-to-surface Harpoon missiles for antisubmarine operations.

Army and Air Force Authorization Act of 1950

Passed on July 10, 1950, this act provided the legislative definition of the organization of the USAF, specifying a maximum strength of 502,000 officers and men and an inventory of 24,000 aircraft. On August 3, 1950, with the KOREAN WAR under way, Congress suspended the limitations on strength in anticipation of necessary expansion during the war.

Army Regulation 95-5 (AR 95-5)

Issued on June 20, 1941, AR 95-5 created the U.S. ARMY AIR FORCES. AR 95-5 significantly enhanced the autonomy of the air arm over its former status as the U.S. ARMY AIR CORPS. The USAAF commander reported directly to the army chief of staff, and the AIR FORCE COMBAT COMMAND (AFCC) replaced the cumbersome GENERAL HEADQUARTERS AIR FORCE (GHQ Air Force). The effect of AR 95-5 and subsequent directives was to make the USAAF the functional (if not statutory) equivalent of the army and navy.

Arnold, Henry Harley ("Hap") (1886–1950)
Air Force general

Hap Arnold guided the transformation of the prewar U.S. ARMY AIR CORPS into the mighty U.S. ARMY AIR FORCES of WORLD WAR II and is justly regarded as the father of the independent USAF. He was born in Gladwyne, Pennsylvania, and received an appointment to West Point, from which he graduated in 1907, after which he was assigned to the infantry as a second lieutenant. Arnold served in the Philippines during 1907–09, but, in 1911, he transferred to the AVIATION SECTION, U.S. ARMY SIGNAL CORPS, and volunteered for flight training with the Wright brothers in Dayton, Ohio. In October of the very next year, he became the first to demonstrate how the airplane could be used for reconnaissance, and, for his pioneering efforts, was awarded the first MacKay flying trophy. He also earned the army's first military aviator's badge and expert aviator's certificate, and he established an early world altitude record of 6,540 feet.

Yet Arnold's remarkable achievements did little to spark the army's interest in the airplane as a weapon, and, in April 1913, Arnold was transferred back to the infantry. Returned to the air service in 1916, he was promoted to captain and put in command of the army's aviation training schools in 1917, when the United States entered WORLD WAR I. Arnold directed aviation training from May 1917 through 1919 and earned a reputation as a great teacher. The armistice of November 1918 brought sharp reductions in military funding, which greatly retarded the development of American military aviation. Never one to be discouraged, however, Arnold continued to work toward the goal of creating a credible U.S. Army Air Corps. He attended Command and General Staff College, from which he graduated in 1929 with the rank of

General Henry H. "Hap" Arnold   (U.S. Air Force)

lieutenant colonel and in 1931 was given command of the 1st Bomb Wing and the 1st Pursuit Wing at March Field, California, a post he held through February 1935. During July and August 1934, he led a flight of 10 B-10 bombers on a round trip from Washington, D.C., to Fairbanks, Alaska, winning a second MacKay Trophy for having demonstrated the endurance capabilities of the modern bomber.

Promoted to brigadier general, Arnold took command of 1st Wing, GENERAL HEADQUARTERS AIR FORCE (GHQ Air Force) in February 1935 and became assistant chief of staff of the USAAC in December of that year. After the death of General Oscar Westover in September 1938, Arnold was promoted to temporary major general and named chief of staff. From this position, he was able to institute a program to improve the combat readiness of the USAAC, despite inadequate funding and the resistance of tradition-bound military planners. Named acting deputy chief of staff of the army for air matters in October 1940, Arnold became chief of the Air Corps, after it was renamed the U.S. Army Air Forces in June 1941.

Shortly after Pearl Harbor (December 7, 1941), Arnold was promoted to the temporary rank of lieutenant general and was soon afterward named commanding general of the USAAF. He was promoted to the temporary rank of general in 1943. His position as commanding general of the USAAF put Arnold at the very highest level of policy and strategic planning in the United States military. A member of the U.S. Joint Chiefs of Staff, he participated in shaping Allied strategy in Europe and the Pacific.

Among the many organizational innovations Arnold introduced was the creation of the TWENTIETH AIR FORCE in April 1944. His purpose in creating this unit was, first and foremost, to conduct an effective bombing campaign against Japan, but he organized the 20AF so that it reported directly to his command as a representative of the Joint Chiefs. This bold stroke took the USAAF closer to becoming a fully independent service.

In December 1944, along with generals Dwight D. Eisenhower, Douglas MacArthur, and George C. Marshall, Arnold was elevated to the special rank of general of the army. He continued to command the USAAF through the end of the war, retiring in March 1946. A year after his retirement, on September 18, 1947, thanks in large part to all he had done, the USAAF became the USAF, an independent service. To honor its "father," the USAF named Arnold the first general of the air force in May 1949—despite his retired status. Arnold died the following year on his ranch in Sonoma, California.

Arnold AFB, Tennessee   See AIR FORCE BASES.

Arnold Engineering Development Center (AEDC)

Located at Arnold AFB, Tennessee, AEDC is the most advanced and largest complex of flight simulation test facilities in the world. Housed here are 58 aerodynamic and propulsion wind tunnels, rocket and turbine engine test cells, space environmental chambers, arc heaters, ballistic ranges, and other specialized units. The mission of the AEDC is to test, evaluate, and troubleshoot aircraft, missile, and space systems and subsystems. AEDC also conducts research to develop advanced testing techniques and instrumentation and to support the design of new test facilities.

The center is named for General of the Air Force HENRY HARLEY ARNOLD, who set into motion the research program that would become the work of this center. The facility was officially dedicated by President Harry S. Truman on June 25, 1951. AEDC is part of the AIR FORCE MATERIEL COMMAND (AFMC).

Aviano AB, Italy   See AIR FORCE BASES.

aviation medicine

The USAF is active in research into the physical and psychological problems associated with avia-

tion and spaceflight. USAF aviation medicine began in 1917 with the work of Colonel Theodore C. Lyster of the AVIATION SECTION, U.S. ARMY SIGNAL CORPS, but, during WORLD WAR I, the army relied on civilian physicians contracted to serve as "flight surgeons." In 1918, a Medical Research Laboratory was established at Hazelhurst Field, New York, to research aviation medicine and to train military physicians in the field. By July 1921, the U.S. ARMY AIR SERVICE graduated 46 flight surgeons from Hazelhurst. The following year, the Medical Research Laboratory was transferred to Mitchel Field, New York, as the School of Aviation Medicine. The school moved to Brooks Field, Texas (see Brooks AFB), in 1926, then to Randolph Field (see Randolph AFB).

The principal early work of USAAS aviation medicine was to prevent accidents and illness related to flight, to improve training, to investigate altitude-induced deafness, to test the effects of cold and low air pressure at high altitudes, and even to improve aviator goggles. In 1944, during WORLD WAR II, the school at Randolph Field expanded to include course work in aeromedical evacuation and to train USAAF nurses.

After World War II, research in aviation medicine expanded and was conducted at the Aero Medical Laboratory at Wright-Patterson AFB; at the Air Force Flight Test Center, Edwards AFB; at the Air Development Center, Holoman AFB. The era of high-speed, high-altitude jet flight brought to prominence more medical issues than ever before. Today, the school, renamed the UNITED STATES AIR FORCE SCHOOL OF AEROSPACE MEDICINE, is located at Brooks AFB, Texas.

Aviation Section, U.S. Army Signal Corps

The first separate U.S. Army unit exclusively devoted to aviation, the Aviation Section was created by act of Congress on July 18, 1914. Its first battle experience came in the PUNITIVE EXPEDITION of 1916 against the Mexican social bandit Pancho Villa, but the performance of its aircraft proved unsatisfactory. It was the Aviation Section that

This E-3 Sentry AWACS from the 966th AWACS, Tinker AFB, Oklahoma, is seen in a training flight over New Mexico.   *(U.S. Air Force)*

struggled to bring U.S. military aviation into WORLD WAR I, and on August 27, 1918, the unit was reorganized as the U.S. ARMY AIR SERVICE.

AWACS (Airborne Warning and Control System)

The predecessor of AWACS, airborne radar, was first used in the VIETNAM WAR on EC-121 "College Eye" aircraft (see AIRCRAFT, VIETNAM WAR). The original EC-121 evolved into the EC-121D, used by the AIR DEFENSE COMMAND (ADC) as part of its early warning system for continental defense. Ultimately, an EC-121T was developed as ASACS (airborne surveillance and control system), which gave way in March 1977 to AWACS, deployed on the E-3 Sentry aircraft. (See also AIRCRAFT, COLD WAR AND AFTER.)

A Boeing 707 modified with large radar dome, the E-3 AWACS provided radar coverage extending from the surface of the earth up to the stratosphere at a range of more than 200 miles—and without the ground clutter that plagues ground-based radar. AWACS has proved invaluable in giving tactical commanders the information required to gain control of air battles as well as CLOSE AIR SUPPORT of ground forces as well as management of interdiction reconnaissance and AIRLIFT operations. AWACS was very extensively used in the PERSIAN GULF WAR.

B

balloons and dirigibles

On November 4, 1782, Joseph-Michel Montgolfier, a French paper manufacturer, filled a taffeta container with hot air and watched it ascend. This was the first recorded practical experiment in ballooning—although as early as 1766, the English scientist Henry Cavendish isolated hydrogen, which led a Scottish chemist named Joseph Black to speculate that if a bladder could be filled with the ultralight gas and both the bladder and the gas weighed less than the air they displaced, the bladder would rise. Neither Cavendish nor Black ever got around to trying the experiment. It was Montgolfier and his brother, Jacques-Étienne, who developed the first practical hot-air balloons, and the French Academy that experimented with the first hydrogen balloons, both in 1783. In that same year, a young physician named Pilâtre de Rozier made the first manned tethered flights in a *Montgolfière,* as the early balloons were called, and a French infantry major, the Marquis d'Arlandes, undertook the first free flight in a balloon on November 21, 1783. Very soon after this, ballooning became the rage in Europe, and Jean-Pierre Blanchard, the first aeronaut-showman, became the most celebrated of the early balloonists. He brought his balloon to America and made an ascension from the yard of the old Walnut Street Prison on January 9, 1793, a flight witnessed by President George Washington, Alexander Hamilton, John Adams, Thomas Jefferson, and James Monroe. After reaching a maxi-

mum altitude of 5,812, Blanchard landed, 46 minutes after liftoff, across the Delaware River near Woodbury, New Jersey. He had introduced aviation to the United States.

Although, after witnessing the flight of the Montgolfiers in France, Benjamin Franklin predicted that the balloon would quickly find military applications, it was not until 1840, during the Second Seminole War, that U.S. Army colonel John H. Sherburne proposed the use of observation balloons to be lofted at night to search for Seminole campfires. Secretary of War Joel Poinsett authorized Sherburne to contact Charles Ferson Durant, a balloonist remembered by some historians of flight as "America's first professional aeronaut." However, Sherburne's commanding officer, General W. K. Armistead, allowed no ascensions. In 1846, during the U.S.-Mexican War, John C. Wise, a balloonist from Lancaster, Pennsylvania, volunteered his services for an assault against Veracruz. That key Mexican city was protected from land assault by a formidable fortress and shielded from seaborne attack by dangerous reefs. Wise proposed an attack from the air, using a balloon tethered by five miles of cable to effect aerial bombardment from an altitude of 5,000 feet. The scheme came to nothing, but the War Department returned to John Wise years later, during the Civil War.

By the time of the Civil War, the United States had produced a host of balloonists in addition to Wise and Durant, including Samuel King, James

Allen, William H. Helme, W. D. Bannister, John Steiner, and John La Mountain. O. A. Gager, with Wise, La Mountain, and an unidentified newspaper reporter, made a spectacular flight from St. Louis, Missouri, to Henderson, New York, on July 20, 1859—a distance of 1,100 miles, which they covered in under 20 hours. Of the small legion of balloonists active in America by 1861, the most flamboyant was Thaddeus Sobieski Constantine Lowe, who flew from Cincinnati to Unionville, South Carolina, a thousand miles, on April 19, 1861. By sheer accident, Lowe's exploit was the first balloon ascent of the Civil War.

On the same day that Lowe made his flight, James Allen, a balloonist with four years' experi-

Union army hot air balloon, 1862   *(National Archives)*

ence, and his friend, a dentist named William H. Helme, both members of the 1st Rhode Island Regiment, volunteered their services to the federal government as balloonists. They traveled to Washington, bringing with them a pair of balloons. On June 9, the two aeronauts inflated one of their balloons at a gas main in central Washington. The craft was towed to a farm a mile north of the city, and Allen and Helme made the Union army's first official captive balloon trial ascent. The army was sufficiently impressed to attempt a reconnoitering mission for General Irvin McDowell on the eve of the First Battle of Bull Run. Allen took the larger of his two balloons to Alexandria, Virginia, where he attempted inflation at a coal gas plant. The balloon, aged and in disrepair, split under pressure. Allen successfully inflated his second balloon, but the craft was destroyed when it struck a telegraph pole. Yet the army's interest in ballooning continued, and, on June 12, 1861, Major Hartman Bache, acting chief of the Topographic Engineers, contacted John Wise to request an estimate of the cost of building and operating a small balloon. Early in July, Wise was hired as a military balloonist and commissioned to construct a balloon for $850. Completed on July 21, the army's first balloon was delivered to the capital, where it was inflated, then walked by a ground crew up Pennsylvania Avenue to Georgetown, thence up the C&O Canal, across the Potomac, and to Fairfax Road. There Albert J. Myer, chief signal officer, tethered it to a wagon for the trip to Manassas, where it was to be used to observe the battle now in progress. Unfortunately, Major Myer, anxious to deliver the balloon to the battle site, ordered the wagon driver to whip up the horses—this despite the protests of John Wise. As the balloonist had feared, the gas bag was soon snagged by overhanging branches, which tore gaping holes in the fabric as Wise attempted to free it. Wise repaired his balloon and made observation ascensions on July 24 at Arlington. On July 26, a crew was towing the balloon to Ball's Crossroads. It hit some telegraph wires, which severed the tow ropes, sending the balloon in free flight toward the Confederate lines. Rather than allow the craft to fall into Confederate hands, Union troops were ordered to shoot it down.

Concluding that the problem with balloons was the necessity of inflating them wherever coal gas was available and then having to transport them while inflated, Wise designed a portable hydrogen gas generator. The army declined to build Wise's generator, but it did accept John La Mountain's offer not only of his services as a balloonist but also two balloons and a ready-made portable hydrogen generator. Major General Benjamin F. Butler, headquartered at Fortress Monroe, Virginia, hired La Mountain as a civilian aerial observer on June 5, 1861. His first ascent, at Hampton, Virginia, on July 25, was hampered by heavy winds that prevented his attaining sufficient altitude to observe the enemy. On July 31, however, he rose to 1,400 feet and, commanding a view 30 miles in radius, was able to inform Butler that Confederate strength around Hampton was much weaker than had been thought. This was the first useful balloon reconnaissance mission for the army. On August 3, La Mountain made the first ascension tethered to a waterborne vessel, and, beginning on October 4, he used prevailing winds in a series of untethered, free-flight reconnaissance missions.

On June 18, 1861, La Mountain's fellow balloonist and rival Thaddeus Lowe made the first telegraph transmission from aloft, demonstrating the feasibility of real-time reconnaissance. President Abraham Lincoln personally persuaded the Union army's superannuated commander Winfield Scott to establish a balloon corps. In September, Lowe used the balloon for artillery spotting, transmitting ranging observations by telegraph. Four new balloons were built by November 10, 1861, and, in January 1862, two more were added, giving the army's still-unofficial balloon corps a total of seven. These craft and the men who tended and flew them were, in effect, the first air arm of the U.S. military.

Having amassed his small fleet of aircraft, Lowe set about staffing his balloon corps. With rivalries among the nation's leading aeronauts running high, Lowe could recruit neither Wise nor La Mountain, the men with the greatest experience, but, instead, chose William Paullin, John R. Dickinson, Ebenezer Seaver (almost immediately dismissed over a salary dispute), John Starkweather, John H. Steiner (who resigned after a year of service), Ebenezer Locke Mason, Jr. (who, like Ebenezer Seaver, was dismissed over pay issues), and the experienced balloonist James Allen, who brought along his brother Ezra. All of the early balloonists were civilian employees of the army, who, in turn, hired civilian assistants, but also used the services of enlisted men attached to the balloon corps either permanently or on an as-required basis. Although the army declined to assign Lowe and his balloon corps official status, Lowe dubbed himself variously "Aeronaut," "Chief Aeronaut," and even "Chief of Aeronautics, Army of the Potomac." The balloon corps itself was shuffled from one military jurisdiction to another, originating at the behest of the Topographic Engineers of the Army, with the Quartermaster furnishing supply (however irregularly); after March 31, 1862, the balloon corps became entirely the province of the Quartermaster until May 25, 1862, when it came under the tactical control of Brigadier General Andrew A. Humphreys, chief topographic engineer on General McClellan's staff. On April 7, 1863, control was transferred to the Army Corps of Engineers under the direction of Captain Cyrus B. Comstock, who immediately informed Lowe that his pay was being cut from 10 dollars a day to six. After making a protest, Lowe resigned—though he volunteered to remain in service until battles in progress had been resolved. On May 7, 1863, he left the corps, and command was briefly given to Brigadier General Gouverneur K. Warren. In June, General Joseph Hooker assigned Chief Signal Officer Colonel Albert J. Myer to take over the "balloon department." Myer, no advocate of aerial observation, protested that he had neither the men nor the appropriation to run the department. In the meantime, General Daniel Butterfield summarily declared, without basis, that balloon operations were of no value, and, in 1863, the balloon corps, never really an official military entity, was disbanded.

The U.S. Army neglected aviation from the disbanding of the balloon corps in 1863 until October 1, 1890, when Congress assigned to the Signal Corps the duty of collecting and transmitting information for the army. In 1891, Chief Signal Officer brigadier general Adolphus V. Greely requested appropriations to create a balloon corps. The following year, a balloon "section" was formally established within the Signal Corps. In 1891, Greely had sent Lieutenant William A. Glassford to Europe to study the latest developments in balloon aeronautics. The lieutenant procured from the French a small balloon, the *General Myer,* equipped with a telephone for air-to-ground communication. At Fort Logan, Colorado, Glassford, promoted to captain, used the *General Myer* in an operational balloon section as part of a Signal Corps telegraph train. When the *General Myer* was destroyed in a severe windstorm in 1897, Glassford directed Sergeant William Ivy—who, in civilian life, had earned a reputation as a stunt balloonist/parachutist under the alias of Ivy Baldwin—to build a new one. Ivy and his wife had completed a balloon, made of silk and with a capacity of 14,000 cubic feet, just the year before, and this Ivy now readied for Signal Corps service. It was destined to be the only balloon used in the Spanish-American War. When the United States declared war on Spain on April 25, 1898, Lieutenant Colonel Joseph E. Maxfield of the Signal Corps was ordered to transport Ivy's balloon to Santiago, Cuba. Maxfield was hurriedly assigned a command of 24 enlisted men and three officers detailed from the Signal Corps and from two infantry units. The balloon train arrived in Santiago on June 22, but disembarkation was delayed until June 28. Logistical problems prevented the balloonists from going ashore with their cumbersome portable hydrogen generator and the even more cumbersome stock of iron filings and sulfuric acid from which the hydrogen was produced. They had to use ready-filled hydrogen cylinders, which meant that the balloon could be inflated only once in the field. The balloon reached headquarters on June 29 and was unpacked. The tropical heat had softened the varnish coating on the fabric envelope, which now stuck together and partially disintegrated, causing a number of large tears that had to be sewn and patched.

Equipped with a patched balloon manned by an inexperienced ground crew, Ivy and Maxfield made their first ascension on June 30. Others followed, which confirmed, among other things, the presence of the Spanish fleet in Manila harbor. Enthusiastically positive reports were made to U.S. expedition commander General William R. Shafter. But even more impressive were the observations made on July 1 during the make-or-break Battle of San Juan Hill. Balloon observers were able to discover a trail that not only relieved congestion, enabling the troops to advance much faster, but also allowed the American and Cuban forces to deploy and coordinate two columns against the Spanish, one along the main road. Observers also proved effective in directing and redirecting artillery fire. Some historians believe that the use of the balloon was a determining factor in this hard-fought victory.

Despite the success of balloon reconnaissance in the Spanish-American War, little was done after the war to develop the balloon corps. In 1900, Congress appropriated $18,500 for a balloon house and administration and instruction buildings at Fort Myer, Virginia. Two years later, a balloon detachment consisting of a dozen enlisted men (later expanded to 22) was organized at Fort Myer under the command of Lieutenant A. T. Clifton. Equipment was modest: a German-built kite balloon, three French-built silk balloons, five small cotton signal balloons, five observer baskets, three nets, an inflation hose, steel tubes, sandbags, a compressor unit, and a hydrogen generator. The balloon detachment did very little ballooning until 1906, when the Signal Corps was able to obtain sufficient compressed hydrogen for regular operations. In August 1906, balloon instruction was expanded from Fort Myer, Virginia, to Fort Leavenworth, Kansas, but much of the training was limited to classroom theory because of chronic equipment shortages. In any case, by this time, balloons were being outmoded by dirigibles, steerable (the word "dirigible" was coined from the Latin *dirigere,* meaning "to direct") balloons, powered by engines.

Count Ferdinand von Zeppelin of Germany designed the first practical dirigibles during 1899–1902. In 1907, Brigadier General James Allen, chief signal officer of the army, met an aerial showman named Thomas Scott Baldwin, who had worked with aviation pioneer Glenn Curtiss, who designed a lightweight four-cylinder engine to propel a new dirigible. General Allen approached Baldwin to supervise the design and construction of an experimental dirigible for the army. On February 24, 1908, he produced U.S. Army Dirigible No. 1 with a 20-horsepower water-cooled gasoline engine developed by Glenn Curtiss. Baldwin trained three officer pilots, Lieutenants FRANK P. LAHM, BENJAMIN D. FOULOIS, and THOMAS E. SELFRIDGE. The first flight was made on September 18, 1908, with Lieutenant Foulois as pilot.

Dirigibles were destined to a short life in the army air service, as they were almost immediately eclipsed by the introduction of heavier-than-air craft, the airplane. The U.S. Navy would, however, go on to develop uses for these "steerable balloons." Nevertheless, both dirigibles and balloons were important in the birth of military aviation and were the seeds from which an American air force would eventually grow.

Barksdale AFB, Louisiana   See AIR FORCE BASES.

Basic Military Training Honor Graduate Ribbon   See DECORATIONS AND MEDALS.

basic training

All USAF basic training—also known as basic military training (BMT)—is conducted at Lackland AFB, Texas. In the USAF, basic training is a six-week course, which consists of academic instruction, physical training (PT), and marksmanship. The object of basic training is to teach enlistees how to adjust to military life, to prepare them for military life, and generally to promote pride in being a member of the USAF. In addition, trainees who have enlisted with an aptitude-area guarantee are given orientation and counseling to help them choose a job specialty that is compatible with both USAF needs and their own skills, education, civilian experience, and desires.

From basic training, graduates proceed to one of the AIR EDUCATION AND TRAINING COMMAND (AETC) technical training centers.

Beale AFB, California   See AIR FORCE BASES.

Berlin Airlift

The alliance between the Western democracies and the Soviet Union forged during WORLD WAR II rapidly disintegrated with the defeat of the common enemy. Occupied Germany was divided into sectors controlled by the United States, France, Britain, and the Soviet Union. As early as the end of March 1948, the Soviets became wary of the strong alliances being formed among the Western allies to coalesce the German sectors they controlled into a separate capitalist state, West Germany. Accordingly, Soviet forces began detaining troop trains bound for West Berlin—the U.S./French/British-controlled sector of the divided German capital, which was deep inside the Soviet-controlled eastern sector of Germany. On June 7, 1948, the Western nations announced their intention to create West Germany. A little more than two weeks after this announcement, on June 24, Soviet forces blockaded West Berlin, protesting that, given its location, the city could never serve as the capital of West Germany.

Declaring that to give up West Berlin would mean relinquishing all of Germany to the Soviets, President Harry S. Truman called on the newly independent USAF to organize a massive emergency AIRLIFT to keep West Berlin supplied. From June 26, 1948, to September 30, 1949, the USAF made 189,963 flights over Soviet-held territory into West Berlin (U.K. forces made 87,606 flights). The USAF flew in a total of 1,783,572.7 tons of food, coal, and other cargo (the British an additional 541,936.9 tons) as well as 25,263 inbound passengers and 37,486 outbound (the British flew in 34,815 and 164,906 out). The result of this unrelenting and extremely hazardous mission was a logistical and political triumph for the West. On May 12, 1949, the Soviets officially lifted the blockade, and East and West Germany were formally created later that very month. The joint Western action in Berlin became the basis of the NATO alliance.

On June 25, 1948, U.S. Army general Lucius D. Clay telephoned Lieutenant General CURTIS EMERSON LEMAY, commander of UNITED STATES AIR FORCES IN EUROPE (USAFE), with a question: "Curt, can you transport coal by air?" LeMay responded: "Sir, the air force can deliver anything." On June 26, LeMay set into motion the marshaling of transport aircraft not only in Europe but from the Alaskan, Caribbean, and Tactical Air Commands, 39 C-54 Skymasters and other passenger and cargo aircraft, together with some 825 aircrews and support personnel. From Hickam AFB, Hawaii, came more C-54s and another 425 personnel. On June 27,

Brigadier General Joseph Smith was appointed to lead the Berlin Airlift Task Force in what was dubbed Operation Vittles. General Smith's tenure as commander lasted approximately one month, during which time he established the extraordinary goal of flying 65 percent of the available aircraft *every* day, a schedule that allowed barely enough time for maintenance and operations personnel to service the aircraft. Second, Smith ordered each plane to make three round trips to Berlin daily. Third, he established a block system, so that aircraft of the same cruising speeds could travel together. Finally, he created an Air Traffic Control Center at Frankfurt to schedule and coordinate the flights.

On July 23, 1948, MILITARY AIR TRANSPORT SERVICE (MATS) took over airlift operations, and Major General William H. Tunner replaced Brigadier General Smith as commander of the operation. Tunner orchestrated the airlift according to what he called a "steady rhythm, constant as the jungle drums." Aiming to move maximum tonnage to Berlin each and every day, Tunner calculated that there were 1,440 minutes in a day and set an ultimate goal of landing an aircraft every minute. Tunner knew this was impossible at the

Transport airplanes taking part in the Berlin Airlift   *(National Archives)*

time, but, on most days, he achieved landings every three minutes.

Tunner insisted on maximum efficiency. He ordered that no crew member was to leave the site of his airplane at Tempelhof and Gatow airports. When a plane touched down, the operations officer would come to the pilot with any necessary information, as did a weather officer. A third jeep rolled up to the plane with hot coffee, hot dogs, and doughnuts. Tunner even hired motion-study experts to analyze loading and unloading. Soon, 12 men could load 10 tons of bagged coal into a C-54 in six minutes flat, while unloading crews reduced 17-minute tasks to five. Similarly, refueling crews learned techniques to cut refueling times from 33 to eight minutes. Ultimately, aircraft turnaround time, which had been an impressive 60 minutes, was cut to a phenomenal 30 minutes.

The machinelike efficiency of the airlift, sustained for nearly a year, forced the Soviet Union to yield, giving the West its first victory of the cold war.

Blesse, Frederick C. ("Boots") (1921–   )
fighter pilot

Blesse flew fighters in the KOREAN WAR and in the VIETNAM WAR, compiling a record of 10 victories, which made him America's sixth-ranking jet ace. For USAF doctrine, he is especially important as the author of an influential essay entitled "No Guts, No Glory," on air superiority jet fighter tactics.

Born in the Panama Canal Zone, Blesse graduated from the U.S. Military Academy at West Point in 1945, too late to fly in WORLD WAR II. In addition to two tours in Korea and 157 sorties flown in the Vietnam War, Blesse won all six trophies in the 1955 Worldwide Gunnery Championship meet, a record yet to be equaled. He retired from the USAF with the rank of major general.

Bolling AFB, Washington, D.C.   See AIR
FORCE BASES.

bombing, strategic

Strategic bombing attacks vulnerable aspects of a whole nation with the objective of disrupting the nation's economy, its ability to produce war materiel, and its ability to feed, clothe, and shelter its citizens. Although strategic bombing is not directed exclusively against civilian targets, such targets do become fair game in achieving the desired objective. The idea, however, is not to "punish" the people of an enemy nation, but to destroy that nation's will and ability to make war.

Military aviation planners in the United States began developing strategic doctrine after WORLD WAR I. The Air Corps Tactical School focused on strategic bombing using large bombers, and the U.S. ARMY AIR FORCES carried out strategic bombing operations against Germany and Japan in WORLD WAR II. In the KOREAN WAR, strategic bombing was not applied, but, in the VIETNAM WAR, it was used in a somewhat abridged form.

The doctrine of strategic bombing has been subject to a great deal of controversy, particularly with regard to its application in World War II. Some studies have suggested that the USAAF's costly campaign of strategic bombing had relatively little effect on Germany's ability (or will) to continue the war, whereas other studies suggest that the campaign was indeed instrumental in the Allied victory. Post–World War II USAAF and USAF opinion was that, when the objective is the unconditional surrender of the enemy, only strategic bombing that makes some use of nuclear weapons can guarantee results. In short, the ultimate objective of strategic bombing must be the total annihilation of the enemy—or, at least, the fully credible threat thereof.

See also BOMBING, TACTICAL.

bombing, tactical

For the air arm, tactical operations are conducted against enemy armed forces, in contrast to strategic operations, which may be conducted against the entire society and social infrastructure of the enemy, civilian as well as military. Typically, tactical air operations are carried out in coordination with friendly surface (land or naval) operations.

Tactical bombing is an aspect of attack aviation. It includes carefully targeted bombing of enemy bases, supply points, convoys, and communication. Interdiction can be carried out against the enemy on the battlefield as well as deep within the enemy's interior. (A sustained campaign of interdiction tends to become a campaign of strategic bombing; see BOMBING, STRATEGIC.) In addition to interdiction, tactical bombing may be carried out in direct support of ground attack. Carpet bombing consists of massive aerial bombardment of enemy troops on the battlefront (see CLOSE AIR SUPPORT).

Following WORLD WAR II, which ended in Japan with a nuclear attack, USAF planners emphasized the development of strategic doctrine and weapons at the expense of tactical doctrine and weapons. Yet the conflicts the USAF was called on to fight after World War II, especially the KOREAN WAR and the VIETNAM WAR, required the extensive use of tactical bombing. The USAF improvised, often with considerable success, as in the "Linebacker" operations of the Vietnam War.

Bong, Richard I. (1920–1945) *World War II ace and test pilot*

Bong, who, having won every possible U.S. ARMY AIR FORCES decoration, was awarded the Medal of Honor in December 1944, was America's ace of aces, with 40 combat victories scored during WORLD WAR II.

Born in Poplar, Wisconsin, he flew P-38s with the 35th Fighter Group and then with the 49th Fighter Group. By November 1943, he had racked up 21 victories. After serving for a time on the operations staff of the FIFTH AIR FORCE, Bong flew

Major Richard Bong—the "ace of aces"—is the highest-scoring U.S. ace of any war.   *(U.S. Air Force)*

in New Guinea, where he achieved another seven victories. After taking a course in aerial gunnery back in the United States, Bong returned to the Pacific and scored a dozen victories in 30 sorties.

After December 1944, Bong returned to the United States and was subsequently assigned as a TEST PILOT for early jets. He was killed in August 1945, testing an F-80 near Burbank, California. In 1986, he was inducted posthumously into the National Aviation Hall of Fame, Dayton, Ohio.

brigadier general   See RANKS AND GRADES.

Brooks AFB, Texas   See AIR FORCE BASES.

C

Cannon AFB, New Mexico   See Air Force bases.

captain   See ranks and grades.

careers

The USAF is a very large organization, which offers opportunities in most of the careers one might find in civilian life and many that are to be found only in the military or in an advanced aerospace organization. Because many USAF activities rely extensively on advanced and complex technology, career opportunities in scientific and technical fields are especially strong.

There are 12 broad USAF occupational groups:

1. Human services;
2. Media and public affairs;
3. Health care;
4. Engineering, science, and technical;
5. Administrative;
6. Service;
7. Vehicle, aircraft, and machinery mechanic;
8. Electronic and electrical equipment repair;
9. Construction;
10. Machine operator and precision work;
11. Transportation and material handling; and
12. Combat specialty

Enlisted Careers

1. **Human Services Occupations**
   Caseworkers and counselors
   Religious program specialists
2. **Media and Public Affairs Occupations**
   Audiovisual and broadcast technicians
   Broadcast journalists and newswriters
   Graphic designers and illustrators
   Interpreters and translators
   Musicians
   Photographic specialists
3. **Health Care Occupations**
   Cardiopulmonary and EEG technicians
   Dental specialists
   Medical laboratory technicians
   Medical record technicians
   Medical service technicians
   Optometric technicians
   Pharmacy technicians
   Physical and occupational therapy specialists
   Radiologic (X-ray) technicians
4. **Engineering, Science, and Technical Occupations**
   Air traffic controllers
   Chemical laboratory technicians
   Communications equipment operators
   Computer programmers
   Emergency management specialists
   Environmental health and safety specialists
   Intelligence specialists

Meteorological specialists
Nondestructive testers
Ordnance specialists
Radar operators
Radio intelligence operators
Space operations specialists
Surveying, mapping, and drafting technicians

5. **Administrative Occupations**
Administrative support specialists
Computer systems specialists
Finance and accounting specialists
Flight operations specialists
Legal specialists and court reporters
Personnel specialists
Postal specialists
Preventive maintenance analysts
Recruiting specialists
Sales and stock specialists
Supply and warehousing specialists
Training specialists and instructors
Transportation specialists

6. **Service Occupations**
Firefighters
Food service specialists
Law enforcement and security specialists
Military police

7. **Vehicle, Aircraft, and Machinery Mechanic Occupations**
Aircraft mechanics
Automotive and heavy equipment mechanic
Divers
Heating and cooling mechanics
Powerhouse mechanics

8. **Electronic and Electrical Equipment Repair Occupations**
Aircraft electricians
Communications equipment repairers
Computer equipment repairers
Electrical products repairers
Electronic instrument repairers
Photographic equipment repairers
Power plant electricians
Precision instrument repairers
Radar equipment repairers
Weapons maintenance technicians

9. **Construction Occupations**
Building electricians
Construction equipment operators
Construction specialists
Plumbers and pipe fitters

10. **Machine Operator and Precision Work Occupations**
Compressed gas technicians
Dental and optical laboratory technicians
Machinists
Power plant operators
Printing specialists
Survival equipment specialists
Water and sewage treatment plant operators
Welders and metal workers

11. **Transportation and Material Handling Occupations**
Air crew members
Aircraft launch and recovery specialists
Cargo specialists
Flight engineers
Petroleum supply specialists
Quartermasters and boat operators
Seamen
Vehicle drivers

12. **Combat Specialty Occupations**
Special operations forces

Officer Careers

1. **Executive, Administrative, and Managerial Occupations**
Communications managers
Emergency management officers
Finance and accounting managers
Food service managers
Health services administrators
International relations officers
Law enforcement and security officers
Management analysts
Personnel managers
Postal directors
Purchasing and contracting managers
Recruiting managers
Store managers

Supply and warehousing managers
Teachers and instructors
Training and education directors
Transportation maintenance managers
Transportation managers

2. **Human Services Occupations**
Chaplains
Social workers

3. **Media and Public Affairs Occupations**
Audiovisual and broadcast directors
Music directors
Public information officers

4. **Health Diagnosing and Treating Practitioner Occupations**
Dentists
Optometrists
Physicians and surgeons
Psychologists

5. **Health Care Occupations**
Dietitians
Pharmacists
Physical and occupational therapists
Physician assistants
Registered nurses
Speech therapists

6. **Engineering, Science, and Technical Occupations**
Aerospace engineers
Air traffic control managers
Chemists
Civil engineers
Computer systems officers
Electrical and electronics engineers
Environmental health and safety officers
Industrial engineers
Intelligence officers
Lawyers
Life scientists
Marine engineers
Meteorologists
Nuclear engineers
Physicists
Space operations officers
Surveying and mapping managers

7. **Transportation Occupations**
Airplane navigators
Airplane pilots
Helicopter pilots

8. **Combat Specialty Occupations**
Missile system officers
Special operations officers

Carswell AFB   See AIR FORCE BASES.

Castle AFB   See AIR FORCE BASES.

chain of command

As in all United States military service branches, the chain of command is a system designed to resolve problems at the lowest possible level. Each link in the chain represents a level of responsibility, extending from the president (as commander in chief) to the secretary of defense, to the SECRETARY OF THE AIR FORCE, to the CHIEF OF STAFF, USAF, then to the relevant commander of a MAJCOM. From here, depending on the command structure of the MAJCOM, the chain descends each supervisory level, ultimately to the noncommissioned officer level of first sergeant. In the chain of command, each level is responsible for the next lower level and accountable to the next higher level.

Chandler, Charles deForest (1878–1939)
U.S. Army pilot

Chandler was the first commander of the USAF's first direct antecedent organization, the AERONAUTICAL DIVISION, U.S. ARMY SIGNAL CORPS, which was created in 1907.

Chandler was a native of Cleveland, Ohio, and was commissioned in the Signal Corps in 1898. In 1907, when he was placed in command of the Aeronautical Division, Chandler was qualified as a balloon pilot. He gained dirigible qualification two years later and, in 1911, became a qualified airplane pilot. A year later he was awarded the rating of Military Aviator.

Chandler was in charge of the Signal Corps aviation schools at College Park, Maryland, and Augusta, Georgia. In 1913, he commanded the 1st Aero Squadron, based at Texas City, Texas, and he established the U.S. Army balloon school at Fort Omaha, Nebraska. In WORLD WAR I, Chandler replaced FRANK P. LAHM as head of the AEF's Balloon Section. He retired with the rank of colonel in 1920.

Chanute AFB, Illinois   See AIR FORCE BASES.

Charleston AFB, South Carolina   See AIR FORCE BASES.

Chennault, Claire L. (1893–1958) *U.S. Army Air Forces general*

Chennault is best remembered as the irascible, resourceful, daring, and always controversial commander of the AMERICAN VOLUNTEER GROUP, the celebrated Flying Tigers, who flew for the Chinese Air Force in WORLD WAR II. He was later promoted to command of the FOURTEENTH AIR FORCE.

Born in Commerce, Texas, Chennault entered the infantry as a first lieutenant in 1917, then transferred to the Signal Corps to become a pilot in 1919. He was assigned as the commander of a pursuit squadron and, from this point on, became a student of fighter strategy and tactics. After graduating from the Air Corps Tactical School in 1931, Chennault served as an instructor there until 1936.

As an advocate of the strategic importance of fighters, Chennault ran afoul of the pre–World War II "bomber mafia," planners who stressed the bomber as the air weapon par excellence. Discouraged, Chennault retired from the army with the rank of captain in 1937.

In 1937, with China embroiled in a desperate war against Japanese invaders, Mme. Jiang Jieshi (Chiang Kai-shek) recruited Chennault to organize

Claire Chennault on the cover of *Life* magazine, October 8, 1942   *(Life)*

and train the American Volunteer Group, the Flying Tigers, which flew already obsolescent P-40s against technologically superior Japanese fighter aircraft. Chennault chose and trained his AVG pilots so skillfully that, despite their handicaps in numbers and quality of aircraft, between December 1941 (when operations began) and July, when the AVG became the 23rd Fighter Squadron of the U.S. ARMY AIR FORCES, the Flying Tigers shot down 299 Japanese aircraft with a loss of 32 planes and 19 pilots. (Some recent scholars believe these figures are variously inflated.)

Chennault returned to U.S. service in April 1942 with the rank of colonel but was soon promoted to brigadier general, and, in July, became commanding general of the USAAF in China. In

March 1943, he was named to command of the 14AF, which supported the China-Burma-India (CBI) theater operations of army general Joseph Stilwell. Even as a U.S. Army commander, however, Chennault remained a maverick, confounding his superiors by dealing directly with China's Jiang Jieshi rather than through the CHAIN OF COMMAND or even with President Roosevelt. Chennault saw the war through, however, and retired in 1945.

After the war, Chennault remained loyal to Jiang, organizing the Chinese National Relief and the Civil Air Transport to assist in the fight against the communists. The USAF acknowledged Chennault's achievements by promoting him to the honorary grade of lieutenant general just nine days before he succumbed to cancer in 1958.

Cheyenne Mountain Air Force Station

Located in southwest Colorado Springs, Colorado, this installation is an underground command center for monitoring the skies and space for hostile incoming weapons. Built in anticipation that it would be a primary target for a nuclear attack, Cheyenne Mountain is perhaps the most heavily fortified large underground installation in the world. It consists of 15 steel buildings, laid out in a 4.5-acre grid *inside* the mountain, and accessed through a tunnel and 30-ton blast doors. The buildings themselves are suspended on 1,300 47-inch steel springs designed to absorb the shock of a nuclear detonation. Thirty days' supplies and 6 million gallons of water are stored inside the installation. About 1,500 people work inside the mountain, which is operated by NORAD and the U.S. Space Command, a unified command headquartered in nearby Peterson AFB.

As thoroughly secured as Cheyenne Mountain is, military planners acknowledge that it could not withstand a direct hit from one of its own nuclear missiles; therefore, a similar facility at Offutt AFB, Nebraska, would be used as a backup in case of a mission failure at Cheyenne Mountain.

chief   See RANKS AND GRADES.

chief master sergeant   See RANKS AND GRADES.

chief master sergeant of the air force   See RANKS AND GRADES.

Chief of Staff, USAF

Created by the NATIONAL SECURITY ACT OF 1947, the position of Chief of Staff, USAF, is the head of the USAF. The Chief of Staff is a general appointed by the president for a four-year term. He or she is a member of the Joint Chiefs of Staff as well as the Armed Forces Policy Council and is an adviser to the president, the National Security Council, the secretary of defense, and to the SECRETARY OF THE AIR FORCE. Ex-officio, the Chief of Staff presides over the AIR STAFF.

Civil Air Patrol (CAP)

CAP performs three main functions: emergency services, aerospace education, and cadet training. CAP was founded on December 1, 1941, and, during WORLD WAR II, its principal purpose was to allow private pilots and aviation enthusiasts to use their light aircraft and flying skills to aid in civil defense efforts. In 1943, the organization came under the control and direction of the U.S. ARMY AIR FORCES and, on July 1, 1946, became a permanent peacetime institution when Public Law 476 established it as a federally chartered, benevolent civilian corporation. Two years later, in May 1948, Public Law 557 made the organization the official auxiliary of the USAF. Known as the CAP Supply Bill, the 1948 law authorized the SECRETARY OF THE AIR FORCE to assign military and civilian personnel to liaison offices at all levels of CAP.

Today, CAP's emergency services include air and ground search and rescue, disaster relief, and civil defense for natural disasters. CAP members fly approximately 85 percent of the search and rescue mission hours directed by the Air Force Rescue and Coordination Center (AFRCC) at Langley AFB. In 1985, CAP agreed to assist the U.S. Customs Service in its counternarcotics efforts by flying air reconnaissance missions along U.S. boundaries, and, in 1989, similar agreements were made with the Drug Enforcement Administration (DEA) and the U.S. Forest Service.

CAP's aerospace education programs provide its members and the educational community information about aviation and space activities through support of some two hundred education workshops for teachers at approximately 100 colleges and universities around the country. CAP conducts the National Congress on Aviation and Space Education, an annual national convention for aerospace teachers.

The CAP Cadet Program is open to U.S. citizens and legal residents of the United States, its territories, and possessions between the ages of 12 and 21. Cadets progress through achievements that include special activities, aerospace education, leadership programs, moral leadership, and physical fitness and may compete for academic and flying scholarships. On completion of initial training, cadets receive the General Billy Mitchell Award, which entitles them to enter the USAF as an airman first class, should they choose to enlist.

CAP is organized into eight geographic regions composed of 52 WINGs, one for each state, Puerto Rico, and the District of Columbia. Wings are subdivided into groups, squadrons, and, sometimes, flights—approximately 1,700 individual units in all. The organization is headquartered at Maxwell AFB and is staffed by military and civilian personnel. CAP membership consists of approximately 26,000 cadets and more than 35,000 adult volunteers. Members operate more than 3,700 privately owned aircraft and 530 CAP-owned aircraft and more than 950 CAP-owned ground vehicles.

Clark AB   See AIR FORCE BASES.

close air support (CAS)

CAS is the use of air power to attack enemy targets (typically personnel, artillery, tanks, and so on) that are close to friendly ground forces. Typically,

the object of CAS is to give friendly ground forces room to maneuver and generally to bolster offensives and counteroffensives. USAF aircraft most frequently used for CAS include the A-10 Thunderbolt II, AC-130H Spectre gunship, and the F-16 Fighting Falcon.

Cochran, Jacqueline (?–1980) *American aviator*

After earning fame as a civilian aviator in the 1930s, Cochran, in 1939, suggested that women be recruited and trained to fly military aircraft. In response, Major General HENRY HARLEY ARNOLD, chief of the U.S. ARMY AIR CORPS, suggested that she recruit women volunteers to serve in Britain's Air Transport Auxiliary, which would give her the experience necessary should the USAAC ever create a women's unit. Cochran recruited 25 American women to serve the ATA and became the chief of these U.S. volunteers.

In October 1942, Arnold instituted training to produce 500 women ferry pilots, principally to fly aircraft from manufacturers to air bases within the continental United States. In June 1943, Cochran was appointed special assistant and director of women pilots for the U.S. ARMY AIR FORCES. This became the WOMEN AIRFORCE SERVICE PILOTS

Jackie Cochran in the cockpit of a Canadair F-86 with Chuck Yeager   *(U.S. Air Force)*

(WASP) on August 5, 1943, but it was deactivated in December 1944.

After the war, Cochran became a lieutenant colonel in the AIR FORCE RESERVE and, in 1953, was the first woman to fly faster than sound. In 1964, she took an F-104 to Mach 2, breaking all speed records for the time. In civilian life, Cochran ran a cosmetics firm and served on the board of directors of Northeast Airlines.

College of Aerospace Doctrine, Research and Education (CADRE)

Headquartered at Maxwell AFB and operating under the aegis of AIR UNIVERSITY (AU), CADRE is charged with assisting in the development of wargaming and the development and analysis of the concepts, doctrine, and strategy of aerospace power, and to educate USAF and joint communities on warfighting at the operational and strategic level through research, wargaming, and military education.

CADRE publishes *Airpower Journal,* the USAF's professional quarterly and primary institutional forum for exchanging ideas about airpower and other matters relating to national defense. CADRE's Public Affairs Center of Excellence conducts public affairs–related research to assist in the development of USAF doctrine. CADRE's wargaming component plans, develops, and conducts war games in support of USAF operational, analytical and educational requirements. The Warfare Studies Institute educates USAF and joint warfighters on issues concerning aerospace warfare, including contingency war planning, joint doctrine air campaign development, information warfare applications, and aerospace power. The CADRE Intelligence Directorate provides intelligence services to the commander and staff organizations of Air University; the commander and staff organizations of the 42nd Air Base Wing, and Air University professional military education (PME) schools and institutes. The Plans and Operations Directorate supports CADRE budget needs and long- and short-range plans, security, and logistics.

colonel See RANKS AND GRADES.

Columbus AFB, Mississippi See AIR FORCE BASES.

Combat Control Team (CCT)

The CCT consists of specially trained personnel airdropped to front lines to provide local air traffic control and to advise on all aspects of landing, airdrop, and extraction zone requirements.

First organized by the USAF as discrete units in 1952, the CCTs evolved into the "Blue Berets" of the VIETNAM WAR. In 1968, there were 485 combat controllers in the USAF, deployed by the Airlift Control Center as needed. Personnel on each were divided into three teams, each headed by an officer and consisting of air traffic controllers and radio maintenance specialists. One team was always on alert status, ready with a jeep, radio, and portable navigational aids to deploy by AIRLIFT within 15 minutes.

The CCTs performed varied missions, such as providing air traffic control at remote airstrips, guiding in airlift craft—the C-130s, C-123s, and C-7s—and accompanying army and marine units to provide control for emergency airdrops of ammo and supplies. Combat controllers were required to maintain proficiency in air traffic control procedures, in packing parachutes, in performing radio maintenance, and in use of weapons (M-16 and CAR-15). Their training included jump school, and courses in control tower, combat control, survival (tropical, arctic, and water), amphibious training, High Altitude, Low Opening (HALO) parachute rigging, and radio maintenance. They also attained proficiency in Ground Proximity Extraction System (GPES) airdrop procedures. The informal motto of the CCTs was "first in, last out."

Combat Readiness Medal See DECORATIONS AND MEDALS.

Comm Squadron

Comm Squadron is an informal term denoting a communications squadron, the unit on a base that is responsible for all communications, including radar, air traffic control, telephone service, and all message centers.

Community College of the Air Force (CCAF)

CCAF is the world's only degree-granting institution of higher learning dedicated exclusively to enlisted people. It offers career-oriented airmen and NCOs the opportunity to earn a job-related, two-year undergraduate degree (Associate in Applied Science) and is open to all active-duty, AIR NATIONAL GUARD, and AIR FORCE RESERVE members.

The college curriculum combines technical and professional military education with off-duty education at civilian institutions. As America's largest community, junior, or technical college, CCAF has awarded more than 125,000 associate in applied science degrees since it first opened in 1972.

Continental Air Command (CONAC)

Activated as a MAJCOM in 1948, CONAC replaced the TACTICAL AIR COMMAND (TAC) and AIR DEFENSE COMMAND (ADC). CONAC also controlled the AIR FORCE RESERVE. Tactical Air Command was reestablished in 1950, during the KOREAN WAR, and Air Defense Command was reactivated as a MAJCOM in 1951. CONAC was relegated to administering the AIR NATIONAL GUARD and the Air Force Reserve. In 1968, CONAC was inactivated.

cruise missile

A small, pilotless jet- or rocket-propelled aircraft with folding wings and fins, a cruise missile may be launched from the ground, from a ship, or dropped from an aircraft. Cruise missiles are typically "smart weapons," guided by highly sophisticated computer programs and navigational systems—incorporating a terrain contour-matching guidance system, an onboard global positioning system (GPS), and an inertial navigation system (INS)—so that they can follow complicated routes to a target. Some cruise missiles are fitted with conventional warheads, some with nuclear devices.

Currently, the USAF cruise inventory includes:

Boeing AGM-86B cruise missile (nuclear warhead) and AGM-86C (conventional warhead) air-launched cruise missile, designed to be dropped by B-52H bombers. The AGM-86B has a range of about 1,500 miles.

McDonnell-Douglas AGM-84D Harpoon, an all-weather, over-the-horizon, antiship missile system. Designed to fly at low altitudes, skimming the sea, the Harpoon uses active radar guidance to reach its target. The missile is designed for launch from B-52H bombers.

D

Davis, Benjamin O., Jr. (1912–2002) U.S.
Air Force general

The son of the first African-American U.S. Army general, Davis became the first African American to graduate from the U.S. Military Academy at West Point in the 20th century and the first African-American general in the U.S. Air Force.

Benjamin O. Davis, Jr., climbs into an advanced trainer at Tuskegee Army Air Base in 1942. *(Library of Congress)*

Davis enrolled in flight training in 1941 at Tuskegee Army Air Field (see TUSKEGEE AIRMEN) as a member of the segregated unit's first class. He went on to become commander of the 99th Pursuit Squadron, a segregated unit he led into combat in North Africa. Despite discrimination practiced against the unit, the 99th excelled, as did Davis's next command, the 332nd Fighter Group.

Using the war record of the Tuskegee Airmen as evidence, Davis, after the war, worked toward the integration of the USAF. President Harry S. Truman's Executive Order 9981, mandating the integration of the armed forces, was issued in 1948, and the following year, HOYT SANFORD VANDENBERG, chief of the USAF, explicitly ordered full integration of the USAF. In the new integrated USAF, Davis was assigned a number of important commands and staff postings, culminating in an appointment as deputy chief of staff for operations of the UNITED STATES AIR FORCES IN EUROPE (USAFE). He held this post until his retirement in 1970. In civilian life, he served as assistant secretary of transportation (environment, safety, and consumer affairs) in the administration of Richard M. Nixon. Davis succumbed to Alzheimer's disease on July 4, 2002.

Davis-Monthan AFB, Arizona   See AIR FORCE BASES.

decorations and medals

Each U.S. military branch has its own medals and decorations, and the U.S. Air Force is no exception. Although USAF personnel are eligible for many awards from the other services, this entry mostly concerns itself with those awards that originated with the U.S. Air Force.

Aerial Achievement Medal

This decoration was established by the SECRETARY OF THE AIR FORCE on February 3, 1988, and is awarded by the DEPARTMENT OF THE AIR FORCE to U.S. military and civilian personnel for sustained meritorious achievement while participating in aerial flight. The achievements must be accomplished with distinction above and beyond that normally expected of professional airmen. Approval authority is delegated to WING commanders for military personnel and to the secretary of the air force for civilians. MAJCOMs identify the missions and positions that qualify for this award.

Air Force Achievement Medal

This award, authorized by the SECRETARY OF THE AIR FORCE on October 20, 1980, is presented to USAF personnel for outstanding achievement or meritorious service rendered specifically on behalf of the USAF. It may also be awarded for acts of courage lesser than those meriting award of the Air Force Commendation Medal.

Air Force
Basic Military Training Instructor Ribbon

The SECRETARY OF THE AIR FORCE established this ribbon on December 7, 1998, to acknowledge military training instructors who display commitment and dedication to the training of USAF personnel. Instructors serving in USAF basic military training and at USAF officer training schools are eligible for the ribbon; however, instructors at technical training schools are ineligible.

Air Force Commendation Medal

Authorized by the SECRETARY OF THE AIR FORCE on March 28, 1958, this medal is awarded to members of any of the armed forces of the United States who, while serving in any capacity with the USAF after March 24, 1958, distinguished themselves by meritorious achievement and service. The degree of merit must be distinctive, though not necessarily unique. Acts of courage that do not involve the voluntary risk of life required for the Airman's Medal may be considered for the AFCM.

Air Force Cross

The decoration was established by Congress, Public Law 88-593, on July 6, 1960, which amended Section 8742 of Title 10, U.S. Code, to change the designation of Distinguished Service Cross to Air Force Cross in cases of awards made under USAF authority. This cross, then, is the USAF version of the Distinguished Service Cross and is awarded for extraordinary heroism, not justifying the award of a Medal of Honor, to any person serving with the USAF while engaged in military operations involving conflict with an opposing foreign force or while serving with friendly foreign forces engaged in conflict against an opposing armed force in which the United States is not a belligerent party.

The first award of the Air Force Cross was a posthumous presentation to Major Rudolf Anderson Jr., for extraordinary heroism in connection with military operations against an armed enemy from October 15, 1962, to October 27, 1962, during the Cuban missile crisis.

Air Force Good Conduct Medal

Authorized by Congress on July 6, 1960, along with other medals for the USAF, the AFGCM was not actually created until June 1, 1963, when the SECRETARY OF THE AIR FORCE established it. It is awarded to USAF enlisted personnel for exemplary conduct during a three-year period of active military service or for a one-year period of service during a time of war. Persons eligible for the award must have had character and efficiency ratings of excellent or higher throughout the qualifying period, including time spent in attendance at service schools, and there must have been no convictions of court-martial during this period.

USAF personnel awarded the Army Good Conduct Medal either before or after June 1, 1963, were permitted to wear both the USAF and army medals.

Air Force Longevity Service Ribbon

DEPARTMENT OF THE AIR FORCE General Order 60, November 25, 1957, authorized this ribbon for award to all USAF members who complete four years of honorable active or reserve military service with any branch of the U.S. armed forces. This ribbon replaces the Federal Service Stripes previously worn on the uniform.

Air Force Organizational Excellence Award

The SECRETARY OF THE AIR FORCE authorized this award on August 26, 1969, to recognize the achievements and accomplishments of USAF organizations and activities. It is awarded to USAF internal organizations that are entities within larger organizations. Such organizations must be unique, unnumbered organizations or activities that perform functions normally conducted by numbered wings, groups, squadrons, and so on.

Air Force Outstanding Unit Award

The Air Force Outstanding Unit Award was authorized by DEPARTMENT OF THE AIR FORCE General Order 1 of January 6, 1954, and is awarded by the SECRETARY OF THE AIR FORCE to numbered units that have distinguished themselves by exceptionally meritorious service or outstanding achievement clearly setting the unit above and apart from similar units. Eligible services include performance of exceptionally meritorious service, accomplishment of a specific outstanding achievement of national or international significance, combat operations against an armed enemy of the United States, or military operations involving conflict with or exposure to hostile actions by an opposing foreign force.

Air Force Overseas Ribbon—Long Tour

The ribbon was authorized by the CHIEF OF STAFF, USAF, on October 12, 1980. Before January 6, 1986, the ribbon was awarded to USAF and AIR FORCE RESERVE members credited with completion of an overseas tour on or after September 1, 1980. USAF and Air Force Reserve members serving as of January 6, 1986, or later are entitled to reflect all USAF overseas tours credited during their career. A service member may wear both the long tour ribbon and the Air Force Overseas Ribbon—Short Tour, if appropriate. The short tour ribbon takes precedence over the long-tour ribbon when both are worn.

Air Force Overseas Ribbon—Short Tour

The ribbon was authorized by the CHIEF OF STAFF, USAF, October 12, 1980. Before January 6, 1986, it was awarded to USAF and AIR FORCE RESERVE members credited with completion of an overseas tour on or after September 1, 1980. USAF and Air Force Reserve members serving as of January 6, 1986, or later are entitled to reflect all USAF overseas tours credited during their careers. A service member may wear both the short tour and the Air Force Overseas Ribbon—Long Tour ribbons, if appropriate. The short tour ribbon takes precedence over the long-tour ribbon.

Air Force Recognition Ribbon

Authorized by the CHIEF OF STAFF, USAF, on October 12, 1980, this ribbon is awarded to individual USAF recipients of special trophies and awards, excluding the Twelve Outstanding Airmen of the Year nominees (see Outstanding Airman Of The Year Ribbon).

Air Force Recruiter Ribbon

On June 21, 2000, the SECRETARY OF THE AIR FORCE established this ribbon to recognize USAF recruiters, both officers and enlisted personnel.

Air Force Training Ribbon

Authorized by the CHIEF OF STAFF, USAF, on October 12, 1980, the ribbon is awarded to USAF service members on completion of initial accession training after August 14, 1974.

Airman's Medal

This decoration, one of a number of USAF awards established by Congress on July 6, 1960, replaces the Soldier's Medal for USAF personnel and is awarded to any member of the armed forces of the United States or of a friendly nation who, while serving in any capacity with the USAF after the date of the award's authorization, shall have distinguished himself or herself by a heroic act, usually at the voluntary risk of his or her life but not involving actual combat.

Air Medal

Established by Executive Order 9158, May 11, 1942, as amended by Executive Order 9242, September 11, 1942, the Air Medal is awarded to military and civilian personnel for single acts of heroism or meritorious achievement while participating in aerial flight. It may be awarded to foreign military personnel in actual combat in support of operations. The magnitude of the achievement is less than that required for the Distinguished Flying Cross, but it must be accomplished with distinction above and beyond that expected of professional airmen.

The Air Medal is not awarded for peacetime sustained operational activities and flights. Approval authority is delegated to MAJCOM for U.S. military personnel and to the SECRETARY OF THE AIR FORCE for civilians and for foreign military personnel. This decoration is the same for all branches of the armed forces, but it is significant to note that the colors of the ribbon—a broad stripe of ultramarine blue in the center flanked on either side by a wide stripe of golden orange, with a narrow stripe of ultramarine blue at the edge—are the original colors of the U.S. ARMY AIR CORPS.

Air Reserves Forces Meritorious Service Medal

Originally established as a ribbon bar by the SECRETARY OF THE AIR FORCE on April 1, 1964, the award was created as a medal by an amendment of May 1, 1973. It is awarded for exemplary behavior, efficiency, and fidelity during a four-year period while serving in an enlisted status in the AIR FORCE RESERVE.

Basic Military Training Honor Graduate Ribbon

Authorized by the CHIEF OF STAFF, USAF, on April 3, 1976, this ribbon is awarded to honor graduates of basic military training (see BASIC TRAINING) who, after July 29, 1976, have demonstrated excellence in all phases of academic and military training. The ribbon is limited to the top 10 percent of the training flight.

Combat Readiness Medal

Authorized by the SECRETARY OF THE AIR FORCE on March 9, 1964, and amended August 28, 1967, the award was originally created as a personal decoration ranking above the commendation medals, lifesaving medals, and the Purple Heart; however, it currently holds the status of an achievement/service medal and is awarded to members of the USAF and AIR FORCE RESERVE (and, after, August 1, 1960, to members of other services) for sustained individual combat or mission readiness or preparedness for direct weapons-system employment. For eligibility, a service member must meet the following criteria: complete an aggregate 24 months of sustained professional performance as a member of USAF combat or mission-ready units subject to combat readiness reporting, or be individually certified as combat or mission ready and have maintained individual readiness the entire period according to a major headquarters, or subject to an individual positional evaluation program according to a higher headquarters standard. "Combat ready" means being professionally and technically qualified in an aircraft crew position in an aircraft that can be used in combat.

Distinguished Flying Cross

This medal is awarded to any officer or enlisted man of the armed forces of the United States who shall have distinguished himself in actual combat in support of operations by "heroism or extraordinary achievement while participating in an aerial flight, subsequent to November 11, 1918." The decoration may also be given for an act performed prior to November 11, 1918, when the individual has been recommended for, but has not received the Medal of Honor, Distinguished Service Cross, Navy Cross, or Distinguished Service Medal.

The first recipient of the Distinguished Flying Cross, authorized by an act of Congress of July 2, 1926 (amended by Executive Order 7786 on January 8, 1938), was Captain Charles A. Lindbergh, U.S. Army Air Corps Reserve, for his solo flight across the Atlantic in 1927. Commander Richard E. Byrd, of the U.S. Navy Air Corps, received the medal on May 9, 1926, for his flight to and from the North Pole. Amelia Earhart received the Distinguished Flying Cross as well—the only instance in which the award was made to a civilian. (An executive order of March 1, 1927, directed that the DFC should not thereafter be conferred on civilians.)

During wartime, members of the armed forces of friendly foreign nations serving with the United States are eligible for the award, which is also given to those who display heroism while working as instructors or students at flying schools.

Medal for Humane Action

This medal was awarded to personnel assigned or attached to and present for duty for at least 120 days during the period of June 26, 1948, to September 30, 1949, inclusive, with any of the units cited in DEPARTMENT OF THE AIR FORCE general orders for participating in the BERLIN AIRLIFT or for direct support of the Berlin Airlift. The Medal for Humane Action may also be awarded to foreign armed forces members and to U.S. and foreign civilians for meritorious participation in the Berlin Airlift. Persons whose lives were lost while participating in the Berlin Airlift, or as a direct result of participating in the Berlin Airlift, may be awarded the Medal for Humane Action without regard to length of service. The medal depicts a C-54 cargo aircraft, the type extensively used in the airlift.

Medal of Honor

Established by Congress on July 6, 1960, as the highest of several awards created specifically for the air force, the Medal of Honor is given in the name of Congress to officers and enlisted members who distinguished themselves by gallantry and intre-

pidity at the risk of their lives, above and beyond the call of duty, in action involving actual combat with an armed enemy of the United States.

The first presentation of the Medal of Honor to a member of the USAF was made by President Lyndon Johnson, on January 19, 1967, to Major Bernard F. Fisher. The Air Force Medal of Honor has been awarded 13 times for actions during the war in Vietnam. Four of these decorations, to Captain Steven L. Bennett, Captain Lance P. Sijan, Captain Hillard A. Wilbanks, and A1C William H. Pitsenbarger, were posthumously awarded. Two were awarded for extraordinary heroism while the recipients were prisoners of war, one to Captain Sijan and the other to Colonel George E. Day, who was the most highly decorated officer in the USAF.

Others who received the medal for their actions in the VIETNAM WAR are Major Merlyn Hans Dethlefsen, Captain James P. Fleming, Lieutenant Colonel Joe M. Jackson, Sergeant John L. Levitow, Lieutenant Colonel Leo K. Thorsness, Captain Gerald O. Young, and Colonel William A. Jones III, who received the medal posthumously.

Four other airmen received the Medal of Honor —before it was created specifically for the USAF— during the KOREAN WAR. Majors George A. Davis Jr., Charles J. Loring Jr., and Louis J. Sebille, and Captain John S. Walmsley Jr., were awarded the medal posthumously. During WORLD WAR II, 35 members of the U.S. ARMY AIR FORCES were presented the nation's top honor for their actions during air missions.

Outstanding Airman of the Year Ribbon

This ribbon is awarded to airmen nominated for competition in the Twelve Outstanding Airmen of the Year Program.

Small Arms Expert Marksmanship Ribbon

This ribbon, authorized by the SECRETARY OF THE AIR FORCE on August 28, 1962, is awarded to USAF members who, after January 1, 1963, qualify as expert in small-arms marksmanship with either the M-16 rifle or issue handgun.

USAF NCO PME Graduate Ribbon

This award, authorized by the SECRETARY OF THE AIR FORCE, August 28, 1962, is presented to graduates of the following certified NCO PME schools: NCO Preparatory Course, Airman Leadership School, NCO Leadership School, NCO Academy, and SRNCO Academy. Graduation from each successive level of PME entitles the member to an oak leaf cluster.

Department of the Air Force

Established by the NATIONAL SECURITY ACT OF 1947, the department provides civilian administrative control over the USAF and reports to the Office of the Secretary of Defense. As originally conceived, the service departments—Department of the Army, Department of the Navy, and Department of the Air Force—wielded a great deal of power relative to the Department of Defense. In 1958, however, the Reorganization Act reduced the authority of the department secretaries and terminated the CHAIN OF COMMAND with the secretary of defense.

Direct Reporting Unit (DRU)   See ORGANIZATION, USAF.

Distinguished Flying Cross   See DECORATIONS AND MEDALS.

division   See ORGANIZATION, USAF.

Doolittle, James Harold ("Jimmy") (1896– 1993) *Army Air Forces general, engineer, test pilot*

A U.S. ARMY AIR FORCES officer, Doolittle is best known for his daring and unprecedented aircraft carrier–launched B-25 raid on Tokyo early in WORLD WAR II.

He was born in Alameda, California, and educated at Los Angeles Junior College, then at UCLA.

James H. "Jimmy" Doolittle   *(U.S. Air Force)*

He joined the Army Reserve Corps in October 1917, after the United States entered WORLD WAR I, and was assigned to the Signal Corps, in which he served as a flight instructor through 1919. In 1920, Doolittle was commissioned a first lieutenant in the U.S. ARMY AIR SERVICE and quickly gained national attention by making the first transcontinental flight—in less than 14 hours—on September 4, 1922. The U.S. ARMY AIR CORPS then sent Doolittle to the Massachusetts Institute of Technology for advanced study in aeronautical science. In 1925, Doolittle earned a doctor of science (Sc.D.) degree, then was assigned to a series of military aviation testing stations. He also became an avid air-race competitor and an aerial demonstration pilot during 1925–30. The object of racing and demonstration was to promote military aviation. Perhaps his single most significant achievement during this period came on September 1929, when he demonstrated the potential of instrument flying by making the first-ever blind instrument landing.

In February 1930, Doolittle resigned his commission to become aviation manager for Shell Oil, where he worked on the development of new high-efficiency aviation fuels. He also continued to race, claiming victories in a number of prestigious competitions, including those for the Harmon (1930) and Bendix (1931) trophies. In 1932, he set a world speed record.

As war loomed, Doolittle returned to active duty in July 1940 as a major in the USAAC. In the weeks and months following the Japanese attack on Pearl Harbor (December 7, 1941), U.S. and Allied forces fought a desperate and dispiriting defensive war in the Pacific theater. In an effort to raise American morale—and to force the Japanese to divert a portion of their air forces to defense—Doolittle planned and commanded an extraordinarily hazardous bombing raid against Tokyo, leading 16 B-25 Mitchell bombers from the aircraft carrier *Hornet* on April 18, 1942. The twin-engine medium bombers were not designed to take off from an aircraft carrier, but Doolittle and the other pilots managed to do just that. They also realized that fuel limitations meant that no round trip was possible, and, in any case, the bombers could not land on an aircraft carrier. They planned to carry out the raid, then land in China, hope to evade capture, and find their way back to Allied lines. Although the damage inflicted on Tokyo and industrial targets was slight, the Doolittle raid was a tremendous morale boost, which, as planned, also served to tie down a portion of the Japanese air force for home defense. Perhaps most remarkable of all was the fact that Doolittle and most of his raiders survived the action and returned to U.S. military control.

After the raid Doolittle was promoted to brigadier general (he was later awarded the Medal of Honor) and was sent to England to organize the TWELFTH AIR FORCE in September 1942. With the temporary rank of major general, he commanded 12AF in Operation Torch, the Allied invasion of French North Africa. From March 1943 to January 1944, he commanded strategic air operations in the Mediterranean theater and was promoted to the temporary rank of lieutenant general in March 1944. During January 1944 to May 1945, he commanded the British-based EIGHTH AIR FORCE's bombing operations against Germany.

After V-E Day, Doolittle returned to the Pacific, where his 8AF provided support in the battle for Okinawa (April–July 1945) and carried out some of the massive bombardment of the Japanese home islands. With the conclusion of the war in the Pacific, Doolittle left active duty (remaining in the reserves) in May 1946 and took a senior executive position with Shell Oil. He was, however, frequently asked by the government to serve on scientific, technological, and aeronautical commissions during 1948–57. After retiring from Shell and the AIR FORCE RESERVE in 1959, he continued to work as a consultant in the areas of technology and aeronautics as well as in the field of national security.

Dover AFB, Delaware   See AIR FORCE BASES.

driver
USAF slang for pilot.
    See also JOCK.

Dyess AFB, Texas   See AIR FORCE BASES.

E

Eastern Air Defense Force

A named air force created in 1949 under Continental Air Command (CONAC), the Eastern Air Defense Force had as its purpose the air defense of the United States. Reassigned to the AIR DEFENSE COMMAND (ADC) in 1951, it was inactivated in 1960 when Air Defense Command was reorganized to eliminate the air force level of organization.

Edwards AFB, California   See AIR FORCE BASES.

Eglin AFB, Florida   See AIR FORCE BASES.

Eielson AFB, Alaska   See AIR FORCE BASES.

Eighteenth Air Force (18AF)

A numbered air force established in 1951, the 18AF was originally designated Eighteenth Air Force (Troop Carrier) and was under the TACTICAL AIR COMMAND (TAC). It was the 18AF that transported French paratroops to Vietnam for the momentous Battle of Dien Bien Phu. The 18AF was originally based at Donaldson AFB, South Carolina, then moved to Waco, Texas, in 1957. It was inactivated the following year.

Eighth Air Force (8AF)

The most celebrated numbered air force in the USAF, 8AF was the nucleus of U.S. ARMY AIR FORCES strategic bombing (see BOMBING, STRATEGIC) missions against Germany during WORLD WAR II.

The antecedent organization of 8AF was the VIII Bomber Command, created in January 1942. It moved from the United States to England in the spring and began combat operations in August. It was not until February 1944 that the VIII Bomber Command was redesignated 8AF. The unit flew B-17 and B-24 heavy bombers and had a Fighter Command made up of 15 fighter groups flying F-47s, F-51s, and P-38s. Whereas the strategic bombing role of 8AF fell short of demonstrating that strategic bombing alone could win a war, the Fighter Command achieved air superiority by effectively destroying the German Luftwaffe, downing 9,275 German aircraft.

Half of USAAF casualties during World War II were incurred by 8AF—more than 47,000 casualties, including more than 26,000 killed. Seventeen Medals of Honor were awarded to 8AF personnel during the war, along with 220 Distinguished Service Crosses, 850 Silver Stars, 7,000 Purple Hearts, 46,000 Distinguished Flying Crosses, and 442,000 Air Medals. The 8AF had 261 fighter aces. After the German surrender, 8AF moved to Okinawa in 1945 and, after the war, in 1946, was headquartered at MacDill Field, Florida, where it served as a STRATE-

GIC AIR COMMAND (SAC) unit. Later in the year, 8AF headquarters was moved to Carswell AFB, Texas, and in 1955 to Westover AFB, Massachusetts. In 1970, 8AF was moved to Andersen AFB, Guam, and conducted B-52 and KC-135 operations during the VIETNAM WAR. In 1975, 8AF moved to Barksdale AFB, Louisiana, and absorbed the functions of the SECOND AIR FORCE. During the PERSIAN GULF WAR, 8AF spearheaded the air war campaign with B-52 strikes directly from Barksdale. Current 8AF units include 2nd Bomb Wing, 5th Bomb Wing, 7th Bomb Wing, 28th Bomb Wing, 509th Bomb Wing, 27th Fighter Wing, 67th Information Operations Wing, 70th Intelligence Wing, 65th Air Base Wing, 85th Group, and 3rd Air Support Operations Group.

See also EIGHTH AIR FORCE HISTORICAL SOCIETY.

Eighth Air Force Historical Society

The EIGHTH AIR FORCE, the most celebrated U.S. ARMY AIR FORCES organization of WORLD WAR II, also holds the record for numbers of Americans who served in a single military organization: more than 1 million. Veterans of the organization formed the Eighth Air Force Historical Society on May 15, 1975, to collect, preserve, and publish the history of this distinguished unit. The society publishes *8th AF News* and has some 15,000 members.

A USAF E-3B Sentry aircraft is readied for flight. *(U.S. Air Force)*

electronic warfare (EW)

The origin of electronic warfare (EW) may be traced as far back as WORLD WAR I, when radio was first used on the battlefield and signals were intercepted. By the time of WORLD WAR II, EW came to include radar technology as well as the use of chaff (metal foil strips released from aircraft) to confound enemy radar returns, LORAN navigation systems, and radio proximity fuses (which use radar to trigger bomb detonation). By the end of the VIETNAM WAR era, EW had assumed such importance that an entire class of USAF aircraft was designated "E" for electronic warfare. These aircraft are equipped with cutting-edge radar and

other detection and imaging equipment as well as computers, to enable the tracking of enemy air and ground resources, to coordinate friendly resources, to direct ground, air, and naval attack, and to jam enemy radio communication and radar operation. The role of EW in USAF operations will almost certainly continue to expand in the future.

element   See ORGANIZATION, USAF.

Eleventh Air Force (11AF)

Originally, this numbered air force was a named air force, the Alaskan Air Force, which was activated in January 1942. Within a month, it was redesignated the 11AF.

During WORLD WAR II, 11AF conducted U.S. ARMY AIR FORCES operations in the Aleutian Islands. In 1945, it was again redesignated as the ALASKAN AIR COMMAND, and a new organization was designated 11AF in June 1946. The new unit was assigned primarily to train AIR FORCE RESERVE personnel. Inactivated in 1948, the 11AF was reactivated in 1990 when it replaced the Alaskan Air Command.

Currently, the 11AF is headquartered at Elmendorf AFB, Alaska, and consists of the 3rd Wing, 354th Fighter Wing, 611th Air Operations Group, and 611th Air Support Group.

Ellsworth AFB, South Dakota   See AIR FORCE BASES.

Elmendorf AFB, Alaska   See AIR FORCE BASES.

England AFB, Louisiana   See AIR FORCE BASES.

Executive Order 9877

Issued by President Harry S. Truman on July 26, 1947, this order unified the U.S. Army and U.S. Navy and established a United States Air Force independent of the U.S. Army. The executive order stated the roles and missions of each service, including the USAF, whereas the NATIONAL SECURITY ACT OF 1947, which went into effect on the same day, stated the principles of the unification of the services and the creation of the USAF.

With regard to the USAF mission, Executive Order 9877 specifically addressed provisions for air superiority, strategic operations, tactical operations, airlift operations, air defense, and assistance to the army and navy.

F

Fairchild AFB, Washington   See AIR FORCE BASES.

Far East Air Forces (FEAF)   See PACIFIC AIR FORCES.

field operating agency (FOA)   See ORGANIZATION, USAF.

Fifteenth Air Force (15AF)

15AF, a numbered air force, was established in November 1943 in Tunisia, assigned to the Mediterranean theater of operations in WORLD WAR II. In December, it moved to Bari, Italy, and served primarily as a strategic bombing organization, hitting targets in Italy, southern France, and the oil refineries at Ploesti, Romania. Major General JAMES HAROLD DOOLITTLE commanded 15AF from 1943 to 1944.

15AF was inactivated in Italy in September 1945, then reactivated in the United States the following year. Assigned to the STRATEGIC AIR COMMAND (SAC) at that time, 15AF was reassigned to AIR MOBILITY COMMAND (AMC) in 1992 and, in 1993, was moved from March AFB to Travis AFB, California. Fifteenth Air Force flew bombers in the KOREAN WAR, then, during the 1960s, added tankers to its complement of aircraft. Between the VIETNAM

WAR and 1991, 15AF commanded reconnaissance aircraft and intercontinental ballistic missiles in addition to tankers, but, on September 1, 1991, it became exclusively a tanker command. When 15AF moved to Travis AFB, it merged its tankers with the AIRLIFT aircraft of the TWENTY-SECOND AIR FORCE, which left Travis for the AIR FORCE RESERVE at Dobbins AFRB, Georgia. Fifteenth Air Force includes 22nd Air Refueling Wing, 60th Air Mobility Wing, 62nd Airlift Wing, 92nd Air Refueling Wing, 317th Airlift Group, 319th Air Refueling Wing, 375th Airlift Wing, 615th Air Mobility Operations Group, 715th Air Mobility Operations Group, and the 302nd Airlift Wing, gained from 22AF.

Fifth Air Force (5AF)

Activated in September 1941 as the Philippine Department Air Force and redesignated the Far East Air Force in October of that year, the unit became 5AF in February 1942. Most of the Far East Air Force's aircraft were destroyed on the ground when the Japanese attacked the Philippines in December 1941. The survivors—personnel and aircraft—retreated to Australia and, in January 1942, the Far East Air Force was sent to Java for combat. In September 1942, 5AF was reorganized to command all U.S. ARMY AIR FORCES units in Australia and New Guinea. Under the command of Major General George Kenney, 5AF used fighters (especially P-38s) to win air superiority in the South

Pacific and also carried out tactical AIRLIFT missions in support of ground offensives in New Guinea. The 5AF was also instrumental in attacks on Japanese naval forces attempting to transport reinforcements to the islands. In August 1944, 5AF played a key role in operations to retake the Philippines. As soon as air fields were available on Okinawa, 5AF moved operations there in order to concentrate on Japanese shipping, the China coast, and Kyushu.

After the surrender of Japan, 5AF took part in the occupation, then moved headquarters to South Korea with the outbreak of war there. The 5AF handled tactical operations during the KOREAN WAR, having flown by the time of the armistice in 1953 more than 625,000 missions, in which 953 North Korean and Chinese aircraft were downed and enough CLOSE AIR SUPPORT had been provided to account for 47 percent of all enemy troop casualties. In Korea, 38 fighter pilots were identified as aces, including Lieutenant Colonel JAMES JABARA, the first U.S. jet ace, and Captain Joseph McConnell, the leading Korean War ace, with 16 confirmed victories.

After the Korean War, 5AF returned to Japan and, during the VIETNAM WAR, operated from there. Since 1990, 5AF has been headquartered at Yakota AB, Japan. It currently includes 18th Wing, 35th Fighter Wing, 374th Airlift Wing, 605th Air Operations Group, 605th Air Operations Squadron, 605th Air Intelligence Squadron, 605th Air Support Squadron, 605th Air Communications Flight, and 20th Operational Weather Squadron.

films, USAF portrayed in

Life in and the exploits of the United States military have long been favorite subjects for the movies, and the USAF and its predecessor organizations have been especially popular because of the glamour, excitement, and danger of combat flight.

The most notable post–WORLD WAR I film was the 1927 *Wings,* directed by William Wellman. The central story, which concerns two American lads who are in love with the same girl and who become World War I pilots, is paper thin, but the aerial combat footage, featuring dogfights, is remarkable for 1927 or, indeed, any era. The movie won the first Academy Award for best picture, and it increased recruitment of U.S. ARMY AIR SERVICE pilots.

WORLD WAR II saw the production of many service-related movies. The best-known films focusing on the U.S. ARMY AIR FORCES include *I Wanted Wings* and *Keep 'Em Flying,* both from 1941, and both focusing on pilot training. Films emphasizing battle action came a bit later in the war. *Flying Tigers* (1942) was a very popular portrayal of the exploits of the AMERICAN VOLUNTEER GROUP in China, and *Thirty Seconds over Tokyo* (1944) told a romanticized version of the daring Doolittle raid against Tokyo (April 18, 1942). Most important from this era was *Air Force,* released in 1943 and directed by the great Howard Hawks. The film is set in the Pacific theater and tells the story of a single B-17 crew. It won a best-picture Academy Award. Perhaps the most effective movie about the USAAF in World War II produced after the war was *Twelve O'Clock High* (1950), which vividly portrays the psychological toll strategic bombing (see BOMBING, STRATEGIC) took on American air crews and their commanders.

The KOREAN WAR occasioned *Sabre Jet* (1953), and the cold war era brought *Strategic Air Command* (1955), which emphasized the sacrifice and the skill of AIR FORCE RESERVE personnel reactivated to meet the needs of the nuclear air arm. The 1960s, heavily influenced by anti-Vietnam War sentiments, produced a spate of films not so much specifically critical of the USAF as of a general "war mentality." *Fail-Safe* (1964) chillingly dramatized the genesis of a thermonuclear accident and the high price of averting World War III. Stanley Kubrick's *Dr. Strangelove, or How I Learned to Stop Worrying and Love the Bomb* (also 1964) exploited the same theme from the perspective of the blackest possible comedy.

Films after the end of the VIETNAM WAR have tended to return to a more celebratory view of the U.S. air arm, although often with a nostalgic historical perspective. The 1990 *Memphis Belle,* for

A movie poster for *Thirty Seconds over Tokyo,* 1944   *(Library of Congress)*

example, evoked the look and feel of the 1940s to tell the story of the first British-based EIGHTH AIR FORCE B-17 crew to complete the 25 missions that entitled the crew members to rotate back to the United States.

First Air Force (1AF)

A numbered air force, 1AF was activated as the Northeast Air District in 1940 before it was redesignated in 1941. Headquarters during WORLD WAR II was Mitchel Field, New York, and the unit functioned as a training organization and, until 1943, also provided air defense for the East Coast. It was moved to Fort Slocum, New York, in 1946 as part of the Air Defense Command, then, in 1948, it was transferred to the CONTINENTAL AIR COMMAND and, in 1949, returned to Mitchel. Inactivated in 1958, it was reactivated in 1966, reassigned to Air Defense Command, and moved to Stewart AFB, New York. At this time, 1AF was responsible for the air defense of the northeastern United States, Greenland, Iceland, and parts of Canada. Inactivated in 1969, 1AF was reactivated in 1986 at Langley AFB, Virginia, and assigned to the TACTICAL AIR COMMAND (TAC). It was now composed of units of the active USAF as well as the AIR NATIONAL GUARD (ANG).

In 1992, 1AF, now headquartered at Tyndall AFB, Florida, became an AIR COMBAT COMMAND

(ACC) organization, and it was the first numbered air force to be made up primarily of ANG personnel. The current mission of 1AF is to plan, conduct, control, coordinate, and ensure the air sovereignty and defense of the United States. The unit primarily operates F-15 and F-16 fighters and consists of the 102nd, 119th, 120th, 125th, 142nd, 144th, 147th, 148th, and 158th Fighter Wings.

first lieutenant   See RANKS AND GRADES.

first sergeant   See RANKS AND GRADES.

flexible response

Flexible response was a cold war doctrine intended to provide the U.S. military, especially the USAF, with credible means to match nonnuclear escalation. The word "flexible" implied the availability of multiple options to use in responding to a crisis. In the volatile climate of the cold war, this was deemed preferable to formulating a handful of hard-and-fast war scenarios.

In practice, flexible response called for the continued European presence of large U.S. conventional forces. These forces would serve as a deterrent to Soviet aggression and would also fight limited wars.

Although flexible response was formulated as an alternative to nuclear war, Secretary of Defense Robert McNamara (in the administration of John F. Kennedy) did not believe that new conventional weapons were needed, and thus the USAF continued to direct most of its resources to developing strategic (nuclear and thermonuclear) weapons. The tactical requirements of the VIETNAM WAR vividly exposed the inadequacies of this development policy, although USAF personnel brilliantly improvised such tactical weapons as AC-47 and AC-130 gunships and the use of B-52s for tactical carpet bombing.

flight (organizational unit)   See ORGANIZATION, USAF.

flight surgeon

A medical officer (M.D.) with special training in aviation medicine, the flight surgeon serves with an aviation unit.

Flying Training Air Force (FLY TAF)

FLY TAF was a named air force established in 1951 and assigned to the Air Training Command (ATC). It trained pilots, navigators, and radar observers. FLY TAF was deactivated in 1958.

folklore

As with many other occupations, the profession of military aviation has developed its own body of occupational folklore involving indoctrination rituals and procedures, rituals and routines to enforce conformity, narrative folklore to share experiences, narrative and other kinds of folklore to reduce anxiety, folklore to cope with authority, and special jargon or folk speech. The folklore of this latter category may be the most important, since a command of the group's folk speech is essential to admission to full membership within the group. Some of the folk speech heard within the USAF is familiar almost exclusively to insiders. A "shit screen," for example, is a fall guy, the person who takes the blame for some foul-up or infraction. "Above my pay grade" is a phrase used to pass responsibility to some higher power: "That decision, George, was made above my pay grade. Sorry." "Brown shoe" is used to describe someone who has been in the service for many years or who takes a rigid position on how standards will be maintained and things done—by the book. (Dress shoes in the old USAAF were brown.) "Check-six" is used by fighter pilots to mean check your tail—the six o'clock position (12 is straight ahead); by figurative extension, the phrase means watch your back and be sure your facts are straight. "Delta Sierra" is the phonetic alphabet version of the initials "DS" and signifies "deep shit"—that is, big trouble. A "fast burner" is a person who is a go-getter, highly capable, and highly respected. A "boot" is a recruit in basic training. A first shirt/first skirt is a male or female first sergeant.

Other elements of military vocabulary have become part of the folk speech of the general population. For example, official military jargon is replete with acronyms. During WORLD WAR II, airmen and other soldiers invented some of their own, the most popular of which was *snafu*—Situation Normal, All Fucked Up. The word, without its obscene connotation and, indeed, without a sense of its even being an acronym, is now in general speech. (Variants on *snafu* never entered general speech and have vanished from military folk speech as well. These include: FUBAR, Fucked Up Beyond All Recognition; TARFU, Things Are Really Fucked Up; and so on.) Almost as popular as *snafu* was *SOS*, which had been adopted in 1908 as the international radiotelegraph Morse Code signal for distress and, some time during World War II, was adopted in the enlisted men's mess as a signal of specifically gustatory distress. A staple of World War II military cuisine was creamed chipped beef on toast, unofficially and universally dubbed Shit On a Shingle: SOS. The utility of this acronym rapidly increased as the expression came to signify any old lies, chores, or routines the U.S. ARMY AIR FORCES dished up day after day: Same Old Shit. In this latter sense, it, too, has entered general folk speech, as have such expressions as *grunt,* which, in the USAF, means an ordinary enlisted person, but, in the general population, means any working stiff; *scut work,* which originated in military folk speech as a label for any disagreeable task (such as cleaning latrines) and is now found outside the military as well; and *down the tubes,* meaning total failure.

Other items of military folk speech have been borrowed *from* general folk speech. In the air arm, for example, *bogey* has long been a term for an unidentified air contact that is assumed to be hostile. The word seems to have come into general use during the early years of jet and electronic air combat—that is, during the KOREAN WAR—and is usually used to describe radar-screen blips interpreted as hostile aircraft, though bogies can also be sighted visually, usually on one's tail (or *six*). The word recalls the bogey or bogey man of fairy tale and nightmare.

Military folk speech also borrows words from general standard English. WORLD WAR I produced the term *dogfight* to describe aerial combat between two or more fighter planes. During the PERSIAN GULF WAR, USAF pilots often used the term *fur ball* to describe the same situation. This latter term aptly evokes the visceral effects of high-speed jet combat, an amalgam of pumping adrenaline, blackout-inducing G-forces, an urge to kill, and ever-churning fear. It is almost certainly descended from pilot slang dating back to the USAAF of World War II, when a close call or frightening situation was referred to as "hairy."

Soldiers in combat are, of course, under great stress, and such emotionally intense circumstances often produce folklore intended to bring luck or explain things that are essentially irrational and terrifying. Thus much military folklore resembles tall tales or miracle narratives and includes stories of near misses, brushes with death, miraculous escapes, and even ghost stories (in the form of the returning spirits of fallen comrades). Widely discussed among military aircrews during World War II were *gremlins,* which were imagined as imps or demons that cause problems with aircraft. To the action of gremlins were attributed mechanical failures and other difficulties that could not be otherwise explained. This was done tongue in cheek, to be sure, yet with an unmistakable edge of earnestness, too. By the middle years of the war, USAAF aircrews even provided descriptions of gremlins, which were depicted as about 20 inches tall and looking like a Jack Rabbit crossed with a bull terrier. Some descriptions clothed the gremlins: "green breeches and red jackets, ornamented with neat ruffles," as well as spats and top hats. Other descriptions depict them more frankly as demons: six inches tall with horns and black leather suction boots. Gremlins were not imagined as primitive beings, but as technically sophisticated saboteurs, who also possessed superhuman strength.

Another subject of aircrew folklore were *foo fighters.* These were strange balls of light and disk-shaped objects that World War II Allied bomber crews reported seeing as they flew missions over

Germany and Japan. The term *foo-fighter* was apparently a pun on the French word *feu* (fire), which appeared in "Smokey Stover," a popular comic strip of the period ("Where there's foo, there's fire," was a frequent Smokey tag line). Foo fighters appeared to dance off the bombers' wingtips, or they kept pace with the aircraft in front and in back. Many explanations for the foo fighters were offered, ranging from static electricity discharges to Japanese and German secret weapons. After a cursory investigation, the EIGHTH AIR FORCE officially (if unconvincingly) dismissed them as "mass hallucination."

Superstitions are common in high-risk, high-anxiety occupations such as combat flying. Many pilots and other aircrew members wore and wear "lucky" scarves, hats, gloves, and items of jewelry. Fighter pilots still typically insist on "mounting" their aircraft as one mounts a horse, always from the left side. "Short timers"—combat aircrew members whose tour of duty is approaching its close—make it a point never to speak of the number of missions remaining, lest misfortune follow.

Foulois, Benjamin D. (1879–1967) *U.S. Army Air Corps general*

The third chief of the U.S. ARMY AIR CORPS, serving from 1931 to 1935, Foulois was an activist on behalf of the creation of an independent air arm.

He was born in Washington, Connecticut, and enlisted in the U.S. Army Engineers in 1898. After serving in the Philippines during the Spanish-American War and afterward, Foulois was commissioned an officer. He left the engineers for the Signal Corps in 1908 and piloted the first dirigible (see BALLOONS AND DIRIGIBLES) purchased by the U.S. government. He taught himself to fly airplanes and, in 1910, was assigned to fly the U.S. Army's first airplane and became the service's first (and, for a time, only) pilot, instructor, and observer. In 1911, he designed the first radio transceiver ever used on an airplane and, with it, became a pioneer in aerial reconnaissance. He was also instrumental in developing early tactical doctrine.

As commander of the 1st Aero Squadron, Foulois served in the PUNITIVE EXPEDITION against Pancho Villa in 1916. The following year he was assigned to Washington as chairman of the Joint Army-Navy Technical Aircraft Committee. With

Benjamin D. Foulois   *(U.S. Air Force)*

America's entry into WORLD WAR I, he was jumped rapidly in rank. A captain in May 1917, he was a brigadier general in July. He was shipped off to France, where he served as chief of the USAAS for the American Expeditionary Force (AEF). Like many officers rapidly promoted during the war, he reverted in rank—to major—after the armistice. Foulois regained his rank as brigadier general in 1927, when he was assigned as assistant to the chief of the USAAC. He became chief in 1931.

In an effort to achieve some degree of independence from the army and establish an air operations identity apart from the navy, Foulois established the GENERAL HEADQUARTERS AIR FORCE. Always pushing to demonstrate the value of air power, he persuaded President Franklin D. Roosevelt to assign to the USAAC the dangerous job of flying the air mail routes. This proved disastrous, and, under congressional pressure over the air mail fiasco and disputes over procurement procedures, Foulois retired from the military in 1935.

Fourteenth Air Force (14AF)

Fourteenth Air Force, which, with the TWENTIETH AIR FORCE, is currently one of two numbered air forces in the AIR FORCE SPACE COMMAND (AFSPC), provides space warfighting forces to U.S. Space Command and is located at Vandenberg AFB, California. The mission of 14AF is to manage space forces to support U.S. Space Command and North American Aerospace Defense Command (NORAD) operational plans and missions.

The organization was first activated in 1943 at Kumming, China, and consisted of the former AMERICAN VOLUNTEER GROUP, the famed "Flying Tigers," plus reinforcing units. The 14AF was a small defensive air force, which (like many Allied military units in the CBI, the China-Burma-India theater) was given low priority and operated mainly to jab at Shanghai and Japanese shipping off the China coast. From 1943 to 1945, 14AF was commanded by CLAIRE L. CHENNAULT, the colorful and irascible commander who had created the American Volunteer Group.

In December 1945, 14AF returned to the United States and was inactivated from January to May 1946. It was assigned to AIR DEFENSE COMMAND (ADC) and then, in 1948, to CONTINENTAL AIR COMMAND (CAC), based at Orlando AFB, Florida. From 1946 to 1960, 14AF supervised AIR FORCE RESERVE and AIR NATIONAL GUARD activities. Inactivated in 1960, it was reactivated in 1966 at Gunter AFB, Alabama, once again as part of the Air Defense Command. When it moved to Colorado Springs in 1968 it was redesignated the Fourteenth Aerospace Force. Moved to Dobbins AFB, Georgia, in 1976, it was returned to its 14AF designation and made a USAFR unit. Fourteenth Air Force finally moved to Vandenberg AFB as part of the AFSPC.

Fourth Air Force (Reserve)

Activated as the Southwest Air District at March Field, California, in 1940, the unit was redesignated Fourth Air Force (4AF), a numbered air force, in 1941 and moved to Hamilton Field, California. The mission of 4AF was to provide air defense for the western continental United States and, until 1943, to train new units. After 1943, the training focus of 4AF rested on replacements for combat units.

After WORLD WAR II, 4AF was assigned in 1946 to AIR DEFENSE COMMAND (ADC) and, in 1948, to CONTINENTAL AIR COMMAND (CAC). It was inactivated in 1960, then reactivated in 1966, again under ADC. Three years later, it was again inactivated, then reactivated in 1976 at McClellan AFB, California, at which time it became an AIR FORCE RESERVE unit. Now located at March AFB, California, 4AF is assigned to AIR MOBILITY COMMAND (AMC) when called to active duty. Units within 4AF include 349th Air Mobility Wing, 433rd Airlift Wing, 434th Air Refueling Wing, 445th Airlift Wing, 446th Airlift Wing, 452nd Air Mobility Wing, 507th Air Refueling Wing, 916th Air Refueling Wing, 927th Air Refueling Wing, 932nd Airlift Wing, and 940th Air Refueling Wing.

Francis E. Warren AFB, Wyoming   See AIR FORCE BASES.

G

general   See RANKS AND GRADES.

General Headquarters Air Force (GHQ Air Force)

Established on March 1, 1935, GHQ Air Force was intended as a means of creating for the U.S. ARMY AIR CORPS a separate mission for reconnaissance and bombardment directly under the U.S. Army chief of staff. In effect, GHQ Air Force was a first step toward creation of an independent air arm. Because GHQ Air Force controlled reconnaissance and bombardment missions only, whereas supply, training, and doctrine remained under control of the chief of the air corps, the organizational scheme had the effect of splitting USAAC functions and soon proved unwieldy. GHQ Air Force was deactivated in 1941, on the eve of United States entry into WORLD WAR II.

General of the Air Force   See RANKS AND GRADES.

George, Harold L. (1893–1986) *Air Force strategist*

George was one of the principal architects of American air power and was a central figure in creating U.S. ARMY AIR FORCES strategic operations, doctrines, and war plans. He radically reconfigured the AIR TRANSPORT COMMAND (ATC) into a force capable of performing tactical and strategic AIRLIFT anywhere in the world, thereby providing the basis from which the MILITARY AIRLIFT COMMAND (MAC) and the AIR MOBILITY COMMAND (AMC) would develop.

A native of Somerville, Massachusetts, George was commissioned a second lieutenant in the AVIATION SECTION, U.S. ARMY SIGNAL CORPS, in 1918. He served during the close of WORLD WAR I as a bomber pilot in the Meuse-Argonne offensive. After the war, George became an ardent disciple of the air power ideas of WILLIAM MITCHELL and was one of the pilots who participated in Mitchell's demonstration bombardment of captured German warships. George carried Mitchell's ideas into his work with the Air Corps Tactical School, where he served as chief of the bombardment section from 1932 to 1934 and as director of air tactics and strategy from 1934 to 1936. A mentor who exercised great influence on the officers who would shape air power strategy and tactics in WORLD WAR II, George was a thoroughgoing advocate of precision daylight bombing as the chief means of conducting strategic operations (see BOMBING, STRATEGIC).

In 1941, George was appointed assistant chief of the AIR STAFF for war plans. In collaboration with other Air Corps Tactical School theorists, George formulated AWPD-1, the bomber-focused plan the USAAF would ultimately employ against Germany.

George was named to head the Ferry Command in 1942, charged with the task of expanding USAAF airlift capabilities to a worldwide scale. When George took command, he had 130 aircraft and 11,000 people. By the end of World War II, he had expanded airlift to the Air Transport Command, with more than 3,000 planes and 300,000 people. The emphasis was on transoceanic operations, so that the reach of the USAAF—and the other services it assisted—became truly and even routinely global.

Goodfellow AFB, Texas   See AIR FORCE BASES.

Grand Forks AFB, North Dakota   See AIR FORCE BASES.

Griffiss AFB, New York   See AIR FORCE BASES.

Grissom AFB, Indiana   See AIR FORCE BASES.

group   See ORGANIZATION, USAF.

H

Hanscom AFB, Massachusetts   See AIR FORCE BASES.

Headquarters Air Force (HAF)

HAF, also called Headquarters Department of the Air Force, and familiarly known as Dash 1, is housed chiefly in the Pentagon and is headed by the SECRETARY OF THE AIR FORCE. Directly reporting to the secretary is a Secretariat, which includes many administrative departments and functions. Also directly responsible to the secretary, but completely separate from the Secretariat, is the AIR STAFF, head by the CHIEF OF STAFF, USAF. Within the Air Staff level are the various field operating agencies (see ORGANIZATION, USAF).

Hickam AFB, Hawaii   See AIR FORCE BASES.

Hill AFB, Utah   See AIR FORCE BASES.

history, overview of USAF

The USAF came into being as an independent service, of equal status with the U.S. Army and U.S. Navy, on September 18, 1947, by virtue of the NATIONAL SECURITY ACT OF 1947; however, its full history may be traced as far back as the Civil War, when, between 1861 and 1863, the Union army made substantial use of tethered BALLOONS for battlefield observation. The army invested $50,000 in a grant to aviation pioneer Samuel P. Langley for development of an airplane during the Spanish-American War in 1898. Langley failed to develop a workable aircraft, and it was not until August 1, 1907—four years after the Wright brothers made their first flight—that President Theodore Roosevelt, an aviation enthusiast, authorized the AERONAUTICAL DIVISION, U.S. ARMY SIGNAL CORPS. A modest organization, the Aeronautical Division was primarily concerned with assessing the capabilities of aircraft for military applications.

On July 18, 1914, the AVIATION SECTION, U.S. ARMY SIGNAL CORPS was formed. This organization brought American military aviation into WORLD WAR I in 1917, but it was unable to manage the necessary expansion of the service. A bigger, more autonomous organization, the U.S. ARMY AIR SERVICE, was established on May 24, 1918. Under this organization, U.S. airmen flew very significant missions during the closing months of World War I. In 1916, the American air arm consisted of 311 men, total. By the end of World War I, the USAAS mustered 195,023 officers and enlisted personnel.

The outstanding individual to emerge during the period of the USAAS was Brigadier General WILLIAM MITCHELL, an abrasive, tireless, and far-seeing advocate of military air power. His demonstration of the effectiveness of aerial bombardment against large naval vessels failed to move the U.S. Army to expand the USAAS, but it did interest the navy in aviation. Although Mitchell's outspoken

Samuel Pierpont Langley and Charles M. Manly (left), chief mechanic on board the houseboat that served to launch Langley's Aerodrome aircraft over the Potomac River near Washington, D.C., in 1903. Even though he was one of the pioneers of flight in America, Langley never saw his dreams fulfilled. He is remembered as one of the most unlucky trail blazers in flight history. *(NASA)*

frustration with his superiors ultimately resulted in his high-profile court martial in 1925, his public agitation did influence the passage of the AIR CORPS ACT OF 1926, which established the U.S. ARMY AIR CORPS on July 2, 1926. With greater autonomy than the USAAS, the USAAC developed aircraft, tactics, strategy, and doctrine, all aimed at establishing the independence of air power in warfighting.

On the eve of the United States' entry into WORLD WAR II, the army recognized the necessity of creating a nearly independent air arm, and, on June 20, 1941, the U.S. ARMY AIR FORCES came into

being. The new service quickly geared up for war, expanding personnel from 23,455 in 1939 to 2,372,292 in 1944. As visionaries like Mitchell had predicted, air power played an extraordinarily important role in the war. It was the USAAF that delivered the first offensive blow against Japan in the form of JAMES HAROLD DOOLITTLE's daring raid on Tokyo on April 18, 1942, and it was USAAF bombers that brought the war to the Germans well before effective Allied offensive action on the ground was possible. While military analysts and historians continue to argue over the effectiveness of strategic bombing (see BOMBING, STRATEGIC) in World War II, it is a fact that two USAAF B-29s brought World War II to an end by delivering nuclear weapons against Japan in August 1945. And the war also made it clear that the time had come to establish an entirely independent air arm, of status equal to that of the navy and the army.

The United States Air Force was born by act of Congress (National Security Act of 1947) on September 18, 1947, and, in a nuclear age, it soon became the principal strategic force of the United States, capable of delivering nuclear—and then thermonuclear—weapons to any target anywhere in the world. While the thrust of USAF development during the Cold War period was in the area of strategic deployment, the first test of the USAF was tactical: the BERLIN AIRLIFT during 1948–49. The success of the airlift marked a major victory against Soviet expansion in Europe, and it served as the impetus for the creation of NATO, in which the USAF would play a major role.

Even as the USAF, through the STRATEGIC AIR COMMAND (SAC), developed as a nuclear deterrent force, the next major challenge was also tactical in nature. The KOREAN WAR (1950–53) called for CLOSE AIR SUPPORT of ground forces, although USAF strategic operations against North Korean irrigation and dam systems were also effective in bringing the communists to the negotiating table.

After Korea and until the escalation of the VIETNAM WAR, the emphasis for the USAF again turned to strategic deterrence, especially after the Soviet Union and, later, Communist China acquired nuclear and thermonuclear weapons. Under General CURTIS EMERSON LeMay, who led the USAF from 1948 to 1965, the service became the chief American means of maintaining a policy of mutually assured destruction (MAD), in which the existence of massive atomic arsenals in U.S. as well as Soviet hands discouraged both sides from declaring war. During this period, the USAF developed the massive B-52 bomber and an arsenal of ICBM (INTERCONTINENTAL BALLISTIC MISSILE) weapons, as well as important advances in aerial reconnaissance, including the U-2, the SR-71, and an array of military satellites.

The escalation of the Vietnam War beginning in 1965 once again showed the shortsightedness of preparing almost exclusively for strategic warfare at the expense of readiness to fight a limited war on a tactical level. The war drew on USAF ingenuity and the ability to improvise as well as to adapt strategic aircraft (most notably the B-52) to a tactical role. As the PERSIAN GULF WAR demonstrated in 1990–91, the USAF had become a tremendously flexible service, capable of maintaining strategic deterrence as well as coordinating with ground and sea forces to achieve a rapid tactical victory. In the "war against terrorism," the campaign against terrorist-held Afghanistan that followed the terrorist attacks against the World Trade Center in New York and the Pentagon outside of Washington, D.C., on September 11, 2001, the USAF again played the major role. At the beginning of the 21st century, there could be no doubt that the USAF was the largest and most effective air force in history.

Holloman AFB, New Mexico   See AIR FORCE BASES.

Howard AFB, Panama   See AIR FORCE BASES.

Hurlburt Field, Florida   See AIR FORCE BASES.

I

Incirlik AB, Turkey   See AIR FORCE BASES.

insignia, aircraft

Once bright and bold, the insignia on USAF combat aircraft since the VIETNAM WAR has been generally gray or black to reduce rather than enhance visibility. This reflects a recognition of the sophistication of air defense weaponry.

The first insignia on U.S. Army aircraft was carried on planes used in the PUNITIVE EXPEDITION led by General John J. Pershing against Pancho Villa in 1916. Planes were marked with a red star, sometimes enclosed within a solid white circle. This insignia was never made official, however, and, in May 1917, the month after the United States entered WORLD WAR I, the official insignia became a white star within a blue circle, with a solid red disk within the star. Aircraft rudders carried vertical red, white, and blue stripes. In 1918, Brigadier General WILLIAM MITCHELL changed the insignia to a roundel with a white disk inside a larger blue ring, which was in an even larger red ring. The change was made to bring the U.S. insignia into line with the insignia of the other Allies, and, in 1919, with the war over, the 1917 star insignia was adopted once again. The rudder insignia changed in 1927, becoming a vertical blue stripe forward with alternating horizontal red and white stripes aft. This was used until 1940.

During WORLD WAR II, in 1942, the red disk was removed from the center of the white star to avoid possible confusion with the Japanese "rising sun" insignia. Also in 1942, some insignia added a narrow yellow ring outside of the blue field, but this was used on an unofficial basis. In 1943, white rectangles ("wings") were added at the sides of the blue circle to heighten visibility, and a red stripe was run around the entire insignia. This was soon replaced by a blue stripe for the rest of the war.

After the war, in 1947, the red outline was restored to the insignia, which now also included a horizontal red stripe in the middle of the "wing" rectangles. This design endured until the advent of the modern, lower-visibility insignia. The insignia on today's "stealth" aircraft barely contrasts with the prevailing color of the aircraft fuselage and air surfaces.

Inter-American Air Forces Academy (IAAFA)

The mission of the IAAFA is to train and support Latin American air forces, in Spanish, so that they may support United States national interests and the security interests of the hemisphere. Located at Lackland AFB, Texas, IAAFA also seeks to promote "inter-Americanism" and to expose students to the American lifestyle. Staffed by Spanish-speaking USAF instructors, IAAFA provides instruction for both officers and enlisted personnel in over 60 supervisory, specialization, and technical-academic courses including aircraft systems and maintenance, helicopter maintenance, electronics, communications, intelligence, supply, logistics, air base ground defense, security, pilot instrument procedures, computer resources, and information systems management. Training is conducted at three geographically separated locations: Lackland AFB, Kelly AFB, and the U.S. Army's Camp Bullis, outside of San Antonio, Texas.

IAAFA is older than the USAF itself, having been established on March 15, 1943, at the request of the Peruvian minister of aeronautics, General Fernando Melgar. In 1943, the newly established academy trained 11 Peruvian students at Albrook Field, Panama Canal Zone. IAAFA expanded during the 1950s and was officially named "The Inter-American Air Forces Academy" in 1966.

intercontinental ballistic missile (ICBM)

The AIR FORCE SPACE COMMAND (AFSPC) manages and controls the USAF's ICBM program, which is one leg of the so-called triad that makes up the United States' strategic forces. (The other two legs are nuclear-capable manned bombers and the U.S. Navy's fleet of nuclear-missile submarines.)

ICBMs are long-range missiles, in contrast to shorter-range IRBM (INTERMEDIATE-RANGE BALLISTIC MISSILE) weapons. ICBMs consist of a rocket engine, fuel, oxidizer, guidance system, and a nuclear or thermonuclear warhead. The missiles are an outgrowth of the German V-2 rockets of WORLD WAR II. After the war, the USAF conducted research on the Atlas ICBM, and, in 1953, the USAF and the U.S. Army independently (and competitively) developed missiles. At last, in 1957, all ICBM programs, operations, and arsenals were put under the direction of the USAF.

ICBMs currently in the USAF inventory include:

The LGM-30G Minuteman. Built by Boeing, the Minuteman has a range of more than 6,000

The Peacekeeper missile   (U.S. Air Force)

miles and can carry nuclear or thermonuclear warheads. The current Minuteman force consists of 500 Minuteman III missiles located at Warren AFB, Wyoming, Malmstrom AFB, Montana, and Minot AFB, North Dakota. If the Start II nuclear limitation treaty is fully implemented, the Minuteman III will become the only land-based ICBM in the triad.

LG-118A Peacekeeper. Built by Boeing and with a range in excess of 6,000 miles, the Peacekeeper was first deployed in 1986. It can deliver 10 independently targeted thermonuclear warheads with great accuracy. Currently, 50 of these $70 million missiles are deployed, but they may be retired if the Start II treaty is fully implemented.

intermediate-range ballistic missile (IRBM)

Although the USAF inventory includes many types of missiles, the only strategic missile weapons in the AIR FORCE SPACE COMMAND (AFSPC) inventory today are ICBM (INTERCONTINENTAL BALLISTIC MISSILE) weapons. Beginning in the 1950s, however, the USAF inventory also included IRBMs with nuclear warheads. The most important of these were:

> *Chrysler PGM-19 Jupiter.* Developed by the army's Ballistic Missile Agency at the Redstone Arsenal, Alabama, under Dr. Wernher von Braun, the Jupiter was placed under USAF control in 1959. Jupiter was a single-stage, liquid-propellant missile using an all-inertial guidance system to direct it toward the target. Its range was 1,500 miles, and Jupiter squadrons of 15 missiles each were deployed at NATO launch sites in Italy and Turkey in 1961. The Jupiter was withdrawn from military use in 1963.

> *Douglas PGM-17 Thor.* The single-stage Thor entered active military service in September 1958 and was the free world's first operational IRBM. The Thor was assigned to the STRATEGIC AIR COMMAND (SAC) and was also deployed to England early in 1959. The Thor was retired from military service in 1963, although it was modified for space research, either as a single-stage booster or in combination with various types of upper stages for such satellite programs as Tiros, Telstar, Pioneer, and Discoverer.

Jabara, James (1923–1966) *fighter pilot*

USAF pilot James Jabara became America's first jet ace, achieving 15 victories against MiGs during two tours in the KOREAN WAR. A native of Muskogee, Oklahoma, Jabara became an aviation cadet in 1942, during WORLD WAR II, and entered the U.S.

ARMY AIR FORCES as a commissioned pilot the following year.

During World War II, Jabara flew with the NINTH AIR FORCE and the EIGHTH AIR FORCE in F-51s, a total of 108 sorties. He was credited with one and a half victories. His first tour in Korea began in 1950 with the 4th Fighter Interceptor Wing of the FIFTH AIR FORCE, flying F-86 jets. Having scored six victories, he returned to the United States in 1951, where he was assigned to USAF headquarters, then, at his request, he served another tour in Korea, scoring nine more victories.

In 1964, as colonel, Jabara commanded the 4540th Combat Crew Training Group at Luke AFB, Arizona, overseeing the training of U.S.-allied foreign pilots in the F-104G. Jabara was killed in an automobile accident.

Japan Air Defense Force (JADF)

A named air force, the unit was created in 1952 to replace the 314th Air Division and was under the FAR EAST AIR FORCES (FEAF). The JADF was created to defend Japan while the FIFTH AIR FORCE, established as the occupying air force of Japan after WORLD WAR II, was in Korea during the KOREAN WAR. JADF was dissolved in 1954.

jock

USAF slang for pilot; typically applied to fighter pilots—"fighter jocks." See also DRIVER.

James Jabara   *(U.S. Air Force)*

Joint Services Survival, Evasion, Resistance, and Escape (SERE) Agency (JSAA)

JSAA is the Department of Defense executive agency for operational evasion and escape matters, for code of conduct and survival, evasion, resistance, and escape (SERE) training, and for the DOD Prisoner of War (POW)/Missing in Action (MIA) program. JSAA headquarters is at Fort Belvoir, Virginia.

Joint Strike Fighter (JSF) Program

The JSF Program (formerly the Joint Advanced Strike Technology (JAST) Program), is a Department of Defense project to define affordable next-generation strike aircraft weapon systems for the USAF, navy, marines, and the forces of our allies. The principal goal of the program is to produce an affordable aircraft that will satisfy the following needs:

> *USAF:* Multirole aircraft (primary-air-to-ground), to replace the F-16 and A-10 and complement the F-22A
>
> *U.S. Navy:* First-day-of-war, survivable strike fighter aircraft to complement F/A-18E/F

Boeing and Lockheed Martin competed for the Joint Strike Fighter contract. This Lockheed-Martin prototype won the contract. *(Lockheed-Martin photo)*

> *U.S. Marine Corps STOVL (short takeoff and vertical landing):* Aircraft to replace the AV-8B and F/A-18 as the only USMC strike fighter
>
> *United Kingdom Royal Navy and Royal Air Force:* STOVL aircraft to replace Sea Harriers and GR.7s as a supersonic strike fighter

The JSF program originated in the early 1990s, and the Joint Advanced Strike Technology (JAST) Program was initiated in late 1993. As of the close of 2001, the JSF program was nearing the end of the concept demonstration. It is anticipated that the USAF will be the largest JSF customer, purchasing 1,763 CTOL (conventional takeoff and landing) aircraft. The U.S. Marine Corps is expected to purchase 609 STOVL aircraft, and the U.S. Navy about 480 carrier-launched aircraft. The U.K. Royal Air Force and Royal Navy will purchase 150 of the STOVL variant. Boeing and Lockheed Martin both produced prototypes, but the final contract was awarded to Lockheed Martin in October 2001.

Joint Surveillance Target Attack Radar System (JSTARS)

Joint STARS or JSTARS is a joint USAF/U.S. Army program that provides air and ground commanders with near real-time wide-area surveillance and deep targeting data on both fixed and moving targets, day or night and under all weather conditions. JSTARS can detect, locate, track, and classify targets in enemy territory beyond the Forward Line of Own Troops (FLOT).

The airborne platform for the JSTARS electronics is the E-8, a specially modified C-18 transport (the military version of the Boeing 707-323C). JSTARS was first used extensively in the PERSIAN GULF WAR of 1990–91.

Jones, David C. (1921–) *Air Force general*

Chairman of the Joint Chiefs of Staff from 1978 to 1982, Jones was the third USAF officer to hold the position. He had served as chief of staff of the

USAF from 1974 until his appointment as JCS chairman.

A native of Aberdeen, South Dakota, Jones was an aviation cadet and entered the U.S. ARMY AIR FORCES through that program in 1943. During WORLD WAR II, Jones served as a flying instructor, and, in the KOREAN WAR, flew more than 300 combat hours in B-29s. Returned to the United States, he served as operations planner and as aide to General CURTIS EMERSON LEMAY at STRATEGIC AIR COMMAND (SAC) headquarters. In 1960, Jones graduated from the National War College and served on the AIR STAFF. He became commander of the SECOND AIR FORCE in 1969, then commander in chief of UNITED STATES AIR FORCES IN EUROPE (USAFE) in 1971.

Jones was an advocate of the B-1 bomber program and an expanded AWACS program. He initiated and directed important USAF organizational changes, including the reduction in the size of numbered air forces and the creation of Allied Air Forces Central Europe under the auspices of NATO. He strengthened the role of the JCS, and, although he retired in 1982, he continued to work successfully toward that end.

Jungle Jim

The name was applied to the 4400th Combat Crew Training Squadron established at Eglin AFB, Florida, in 1961. The unit's purpose was to train airmen for guerrilla warfare and air commando operations. A Jungle Jim detachment was deployed to South Vietnam in October 1961, ostensibly as part of U.S. military advisory forces to train South Vietnamese personnel. In the VIETNAM WAR, the Jungle Jim detachment was called Farm Gate and flew U.S. aircraft bearing Vietnamese air force markings.

K

Kadena AB, Japan   See AIR FORCE BASES.

Keesler AFB, Mississippi   See AIR FORCE BASES.

Kelly AFB, Texas   See AIR FORCE BASES.

Kenly, William L. (1864–1928) *U.S. Army Air Service director*

The first head of the U.S. ARMY AIR SERVICE, Kenly was born in Baltimore and graduated from West Point in 1889. Originally commissioned in the artillery, he attended San Diego Signal Corps Aviation School shortly before the United States entered WORLD WAR I. Although he shipped out to France as commander of an artillery unit, he was subsequently appointed chief of the USAAS. In November 1917, General BENJAMIN D. FOULOIS relieved him, and, after briefly serving in artillery again, Kenly returned to the United States early in 1918 to head the Division of Military Aeronautics, effectively commanding the USAAS through the end of World War I. Kenly had little effect on the USAAS because funding was drastically reduced with demobilization. He retired in 1919.

Key West Agreement of 1948

Although EXECUTIVE ORDER 9877 of July 26, 1947 clearly specified the roles of the newly created USAF,

a dispute arose among the services, all of which wanted to use air power. Particularly acrimonious was the conflict between the navy and the USAF. The navy rejected the idea of using heavy bombers to fulfill the strategic role and favored the use of carrier-based aircraft. The USAF continued to champion the role of the heavy bomber. Somewhat less acute was the dispute between the army and the USAF. The army saw coastal air defense as its mission, and the army also sought control over ICBM (INTERCONTINENTAL BALLISTIC MISSILE) weapons.

In an effort to resolve the disputes, Secretary of Defense James V. Forrestal convened conferences with the Joint Chiefs of Staff to be held in Key West, Florida, in March 1948. The conferences produced an agreement (historically referred to as the Key West Agreement—although no official document was so titled) that the USAF held prime responsibility for strategic operations and the navy for control of the seas. Air defense was assigned to the USAF, but the army was given the function of organizing, equipping, and training air defense units.

The Key West Agreement did not definitively settle the USAF-army controversy over ICBM and surface-to-air operations. In 1949, control of surface-to-air missiles with up to a 100-mile range was given to the army, whereas the USAF controlled those with ranges exceeding 100 miles. In 1956 the secretary of defense settled the matter of which service would control ICBMs by assigning to the

USAF control over all ballistic missiles with a range in excess of 20 miles.

Kirtland AFB, New Mexico See AIR FORCE BASES.

Korean War

Background of the War

The Korean War of 1950–53 had its immediate cause in the invasion of South Korea by forces from the communist North. However, Korea had an ancient heritage of internal conflict and, through the centuries, was also often subject to invasion by China or Japan. In 1910, Japan, expanding its empire, annexed Korea without incurring objection from the rest of the world, including the United States. After the December 7, 1941, Japanese attack on Pearl Harbor, however, the United States' declaration of war acknowledged, among many other things, that Japan had made Korea one of its first victims of imperialist aggression, and, from this point on, the fate of Korea became a subject of interest to America. At the 1943 Cairo Conference among China, Great Britain, and the United States, the Allies agreed to include the independence of Korea among the objectives of their joint prosecution of WORLD WAR II. At the Potsdam Conference (July 27–August 2, 1945), Soviet premier Joseph Stalin declared his intention to abide by the Potsdam agreement to establish an international trusteeship for Korea after the defeat of Japan. The sudden surrender of Japan on August 14, 1945, after the atomic bombings of Hiroshima and Nagasaki, made an Allied occupation of Korea unnecessary. Nevertheless, the United States proposed that the Soviets receive Japan's surrender in Korea north of the 38th parallel while the United States accept surrender south of this line. The idea was that this de facto partition would be strictly temporary and would remain in place only until Korea could be restored to a full peacetime footing. The Soviets, however, seized on it to divide Korea and bring the northern portion into the communist sphere. The

38th parallel became a fortified line, and, in September 1947, the United States requested that the United Nations intervene to bring about Korean unification. Over a Soviet objection, the UN decided that a unified government be established for Korea following a general election. Moreover, it was resolved that, after the government had been established, the UN would dispatch a security force to Korea to protect it. Encouraged by the Soviets, the North Korean communists barred the UN commission from holding elections north of the 38th parallel. South of the parallel, the 1948 elections created the Republic of Korea (ROK) under President Syngman Rhee. In response, on May 25, 1948, Soviet-sponsored elections in the north created a Supreme People's Assembly, which purported to represent all of Korea. The People's Democratic Republic of Korea (DRK) was put under the leadership of Kim Il Sung, a Soviet-trained Korean communist.

Having set up a North Korean government, the Soviets pledged to withdraw Red Army troops from the country by January 1, 1949. Although heartened by this announcement, the United States began to train and equip an indigenous Korean security force for the South and provided economic aid. The situation was delicate, because the United States wanted neither to abandon South Korea nor to give the appearance of sponsoring South Korean aggression, which might trigger a new world war. Accordingly, the United States supplied defensive weapons only. President Rhee protested that his nation needed much more, and he even hired as a military adviser CLAIRE L. CHENNAULT, the famed U.S. ARMY AIR FORCES major general, retired, who had commanded China's "Flying Tigers" (see AMERICAN VOLUNTEER GROUP) during WORLD WAR II. Rhee asked Chennault to plan a South Korean air force.

The United States completed its official military withdrawal from Korea on June 29, 1949, leaving behind only a 500-man U.S. Korean Military Advisory Group (KMAG).

War Begins

During May 1950, KMAG reported a military buildup on the northern side of the 38th parallel. At four o'clock on the morning of June 25, 1950, these forces invaded, crossing the 38th parallel and brushing aside the inferior South Korean army. The main invading force headed toward Seoul, the South Korean capital, about 35 miles below the parallel, while smaller forces moved down the center of the Korean peninsula and along the east coast. The North Korean People's Army (NKPA) took Seoul, whereupon President Harry S. Truman ordered General Douglas MacArthur, commander of the U.S. Far East Command, to supply the ROK with equipment and ammunition, because most supplies had been abandoned in the retreat of ROK forces.

USAF elements were the first U.S. military units to respond to the invasion. By the afternoon of June 25, North Korean fighters attacked South Korean and USAF aircraft and facilities at Seoul airfield and Kimpo AB, just south of the capital. On June 26, FAR EAST AIR FORCES (FEAF) fighters provided protective cover while ships evacuated American nationals from Inchon, 20 miles west of Seoul. On June 27, as the communists closed in on Seoul, FEAF transports evacuated more Americans, and FIFTH AIR FORCE fighters, escorting the evacuation transports, shot down three North Korean MiGs—the first aerial victories of the war.

The U.S. delegation to the United Nations secured a Security Council resolution that UN members assist the ROK. Armed with this, President Truman mobilized U.S. air and naval forces. On June 28, FEAF, under the command of Lieutenant General George E. Stratemeyer, began flying interdiction missions between Seoul and the 38th parallel, photo-reconnaissance and weather missions over South Korea, airlift missions from Japan to Korea, and CLOSE AIR SUPPORT missions for the ROK troops. On June 29, the 3rd Bombardment Group made the first American air raid on North Korea, bombing the airfield at Pyongyang, and FEAF Bomber Command followed with sporadic B-29 missions against North Korean targets through July. At last, in August, major B-29 raids were launched against North Korean marshaling yards, railroad bridges, and supply dumps.

U.S. ground forces were committed to war on June 30, 1950. On July 7, the UN established an allied command under President Truman, who named General MacArthur as UN commander in chief. In the meantime, the 5AF, under Major General Earl E. Partridge, established an advanced headquarters in Taegu, South Korea, 140 miles southeast of Seoul, also the location of Eighth Army headquarters. However, during this early period of the war, most FEAF bombers and fighters operated from bases in Japan, which was a major disadvantage in flying short-range F-80 jet aircraft. Nevertheless, USAF pilots worked in concert with carrier-launched naval aircraft to attack enemy airfields, destroying much of the small North Korean air force on the ground. Before the end of July, USAF and navy and marine air units claimed air superiority over North and South Korea.

By August 5, the relentless retreat of UN ground forces had stopped, and FEAF air support, effective ground action, and the unsupportable lengthening of North Korean supply lines ended the communist offensive. The UN troops held a defensive perimeter in the southeastern corner of the peninsula, in a 40- to 60-mile arc about the seaport of Pusan. Holding the Pusan perimeter required careful coordination between ground action and close air support.

UN Forces Take the Offensive

Beginning on September 15, 1950, UN forces assumed the offensive when the U.S. X Corps made a spectacular amphibious assault landing at Inchon, 150 miles north of the battle front. In the south, the U.S. Eighth Army (including U.S., ROK, and British forces) counterattacked on September 16. The 5AF provided close air support, while, far to the north, FEAF bombed Pyongyang, the capital of North Korea, and Wonsan, an east coast port 80 miles north of the 38th parallel.

U.S. Marines retook Kimpo AB on September 17. On the 19th, the first FEAF cargo aircraft landed there. From this point on, the AIRLIFT of supplies, fuel, and troops would be virtually continuous. Air controllers accompanied advancing Eighth Army tank columns to support tank commanders with aerial reconnaissance and to call in close air support. Seoul was recaptured on September 26, and, on September 28, fighter-bombers returned permanently to Taegu. Engineers also rebuilt other airfields, beginning with Pohang, on the east coast 50 miles northeast of Taegu, and, on October 7, USAF flying units returned to Pohang and to other rebuilt airfields at Kimpo and at Suwon, 20 miles south of Seoul. The ability to operate from bases in Korea greatly increased the effectiveness of the limited-range jet fighters.

On October 9, UN forces took the war into North Korea when the Eighth Army crossed the 38th parallel near Kaesong. American and South Korean forces entered Pyongyang on October 19 while FEAF B-29s and B-26s continued to bomb transport lines and military targets in North Korea,

and B-26s, F-51s, and F-80s provided close air support to the advancing ground troops. FEAF also continuously supplied photo reconnaissance, airlift, and air medical evacuation.

On the east coast of Korea in the meantime, ROK forces crossed the 38th parallel on October 1 and captured Wonsan on October 11. On October 26 South Korean forces reached the Yalu River, the border with China, at Chosan, 120 miles north of Pyongyang.

Chinese Intervention

On the night of November 25, 1950, Chinese forces, in great strength, attacked the Eighth Army on its center and right. Two days later, even more

This photo shows the results of dropping a 2,000-pound bomb on the Korean side of a bridge across the Yalu River into Manchuria, on November 15, 1950. *(National Archives)*

powerful Chinese attacks overran units of X Corps on its left flank. By November 28, UN positions were caving in as about 300,000 Chinese troops entered North Korea.

UN troops rapidly withdrew, and even UN air superiority vanished as Soviet-built Chinese MiG-15 jet fighters easily outflew U.S. piston-driven craft. By December 15, UN forces had withdrawn all the way to the 38th parallel and were now establishing a defensive line across the breadth of the Korean peninsula.

5AF provided close air support to cover the withdrawal, and U.S. F-80s did their best against the Chinese MiG-15s. During November, FEAF medium and light bombers, along with U.S. Navy aircraft, attacked bridges over the Yalu River and supply centers along the Korean side of the river —operations severely hampered by orders to avoid violating Chinese air space. Despite the handicap, on November 25, bombers destroyed key bridges, but the communists responded by rapidly erecting pontoon bridges. As winter set in, they also crossed the ice of the frozen Yalu. B-29 raids were effective against North Korean supply dumps, however.

In response to the introduction of Chinese MiG 15s, USAF commanders requested and received rush consignments of the newest and best jet fighters. On December 6, the 27th Fighter-Escort Wing, flying F-84 Thunderjets, arrived at Taegu. On December 15, the 4th Fighter-Interceptor Wing flew its first mission in Korea using the most advanced aircraft, the F-86 Sabre. It was the timely introduction of the Sabres that allowed UN forces to regain and maintain air superiority.

As 1950 came to a close, FEAF flew interdiction and armed reconnaissance missions to slow the advancing Chinese. 5AF pilots killed or wounded some 33,000 enemy troops during December, forcing the Chinese to move only by night. Yet the communist advance continued, and, on January 1, 1951, Chinese forces crossed the 38th parallel. They entered Seoul three days later. On January 15 UN forces halted the Chinese and North Korean armies 50 miles south of the 38th parallel, on a line from Pyongtaek on the west coast to Samchok on the east coast.

UN Counteroffensive

UN forces began a counteroffensive on January 25, 1951, with the object of wearing down the overextended enemy. On February 10, Kimpo AB was again recaptured, and, when thawing roads made ground transport impossible, the 315th Air Division airdropped supplies to the ground forces. UN forces reoccupied Seoul on March 14. On the 23rd, FEAF airlift forces dropped a reinforced regiment at Munsan, 25 miles north of Seoul.

Up north, between the Chongchon and Yalu rivers, communist forces established an air presence so formidable that 5AF pilots called the region "MiG Alley." By March 10, Sabres were fighting in MiG Alley while also escorting FEAF B-29 attacks against area targets. From April 12 to 23 the FEAF bombers attacked rebuilt airfields on the outskirts of Pyongyang. By this time, Eighth Army ground units had regained the 38th parallel. Between April 17 and 21, with close air support, ground units penetrated beyond the 38th parallel.

Communist Chinese Spring Offensive

On April 22, 1951, Chinese forces began a new offensive with an assault on ROK army positions 40 to 55 miles northeast of Seoul. U.S. Army and marine forces, in concert with British ground troops, stopped the new communist drive by May 1. Two weeks later, however, the Chinese and North Koreans attacked near Taepo, between the east coast and Chunchon, 45 miles northeast of Seoul. The advance was halted by May 20, and, on May 22, UN Command (now under the overall direction of General Matthew Bunker Ridgway, who had replaced General MacArthur—removed by President Truman for insubordination) launched a counterattack. FEAF and navy fliers maintained air superiority during this period by means of aerial combat and continual bombing of North Korean airfields. The 5AF and a U.S. Marine air wing extended airfield attacks on May 9 to include Sinuiju airfield in the northwest corner of Korea.

The attacks were devastating to communist air power in the region.

General Stratemeyer, FEAF commander, suffered a heart attack in May 1951, and Lieutenant General O. P. Weyland took over FEAF. Throughout most of this period, Chinese pilots stayed on the Manchurian side of the Yalu River, but, on May 20, 50 MiGs engaged 36 Sabres in aerial combat. It was during this fight that Captain JAMES JABARA shot down two MiGs, which, added to his four prior kills, made him the first jet ace in aviation history.

FEAF, marine, and navy air forces coordinated carefully to help force the North Koreans and Chinese to restrict their movements and attacks to periods of darkness and bad weather. FEAF also supplemented sealift with airlift during this period. In late May, FEAF began Operation Strangle to interdict the flow of communist supplies south of the 39th parallel, and, in June, the campaign was extended to attacks against railroads.

Negotiations Begin

In July 1951, delegations began cease-fire negotiations at Kaesong, North Korea, on the 38th parallel. During these talks, UN forces continued pushing the communist troops northward, until, by July 8, the front had returned to the 38th parallel.

Negotiations formally began on July 10, 1951, and broke down on August 23, whereupon the UN Command launched an offensive in central Korea. FEAF settled in for a war of attrition and devoted much effort to rebuilding and improving its Korean airfields. Beginning late in July, the Chinese air force conducted an air campaign to challenge UN air superiority. In September they targeted the 5AF, whose pilots, however, shot down 14 MiGs, while suffering 6 losses.

Despite U.S. victories, the Chinese air offensive forced the 5AF to suspend fighter-bomber interdiction in MiG Alley until the winter. During this period, UN air command concentrated on railroad targets outside of MiG Alley and on new North Korean airfields. These raids proved unsuccessful. However, on November 12, 1951, truce negotiations resumed, now at Panmunjom, and UN ground forces ceased offensive action, settling into a war of containment.

Stalemate

While negotiations dragged on, the USAF received more F-86 Sabres to counter the Chinese air force. Beginning in December 1951, members of the 51st and 4th Fighter-Interceptor Wings downed 26 MiGs in two weeks, breaking the back of the Chinese air offensive. For the rest of the winter, MiG pilots generally avoided aerial combat. Despite this, pilots of the 5AF destroyed 127 communist aircraft in aerial combat between January and April 1952. USAF losses were only nine planes. 5AF B-29 raids also continued during this period. However, during the winter of 1951–52, with battle lines static, the need for the close air support mission was greatly diminished. USAF commanders concentrated instead on aerial bombardment of enemy positions alternating on a daily basis with artillery attacks on those same positions. The communist response was to dig in, rendering both aerial and artillery bombardment fairly ineffective.

In an effort to end the stalemate at Panmunjom, UN air commanders resolved to attack targets previously exempted or underexploited. Accordingly, in May 1952 the 5AF shifted from interdiction of transportation to attacks on supply depots and industrial targets. Beginning on June 23, U.S. Navy and 5AF units also made coordinated attacks on the electric power complex at Sui-ho Dam, on the Yalu River near Sinuiju, followed by strikes against the Chosin, Fusen, and Kyosen power plants. On July 11, Pyongyang was bombed by aircraft of the Seventh Fleet, the 1st Marine Air Wing, the 5AF, the British Navy, and the ROK air force. At night, FEAF sent in B-29s. Allied air forces returned to Pyongyang again on August 29 and 30, and, in September, 5AF attacked troop concentrations and barracks in northwest Korea, while FEAF bombed similar targets near Hamhung in northeast Korea.

During the summer of 1952, many F-86Es were upgraded to more powerful and more maneuverable F-86Fs. MiG activity increased during August and September, but U.S. pilots achieved an 8-to-1 ratio of victories to losses.

Despite the pressure of the air campaign, the Panmunjom talks produced nothing, and the war entered its third winter.

Continued Stalemate

While the stalemate continued, USAF Sabre pilots continued to shoot down MiGs, even though they were generally outnumbered and flew aircraft that were still technically inferior to the MiG-15, at least at high altitude. On February 18, 1953, near the Suiho Reservoir on the Yalu River, four F-86Fs attacked 48 MiGs, shot down two, and caused two others to crash while taking evasive action. All four Sabres returned safely to base.

The success of 5AF Sabres was not matched by that of the aging B-29s of FEAF Bomber Command. The big bombers increasingly fell victim to interceptor and antiaircraft artillery attacks at night. Missions were curtailed, although important industrial targets continued to be targeted.

In the spring of 1953, a POW exchange agreement broke the stalemate at Panmunjom, and productive talks continued.

The War Winds Down

During the renewed talks, the communists sought to improve their position with a major assault on June 10 against the ROK II Corps near Kumsong, a small town in central Korea. In combating this offensive, FEAF flew a record-breaking 7,032 sorties, mostly to deliver close air support. When the offensive was renewed, FEAF flew another 12,000 combat sorties, again mostly in close air support.

During the offensives, the 315th Air Division airlifted an Army regiment (3,252 soldiers and 1,770 tons of cargo) from Japan to Korea, and, from June 28 through July 2, airlifters flew almost 4,000 more troops and over 1,200 tons of cargo from Misawa and Tachikawa air bases in Japan to Pusan and Taegu airfields in Korea. These were the last major airlift operations of the Korean conflict. During May, June, and July 1953, Sabre pilots achieved 165 aerial victories with only three losses—a magnificent achievement.

The war ended not in victory or defeat, but with the armistice of July 27, 1953. The number of Chinese and North Korean troops killed is unknown, but estimates range between 1.5 and 2 million, in addition to at least a million civilians killed. South Korean civilian casualties probably equaled those of North Korea. United States losses were 142,091 casualties, including 33,629 deaths and 7,140 captured. USAF losses were fairly light, 1,841 casualties including 379 killed in action, 11 deaths from wounds, and 821 missing in action and presumed dead. In addition, 224 fliers were captured.

UN and U.S. action in the Korean War did succeed in confining communist rule to North Korea, but, beyond this, the conflict ended inconclusively.

Kunsan AB, Republic of Korea   See AIR FORCE BASES.

L

Lackland AFB, Texas   See AIR FORCE BASES.

Lafayette Escadrille
This celebrated WORLD WAR I unit of American volunteer aviators was originally a French unit staffed by U.S. volunteers and commanded by a French officer and assistant. It was officially designated N. 124 when it flew the Nieuport 28, and, later, S. 124 when it flew the Spad XIII. Its mission was reconnaissance, patrol, and fighter escort.

Lafayette Escadrille was mainly the brainchild of Bostonian Norman Prince, who had volunteered early in the war (1915) to fly for the French. (Prince would die in a night landing accident on October 12, 1916.) He lobbied his commanders to create an all-American flying unit, which was authorized on March 21, 1916. The French wanted to call it the "American Escadrille," but the requirements of U.S. neutrality prompted a name change to "Lafayette Escadrille." The unit was dispatched to the front in April 1916 and operated until February 1918, when it became the 103rd Aero Squadron and was placed fully under U.S. military control.

During the course of its service, the Lafayette Escadrille roster had 38 U.S. pilots, suffered approximately a 30 percent casualty rate (killed in action), and was credited with 37 victories—a middling record, and 17 of those kills were credited to a single pilot, Raoul Lufbery.

Lahm, Frank P.   (1877–1963) *U.S. Army pilot*
The first person to earn a pilot's rating in the first USAF antecedent organization, the AERONAUTICAL DIVISION, U.S. ARMY SIGNAL CORPS, Lahm flew BALLOONS as well as airplanes. He was born in Mansfield, Ohio, and graduated from the U.S. Military Academy at West Point in 1901. Eight years later, he soloed in an airplane, having already set an endurance record of one hour, 12 minutes in a flight with Orville Wright. Lahm later flew the Aeronautical Division's first flight cross country.

In WORLD WAR I, Lahm commanded balloon units and served on the General Staff during the major Saint-Mihiel and Meuse-Argonne offensives. In 1926, he was appointed assistant chief of the U.S. ARMY AIR CORPS and organized and trained the Air Corps Training Center. He retired in 1941 as chief of aviation for the First Army.

Lajes Field, Azores, Portugal   See AIR FORCE BASES.

Langley AFB, Virginia   See AIR FORCE BASES.

Laughlin AFB, Texas   See AIR FORCE BASES.

LeMay, Curtis Emerson (1906–1990) *Air Force general and Chief of Staff*

LeMay was born in Columbus, Ohio, and set out to obtain an appointment to West Point. When he was disappointed in this attempt, he enrolled at Ohio State University, leaving that institution in 1928, to join the army after having completed the ROTC program. In September, LeMay became a cadet in the U.S. ARMY AIR CORPS Flying School and earned his wings on October 12 of the following year. He was commissioned a second lieutenant in January 1930 and posted to the 27th Pursuit Squadron, headquartered in Michigan.

Under army sponsorship, LeMay spent several years completing the civil engineering degree he had begun at Ohio State. Awarded that degree in 1932, he was seconded by the army to the Depression-era CCC (Civilian Conservation Corps) public works program, and he flew the air mails when President Franklin D. Roosevelt assigned Army fliers to air mail operations in 1934. After promotion to first lieutenant in June 1935, LeMay attended an over-water navigation school in Hawaii. In 1937, he transferred from pursuit planes to the 305th Bombardment Group at Langley Field, Virginia, and became involved in exercises demonstrating the ability of aircraft to find ships at sea.

Curtis LeMay was one of the first army pilots to fly the new B-17 bomber. He led a flight of them on a goodwill tour to Latin America during 1937–38. After returning from this tour, he attended the Air Corps Tactical School (1938–39) and, in January 1940, was promoted to captain and given command of a squadron in 34th Bomb group. In 1941, he was promoted to major. With the U.S. entry into WORLD WAR II following Pearl Harbor (December 7, 1941), promotion came even faster. By January 1942, LeMay was a lieutenant colonel, and three months later was promoted to colonel. At this point, in April, he assumed command of the 305th Bombardment Group in California and brought that unit to Britain as part of what became the EIGHTH AIR FORCE.

Once in place in Britain, LeMay set about improving precision bombing tactics by the extremely

Curtis LeMay   *(U.S. Air Force)*

risky means of abandoning evasive maneuvering over targets and by also introducing careful target studies prior to missions. The combination of these tactics soon doubled the number of bombs placed on target, and, in June 1943, LeMay was assigned to command the 3rd Bombardment Division, which he led on the so-called shuttle raid against Regensburg in August. The following month, LeMay was promoted to temporary brigadier general, followed by promotion to temporary major general in March 1944. He was then sent to China to lead the 20th Bomber Command against the Japanese.

LeMay took command of the 21st Bomber Group on Guam in January 1945. He stunned his air crews by modifying their B-29s to carry more bombs, stripping the aircraft of defensive guns (as well as gun crews and ammunition). LeMay further ordered the aircraft to attack targets not in formation but singly, and at low level. Crews feared a heavy casualty toll, but, remarkably, their survival rate actually improved, and bombing effectiveness was dramatically increased. Under LeMay's command, the 21st annihilated four major Japanese cities—including Tokyo—with incendiary bombs. Indeed, LeMay's fire-bombing raids were far more immediately destructive than the atomic bombing of Hiroshima and Nagasaki.

As the war drew to a conclusion in the Pacific, LeMay was named commander of the TWENTIETH AIR FORCE in July 1945 and then deputy chief of staff for research and development, a post he held through 1947. In that year, he was promoted to temporary lieutenant general in the newly independent USAF and was given command of the UNITED STATES AIR FORCES IN EUROPE (USAFE) on October 1, 1947. LeMay was a key planner in the great BERLIN AIRLIFT of 1948–49, which kept Berlin supplied during the Soviet blockade of the city.

In October 1948, LeMay returned to the United States as head of the newly created STRATEGIC AIR COMMAND (SAC), the USAF unit tasked with waging nuclear and thermonuclear war. Under LeMay, the USAF greatly expanded and entered the jet age with B-47 and B-52 bombers and in-air refueling tankers (KC-135s). By the 1950s, LeMay oversaw the introduction of ICBM (INTERCONTINENTAL BALLISTIC MISSILE) weapons into the USAF inventory of strategic hardware. He was promoted to general in October 1951, becoming the youngest four-star general since Ulysses S. Grant.

In 1957, Curtis LeMay was named vice chief of staff of the air force and became CHIEF OF STAFF, USAF, in 1961. During the 1960s, his hard-nosed conservatism frequently brought him into conflict with the administrations of John F. Kennedy and Lyndon Johnson, and his relations with Secretary of Defense Robert S. McNamara were strained and, at times, bitter. LeMay never mellowed; rather, he became increasingly irascible, and, on February 1, 1965, he retired from the USAF. His political conservatism drove him to become the running mate of segregationist George Wallace in his failed 1968 bid for the presidency. It was an

association that, many felt, tarnished LeMay's remarkable career.

An uncompromising commander, LeMay always demanded "maximum effort" from his air crews and from their aircraft. He was also a forward-thinking planner who shaped the modern USAF and established its place as the most strategic of the three services. The modern doctrines of precision bombing and strategic bombing (see BOMBING, STRATEGIC) were largely his work, and it was under his leadership that the USAF was ushered into both the jet age and the nuclear age.

lieutenant colonel   See RANKS AND GRADES.

lieutenant general   See RANKS AND GRADES.

literature, USAF portrayed in

Like movie makers (see FILMS, USAF PORTRAYED IN), novelists have seen the air arm as an exciting subject for fiction. The first notable air service fiction was written by Elliott White Springs, who achieved ace status flying with the U.S. ARMY AIR SERVICE in WORLD WAR I, and who published widely in magazines during the 1920s. During the 1920s and 1930s, popular magazines published a good deal of fiction portraying the air service in World War I. Novel-length fiction did not emerge until after WORLD WAR II, however. Important books include the 1947 *Command Decision,* by William Wister Haines, about the EIGHTH AIR FORCE. The "command decision" in question was whether to bomb a German jet aircraft factory, even though the mission was sure to result in terrible losses among bomber crews. Another Eighth Air Force story was *Twelve O'Clock High* from 1948. Written by Beirne Lay, Jr., and Sy Bartlett, the novel focused on the emotional toll of strategic bombing. Perhaps the most enduring of the immediate postwar air force novels was James Gould Cozzens's 1948 *Guard of Honor,* which concerned relationships among commanders and subordinates, with particular emphasis on racial tensions. The novel was awarded the Pulitzer Prize. The 1959 novel *The War Lover,* by John Hersey, author of the powerful documentary *Hiroshima,* was a best-selling antiwar treatment, again depicting the world of the Eighth Air Force.

The 1950s saw several important KOREAN WAR novels, including *Don't Touch Me* (1951) by MacKinlay Kantor and *MiG Alley* (1959) by Robert Eunson. But the decade also introduced novels speculating about war in the future—thermonuclear war. Peter Bryant's 1958 *Red Alert* was the first significant contribution to this genre, and the next decade saw the chilling *Fail-Safe* (1962), an imagination of a computer glitch that unleashes a thermonuclear catastrophe.

The general antiwar feeling of the 1960s produced several notable novels satirically hostile to the air arm, including Joseph Heller's *Catch-22* (1961), which was subsequently made into a motion picture, and *Dr. Strangelove, or How I Learned to Stop Worrying and Love the Bomb,* which, in 1964, was adapted into novel form from the Stanley Kubrick motion picture screenplay. The VIETNAM WAR gave rise to *Sweet Vietnam* (1984), by Richard Parque, and an important semi-documentary series by Cat Branigan, *Wings over Nam, The Wild Weasels, Linebacker,* and *Bird Dog,* all published between 1989 and 1990.

Little Rock AFB, Arkansas   See AIR FORCE BASES.

Los Angeles AFB, California   See AIR FORCE BASES.

Love, Nancy Harkness (1914–1976) *Aviator*

A prominent female aviator in the 1930s, Nancy Harkness Love successfully proposed the use of women as ferry pilots for the U.S. ARMY AIR FORCES and became director of the WOMEN'S AUXILIARY FERRYING SQUADRON (WAFS). Unlike JACQUELINE COCHRAN, whose similar proposal ultimately resulted in the creation of the WOMEN AIRFORCE SERVICE PILOTS (WASP), Love did not advocate training women pilots, but, rather, recruiting already highly qualified female commercial aviators.

Love came to flying early, earning her license at age 16 and working as an activist in the creation of student flying clubs. She earned her transport license at age 18 and her commercial license a year later, in 1933. With her husband, Robert Maclure Love, she operated Inter City Aviation and often personally delivered planes to customers. Love was a TEST PILOT in the later 1930s and was instrumental in the development of tricycle landing gear, which proved essential for medium and heavy bombers.

Love not only directed the WAFS, she personally flew ferrying missions and was the first woman in U.S. military aviation to fly a bomber, a B-25, taking it from the West Coast to the East Coast in record time. She was the recipient of the Air Medal.

Luke AFB, Arizona   See AIR FORCE BASES.

M

MAJCOM   See ORGANIZATION, USAF.

major   See RANKS AND GRADES.

major general   See RANKS AND GRADES.

Malmstrom AFB, Montana   See AIR FORCE BASES.

master sergeant   See RANKS AND GRADES.

Maxwell AFB, Alabama   See AIR FORCE BASES.

Maxwell AFB, Gunter Annex, Alabama See AIR FORCE BASES.

McChord AFB, Washington   See AIR FORCE BASES.

McClellan AFB, California   See AIR FORCE BASES.

McConnell AFB, Kansas   See AIR FORCE BASES.

McGuire AFB, New Jersey   See AIR FORCE BASES.

Medal for Humane Action   See DECORATIONS AND MEDALS.

Medal of Honor   See DECORATIONS AND MEDALS.

Military Airlift Command (MAC)

MAC was absorbed, with the STRATEGIC AIR COMMAND (SAC), into the AIR MOBILITY COMMAND (AMC) in June 1992. Before this, it was a MAJCOM in its own right, responsible for USAF AIRLIFT operations. MAC was headquartered at Scott AFB, which is now home to the AMC.

MAC's first predecessor organization was the Air Corps Ferrying Command (ACFC), created in May 1941, and the AIR TRANSPORT COMMAND (ATC), activated in July 1942. In 1948, ATC was redesignated the MILITARY AIR TRANSPORT SERVICE (MATS), which, in turn, became MAC in 1966. Up to 1974, MAC was responsible for strategic airlift; in 1974, it was also assigned a tactical airlift role.

Military Air Transport Service (MATS)

MATS was created in June 1948 when the AIR TRANSPORT COMMAND (ATC) was redesignated. The ATC had been created from Air Corps Ferrying Command in July 1942. The greatest test of MATS was the BERLIN AIRLIFT, beginning in 1948. MATS was redesignated the MILITARY AIRLIFT COMMAND (MAC) in 1966. In turn, MAC was absorbed (with the STRATEGIC AIR COMMAND [SAC]) into the AIR MOBILITY COMMAND (AMC) in June 1992.

Minot AFB, North Dakota   See AIR FORCE BASES.

Misawa AB, Japan   See AIR FORCE BASES.

missiles, strategic

The USAF is an aerospace force, with an arsenal that includes manned aircraft as well as unmanned missiles. Strategic missiles are those designed to carry nuclear and thermonuclear warheads. A missile capable of intercontinental range is an ICBM (INTERCONTINENTAL BALLISTIC MISSILE), while a missile of shorter, but still strategic, range is an IRBM (INTERMEDIATE-RANGE BALLISTIC MISSILE).

Navaho: This early USAF missile project was inspired by the German V-1 and V-2 rockets of WORLD WAR II. The Navaho was to combine the CRUISE MISSILE characteristics of the V-1 with the ballistic missile characteristics of the V-2, principally by adding wings to what was essentially a V-2 body and combining a ramjet with a booster engine. The object was to give a cruise missile intercontinental range.

North American Aviation produced the Navaho prototype, which first flew in 1956—unsuccessfully. After 11 more attempts, the missile did fly in 1957, but the program was cancelled before any Navahos went into production. Had it reached production, the Navaho was intended to achieve a 5,500-mile range carrying a 7,000-pound warhead.

Jupiter: The Jupiter was designed in the 1950s as an IRBM not by the USAF but by the Army Ballistic Missile Agency (ABMA); it was designated SM-78. Late in 1955, Secretary of Defense Charles E. Wilson directed the ABMA to work in conjunction with the U.S. Navy to develop both a land-based and a sea-based version of the Jupiter, but in 1956, Wilson transferred to USAF control all missiles with a range of over 200 miles. In fact, the Jupiter became something of an orphan under USAF control because its development had competed with the USAF-developed Thor. Nevertheless, it would be the Jupiter that became the nation's first IRBM.

Jupiter was built by Chrysler, which began delivery to the USAF in 1957. The first test occurred on April 26 of that year. The missile was retired in 1964.

In addition to its role as a weapon, the Jupiter led to the development of the *Juno I* rocket, which launched America's first satellite into orbit. Approximately 60 feet long, the Jupiter had a range of 1,976 miles.

Thor (SM-75, PGM-17): Development of this IRBM began in November 1955, leading to an intense rivalry between USAF and U.S. Army missile programs. Douglas Aircraft completed design of the missile in July 1956 and delivery began in October. Fuel was liquid oxygen/RP-1 (kerosene), which produced 150,000 pounds of thrust at launch through two Rocketdyne vernier engines. However, the first four test launches, beginning on January 25, 1957, failed. It was 1959 before Thor was declared operational. Thor missiles served until 1965. The 65-foot-long Thor had a range of 1,976 miles.

Atlas: With a range 11,500 miles (Atlas E and F), the Atlas was the first U.S. ICBM. Built by General Dynamics, the missile was operational with the USAF from 1958 to 1965. The first three versions, A, B, and C, were test vehicles only; D, E, and F were the operational models.

The Atlas pioneered a unique, two-booster propulsion system and a super-thin, frameless propellant tank. Fuel was a mixture of RP-1 (kerosene) and liquid oxygen. In addition to its role as a nuclear weapons platform, the Atlas launched the first American astronauts into orbit, beginning with John Glenn.

Titan: In 1955 a decision was made to develop a successor to the Atlas ICBM. The two major improvements desired were a two-stage propulsion system and a self-stabilized light alloy frame that would not need to be pressurized to remain rigid. The missile also used a pure inertial guidance system and was designed to be housed in underground silos exclusively. Built by Martin Marietta, the result was the biggest (98 feet long) ICBM in the USAF inventory, capable of a range of 8,000 miles.

The first test launch was made on February 6, 1959, and the missile became operational at Lowry AFB, Colorado, on April 18, 1962. The Titan I fleet was deactivated by 1966 and replaced by the Titan II. Unlike the Titan I, which was stored in an underground silo but lifted out for launch, the Titan II was launched directly from the silo. It used a new fuel, hydrazine and unsymmetrical dimetheylhydrazine plus nitrogen tetroxide, which significantly increased thrust. The Titan II could deliver a 10-megaton thermonuclear warhead over 9,300 miles.

Skybolt: Designated GAM-87A, the Skybolt was an air-launched ballistic missile, designed to be carried by B-52H bombers. Douglas Aircraft began design in 1959, and the first launch came in 1961. Although the missile was successful, the Skybolt program was cancelled in December 1962 before full production began. The missile had a range of 1,000 miles.

Snark (SM-62): The Snark was designed as a ground-launched intercontinental cruise missile. North American began design in 1946, basing the missile on a German World War II prototype, the A-10, which had never entered production. The first flight came in 1951, but, because of multiple test failures, the Snark did not enter service until 1961. It was retired before the end of the year, 30 having been built. The idea of an intercontinental cruise missile was replaced by reliance on the ICBM for long-range delivery of nuclear weapons.

Snark was subsonic, with a top speed of 524 mph and a range of 6,000 miles.

Minuteman: The Minuteman was the world's first solid-fuel ICBM, and, in its LGM-30G Minuteman III configuration, it remains a key element of the U.S. strategic deterrent forces. The Minuteman was designed by Boeing beginning in the late 1950s, and the first Minuteman I was launched on February 1, 1961. The solid-fuel Minuteman reacts much more quickly than earlier liquid-fuel missiles, making it more survivable in a thermonuclear exchange. At its peak, about 1,000 Minuteman missiles were deployed; today's inventory consists of 500 Minuteman III's located at Warren AFB, Malmstrom AFB, and Minot AFB.

The Minuteman III has three solid-propellant rocket motors and is capable of flying more than 6,000 miles at about 15,000 mph (Mach 23). Ceiling is 700 miles. Production ended in December 1978.

Peacekeeper (MX): Development of this four-stage ICBM began in 1972 and was designated "ICBM Missile-X," or "MX," a name that stuck. The principal purpose of the missile was as a counterforce hard-target weapon: a missile to kill enemy missile silos. A MIRV (multiple independent reentry vehicle) weapon, the MX was designed to carry 10 independently targeted thermonuclear warheads. First flight came in 1983, and, after much controversy over how and where the MX would be based, the missiles were deployed in converted Minuteman silos at Warren AFB in October 1986. By December 1988, all 50 MX missiles in the USAF inventory had been deployed. Range is nearly 7,000 miles at a velocity of 15,000 mph (Mach 23) and a ceiling of 500 miles. Under the terms of the START II arms-reduction treaty, the Peacekeeper missile was slated for retirement, but renegotiation of the weapons-reduction agreement modified this goal to reduction rather than elimination.

AGM-86B Air-Launched Cruise Missile (ALCM): Boeing's ALCM is equipped with a nuclear warhead and can be launched from the B-52 or the

B-1B. Between 1980 and 1986, 1,715 were produced. Speed is 550 mph, range 1,500 miles.

missiles, tactical

Tactical missiles are of relatively short-range—compared with IRBM (INTERMEDIATE-RANGE BALLISTIC MISSILE) and ICBM (INTERCONTINENTAL BALLISTIC MISSILE) weapons—and carry conventional (nonnuclear) warheads or relatively low-yield (tactical) nuclear warheads. Weapons of this type may be launched from aircraft against other aircraft (air-to-air), from aircraft to surface targets (air-to-surface), from the surface to air (surface-to-air), or from the surface to surface (surface-to-surface).

Air Decoy Missile (ADM)
and Air-Ground Missiles (AGM)

ADM-20 Quail: This Air Decoy Missile was built by McDonnell, first flew in 1958, and entered service in 1960. Designed to be launched from the B-52, the Quail was intended to decoy enemy radar by mimicking the actions of the B-52. It had no warhead. The missile was retired in 1978.

AGM-12 Bullpup: Martin Marietta's Bullpup entered service in 1959 as an air-to-surface guided missile capable of delivering a conventional or nuclear warhead or a special antipersonnel warhead. During the Vietnam era, it was replaced by the AGM-6 Maverick. Speed was Mach 1.8, range 10 miles.

AGM-28 Hound Dog: This early CRUISE MISSILE was built by North American Aviation and was designed to be launched from a B-52; two Hound Dogs could be carried under the bomber's wings. The Hound Dog's engines were used to assist B-52 takeoff, thereby compensating for its own weight. The missile entered service in 1960 and was retired in 1976. It reached Mach 2.1 and had a 700-mile range.

AGM-45 Shrike: Designed and built by the Naval Weapons Center, the Shrike was an early antiradar or antiradiation missile, designed to passively home in on enemy radar. The AGM-45 was used by the USAF in the VIETNAM WAR, launched

from F-105G Wild Weasels. Production stopped in 1978, by which time some 12,000 had been received into the USAF inventory. It is still in use by the USAF and the U.S. Marine Corps. Range is about 25 miles.

AGM-65 Maverick: This air-to-surface missile is extensively used by the USAF and allied air forces. Developed by Hughes Missiles Systems Group in the 1970s (first delivered in 1972), it is expected to be in use well into the 21st century. The "D" version of the missile is especially designed to work with the LANTIRN (Low-Altitude Navigation and Targeting Infrared Night) sight used on the F-16. The "G" version uses infrared and improved flight controls. Both the D and G versions are still in production. Range is about 14 miles.

AGM-69 Short-Range Attack Missile (SRAM): Boeing's air-to-surface SRAM was produced from 1971 to 1975 and acquired in a quantity of about 1,500. Designed to be launched from B-52s and other bombers, the AGM-69 strikes SAM (surface-to-air missile) sites and other ground targets. Speed is Mach 2.5; range from high altitude is 100 miles, from low altitude, 35 miles.

AGM-78 Standard Antiradiation Missile (Standard ARM): Built by General Dynamics, the missile went into production in 1968 and was intended, like the AGM-45 Shrike, as an antiradar or antiradiation air-to-surface missile. The missile was not produced in large numbers and was retired in 1986. Top speed was Mach 2; range was 15 miles.

AGM-84A-1 Harpoon: This antiship missile, made by McDonnell Douglas, was designed for the U.S. Navy, but it was also adopted by the USAF in the mid 1980s. It can be launched from ships, submarines, or aircraft—although the only USAF aircraft equipped to carry it is the B-52. With a high subsonic speed, it has a range of nearly 60 miles.

AGM-88A High-Speed Antiradiation Missile (HARM): This Texas Instruments HARM missile homes in on enemy radar and destroys it. It was first deployed in 1986 against Libya. Top speed is Mach 2, and range is over 10 miles.

AGM-129A Advanced Cruise Missile (ACM): Built by General Dynamics, the AGM-129 was developed from the AGM-109 Tomahawk and is intended to deliver a conventional or tactical nuclear (200-kiloton) warhead. The missile incorporates advanced stealth technology, so that it is virtually impossible to detect by radar or other means. Range is 1,550 miles and propulsion is by a turbofan jet.

AGM-131A Short-Range Attack Missile (SRAM II): The Boeing SRAM II replaces the AGM-69 and is designed to be carried in rotary launchers on B-52, B-1, and B-2 bombers. The ground-attack missile incorporates stealth and a laser inertial guidance system.

AGM-136A Tacit Rainbow: The Northrup Ventura AGM-136A was designed in the early 1980s as a jet-powered drone for finding and destroying enemy ground-based radars. The vehicle was intended for low-cost production, so that it could be used in great numbers—"swarms"—against dense enemy air defense networks. Once launched, the missile traveled to the target area, then "loitered" until it sensed enemy radar transmission. This triggered attack.

The first Tacit Rainbow was test launched on July 30, 1984, but the missile failed to reach production before the program was cancelled for budget reasons in 1991. Speed was subsonic and range was in excess of 50 miles.

AGM-142A Have Nap: The Have Nap is a USAF version of the Israeli-made air-to-surface Popeye guided missile and was acquired in 1988. The missile is guided by television and is launched and guided from the B-52. Range is 50 miles.

Air Interceptor Missiles (AIM)

AIM-4 Falcon and Super Falcon: The Falcon was the world's first air-launched guided (SARH, semiactive radar homing) missile. Built by Hughes, it became operational in 1956 and was launched from F-89 and F-102 aircraft. The Super Falcon improved range and accuracy. The Super Falcon was not retired until 1988. Top speed was Mach 2.5 over a range of seven miles.

AIM-7 Sparrow: The AIM-7 is used by the U.S. Navy, the USAF, and NATO forces. Made by Raytheon, it is radar-guided and, in its earliest version, was developed in the 1950s. The AIM-7M is the latest version and is widely used. Most of its specifications are classified.

AIM-9 Sidewinder: The Sidewinder is the most successful air-to-air missile in the USAF inventory

An F-16C Fight Falcon fires an AIM-9M Sidewinder heat-seeking missile. *(U.S. Air Force)*

and is the most important air-to-air missile ever made. Production has approached 200,000 units, and it is used by all the U.S. services as well as by many foreign countries. It was developed by General Dynamics in the early 1950s, first flew in 1953, and entered USAF service in 1956. It is supersonic and heat seeking. The current version is the AIM-9M, and, despite the age of the basic design, it is expected to serve well into the 21st century. Top speed is in excess of Mach 2, with a range of more than 10 miles.

AIM-120 Advanced Medium-Range Air-to-Air Missile (AMRAAM): Faster, smaller and lighter than the AIM-7 Sidewinder, and with improved capabilities against low-altitude targets, the AIM-120 is intended as a follow-on replacement for the AIM-7. With all-weather, beyond-visual-range capability, the missile can be carried by the F-15, F-16, and F-22 fighters. It uses active radar with an inertial reference unit and microcomputer system, so that, once the missile closes on a target, its active radar guides it to intercept. This gives the pilot the ability to aim and fire several missiles simultaneously at multiple targets. While the missiles guide themselves to their targets, the pilot can perform any necessary evasive maneuvers.

Hughes Aircraft and Raytheon developed the missile, which began production in 1987 and was deployed beginning in 1991. It was used in Operation Southern Watch and in Bosnia. Speed is supersonic.

Air-Intercept Rocket (AIR)

Air-2A Genie: This air-intercept rocket was developed by Douglas Aircraft in 1955 to be launched from the F-106. It was mated with a small nuclear warhead. The rocket can best be described as a semi-guided weapon: the system acquired a target, computed a launch point and flight time, programmed a timer within the missile, alerted the pilot to arm the warhead, then fired the missile at the correct time. The Genie went out of service with the F-106, which was retired in 1988. Speed was Mach 3 and range six miles.

Other Tactical Missiles

BGM-109G Gryphon Ground-Launched Cruise Missile (GLCM): This small cruise missile, built by General Dynamics, carried a 200-kiloton tactical nuclear warhead. It was designed to be launched from a mobile launcher and was capable of great accuracy, flying at low altitudes and high subsonic speeds. The first GLCMs were deployed as part of the NATO defense of Europe beginning in 1983. This deployment was highly controversial and was instrumental in bringing about the Intermediate Nuclear Forces (INF) Treaty between the United States and the USSR—the first nuclear forces reduction in history. Under the terms of the 1988 treaty, all USAF GLCMs were eliminated. Speed was about 500 mph and range 1,500 miles.

GBU-15: Built by Rockwell International, the GBU-15 is a Guided Bomb Unit used to convert an Mk-84 bomb into a guided weapon.

IM-99 BOMARC: Produced in the late 1950s, this "interceptor missile" was the product of design research carried out by Boeing Airplane Company and the University of Michigan's Aeronautical Research Center—hence, the name BOMARC. It was a ground-launched interceptor and figured as an important element in the defense of the continental United States. The missile was retired during the early 1970s. Top speed exceeded Mach 2, ceiling was 80,000 feet, and range over 400 miles—all of which made the BOMARC effective against incoming bombers.

JB-2 Loon: An early step in the USAF cruise missile program, the JB-2 was a copy of the World War II German V-1 buzz bomb and began development, under the U.S. ARMY AIR FORCES, in 1944. Willys-Overland, the jeep manufacturer, was awarded a contract for 50,000 JB-2s, but none reached production before the end of the war. Most of the planned production was cancelled, and those produced were used as target drones (designated KUW-1).

TM-61 Matador and Mace: This air-breathing, turbojet-propelled cruise missile was designed by the Glenn L. Martin Company in 1945, The first flight (unsuccessful) came in 1949, and the missiles were deployed to Europe during 1955–62. The original Matador guidance system was subject to jamming, and the missile had a very limited range of 250 miles. The TM-61B Mace, introduced in 1954, substantially improved the guidance system and greatly extended range to 1,288 miles at high altitude (ceiling, 42,000 feet). Top speed for the Mace was Mach 0.85. The Mace was deployed in Europe from 1959 to 1966 and in Okinawa from 1961 to 1969.

Mitchell, William ("Billy") (1879–1936)
U.S. Army general and military aviation advocate

Mitchell was born, in Nice, France, to John Lendrum Mitchell, who later became U.S. senator from Wisconsin. Young Mitchell was raised in Milwaukee and educated at Racine University and Columbian (later George Washington) University, then enlisted in the 1st Wisconsin Infantry at the outbreak of the Spanish-American War in 1898. He fought in Cuba, rising to lieutenant of volunteers and was subsequently commissioned a lieutenant in the regular army. Assigned to the Signal Corps, he attended the Army Staff College at Fort Leavenworth, Kansas, from 1907 to 1909, then served for a short time on the Mexican border before securing an assignment to the General Staff in 1912. Three years later, Mitchell resigned the coveted staff post to join the AVIATION SECTION, U.S. ARMY SIGNAL CORPS. Enrolling in flight school at Newport News, Virginia, he earned his wings in 1916 and was immediately sent to Europe as an observer. In April 1917, with U.S. entry into WORLD WAR I, Mitchell was appointed air officer of the American Expeditionary Force (AEF) and promoted to lieutenant colonel in June. In May 1918, he became air officer of I Corps with the rank of colonel and was the first U.S. officer to fly over enemy lines.

Mitchell's principal command was large-scale bombing. In September 1918 he led a successful Franco-American bombing mission consisting of 1,500 aircraft—the greatest number of planes ever massed to that time—against the Saint-Mihiel

Billy Mitchell   *(U.S. Air Force)*

salient. The mission demonstrated the utility of air support of ground action. Appointed next to command the combined Franco-American air services for the Meuse-Argonne offensive and promoted to brigadier general, Mitchell led another massive formation against targets behind enemy lines on October 9.

After the armistice, Mitchell was named assistant chief of the U.S. ARMY AIR SERVICE in 1919, and he embarked on an intensely heated and controversial campaign to create a separate and independent air force. Beyond this, Mitchell was also a vocal advocate of unified control of military air power. Even more than his call for an independent air arm, his advocacy of unified control put him at odds with the military establishment. Of a confrontational disposition, Mitchell tweaked navy officials by boasting that the airplane had rendered the battleship obsolete. He purported to demonstrate this by bombing the captured German dreadnought *Ostfriesland* and sinking it in 21 1/2 minutes in 1921. To the credit of the navy, officials responded to the demonstration by conducting further tests, which initiated the navy's development of the aircraft carrier as an offensive weapon.

In the meantime, Mitchell continued a relentless campaign for enlargement of the present USAAS and the eventual creation of an independent air force. Frustrated superiors attempted to discourage and block Mitchell by demoting him to colonel and reducing his command responsibility to an assignment as air officer of the VIII Corps area in San Antonio, Texas (in April 1925). With single-minded dedication, however, he refused to back down. On the contrary, he fanned the flames of controversy by appealing directly to the press.

When the navy dirigible *Shenandoah* crashed in a thunderstorm on September 3, 1925, Mitchell went to the papers with accusations of War and Navy Department "incompetency, criminal negligence, and almost treasonable administration of the National Defense." This "betrayal" proved to be the last straw. Mitchell was court-martialed and, in a highly publicized trial, was convicted of insubordination in December 1925. Sentenced to five years' suspension from duty without pay, Mitchell decided to resign his commission, effective February 1, 1926. A private citizen, he continued to speak out on air power from his Middleburg, Virginia, home.

As an advocate and strategist in the field of military air power, Billy Mitchell was clearly ahead of his time. WORLD WAR II, which Mitchell did not live to see, proved most of his theories true, including his remarkable (and much derided) assessment, made in the 1920s, that the navy's fleet at Pearl Harbor in the Hawaiian Islands was vulnerable to a carrier-launched air attack and that the attack would be made by Japan.

Working against Mitchell was his almost deliberately caustic and provocative manner, and it was not until after his death that his positions were largely vindicated. He was—posthumously—recognized as one of the founding fathers of U.S. air

power in general and the USAF in particular. His memory was honored in World War II when the twin-engine B-25 bomber, one of the ablest aircraft of the conflict, was named for him: the Mitchell bomber.

Moody AFB, Georgia   See AIR FORCE BASES.

Mountain Home AFB, Idaho   See AIR FORCE BASES.

museums, USAF

The principal USAF museum is the UNITED STATES AIR FORCE MUSEUM at Wright-Patterson AFB, the oldest and largest aviation museum in the world, established in 1923 (and given its current name in 1956). More than 300 aircraft are on display at the museum, which is dedicated to the history of flight in general and military aviation in particular.

Other USAF museums include:

- Davis-Monthan AFB Museum, Davis-Monthan AFB, Arizona
- AF Flight Test Center Museum, Edwards AFB, California
- Castle AFB Museum, Castle AFB, California
- 475 Fighter Group Museum, March AFB, California
- Travis AFB Museum, Travis AFB, California
- Air Force Academy Visitors Center, UNITED STATES AIR FORCE ACADEMY, Colorado
- Peterson AFB Museum, Peterson AFB, Colorado
- Air Mobility Command Museum, Dover AFB, Delaware
- USAF Armament Museum, Eglin AFB, Florida
- Museum of Aviation, Warner Robins AFB, Georgia
- Reflections of Freedom Air Park, McConnell AFB, Kansas
- Eighth Air Force Museum, Barksdale AFB, Louisiana

- Sawyer AFB Museum, Sawyer AFB, Michigan
- National Aviation Hall of Fame, Wright-Patterson AFB, Ohio
- Museum of Aerospace Medicine, Brooks AFB, Texas
- Hill AFB Museum, Hill AFB, Utah

In addition to museums administered by the USAF, many aviation museums located throughout the United States are run by civilian organizations or by other military services. Many of these include material relevant to the history and present operations of the USAF.

mustang

Slang term for a noncommissioned officer with prior enlisted service.

N

named air forces   See ORGANIZATION, USAF.

National Security Act of 1947

The National Security Act reorganized the Department of Defense, providing for unification of the armed forces, and created the USAF as an independent service. The law went into effect as Public Law 253, on July 26, 1947, the same day that President Harry S. Truman signed EXECUTIVE ORDER 9877, which addressed the administrative details and missions of the unified armed forces and the newly created USAF. Pursuant to the act, the USAF came into existence on September 18, 1947.

The National Security Act and the executive order provided for a single secretary of defense; the Department of the Army, the Department of the Navy, and the Department of the Air Force; the creation of a National Security Council, a National Security Resources Board, the Joint Chiefs of Staff, a Research and Development Board, a Munitions Board, and the Central Intelligence Agency, in addition to the creation of the USAF.

Nellis AFB, Nevada   See AIR FORCE BASES.

Newark AFB, Ohio   See AIR FORCE BASES.

"New Look" Air Force

The "New Look" was a term applied to all of the armed services pursuant to a reevaluation of the role of the military during the administration of President Dwight David Eisenhower in the 1950s. The "New Look" Air Force emphasized strategic (i.e., nuclear) operations and, as such, fostered development of a strategic bomber (the B-52) and an array of ICBM (INTERCONTINENTAL BALLISTIC MISSILE) weapons. General Nathan F. Twining, fourth CHIEF OF STAFF, USAF, from 1953 to 1957, oversaw the introduction and early development of the New Look.

Nineteenth Air Force (19AF)

Formed in 1955 at Foster AFB, Texas, the 19AF was a subcommand of the TACTICAL AIR COMMAND (TAC). In 1958, 19AF headquarters moved to Seymour Johnson AFB. The unit was inactivated in 1973. 19AF was intended as a mobile task force headquarters for the Composite Strike Force, a special force combining the services for response to crises. In addition, 19AF conducted joint field training with the U.S. Army.

Ninth Air Force (9AF)

This unit was formed during WORLD WAR II, in November 1942, from what had been designated as the Middle East Air Force. The 9AF operated B-17 and B-24 bomber aircraft and P-40 fighter escorts. Later, F-47s and P-38s were added. Until it moved to England late in 1943, the 9AF supported Allied actions in North Africa and then Sicily. The unit played a major role in supporting the Normandy invasion ("D-day") during 1944 and was instrumental in supporting the spectacular breakout and advance of George S. Patton's Third Army. At the time of its inactivation in December 1945, 9AF was the largest tactical air force in the world.

In March 1946, 9AF was reactivated and has since served as a tactical unit. Today the 9AF is part of CENTAF and is headquartered at Shaw AFB, South Carolina. The unit is responsible for six active-duty flying wings and for overseeing the operational readiness of 30 designated units of the AIR NATIONAL GUARD and AIR FORCE RESERVE. The primary mission of today's 9AF is to project decisive air and space power for United States Central Command and America; 9AF has the dual role of serving also as the headquarters for U.S. Central Command Air Forces to conduct U.S. air operations throughout Southwest Asia.

North American Aerospace Defense Command (NORAD)

NORAD—the North American Aerospace Defense Command—is a binational U.S. and Canadian military organization charged with the missions of aerospace warning and aerospace control for North America. The aerospace warning mission includes monitoring artificial objects in space as well as the detection, validation, and warning of attack against North America by aircraft, missiles, or space vehicles. The aerospace control mission includes surveillance and control of the airspace of Canada and the United States.

NORAD is under command of a commander in chief (CINC) appointed by both the president of the United States and the prime minister of Canada. The CINC maintains headquarters at Peterson AFB, Colorado, with a command and control center nearby at Cheyenne Mountain Air Station. It is Cheyenne Mountain that serves as the

central collection and coordination facility for a worldwide system of sensors that provide an accurate picture of any aerospace threat. In addition, three subordinate regional headquarters at Elmendorf AFB, Alaska (Alaska NORAD Region, ANR), Canadian Forces Base Winnipeg, Manitoba (Canadian NORAD Region, CANR), and Tyndall AFB, Florida (Continental U.S. NORAD Region, CONR) control air operations within their geographical areas of responsibility.

NORAD provides to the governments of Canada and the United States integrated tactical warning and attack assessment of an aerospace attack on North America. NORAD's aerospace control mission includes detecting and responding to any air-breathing threat to North America. NORAD uses a network of ground-based radars and fighter aircraft to detect, intercept, and engage any air-breathing threat to the continent. NORAD also assists civilian agencies in the detection and monitoring of aircraft suspected of illegal drug trafficking.

NORAD was activated on September 12, 1957, and superceded earlier U.S.-Canadian binational defense and early warning programs known as the Pinetree Line (a network of radar stations), followed in 1957 by the Mid-Canada Line and the DEW Line, or distant early warning system.

Northeast Air Command (NEAC)

NEAC was established as a MAJCOM in 1950 as a means of monitoring and intercepting Soviet transpolar air attacks on the United States. The predecessor organization was the Newfoundland Base Command, which started operations in WORLD WAR II. NEAC worked in cooperation with Canada and Denmark and operated Thule AFB in Greenland. In 1957, NEAC was inactivated, its mission and resources divided between the AIR DEFENSE COMMAND (ADC) and the STRATEGIC AIR COMMAND (SAC).

numbered air forces (NAFS)   See ORGANIZATION, USAF.

Offutt AFB, Nebraska   See AIR FORCE BASES.

organization, USAF

The DEPARTMENT OF THE AIR FORCE was created when President Harry S. Truman signed the NATIONAL SECURITY ACT OF 1947, which became effective on September 18, 1947, after Chief Justice Fred M. Vinson administered the oath of office to the first SECRETARY OF THE AIR FORCE, W. Stuart Symington. The National Security Act transferred the functions assigned to the U.S. ARMY AIR FORCES' commanding general to the Department of the Air Force over a two-year transfer period. Later, pursuant to the Department of Defense Reorganization Act of 1958, the departments of Army, Navy, and Air Force were eliminated from the chain of operational command, and commanders of unified and specified commands became responsible to the president and the secretary of defense through the Joint Chiefs of Staff.

The mission of the air force is to defend the United States and protect its interests through aerospace power. The Department of the Air Force incorporates all elements of the air force. It is administered by a civilian secretary appointed by the president and is supervised by a military CHIEF OF STAFF, USAF. The Secretariat and AIR STAFF help the secretary and the Chief of Staff direct the air force mission.

The secretary of the Air Force has authority to conduct all affairs of the Department of the Air Force, including training, operations, administration, logistical support and maintenance, and welfare of personnel. The secretary's responsibilities include research and development, as well as any other activity prescribed by the president or the secretary of defense. The secretary of the Air Force exercises authority through civilian assistants and the Chief of Staff but retains immediate supervision of activities that involve vital relationships with Congress, the secretary of defense, other governmental officials, and the public. Principal civilian assistants within the Secretariat are:

- Under Secretary of the Air Force
- Deputy Under Secretary for International Affairs
- Assistant Secretary for Acquisition
- Assistant Secretary for Space
- Assistant Secretary for Manpower, Reserve Affairs, Installations, and Environment
- Assistant Secretary for Financial Management

The Office of the Secretary of the Air Force includes a general counsel, auditor general, inspector general, administrative assistant, public affairs director, legislative liaison director, small and disadvantaged business utilization director, and certain statutory boards and committees.

The Chief of Staff, USAF, is appointed by the president, with the advice and consent of the Senate, from among air force general officers, normally for a four-year term. The Chief of Staff serves as a member of the Joint Chiefs of Staff and the Armed Forces Policy Council. As a member of the Joint Chiefs, the chief serves as a military adviser to the president, the National Security Council, and the secretary of defense, as well as to the secretary of the Air Force. The Chief of Staff presides over the Air Staff, transmits Air Staff plans and recommendations to the secretary of the Air Force, and acts as the secretary's agent in carrying them out. The chief is responsible for the efficiency of the USAF and the preparation of its forces for military operations. The chief supervises the administration of personnel and supervises support of forces as directed by the secretary of defense. In addition, the chief has responsibility for activities assigned to the air force by the secretary of defense.

Other members of the Air Staff include:

- Vice Chief of Staff
- Assistant Vice Chief of Staff
- CHIEF MASTER SERGEANT OF THE AIR FORCE
- Deputy Chief of Staff for Personnel
- Deputy Chief of Staff for Plans and Programs
- Deputy Chief of Staff for Air and Space Operations
- Deputy Chief of Staff for Installations and Logistics
- Air Force Historian
- Chief Scientist
- Chief of the AIR FORCE RESERVE
- Chief of the National Guard Bureau
- U.S. AIR FORCE SCIENTIFIC ADVISORY BOARD
- Judge Advocate General
- Director of Test and Evaluation
- Surgeon General
- Chief of Chaplain Service

Air Force Field Organization

Eight MAJCOMS (major commands), 35 field operating agencies, four direct reporting units, and their subordinate elements constitute the air force field organization. Additionally, there are two reserve components, the AIR FORCE RESERVE, which is also a MAJCOM, and the AIR NATIONAL GUARD.

MAJCOM (Major Command)

MAJCOMs, or major commands, are organizations that group similar functions together and provide a command level intermediate between base-level operations and HEADQUARTERS AIR FORCE (HAF). The MAJCOMs are organized by function and, in overseas areas, by geographical location. They perform either operational or support missions. Since major restructuring in 1991, the USAF currently has eight MAJCOMs, each of which is treated in a separate entry:

- AIR COMBAT COMMAND (ACC)
- AIR MOBILITY COMMAND (AMC)
- AIR FORCE SPACE COMMAND (AFSPC)
- PACIFIC AIR FORCES (PACAF)
- UNITED STATES AIR FORCES IN EUROPE (USAFE)
- AIR EDUCATION AND TRAINING COMMAND (AETC)
- AIR FORCE MATERIEL COMMAND (AFMC)
- AIR FORCE SPECIAL OPERATIONS COMMAND (AFSOC)

In descending order of command, elements of major commands include numbered air forces, wings, groups, squadrons, and flights.

Air Force

Until the air force underwent a major organizational restructuring in 1993, "air forces" were organizational units that equated to an "army" in the U.S. Army. They were subordinate to operational and support commands, but superior to a division. There have been numbered air forces and named air forces—as many as 23 numbered air forces and 13 named air forces. After 1993, only the numbered air forces (NAFs) were retained, and these were restructured for strictly warfighting and operational roles; all support functions were allocated elsewhere. Today, an NAF is typically commanded by a major general or lieutenant general, and its staff (about half the pre-1993 strength) is dedicated to operational planning and employment of forces for several wings within the NAF.

In the U.S. ARMY AIR FORCES, before the air force became an independent service arm (in

1947), the NAFS were the equivalent of today's MAJCOMs.

Named Air Forces

Formerly, air force organizational units consisted of numbered air forces and named air forces. The named air forces have been phased out, and only the numbered air forces continue to be used.

Numbered Air Forces (NAFs)

After restructuring of USAF organization during 1991–93, numbered air forces (NAFs) became strictly operational and warfighting units, without support functions. Two or more wings are typically grouped with auxiliary units to form a NAF, usually commanded by a major general or lieutenant general. There have been 23 numbered air forces.

Wing

The basic unit for generating and employing combat capability is the wing, the air force's principal war-fighting instrument. Composite wings operate more than one kind of aircraft, and they may be configured as self-contained units designated for quick air intervention anywhere in the world. Other wings continue to operate a single aircraft type, ready to join air campaigns anywhere they are needed. Air base and specialized mission wings— such as training, intelligence, and testing—also support the air force mission.

Group

A group is an organizational unit intermediate between a wing and a squadron. Typically, groups are identified with up to three Arabic digits, although a few specialized-mission groups are named for their mission and do not have a number. Groups under a wing carry the number of the wing followed by the group's task—for example, the unit responsible for maintenance functions within the 28th Bomb Wing may be designated the 28th Maintenance Group.

In the U.S. ARMY AIR FORCES, the distinction between group and wing was blurred, and a USAAF group was approximately equivalent to a USAAF wing.

Squadron

The squadron is subordinate to a group and superior to a flight. With the single exception of the USAF Demonstration Squadron (the THUNDER-BIRDS), air force squadrons are numbered (using Arabic numerals).

Flight

A flight is an operational flying unit generally consisting of four aircraft. The unit is typically used in fighter operations, in which it is composed of two two-airplane subunits, or elements.

The flight was extensively used as an operational unit during WORLD WAR II (it had been developed by German combat aviators in the 1930s during the Spanish Civil War) and well into the KOREAN WAR. In more recent years, by the late 1980s, faster, more maneuverable fighters called for a more flexible unit than the flight, and today the basic air force combat unit for fighters is the element.

Two alternative senses of *flight* are as a subordinate administrative unit of a squadron and as a term applied to certain units used in parades and ceremonies.

Element

An informal subunit, the element is able to operate by itself and, traditionally, has consisted of half a fighter flight—that is, two aircraft in formation, a

An F-15E pilot checks his wingman   *(U.S. Air Force)*

leader, and a wingman (follower). The element is a tactical team, in which the leader is the attacker and the wingman the defender, who covers the attacker and warns him of any threats. Generally, the senior pilot serves as the element leader, and the less experienced or less qualified pilot as wingman.

Field Operating Agencies and Direct Reporting Units

Field operating agencies and direct reporting units are additional air force organizational subdivisions, which report directly to Headquarters Air Force (HAF). They are assigned a specialized mission, which, in contrast to the mission of a MAJCOM, is restricted in scope. Field operating agencies carry out field activities under the operational control of a HAF functional manager, whereas direct reporting units are not under the operational control of a HAF manager because of a unique mission, legal requirements, or other factors.

The USAF field operating agencies include:

- AIR FORCE AUDIT AGENCY
- AIR FORCE BASE CONVERSION AGENCY
- AIR FORCE CENTER FOR ENVIRONMENTAL EXCELLENCE
- AIR FORCE CIVIL ENGINEER SUPPORT AGENCY
- AIR FORCE COMMUNICATIONS COMMAND
- AIR FORCE COST ANALYSIS AGENCY
- AIR FORCE FLIGHT STANDARDS AGENCY
- AIR FORCE FREQUENCY MANAGEMENT AGENCY
- AIR FORCE HISTORICAL RESEARCH AGENCY
- AIR FORCE HISTORY SUPPORT OFFICE
- AIR FORCE INSPECTION AGENCY
- AIR FORCE LEGAL SERVICES AGENCY
- AIR FORCE LOGISTICS MANAGEMENT AGENCY
- AIR FORCE MANPOWER AND INNOVATION AGENCY

- AIR FORCE MEDICAL OPERATIONS AGENCY
- AIR FORCE MEDICAL SUPPORT AGENCY
- AIR FORCE NATIONAL SECURITY EMERGENCY PREPAREDNESS Office
- AIR FORCE NEWS AGENCY
- AIR FORCE NUCLEAR WEAPONS AND COUNTERPROLIFERATION AGENCY
- AIR FORCE OFFICE OF SPECIAL INVESTIGATIONS
- AIR FORCE OPERATIONS GROUP
- AIR FORCE PENTAGON COMMUNICATIONS AGENCY
- AIR FORCE PERSONNEL CENTER
- AIR FORCE PERSONNEL OPERATIONS AGENCY
- AIR FORCE REAL ESTATE AGENCY
- AIR FORCE REVIEW BOARDS AGENCY
- AIR FORCE SAFETY CENTER
- AIR FORCE SECURITY FORCES CENTER
- AIR FORCE SERVICES AGENCY
- AIR FORCE STUDIES AND ANALYSES AGENCY
- AIR FORCE TECHNICAL APPLICATIONS CENTER
- AIR FORCE WEATHER AGENCY
- AIR INTELLIGENCE AGENCY
- AIR NATIONAL GUARD Readiness Center

Air force direct reporting units include:

- 11th Wing
- AIR FORCE DOCTRINE CENTER
- AIR FORCE OPERATIONAL TEST AND EVALUATION CENTER
- UNITED STATES AIR FORCE ACADEMY

Osan AB, Republic of Korea   See AIR FORCE BASES.

Outstanding Airman of the Year Ribbon
See DECORATIONS AND MEDALS.

P

Pacific Air Forces (PACAF)

PACAF is the chief air component of the U.S. Pacific Command (PACOM), a unified command of U.S. armed forces. The PACAF mission is to plan, conduct, control, and coordinate offensive and defensive air operations in the Pacific and Asian theaters, as well as arctic areas under U.S. control, encompassing Alaska and the west coast of the Americas to the east coast of Africa, and from the Arctic to the Antarctic. It is headquartered at Hickam AFB, Hawaii.

Patrick AFB, Florida   See AIR FORCE BASES.

Persian Gulf War

Background

The origin of the Persian Gulf War may be traced to August 2, 1990, after talks between Iraq and Kuwait failed to resolve a conflict over oil pricing. On that date, Iraq's president, Saddam Hussein, invaded Kuwait, a small, all-but-defenseless country when matched against its neighbor, which had the fifth-largest army in the world.

Operation Desert Shield Commences

On August 2, President George H. W. Bush proclaimed an economic embargo against Iraq, and United Nations Security Council action followed. When Saddam Hussein refused to withdraw from Kuwait, President Bush ordered the commencement of Operation Desert Shield on August 7. The action involved a buildup of U.S. and UN forces in the region that was intended ultimately to liberate Kuwait.

The operation was put under the direction of Headquarters U.S. Central Command (CENTCOM) and was commanded by U.S. Army general H. Norman Schwarzkopf. CENTCOM's immediate mission was to oversee and coordinate U.S. force deployment to the Persian Gulf and to ensure the security of Saudi Arabia as well as other Arab states. Supreme air command was assigned to USAF lieutenant general Charles A. Horner, who established Headquarters Central Command Air Forces (Forward) in Saudi Arabia. Five fighter squadrons, a contingent of AWACS, and part of the 82nd Airborne Division moved into the theater within five days. Twenty-five fighter squadrons flew nonstop to the theater, and, within 35 days, the USAF had deployed a fighter force equal in number to that of the Iraqi air force.

Late in August, President Bush authorized the call-up of reserves for active duty. The AIR FORCE RESERVE and AIR NATIONAL GUARD would play central roles in strategic and tactical AIRLIFT, in fighter and reconnaissance operations, and in flying tanker support.

As U.S. and coalition forces were built up and deployed, President Bush set a deadline of January 15, 1991, for the withdrawal of Iraqi forces from

Kuwait. When that deadline came and went, Operation Desert Shield entered the attack phase as Operation Desert Storm. The Persian Gulf War began.

Air Power Opens Operation Desert Storm

On January 16, 1991, coalition aircraft began the SURGICAL BOMBING of principal Iraqi military targets, including command and communications centers, missile launch sites, radar facilities, airports, and runways. Also targeted were Iraqi ground forces. Using highly advanced guided missile and smart bomb technologies and guided by AWACS and JOINT SURVEILLANCE TARGET ATTACK RADAR SYSTEM (JSTARS) aircraft, the air strikes were massive, but they were targeted precisely against military objectives. During the first 10 days of the war, 10,000 air sorties were flown. Within this brief time period, Iraq's nuclear, biological, and chemical weapons development programs were either destroyed or badly damaged, and its air defenses and offensive air and ballistic missile capability were drastically degraded. By February 25, after continual air attack, the ground war began. Within 100 hours, Kuwait had been liberated, and the Iraqi army was totally and unconditionally defeated.

Key Statistics

Operations Desert Shield and Desert Storm involved more than 55,000 USAF personnel in theater. In addition to executing the combat role, USAF engineers erected more than 5,000 tents, built buildings totaling more than 300,000 square feet, and laid more than 1,600,000 square feet of concrete and asphalt. The USAF deployed to the theater 15 air transportable hospitals with a total 750-bed capacity and one 1,250-bed contingency hospital.

For the first time, the USAF employed cutting-edge space and intelligence assets. Space support included the satellite-based Defense Meteorological Support Program, which accurately predicted weather—critical in Desert Storm, since during the period of the conflict the area experienced the worst weather in 14 years. It also included the

Global Positioning System (GPS), essential to accurate navigation to targets. The Defense Satellite Communications System provided secure voice and data communications for more than 100 ground terminals for Desert Shield/Desert Storm commanders.

USAF intelligence systems included the Mission Support System, which provided integrated mission planning support for USAF pilots. This system reduced mission planning from a matter of days to a total of four hours per mission. Another aspect of advanced USAF communication was tactical digital facsimile, which provided the capability to send high-resolution pictures and other data nearly in real time.

From the January 16, 1991, commencement of the offensive until the February 27 cease-fire, the USAF continuously deployed four AWACS aircraft to control more than 3,000 coalition sorties daily. Two JSTARS E-8 aircraft—at the time still in the late testing phase—were also deployed and supported all mission taskings. One of the two aircraft was in the air every day, its mission to track *every* vehicle that moved on the ground, and to identify and target Iraqi Scud missiles and launchers, convoys, trucks, tanks, surface-to-air missile sites, and artillery pieces.

USAF strategic airlift to the Persian Gulf was the largest since WORLD WAR II. By the time of the cease-fire, USAF airlifters had moved 482,000 passengers and 513,000 tons of cargo—the equivalent to repeating the 56-week BERLIN AIRLIFT every six weeks. Within theater, more than 145 C-130 aircraft were deployed to move units to forward bases. The tactical airlift aircraft flew 46,500 sorties and moved more than 209,000 people and 300,000 tons of supplies within the theater. During the 100 hours of the ground campaign, C-130s flew more than 500 sorties a day.

Air refueling operations during Operation Desert Shield and Operation Desert Storm were massive. The USAF deployed 256 KC-135 and 46 KC-10 tankers to the Persian Gulf.

AIR FORCE SPECIAL OPERATIONS COMMAND (AFSOC) units were also deployed to Desert

Air Force F-15 fighters fly over a Kuwait oil field that has been set ablaze by retreating Iraqi troops during the Gulf War, 1991.   *(Hulton/Archive)*

Storm, in which they performed such missions as infiltration, exfiltration, and resupply of Special Operations Forces teams on direct action missions. Also included among Special Operations responsibilities was the rescue of downed crew members, psychological operations broadcasts, the dropping of 15,000-pound "daisy cutter" antipersonnel bombs, and supporting counterterrorist missions.

Combat aircraft deployed during Operation Desert Shield and Desert Storm included 120 F-15C/Ds. Every Iraqi fixed-wing aircraft destroyed in air-to-air combat, including five Soviet-made MiG-29 Fulcrums, were downed by F-15Cs. No coalition aircraft were lost to Iraqi fighters. In addition, 48 F-15E Strike Eagles were deployed to the theater; two were lost in combat. The USAF sent 144 A-10s to the Persian Gulf. These flew 30 percent of the total USAF sorties, but they accounted for more than

half of the confirmed Iraqi equipment losses. In 8,000 sorties, five A-10s were lost in combat.

The F-117 Stealth Fighter flew more than 1,250 sorties, dropping more than 2,000 tons of bombs. These aircraft were assigned to bomb strategic targets in downtown Baghdad. No F-117 was damaged by enemy air defenses.

The venerable B-52 Stratofortress flew 1,624 missions and dropped more than 25,700 tons of ordnance on Kuwait and southern Iraq, hitting airfields, industrial targets, and storage areas—41 percent of all USAF bombs dropped during the conflict.

F-111F aircraft targeted chemical, biological, and nuclear sites, as well as airfields, bunkers, and command, control and communications facilities as well as parts of the integrated air defense system. In more than 4,000 sorties, only one F-111F was damaged by enemy air defenses.

Eighteen EF-111 Ravens were deployed to jam enemy radar. F-4G Wild Weasels—48 in number—flew 2,500 sorties with high-speed antiradar missiles (HARM), which effectively suppressed Iraqi use of radar. The F-16 Fighting Falcon was deployed in great numbers—249 aircraft—and flew in excess of 13,450 sorties, more than any other aircraft in the war.

From D-day to cease-fire, the USAF flew 59 percent of all sorties with 50 percent of the aircraft and had 37 percent of the losses. At the beginning of the conflict, coalition air forces faced Iraqi assets consisting of 750 combat aircraft, 200 support aircraft, Scud surface-to-surface missiles, chemical and biological weapon capability, excellent air defenses, 10 types of surface-to-air missiles, some 9,000 antiaircraft artillery pieces, and untold thousands of small arms. USAF fighters were credited with 36 of the 39 Iraqi fixed-wing aircraft and helicopters downed during Desert Storm. In all, Iraq lost 90 aircraft to coalition air forces; 122 were flown to Iran, making for a total loss of 234 aircraft. Beyond this, of Iraq's 594 hardened aircraft shelters, 375 were damaged or destroyed, and it is believed that 141 additional aircraft were destroyed within these shelters.

Peterson AFB, Colorado   See AIR FORCE
BASES.

Pope AFB, North Carolina   See AIR FORCE
BASES.

precision bombing   See SURGICAL BOMBING.

Project Blue Book

In the late 1940s, during a rash of public sightings
of unidentified flying objects (UFOs), the USAF
was tasked with investigating the phenomena. Best
known of its investigation programs was Project
Blue Book, the successor to three earlier programs,
Project Sign, Project Grudge, and Project Twinkle
(a suboperation under Project Grudge). From its
origin in Project Sign in 1947, until it was officially
shut down in 1969, Project Blue Book was the
focus of much UFO folklore, controversy, and even
conspiracy theory, as UFO enthusiasts saw Project
Blue Book as the nucleus of a government effort to
cover up information about UFOs and even visita-
tion and contact by extraterrestrials.

Project Blue Book (officially the Aerial Phenomena Group) was formally created in September 1951 and headquartered at Wright-Patterson
AFB. A small unit, it employed USAF electronics
and radar personnel, as well as civilian science
advisers from the Battelle Memorial Institute and
Ohio State University, in addition to Dr. J. Allen
Hynek, a Northwestern University astronomer and
the most highly respected student of UFO phenomena. Intelligence officers at USAF bases
throughout the world were ordered to report all
sightings to Blue Book, and Blue Book in turn was
given the authority to communicate directly with
any USAF base or unit without going through the
normal CHAIN OF COMMAND.

The public generally regarded as authoritative
Project Blue Book's pronouncements on UFOs; the
unit dismissed most reports as natural phenomena, weather balloons, conventional aircraft sight-

ings, or hoaxes. On March 20, 1966, however, Project Blue Book became the target of intense public
and official criticism after its chief adviser, Hynek,
dismissed a Michigan mass sighting as the effect of
"swamp gas." Gerald R. Ford, at the time a Michigan congressman, called for hearings, which were
held by the House Armed Services Committee in
April 1966. The hearings concluded that the USAF
should review Project Blue Book. In the end, the
unit was discredited, and the USAF admitted that
its 19 years of investigation had been inadequate.
An attempt was made to revitalize Project Blue
Book, but a USAF-sponsored commission headed
by the distinguished physicist Edward Uhler Con-
don independently concluded in 1969 that UFOs
were "not of significance for scientific study." Taking this as leave to get out of the flying saucer business, the USAF terminated Project Blue Book on
December 17, 1969.

Punitive Expedition (1916)

In 1911, Mexico's hated president Porfirio Díaz
was deposed, creating a power vacuum that, gradually, Francisco "Pancho" Villa (1877–1923), with
some American support, came to fill. In 1915,
however, the troops of Álvaro Obregón defeated
Villa's forces and installed as Mexico's acting president Villa's bitter enemy, Venustiano Carranza. In a
swift about-face, the United States repudiated Villa
and recognized the Carranza government. Out-
raged, Villa launched attacks against Americans in
Mexico; then, on March 9, 1916, his forces crossed
the border into the United States, raiding the hamlet of Columbus, New Mexico, and killing as many
as 17 (history records anywhere from 12 to 17)
U.S. citizens. The next day, President Woodrow
Wilson ordered Brigadier General John J. Pershing
to organize a force to protect the border and to
apprehend Villa—dead or alive. Hoping that aerial
reconnaissance would be an invaluable asset in a
border-country manhunt, Pershing directed the
1st Aero Squadron of the AVIATION SECTION, U.S.
ARMY SIGNAL CORPS, to accompany his forces to
Columbus.

The 1st Aero Squadron consisted of 11 pilot-officers, 82 enlisted men, one civilian mechanic, a medical officer, and three enlisted medical corpsmen. Equipment consisted of eight Curtiss JN-3 "Jennys," 12 trucks, and an automobile. The first reconnaissance flight from Columbus into Mexico was made on March 16. By April 19, only two of the eight planes were in working condition. The rest had fallen victim to landing accidents and forced landings and had generally succumbed to heat and sand. Overweight and underpowered, the Jennys had trouble climbing in the hot, dry, thin air of the high country (elevation 12,000 feet). On April 20, after four brand-new Curtiss N8s were received at Columbus, the remaining two JN-3s were condemned. After a week of testing, the N8s were likewise condemned on May 9. Between May 1 and May 25, a dozen new Curtiss R-2s arrived. More adequately powered with 160-horsepower engines, the R-2s were declared satisfactory, but, once in the field, they were found to have defective propellers, engine parts, and various construction flaws. Aviation Section mechanics worked heroically on the aircraft from May through July under extremely adverse conditions in a successful effort to keep at least some of the aircraft flying. Near the end of August, 18 new aircraft arrived in Columbus, including 12 Curtiss H-2s and six Curtiss twin-engine craft. The latter planes were declared unsuitable for desert flying and were returned to Fort Sam Houston.

The many mechanical, structural, and logistical problems that beset the 1st Aero Squadron did not make for a promising maiden battle for the Aviation Section. Nevertheless, between March 15 and August, the squadron flew 540 reconnaissance sorties in Mexico for a total of 346 hours of flying time covering 19,533 miles. This aerial reconnaissance was no more successful than Pershing's ground forces in locating and neutralizing Pancho Villa (although Pershing did eliminate a number of Villa's top commanders and inflicted substantial casualties on his forces). The Punitive Expedition was recalled in February 1917.

R

RAF Lakenheath, United Kingdom See
AIR FORCE BASES.

RAF Mildenhall, United Kingdom See AIR
FORCE BASES.

rainbow

Term used for a new airman at basic training
before he or she is issued a uniform; that is, he or
she still wears multicolored civilian clothing and
not the green fatigue uniform. See RANKS AND
GRADES.

Ramstein AB, Germany See AIR FORCE BASES.

Randolph AFB, Texas See AIR FORCE BASES.

ranks and grades

USAF personnel hold rank and grade either as a
commissioned officer, a noncommissioned officer,
or an airman.

Commissioned Officers
(in descending order)

General of the Air Force

The highest rank in the USAF, ranking above general (grade O-10), but, in practice, very rarely

awarded. As of 2002, the late HENRY HARLEY ARNOLD
remained the only general ever to have held this
rank. It is the equivalent of general of the army.

General

Although applied to all general officers in the
USAF, a general is, strictly speaking, a four-star
general, ranking below only general of the air force
(five stars), a rank seldom awarded, so that, effectively, general is the highest rank in the USAF and
equivalent to a naval admiral. The pay grade for
general is O-10.

Lieutenant General

In the USAF (and army and marines), a lieutenant
general is a commissioned officer (grade O-9) who
ranks above a major general (O-8) and below a
general (O-10). The insignia is three silver stars,
and it is equivalent to a naval or coast guard vice
admiral.

Major General

A general officer of grade O-8, who ranks above a
brigadier general and below a lieutenant general.
The insignia of rank is two silver stars. The equivalent naval rank is rear admiral upper.

Brigadier General

The lowest-ranking general officer in the USAF, the
brigadier ranks above a colonel (grade O-6) and
below a major general (grade O-8). Insignia is a
single star in silver. The equivalent naval rank is
rear admiral, lower.

Colonel

This field-grade USAF officer (O-6) ranks below a brigadier general and above a lieutenant colonel. Insignia of rank is a silver eagle.

Lieutenant Colonel

In the USAF (as in the army and marines), a lieutenant colonel is a commissioned officer (grade O-5) who ranks above a major but below a colonel. The equivalent naval rank is commander. Insignia is a silver oak leaf.

Major

An officer of grade O-4, ranking below a lieutenant colonel and above a captain. The insignia is a gold oak leaf, and the naval equivalent is a lieutenant commander.

Captain

In the USAF, as in the army and marines, a captain is a company-grade officer (grade O-3), ranking below a major and above a first lieutenant. This rank is equivalent to a naval or coast guard lieutenant. (In the navy or coast guard, captain is equivalent to a USAF, army, or marine colonel.) The insignia of rank is two silver bars.

First Lieutenant

In the USAF, army, and marines, first lieutenant, grade O-2, ranks above second lieutenant and below captain. Insignia is a single silver bar. The naval and coast guard equivalent is lieutenant (j.g.).

Second Lieutenant

The lowest-ranking commissioned officer in the USAF (grade O-1), the second lieutenant is equivalent to a naval and coast guard ensign. Insignia of rank is a single gold bar.

Noncommissioned USAF Officers (in descending order)

Chief Master Sergeant of the Air Force

Chief master sergeant of the air force is a unique position in the USAF and the highest noncommissioned officer grade (E-9). The CMSgtAF advises the CHIEF OF STAFF, USAF, and the SECRETARY OF THE AIR FORCE on matters concerning the effective utilization, welfare, and progress of the enlisted members of the USAF. Insignia is three chevrons above five inverted chevrons with a USAF device in the middle of the lower chevrons.

Chief Master Sergeant

With first sergeant, chief master sergeant is the highest noncommissioned grade in the USAF (E-9). The insignia is three chevrons above five inverted chevrons.

First Sergeant

In the USAF, a first sergeant is a noncommissioned officer of grade E-8 or grade E-9, ranking above a master sergeant (E-7) and equivalent to a senior master sergeant (also E-8) or a chief master sergeant (E-9). Insignia for the E-8 first sergeant grade is five inverted chevrons below three chevrons, with a diamond device in the center. Insignia for the E-9 grade adds a third chevron above the V (inverted) chevrons, also with a diamond device in the center.

Senior Master Sergeant

A senior noncommissioned officer (grade E-8) ranking above all other enlisted personnel except for chief master sergeant (E-9). Insignia of rank is two chevrons over five inverted chevrons. The USAF senior master sergeant is equivalent to an army or marine master sergeant or first sergeant and to a senior chief petty officer in the navy or coast guard.

Master Sergeant

In the USAF, a master sergeant is a noncommissioned officer of grade E-7, in contrast to this grade in the army and marines, which is E-8. The USAF master sergeant ranks above a technical sergeant (E-6) and below senior master sergeant (E-8) and an E-8 first sergeant (the USAF has E-8 and E-9 first sergeant grades). Insignia of rank is one upright chevron over five chevrons. Equivalent naval noncommissioned grade is senior chief petty officer.

Technical Sergeant

In the USAF, a technical sergeant (grade E-6) ranks below master sergeant (E-7) and above staff sergeant (E-5). Insignia is five stacked V (inverted) chevrons with a star above the middle. A USAF technical sergeant is equivalent to an army and marine staff sergeant and a navy petty officer, first class.

Staff Sergeant
In the USAF, a staff sergeant ranks (E-5) above a sergeant or senior airman (both E-4) and below a technical sergeant (E-6). The USAF staff sergeant is equivalent to the army sergeant (the army staff sergeant is equivalent to a USAF technical sergeant), to the marine sergeant, and to the navy and coast guard petty officer, second class. Insignia is four inverted chevrons with a star above the lowest chevron stripe.

Sergeant/Senior Airman
Promotion to sergeant/senior airman (SrA) depends on vacant positions and is open to airmen first class who meet certain eligibility requirements, including a skill level 5 within their AIR FORCE SPECIALTY CODE (AFSC) classification (or skill level 3, if no skill level 5 exists in the applicable AFSC); 36 months time in service (TIS) and 20 months time in grade (TIG) or 28 months TIG, whichever occurs first; and recommendation by the promotion authority. A special Below-the-Zone Promotion Program also offers an opportunity for early promotion. Grade is E-4. Insignia is three inverted chevron stripes emanating from an encircled star.

Airman (in descending order)

Airman First Class
Promotion to airman first class (A1C) is made on a noncompetitive basis generally after 10 months' time-in-grade as an airman. Grade is E-3. Insignia is two inverted chevrons emanating from an encircled star.

Airman
USAF enlisted recruits begin at the grade of E-1 with the title of Airman basic and are promoted to airman on a noncompetitive basis generally after six months as an airman basic. Insignia is a single chevron stripe emanating from an encircled star. Grade is E-2.

Airman Basic
USAF enlisted recruits begin at the grade of E-1 with the title of airman basic (AB) and are promoted to airman on a noncompetitive basis generally after six months as an airman basic. This rank carries no insignia.

recruiting policies and practices
Like the other services, today's USAF is an all-volunteer organization. More than any other service, its personnel needs call for relatively high to very high degrees of technical training. Accordingly, USAF recruiters look for applicants of substantial aptitude and motivation. In return, the USAF offers extensive education and training, typically in fields that readily transfer to the civilian world. As with any branch of the military service, an emphasis is put on patriotism and service to the nation as well as defense of freedom; however, emphasis is also placed on opportunity for personal development and growth through education, vocational experience, and career development.

The official USAF recruiting website (http://www.airforce.com/index_fr.htm) outlines five "mission" areas to interest potential recruits: humanitarian, health care, flight, aerospace, and scientific research. The image presented is of a professional organization, both committed and cutting edge. Warfighting and combat roles do not receive top billing.

In all of today's armed services, the Internet and mass media advertising have greatly supplemented and extended the reach of the individual recruiter. However, the brunt of the recruitment mission still falls on this highly motivated enlisted person (grade E-5 to E-7), whose job is simultaneously to "sell" prospects on the USAF while also identifying prospects worthy of the service. The recruiter's job is grueling—often 60 to 70 hours per week—and is spent largely in the civilian world rather than within the confines of an air base. No sales person enjoys rejection, and recruiters learn to accept a rejection rate of about 95 percent on a daily basis. The recruiter's performance is evaluated by the number of recruits he brings into the service (typically, each recruiter is expected to bring in three or four per month) and by the performance of those recruits at least through basic training. The special demands of the recruiter's job are recognized by the Air Force Recruiter Ribbon, a decoration authorized on June 21, 2000.

See also AIR FORCE RECRUITING SERVICE.

Reese AFB, Texas   See AIR FORCE BASES.

Rhein-Main AB, Germany   See AIR FORCE BASES.

Rickenbacker, Captain Edward V. (Eddie)
(1890–1973) *ace fighter pilot, airline executive*

One of the most famous American military aviators, Eddie Rickenbacker became the U.S. ace of aces in WORLD WAR I, racking up 26 victories to become the seventh-ranking U.S. ace of all time.

Born Edward Rickenbacher in Columbus, Ohio, he changed the "h" to "k" to anglicize his name, and he also added Vernon as a middle name, because he thought it sounded more distinguished. Before U.S. entry into World War I, Rickenbacker earned fame as a race car driver. He enlisted in the Signal Corps in 1917 and was assigned to France as the personal driver of General John J. Pershing, commander of the American Expeditionary Force (AEF). In this position, he was promoted to sergeant first class.

Rickenbacker persistently agitated for assignment to flight training, and, in October 1917, he was graduated as a pilot and commissioned a first lieutenant. However, Rickenbacker was assigned as an engineering officer, not a combat pilot, at Issoudon, the principal U.S. air training and supply base, under Major CARL A. SPAATZ. Rickenbacker now urgently requested combat duty, but Spaatz did not assign him to the front until March 1918, when he joined the 1st Pursuit Group's 94th Aero Squadron, nicknamed the "Hat-in-the-Ring-Squadron," after its distinctive insignia.

Rickenbacker scored his first victory on April 25 and made ace by May 30. Stricken with a mastoid infection in the summer of 1918, he was out of service for two months. When he returned to the 94th it was as commander. He scored six victories in September and 14 more in October. (Rickenbacker was awarded the Air Force Medal of Honor in 1930 for an action of September 25, 1918, in which he singlehandedly attacked five fighters escorting two observation planes; he shot down one fighter and one observation plane.)

Rickenbacker started an automobile manufacturing company after the war, but, following initial success, the company failed in 1927. Seeking a way out of debt, Rickenbacker returned to auto racing and became president of the Indianapolis Speedway. In 1934, he became general manager of East-

Edward "Eddie" Rickenbacker   *(U.S. Air Force)*

ern Air Lines, which he soon took from the edge of bankruptcy to profitability. In 1938, he was able to purchase Eastern and ran it as president until he was nearly 70.

During WORLD WAR II, Rickenbacker traveled internationally on a morale-boosting tour of U.S. ARMY AIR FORCE units. During one of these trips, the B-17 transporting him ditched in the South Pacific. Thanks in large part to his leadership, Rickenbacker and all but one of the crew survived for 24 days in open rafts. Rickenbacker died of heart failure in 1973 and, at his funeral, was honored by a "missing man" formation flight of USAF F-4s.

Robins AFB, Georgia See AIR FORCE BASES.

S

Schriever AFB, Colorado See Air Force Bases.

Scott AFB, Illinois See Air Force bases.

Second Air Force

The predecessor unit of 2AF was the Northwest Air District, created in 1940. Early in 1941, it was redesignated 2AF and assigned to air defense and training. During World War II, beginning after 1942, 2AF conducted training for heavy and very heavy bombers. Inactivated in March 1946, 2AF was reactivated in June of that year and assigned to Air Defense Command (ADC). Inactivated again in 1948, it was reactivated the following year and assigned to the Strategic Air Command (SAC), charged with the mission of training personnel for strategic operations. Headquartered at Barksdale AFB, 2AF was permanently inactivated in 1975.

second lieutenant See ranks and grades.

secretary of the Air Force

The National Security Act of 1947, which, among other things, created the USAF as an independent service, created the position of secretary of the air force. Appointed by the president of the United States, the secretary of the air force serves under the secretary of defense, but also has direct access to the president and to the director of the budget. The secretary of the air force does not direct USAF operations, but manages funding, procurement, and legal plans and programs.

Selfridge, Thomas E. (1882–1908) *army aviator*

Second Lieutenant Thomas E. Selfridge was the first military officer of any nation to make a solo flight. He was also the first person killed in a powered airplane crash.

Born in San Francisco, he graduated from the U.S. Military Academy (West Point) in 1903 and in 1907 was detailed by the army to work with Alexander Graham Bell and Glenn H. Curtiss to design and build aircraft. On May 19, 1908, he flew the "White Wing" aircraft at Hammondsport, New York, thereby becoming the first military officer to solo in an airplane. Selfridge was next sent to Fort Myer, Virginia, as an official observer at the acceptance trials of the Wright Flyer, which was being considered for purchase by the U.S. Army Signal Corps. On a flight of September 17, 1908, with Orville Wright piloting and Selfridge as passenger, the Flyer crashed, seriously injuring Wright and killing Selfridge—the first fatality to result from a powered crash.

Sembach AB, Germany   See AIR FORCE BASES.

senior airman   See RANKS AND GRADES.

senior master sergeant   See RANKS AND GRADES.

separate operating agency (SOA)   See ORGANIZATION, USAF.

service associations
The leading USAF-related service associations include the following:

Air Force Association: See AIR FORCE ASSOCIATION.

Air Force Enlisted Widows: Founded in 1967 by a group of active duty and retired Air Force NCOs to provide a home for the surviving spouses of enlisted USAF personnel.

Air Force Historical Foundation: See AIR FORCE HISTORICAL FOUNDATION.

Air Force Sergeants Association: A lobbying and special-interest organization dedicated to the USAF NCO.

Air Force Memorial Foundation: The Air Force Memorial Foundation's goal is to establish a permanent Memorial to recognize the many significant contributions to peace and freedom rendered by the United States Air Force and its predecessors, such as the Army Air Corps.

Airmen Memorial Foundation: The Airmen Memorial Foundation was created in 1983 to solve contemporary problems among all components of the Air Force Enlisted Force through the provision of programs and services, conceived from the enlisted perspective, that no one else provides.

Association of Air Force Missileers: Organization for those who have earned the USAF Missile Badge or the Missile and Space Badge, as well as others with an interest in past or current USAF missile and space systems.

United States Air Force Academy Association of Graduates: The alumni association for the UNITED STATES AIR FORCE ACADEMY.

Seventeenth Air Force (17AF)
Established in 1953 as a UNITED STATES AIR FORCES IN EUROPE (USAFE) unit, 17AF was first located at Rabat-Sale, French Morocco, then moved to Wheelus AB, Libya, in 1956. In 1959, it relocated to Ramstein AB, Germany, then to Sembach AB, Germany, in 1972. The 17AF controlled USAF tactical operations forces in Germany until it was inactivated on September 30, 1996.

Seventh Air Force (7AF)
The 7AF is one of the four numbered air forces in the PACIFIC AIR FORCES (PACAF). It was activated on November 1, 1940, as the Hawaiian Air Force and was ultimately redesignated 7AF on February 5, 1947.

The unit was heavily involved in the Pacific theater during WORLD WAR II, executing bombing missions against the Gilberts, the Marshalls, the Carolines, the Marianas, Iwo Jima, and Okinawa, all targets across the Central Pacific.

Inactivated in 1949, 7AF was reactivated on March 28, 1966, and was designated a combat command at Ton Son Nhut AB, Republic of Vietnam. From April 1966 until 1973, 7AF assumed responsibility for most USAF operations in Vietnam and (as the 7/13AF) shared responsibility with the THIRTEENTH AIR FORCE for operations conducted from Thailand. On March 29, 1973, 7AF transferred to Nakhon Phanom Royal Thai AB, Thailand, from which it controlled air assets and operations in Thailand until its second inactivation on June 30, 1975.

In September 1986, 7AF was again reactivated and has served since then as the USAF component to the U.S. and Republic of Korea Combined Forces Command's Air Component Command, a force charged with deterring aggression from

North Korea. The 7AF currently plans, directs, and conducts combined air operations in the Republic of Korea and in the Northwest Pacific in support of PACAF, U.S. Pacific Command, United Nations Command, U.S.-ROK Combined Forces Command, and U.S. Forces Korea. Headquarters consists of about 10,000 USAF personnel located primarily at Osan AB, Kunsan AB, and five other operating bases throughout the Republic of Korea. Aircraft flown include the F-16 Falcon and the A/OA-10 Thunderbolt.

Seymour Johnson AFB, North Carolina
See AIR FORCE BASES.

Shaw AFB, South Carolina   See AIR FORCE BASES.

Shemya AFB, Alaska   See AIR FORCE BASES.

Sheppard AFB, Texas   See AIR FORCE BASES.

Sixteenth Air Force (16AF)
Headquartered at Aviano AB, Italy, 16AF is one of two numbered air forces of the UNITED STATES AIR FORCES IN EUROPE (USAFE). It also functions as the southern air component of the U.S. European Command. The mission of 16AF is to execute aerospace operations through expeditionary force command and control in support of USAFE and NATO. The organization plans and executes combat air operations in southern Europe and portions of the Middle East and northern Africa. It supports about 11,000 USAF and civilian members at two main operating bases, four support bases, and other sites in Spain, France, Germany, Italy, Croatia, Kosovo, Bosnia-Herzegovina, Hungary, Former Yugoslav Republic of Macedonia, Greece, Turkey, and Israel.

Equipment assets of the 16AF include the F-16 Fighting Falcon, with contingency support to the F-15 Eagle, KC-135 Stratotanker, E-3B Sentry (AWACS), U-2 Dragonlady, MC-130P Combat Shadow, HH-60 Pave Hawk, RQ-1A Predator, and a full complement of conventional weapons. 16AF operates two main bases: Aviano AB, Italy, home to the 31st Fighter Wing; and Incirlik AB, Turkey, home to the 39th Wing. In addition, 16AF operates three expeditionary wings: the 31st Air Expeditionary Wing, Aviano AB, Italy; the 39th Air and Space Expeditionary Wing, Incirlik AB, Turkey; and the 16th Air Expeditionary Wing, Aviano. This latter unit operates expeditionary sites at Camp Bondsteel, Kosovo; Camp Able Sentry, the Former Yugoslav Republic of Macedonia; Sarajevo and Tuzla AB, Bosnia-Herzegovina; Taszar AB, Hungary; Zagreb, Croatia; Istres AB, France; and Naval Air Station Sigonella and San Vito Air Station, Italy; in addition to a contingency processing center at Rhein-Main AB, Germany. 16AF also operates support bases in Spain, Italy, Greece, and Turkey.

The predecessor organization to 16AF was the Air Administration, established in Madrid, Spain, in 1954. This unit was redesignated as Headquarters, 16AF. In addition, 16AF operated STRATEGIC AIR COMMAND (SAC) bases in Morocco from 1958 through 1963. In 1966, a year after SAC withdrew its B-47 alert force from Spain, 16AF was reassigned to USAFE.

Sixth Air Force (6AF)
Activated in 1940 as the Panama Canal Air Force and redesignated the Caribbean Air Force in 1941, the unit became the 6AF in 1942 and was charged with the defense of the Panama Canal as well as conducting antisubmarine operations. After WORLD WAR II, in 1946, 6AF was inactivated as a numbered air force and was redesignated Caribbean Air Command, based at Albrook Field, Canal Zone. It is no longer active.

Small Arms Expert Marksmanship Ribbon
See DECORATIONS AND MEDALS.

Soesterberg AB, Netherlands   See AIR
FORCE BASES.

Spaatz, General Carl A. ("Tooey") (1891–
1974) *Army Air Forces general*

The last commanding general of the U.S. ARMY AIR
FORCES, Carl Spaatz was also the first CHIEF OF
STAFF, USAF, and, with General of the Air Force
HENRY HARLEY ARNOLD, is considered one of the
fathers of the independent air arm.

Born in Boyertown, Pennsylvania, Spaatz graduated from the U.S. Military Academy (West Point)
in 1914, took flight training, became a pilot, and
was assigned to the 1st Aero Squadron during the
PUNITIVE EXPEDITION against Pancho Villa. With
U.S. entry into WORLD WAR I in 1917, Spaatz was
sent to France as commander of the 3rd Aviation
Instruction Center at Issoudon. During the last
three weeks of the war, he served in combat and
was credited with two victories in air-to-air
engagements.

Between the wars, Spaatz worked closely with
Brigadier General WILLIAM MITCHELL and commanded the successful 1929 "Question Mark" experiment in-air refueling. On the eve of U.S. entry
into WORLD WAR II, Spaatz was sent abroad, during
the summer of 1940, as an observer of the Battle of
Britain. When the United States entered the war,
Spaatz was named principal combat commander
of the U.S. ARMY AIR FORCES and was primarily
responsible for the massive buildup of the EIGHTH
AIR FORCE. He also served directly under General
Dwight D. Eisenhower as air commander for the
African, Sicilian, and Italian campaigns. Spaatz
then presided over the planning and execution of
air support in Operation Overlord, the "D-day"
invasion of western Europe. It was under Spaatz's
command that the USAAF achieved air superiority
over the Luftwaffe, and it was Spaatz who successfully insisted on targeting the German oil industry
for strategic bombing.

Directly after V-E Day, Spaatz transferred to the
Pacific theater, where he commanded the B-29

W. Stuart Symington, first secretary of the Air Force, and General Carl Spaatz, first Air Force Chief of Staff, at a press
conference announcing the new organizational setup for the Department of the Air Force, 1947.   *(U.S. Air Force)*

strategic bombing campaign against Japan. It was Spaatz who supervised the nuclear raids on Hiroshima and Nagasaki. With the creation of the USAF in 1947, Spaatz became the new air arm's first chief of staff. He retired the following year.

space doctrine

The DEPARTMENT OF THE AIR FORCE is charged with the primary responsibility to organize, train, and equip for prompt and sustained offensive and defensive operations in space. Beginning in 2001, the SECRETARY OF THE AIR FORCE ordered a major "realignment" of headquarters and field commands "to more effectively organize, train, and equip for prompt and sustained space operations." AIR FORCE SPACE COMMAND (AFSPC) was assigned responsibility for space research, development, acquisition, and operations.

As of early 2002, the development of space doctrine is a major ongoing USAF initiative.

Spangdahlem AB, Germany   See AIR FORCE BASES.

Special Experience Identifiers (SEIs)

SEIs identify special experience and training that are not otherwise identified by AIR FORCE SPECIALTY CODES (AFSC). The SEIs are used to identify positions requiring unique experience or training and to track individuals who possess this experience or training.

Special Operations   See AIR FORCE SPECIAL OPERATIONS COMMAND.

Special Weapons Command (SWC)

In the postwar years, nuclear, biological, and chemical weapons were grouped together under the rubric "special weapons," and in 1949 the USAF formed the Special Weapons Command as a MAJ-COM charged with supervising units that handled

such weapons. Redesignated Air Force Special Weapons Center in 1952, Special Weapons Command became part of the AIR RESEARCH AND DEVELOPMENT COMMAND (ARDC) and, as such, lost its own status as a MAJCOM. The Special Weapons Center was in turn inactivated in 1954.

squadron   See ORGANIZATION, USAF.

staff sergeant   See RANKS AND GRADES.

stealth aircraft

Stealth is the general term for the science of designing an aircraft (or naval vessel) such that its detectability by visual and electronic means is significantly degraded. Ideally, the aircraft (or vessel) is rendered virtually invisible to the enemy.

In aircraft design, stealth technology combines innovative aerodynamics with the use of radar-absorbent materials and paints, and technologies to mask active emissions (especially acoustical and

The Boeing B-2 Spirit is the USAF's only full-stealth bomber.   *(U.S. Air Force)*

infrared). The most notable USAF stealth aircraft are the F-117 Nighthawk and the B-2 bomber and the emerging YF-22 and YF-23.

Strategic Air Command (SAC)

Until it was absorbed by AIR COMBAT COMMAND (ACC) on June 1, 1992, SAC was the USAF MAJ-COM charged with conducting strategic—that is, nuclear and thermonuclear—operations.

SAC was established on March 21, 1946. It was intended to deter other nations from starting World War III, and, under the leadership of Lieutenant General CURTIS EMERSON LEMAY, pursuant to the nuclear deterrent policy established by President Harry S. Truman, SAC became a mighty deterrent force. During the decade of the 1950s, it added ICBMs (see INTERCONTINENTAL BALLISTIC MISSILES) to complement its force of long-range bombers and became responsible for two-thirds of the "triad" that formed the U.S. nuclear deterrent (the navy's fleet of guided missile submarines was the final third). During this same period, the USAF emphasis on SAC certainly retarded development of tactical assets, and the USAF found itself scrambling to improvise in order to fight conventional wars in Korea and Vietnam (see KOREAN WAR and VIETNAM WAR).

SAC's first long-range bomber was the B-29, which was followed by the hybrid piston-jet B-36 Peacemaker, introduced in 1948, and the B-52 Stratofortress in the mid-1950s. The B-52 became the mainstay of SAC's piloted nuclear deterrent force (see AIRCRAFT, COLD WAR AND AFTER). Added to this were ICBMs, including the Minuteman II and III and the Peacekeeper.

At the time of its absorption into ACC, SAC had two numbered air forces under it, the EIGHTH AIR FORCE (Barksdale AFB, Louisiana) and the FIF-TEENTH AIR FORCE (March AFB, California).

Strategic Defense Initiative (SDI; "Star Wars")

SDI was announced in March 1983 by President Ronald Reagan as a plan for a system to defend against nuclear weapons delivered by ICBM (IN-TERCONTINENTAL BALLISTIC MISSILE). As planned, SDI would constitute an array of space-based vehicles that would destroy incoming missiles in the suborbital phase of attack.

The plan was controversial on three broad fronts. First, the Soviet Union, at the time the world's other great nuclear super power, saw SDI as a violation of the 1972 SALT I Treaty on the Limitation of Anti-Ballistic Missile Systems and therefore an upset to the balance of power. Second, proponents of the policy of mutually assured destruction ("MAD"), who saw the policy as the chief deterrent to nuclear war, criticized SDI as a means of making nuclear war appear as a viable strategic alternative. Third, a great many scientists and others believed SDI was far too complex and expensive to work. These critics dubbed the "futuristic" program "Star Wars," after the popular science fiction movie, and the label was widely adopted by the media.

Indeed, the technical problems involved in SDI were daunting. Multiple incoming missiles, which could be equipped with a variety of decoy devices, had to be detected and intercepted in space. Even those friendly to the project likened this to "shooting a bullet with a bullet." Congress, unpersuaded, refused to grant funding for the full SDI program, although modified and spin-off programs consumed billions of dollars in development.

The collapse of the Soviet Union beginning in 1989 seemed to many to render SDI a moot point—although others pointed out that a Russian arsenal still existed and that other nations had or were developing missiles of intercontinental range. There were, during the early 1990s, accusations and admissions that favorable results of some SDI tests had been faked, and former secretary of defense Caspar Weinberger asserted that while the SDI program had failed to produce practical weapons and had cost a fortune, its very existence forced the Soviet Union to spend itself into bankruptcy. In this sense, SDI might be seen as the most effective weapon of the cold war.

In the administration of George W. Bush, beginning in 2001, SDI was revived, and the USAF resumed development and testing of components of the system. As of 2005, Congress debated ongoing investment in SDI.

support command

A support command provides supplies, services, maintenance, administration, transportation, training, or other similar nonoperational (noncombat) functions.

surgical bombing

Also known as precision bombing, surgical bombing is the extremely accurate bombing of a specific target to destroy that target while reducing the possibility of damaging or destroying nearby buildings or killing civilians. Surgical bombing tactics and techniques were first applied in the VIETNAM WAR and were used most dramatically in the 1986 attacks on Libya, in which F-111s hit Mohammar Qaddafi's principal headquarters without damaging nearby buildings in downtown Tripoli. The use of computer-guided "smart weapons" in the 1991 PERSIAN GULF WAR bought surgical bombing to a new height of development, and the selective bombing of targets in Baghdad during Operation Iraqi Freedom (2003) demonstrated the latest state of the art.

Survival, Evasion, Resistance, and Escape (SERE)

SERE (survival, evasion, resistance, and escape) is an important part of USAF pilot training. It teaches survival skills, as well as tactics to evade and to resist enemy capture, and to escape if captured. In 1991, after the PERSIAN GULF WAR, a sexual assault component was added to SERE training, but it was modified in 1995 following complaints that SERE rape demonstrations were too realistic and, in themselves, approached the level of sexual assault.

In the USAF, SERE training is part of the UNITED STATES AIR FORCE ACADEMY curriculum and is also conducted by the U.S. Air Force Survival School under the 336th Training Group. Elements of the 66th Training Squadron, based at Fairchild AFB, Washington, Eielson AFB, Alaska, and Naval Air Station Pensacola, Florida, is responsible for all training of USAF personnel who specialize in the SERE career field as experts and instructors. SERE course work includes instruction in basic survival, medical, land navigation, evasion, arctic survival, teaching techniques, roughland evacuation, coastal survival, tropics/river survival, and desert survival. Water-survival training includes instruction in signaling rescue aircraft, hazardous marine life, food and water procurement, medical aspects of water survival, personal protection, and life raft immediate-action procedures. SERE experts are also trained in surviving in the four extreme biomes: barren arctic, barren desert, open ocean, and jungle.

USAF SERE training conforms to standards established by an interservice agency, the Joint Services SERE Agency (JSSA).

T

Tactical Air Command (TAC)

Until it was absorbed with STRATEGIC AIR COMMAND (SAC) into AIR COMBAT COMMAND (ACC) on June 1, 1992, TAC was a USAF MAJCOM responsible for coordinating offensive and defensive air operations with land and sea forces.

TAC was created in 1946, activated at Tampa, Florida, then moved to Langley Field (Langley AFB), Virginia, in order to be nearer the headquarters of the other military service branches. TAC trained and equipped air units for tactical operations worldwide. It conducted operations from three numbered air forces, FIRST AIR FORCE (at Langley), NINTH AIR FORCE (at Shaw AFB, South Carolina), and TWELFTH AIR FORCE (at Bergtrom AFB, Texas). Under TAC control were the USAF Tactical Fighter Weapons Center, the 28th Air Division, and the Southern Air Division (at Howard AFB, Panama).

Tactical Air Control Party (TACP)

The TACP is a ground-based CLOSE AIR SUPPORT team tasked with controlling aircraft and providing air liaison to land forces. TACPs first saw duty in the VIETNAM WAR, beginning in 1961 as the USAF's tactical liaison with the U.S. Army. Personnel lived and worked on army posts, wore the green fatigues of the army, and even had army patches on their shoulders. TACPs kept the army commander informed of what air support could do for him and coordinated close air support from the point of view of the troops on the ground. "In a sense," a 1966 *Airman* magazine article put it, "they run the air war in South Vietnam."

At brigade level, the TACP consisted of three USAF officers—ALO (airlift officer), FAC (forward air controller), and TALO (tactical airlift officer)—and three airmen; at battalion level, there were two officers (ALO and FAC) and two airmen.

technical sergeant   See RANKS AND GRADES.

Technical Training Air Force (TECH TAF)

TECH TAF was established as part of the former Air Training Command (ATC) (now AIR EDUCATION AND TRAINING COMMAND) in April 1951 to conduct basic, preofficer, and technical training. It was inactivated in 1958.

Tenth Air Force (10AF)

The 10AF was created to conduct air combat in India and Burma during WORLD WAR II and was built up in India in 1942. With the FOURTEENTH AIR FORCE, the 10AF constituted the major American combat forces in the China-Burma-India (CBI) theater. Both the 10AF and 14AF were disbanded in December 1945, but 10AF was reactivated on May 24, 1946, at Brooks Field (Brooks AFB), Texas, and was assigned to Air Defense Command (see AERO-SPACE DEFENSE COMMAND [ADC]). It moved to Offutt AFB, Nebraska, on July 1, 1948; then to Fort Benjamin Harrison (later, Benjamin Harrison AFB), Indiana, on September 25, 1948. Assigned to CONTINENTAL AIR COMMAND (CAC) on December 1, 1948, 10AF moved to Selfridge AFB, Michigan, on January 16, 1950. The organization was inactivated on September 1, 1960, then reactivated on January 20, 1966, and assigned to Air Defense Command. Based at Richards-Gebaur AFB, Missouri, the unit was again inactivated on December 31, 1969.

In 1976, 10AF was reactivated and assigned to the AIR FORCE RESERVE and AIR NATIONAL GUARD, with headquarters at Bergstrom AFB, Texas. On October 1, 1993, the unit assumed management responsibility for the AFR rescue mission and for AFR B-52 bomber operations at Barksdale AFB, Louisiana. On July 1, 1994, 10AF assumed command and control of all FOURTH AIR FORCE C-130 AIRLIFT, special operations, and weather units, and, in October, took over all TWENTY-SECOND AIR FORCE C-130 units. In 1996, 10AF was functionally transferred to Naval Air Station Fort Worth Joint Reserve Base, Texas, where it now directs activities of some 11,400 reservists located at more than 23 military installations throughout the United States. There are six fighter wings, three geographically dispersed rescue units, one bomber unit, one AWACS (Airborne Warning and Control System) associate unit, one special operations wing, one space group, one Regional Support Group, and more than 120 nonflying units in logistics and support roles. Flying organizations within 10AF include fighter units equipped with the F-16 Fighting Falcons and A-10 Thunderbolt IIs, air rescue units equipped with the HC-130 Hercules tankers and the HH-60 Blackhawk helicopters, a bomber unit equipped with the B-52H Stratofortresses, and a special operations unit equipped with the C-130 Combat Talon/Combat Shadow aircraft.

test pilots

USAF test pilots are highly qualified (1,000+ flying hours) and highly trained pilots who fly new or experimental aircraft to ensure they perform as expected and planned. The USAF maintains the AIR FORCE FLIGHT TEST CENTER (AFFTC) at Edwards AFB, California, which runs the UNITED STATES AIR FORCE TEST PILOT SCHOOL. USAF testing takes place at Edwards and at Nellis AFB, Nevada. Typically, aircraft manufacturers employ civilian test pilots, who may work under the supervision of the USAF for a particular aircraft test.

Third Air Force (3AF)

Headquartered at RAF Mildenhall, United Kingdom, 3AF is one of two numbered air forces in UNITED STATES AIR FORCES IN EUROPE (USAFE), and is responsible for all USAF operations and support activities north of the Alps. Its area of responsibility includes missions and personnel in the United Kingdom, Germany, the Netherlands, Norway, Belgium, Denmark, Luxembourg, and parts of France.

With Allied victory in Europe and the end of WORLD WAR II came the demobilization and withdrawal of all U.S. air units from the United Kingdom. Their absence, however, was short-lived. In 1948, in response to the Berlin blockade, the U.S. deployed long-range B-29 strategic bombers to four East Anglian bases. Third Air Division was activated to receive, support, and operationally control the B-29 units.

The 3AF was activated on May 1, 1951, to oversee tactical air operations in much of Europe during the cold war. Throughout much of the period 3AF controlled strategic and tactical resources, including bombers and missiles, as part of the United States' NATO presence. The unit participated in Operations Desert Shield and Desert Storm before and during the PERSIAN GULF WAR in 1990–91, playing a major support role and deploying half its combat aircraft, several thousand vehicles, and approximately 50,000 tons of munitions to the theater.

In March 1996, the SEVENTEENTH AIR FORCE was inactivated, leaving 3AF with sole responsibility for overseeing all USAF units north of the Alps. This included taking on two main operating bases, Ramstein AB and Spangdahlem AB, both in Germany, and five geographically separated units. Currently, 3AF consists of 25,000 military personnel and more than 200 aircraft, including KC-135s, F-15s, A-10s, F-16s, C-9s, C-20s, C-21s, and C-130Es.

Thirteenth Air Force (13AF)

Called the "Jungle Air Force" because it was a major component of the WORLD WAR II "island hopping" strategy in the Pacific theater and because it was always remotely headquartered during the war, the 13AF was activated at New Caledonia in the Coral Sea on January 13, 1943, and was initially assigned to defend against advancing Japanese forces. Soon, however, it played a key role in the Pacific offensive, traveling northeast from the Solomons to the Admiralty Islands, New Guinea, Morotai, and, finally, the Philippines. Its first postwar headquarters was at Clark Field (Clark AFB), Philippines, established in January 1946. In December 1948, 13AF moved to Kadena AB, Okinawa, then returned to Clark in May 1949.

During the KOREAN WAR, 13AF provided staging areas for Korea-bound units. After the war, its principal role was training and surveillance. With the beginning and escalation of the VIETNAM WAR, 13AF managed staging and logistics. Its combat units and facilities were expanded in Thailand, and, at the height of 13AF involvement in the Vietnam War, the unit consisted of seven combat wings, nine major bases, 11 smaller installations, and more than 31,000 military members.

The 13AF provided aircraft and support before and during the PERSIAN GULF WAR of 1990–91 and is currently responsible to PACIFIC AIR FORCES (PACAF) for planning, executing, and controlling aerospace operations throughout the Southwest Pacific and Indian Ocean areas. The unit is now headquartered at Andersen AFB, Guam. It consists of the 36th Air Base Wing, the 613th Air Communications Squadron (613 ACOMS), the 613th Air Intelligence Flight (613 AIF), the 613th Air Operations Squadron (613 AOS), and the 613th Air Support Squadron (613 ASUS), all at Andersen. In addition, 13AF is responsible for the 497th Combat Training Squadron (497 CTS), Paya Labar, Sin-gapore, and Detachment 1 of the 613th Air Support Squadron (DET1/613 ASUS), Diego Garcia. The unit has never been stationed in the United States.

Thunderbirds

The Thunderbirds constitute the U.S. Air Force Air Demonstration Squadron and perform precision aerial maneuvers demonstrating the capabilities of USAF high-performance aircraft to people throughout the world. The squadron also exhibits the professional qualities the USAF develops in the people who fly, maintain, and support these aircraft. Squadron objectives include:

- Support of USAF recruiting and retention programs
- Reinforcement of public confidence in the USAF
- Public demonstration of the professional competence of USAF members
- Strengthening of USAF morale and esprit de corps
- Support of USAF community and public relations
- Representation of the United States and its armed forces to foreign nations

Thunderbirds squadron is an AIR COMBAT COMMAND (ACC) unit composed of eight pilots (including six demonstration pilots), four support officers, three civilians, and more than 130 enlisted personnel. A Thunderbirds air demonstration combines formation flying with solo routines. For example, the four-aircraft diamond formation demonstrates the training and precision of USAF pilots while the solo aircraft highlight the maximum capabilities of the F-16. Approximately 30 maneuvers are performed in each demonstration during a show that runs about one hour and 15 minutes. The demonstration season lasts from March to November; new members are trained during the winter months. Officers serve a two-year assignment with the squadron, while enlisted personnel serve three to four. More than 280 million people in all 50 states and 57 foreign countries

The U.S. Air Force Demonstration Squadron, the Thunderbirds, flies the F-16C Fighting Falcon.   *(U.S. Air Force)*

have seen the red, white, and blue jets in more than 3,500 aerial demonstrations.

The Thunderbirds were activated on June 1, 1953, as the 3600th Air Demonstration Team at Luke AFB. At this time, the team flew the straight-winged F-84G Thunderjet. Early in 1955 the team transitioned to the swept-winged F-84F Thunderstreak, and, the following year, after moving to its current home at Nellis, the Thunderbirds traded the F-84 for the world's first supersonic fighter, the F-100 Super Sabre. This was the Thunderbird aircraft of choice for the next 13 years, except for a brief interval during which the Republic F-105 Thunderchief was used.

From 1969 to 1973, the Thunderbirds flew the F-4E Phantom, converted in 1974 to the T-38 Talon, the world's first supersonic trainer. Early in 1983, the team reinstituted its traditional role of demonstrating USAF frontline fighter capabilities by adopting the F-16A. The team converted to the F-16C in 1992.

Tinker AFB, Oklahoma   See Air Force bases.

top three

The top three enlisted ranks or grades in the USAF include master sergeant (e-7), senior master sergeant (e-8), and chief master sergeant (e-9).

Travis AFB, California   See Air Force bases.

Tuskegee Airmen

Like the other services (except, to a limited degree, the USN), the U.S. Army Air Forces were racially segregated before and during World War II. As an experiment in providing greater opportunity for African Americans in the service, on July 19, 1941, the USAAF initiated a program to train black men—separately from whites—as military pilots. Most of the men selected for admission to the cadet program were college graduates or undergraduates. Others could gain admission by demonstrating academic qualifications on rigorous entrance examinations. The black candidates had to meet the same standards as their white counterparts. In addition to training pilots, the program was open to enlisted personnel for such ground-support functions as aircraft and engine mechanics, armament specialists, radio repairmen, parachute riggers, control tower operators, security police, administrative clerks, and so on.

Primary flight training was conducted by the Division of Aeronautics of Tuskegee Institute, the black vocational school and college founded in Alabama by Booker T. Washington in 1881. After completing primary training at Tuskegee's Moton Field, cadets were sent to Tuskegee Army Air Field to complete flight training and to make the transition to combat aircraft.

The first cadet class began in July 1941 and was completed nine months later in March 1942. Of the 13 cadets who enrolled in the first class, five completed the training, including Captain BEN-JAMIN O. DAVIS, JR., a West Point graduate, son and namesake of the army's only African-American general officer, and destined to command the all-black 332nd Fighter Group. Between 1942 and

1946, 992 pilots graduated from the Tuskegee program and received commissions and pilot's wings. On other bases, in Texas and New Mexico, African-American navigators, bombardiers, and gunnery crews were trained. Mechanics were trained at Chanute Air Base in Rantoul, Illinois, until adequate training facilities were completed at Tuskegee late in 1942.

The first Tuskegee airmen were trained as fighter pilots and joined the segregated 99th Fighter Squadron, which flew already obsolescent P-40 Warhawks in North Africa, Sicily, and the Italian mainland from April 1943 until July 1944, when they were transferred to the 332nd Fighter Group in the FIFTEENTH AIR FORCE. Under the command of Davis, who had been promoted to colonel, the 332nd Fighter Group originally consisted of the 100th Fighter Squadron, 301st Fighter Squadron, and 302nd Fighter Squadron. These units underwent combat training at Selfridge Air Base, Michigan, from March 1943 until December

Major James A. Ellison returns the salute of Mac Ross of Dayton, Ohio, as he passes down the line during review of the first class of Tuskegee cadets, U.S. Army Air Corps basic and advanced flying school, Tuskegee, Alabama, 1941. *(U.S. Air Force)*

1943, using P-40s and even older P-39 Airacobras. The group, as originally constituted, saw its first overseas combat operations near Naples, Italy, assigned to the TWELFTH AIR FORCE, beginning in February 1944. In April 1944, the 332nd Fighter Group transferred to the Adriatic shore at Ramitelli Air Strip, near Foggia, Italy, and was assigned to the 15th AF to conduct long-range heavy bomber escort missions in the new P-51 Mustangs. In July 1944, the 99th Fighter Squadron was transferred to Ramitelli as the fourth squadron of 332nd, which thereby became the largest fighter escort group in the 15th AF. Incredibly, the group flew all of its escort missions, mostly over central and southern Europe, without losing a single bomber to enemy aircraft.

In September 1943, black pilots also began training to fly twin-engine aircraft, but the war was over before any of these fliers saw combat. Of the 992 Tuskegee graduates, 450 saw combat, completing a total of 15,553 sorties and 1,578 missions, and earning from the Germans the admiring epithet, *Schwartze Vogelmenschen* (Black Birdmen). At first many American bomber crews resented and derided the members of the 332nd; before long, however, these crews took to calling them "The Black Redtail Angels" because of the bold red marking that distinguished the tail assembly of their aircraft and because they earned a reputation, on escort duty, of defending bombers with uncommon skill and determination.

In addition to bomber escort duty, the 332nd attacked rail and road traffic, as well as coast watching surveillance stations. Sixty-six Tuskegee pilots were killed in action and 32 were made prisoners of war. Members of the 332nd were awarded 150 Distinguished Flying Crosses and Legions of Merit as well as the Red Star of Yugoslavia.

Acceptance was not so forthcoming for many of those Tuskegee airmen who remained in training in the United States. In 1945, black officers ordered to stay out of the segregated officer's club at Freeman Field, Indiana, protested what they considered an illegal and immoral order by attempting to enter the club; 103 were arrested and charged with insubordination. Court-martial proceedings were immediately dropped against 100 of the officers and eventually dropped against two others as well. A third, Lieutenant Roger "Bill" Terry, was convicted, a stain that was not removed from his record until 1995 (see AFRICAN AMERICANS IN THE U.S. AIR FORCE).

Tuskegee Army Air Field continued to train African-American airmen after the war, until 1946. African-American women were also accepted for training in some ground-support functions. Although the newly independent USAF planned as early as 1947 to institute racial desegregation, actual integration of African-American personnel into white units did not begin until 1948, after President Harry S. Truman signed Executive Order 9981, barring the military services from racial discrimination.

Twelfth Air Force (12AF)

The 12AF was formed in WORLD WAR II as part of the force being readied for Operation Torch, the U.S. and Allied invasion of North Africa. The unit was activated at Bolling Field (Bolling AFB) on August 20, 1942, and, under the command of General JAMES HAROLD DOOLITTLE, participated in Operation Torch, as planned. Subsequently, 12AF saw extensive action in Sicily, mainland Italy, and southern France. The unit was inactivated after V-E Day, on August 31, 1945, but it was reactivated at March Field (March AFB), California, on May 17, 1946, and became a training command under the TACTICAL AIR COMMAND (TAC). On January 21, 1951, 12AF was installed at Wiesbaden, Germany, assigned to UNITED STATES AIR FORCES IN EUROPE (USAFE), and was the first USAFE unit to be committed to NATO. The unit was relocated to Waco, Texas, on January 1, 1958, returned to TAC, and assigned the mission of training tactical air crews. The 12 AF moved to Bergstrom AFB, Texas, in 1968 and, during the VIETNAM WAR, served as a principal source of tactical fighter, reconnaissance, and AIRLIFT forces.

Today, 12AF furnishes the USAF component of the U.S. Southern Command (USSOUTHCOM), a unified command responsible for Central and

South America, and is referred to, in this role, as U.S. Southern Command Air Forces, or SOUTHAF. One of its principal missions is involvement in interdicting illegal narcotics trafficking.

On July 13, 1993, 12AF headquarters moved from Bergstrom to Davis-Monthan AFB, Arizona, from which the unit oversees the activities of 10 active-duty wings and 21 AIR FORCE RESERVE and AIR NATIONAL GUARD units.

Twentieth Air Force (20AF)

Located at Francis E. Warren AFB, Wyoming, 20AF operates the ICBM (INTERCONTINENTAL BALLISTIC MISSILE) weapons systems of the AIR FORCE SPACE COMMAND (AFSPC). The unit includes three operational space wings with more than 9,500 people and 500 Minuteman II and 50 Peacekeeper missiles broadcast across 45,000 square miles in parts of Colorado, Montana, Nebraska, North Dakota, and Wyoming. Today, these constitute the only on-alert strategic forces of the United States.

Major 20AF units are the 90th Space Wing (at F. E. Warren AFB), the 91st Space Wing (at Minot AFB, North Dakota), and the 341st Space Wing (Malstrom AFB, Montana). The 625th Space Operations Flight at Offutt AFB, Nebraska, verifies missiles targeting, trains airborne launch control crews, and oversees the operation and integrity of communication networks between the missile sites and national command authorities.

The unit was activated in April 1944 for action in the Asian and Pacific theaters of WORLD WAR II. Headquartered in Washington, D.C., until July 1945, when it was moved to Harmon Field, Guam, 20AF moved to Kadena AB, Japan, in 1949. It was inactivated in 1955, until it assumed its current role.

Twenty-first Air Force (21AF)

With headquarters at Mcguire AFB, New Jersey, 21AF is one of two numbered air forces in AIR MOBILITY COMMAND (AMC). The unit commands and assesses the combat readiness of assigned air mobility forces over the Atlantic half of the globe in support of the "Global Reach" mission. This encompasses forces at more than 55 locations in eight countries, and 21AF major units include six active duty wings, two operational flying groups, and two mobility operations/support groups. The unit also serves as liaison to 40 AIR FORCE RESERVE component wings.

The 21AF operates a strategic AIRLIFT force consisting of C-5 Galaxy, C-17 Globemaster III, C-130 Hercules, and the C-141 Starlifter aircraft. It also operates a tanker force consisting of KC-10 Extenders and KC-135 Stratotankers. The 12AF's 89th Airlift Wing, base at Andrews AFB, Maryland, provides presidential airlift (see AIR FORCE ONE) as well as administrative airlift support to other top government officials. Also under 12AF direction is the Andrews-based Malcolm Grow USAF Medical Center.

At Dover AFB, Delaware, the 436th Airlift Wing flies the C-5. The 437th Airlift Wing at Charleston AFB, South Carolina, flies the C-141 and the newly acquired C-17. The 305th Air Mobility Wing (McGuire) flies the C-141 and KC-10 aircraft. The 6th Air Refueling Wing (Macdill AFB, Florida) and the 19th Air Refueling Group (Robins AFB, Georgia) fly KC-135s. The 43rd Airlift Wing (Pope AFB, North Carolina) and the 463rd Airlift Group (Little Rock AFB, Arkansas) fly the C-130.

In Europe, 21AF directs a network of organizations in support of AMC operations throughout Europe, Africa, and South America, including 621st Air Mobility Support Group (Ramstein AB, Germany), and 621st Air Mobility Operations Group (McGuire). Airlift support squadrons are located at Incirlik AB, Turkey; Lajes Field, Azores; Rota Naval Air Station, Spain; Rhein Main AB, Germany; and RAF Mildenhall, England.

The 21AF predecessor units were the 23rd Army Air Forces Ferrying Wing (created in June 1942), which became the North Atlantic Wing of the AIR TRANSPORT COMMAND (ATC) in February 1944. Redesignated the North Atlantic Division in June, it became the Atlantic Division in September 1945 and was moved to Fort Totten, New York. With creation of the USAF in 1947, 21AF was assigned to the AIR TRANSPORT SERVICE (ATS) and moved to Westover Field, Massachusetts. A year later, it was assigned to MILITARY AIR TRANSPORT SERVICE (MATS). After moving to McGuire AFB, New Jersey, in 1955, it was redesignated a named air force in 1958, becoming the EASTERN TRANSPORT AIR FORCE. It became the 21AF in 1966.

On October 1, 2003, the 21AF was redesignated as the Twenty-first Expeditionary Mobility Task Force

Twenty-first Expeditionary Mobility Task Force   See TWENTY-FIRST AIR FORCE.

Twenty-second Air Force (22AF)

The first predecessor organization of the 22AF was Domestic Division, Air Corps Ferrying Command, activated on December 28, 1941, in Washington, D.C., and assigned to Air Corps Ferrying Command. On February 26, 1942, the unit was redesignated as Domestic Wing, Air Corps Ferrying Command and then, on March 9, 1942, as Domestic Wing, Army Air Forces Ferry Command. It became Domestic Wing, Army Air Forces Ferrying Command, on March 31, 1942, and Ferrying Division, AIR TRANSPORT COMMAND (ATC), on June 20, 1942. After WORLD WAR II, on October 10, 1946, the unit moved to Cincinnati, Ohio, and was subsequently redesignated Continental Division, Air Transport Command, then discontinued shortly afterward. It was not until March 29, 1979, that the unit was reactivated, this time consolidated with the Continental Division, MILITARY AIR TRANSPORT SERVICE (MATS), which had been organized at Kelly AFB, Texas, in July 1948.

In 1958, it moved to Travis AFB, California, and, later that year, was redesignated Western Transport Air Force. On January 8, 1966, it became 22AF.

With the termination of the MILITARY AIRLIFT COMMAND (MAC) in 1992, 22AF was assigned to AIR MOBILITY COMMAND (AMC) on June 1. A year later, 22AF was inactivated at Travis and reactivated at Dobbins Air Reserve Base, Georgia, with a change in assignment to the AIR FORCE RESERVE. Today, 22AF is under the peacetime command of Headquarters Air Force Reserve Command at Robins AFB, Georgia, and manages more than 25,000 reservists and has 149 aircraft, including C-141Bs, C-130s, C-17s, C5A/Bs, and KC-10As. Fifteen reserve wings, 24 flying squadrons, and more than 225 support units are spread throughout 14 states, from New York to Mississippi, and from Massachusetts to Minnesota.

In peacetime, the 22AF recruits and trains reservists and maintains subordinate units. In war, the 22AF provides combat-ready airlift and support units and augments personnel requirements of the Air Mobility Command in the United States. In war, 22AF would come under the operational control of the TWENTY-FIRST AIR FORCE (now Twenty-first Mobility Task Force).

Twenty-third Air Force (23AF)

The 23AF was the last numbered air force, organized on February 10, 1983, and activated on March 1, 1983. It was redesignated as a MAJCOM, AIR FORCE SPECIAL OPERATIONS COMMAND (AFSOC), on May 22, 1990.

Tyndall AFB, Florida   See AIR FORCE BASES.

U

uniforms

When the USAF was created as an independent service arm in 1947, a distinctive uniform was contemplated. Although army officers speculated that the "flyboys" would chose something garish, the choice, ultimately, was quite conservative, a new and distinctive blue dress (Class A) uniform (in a shade similar to that worn by the RAF of Great Britain) designed (as General HOYT S. VANDENBERG said) to look like a "military business suit." Some insignia were also designed to be distinct from those of the army. Oxidized silver was used in lieu of army brass, and, for enlisted personnel, the USAF adopted V-type grade insignia (suggesting wings) to replace the army chevron stripes. The uniforms were approved by the secretaries of the army and navy in 1949 and had officially replaced the army-style uniforms by 1951. Fatigue (later called utility) uniforms were identical to those worn by USA personnel, except for the distinctive USAF V-type rank insignia.

Even before it achieved independent status, the air arm introduced uniform elements to distinguish its members. Aviator badges were introduced in 1913, and, after the United States entered WORLD WAR I in 1917, pilots spurned the choke-collar army uniforms for uniforms with open lapels. During this era, however, sticklers for spit-and-polish insisted that flying officers retain the riding boots and spurs worn by cavalry officers. Pilots were willing to wear the boots, but they pointed out that the spurs interfered with operation of rudder pedals and even tore through fuselage fabric. The army never officially relented, but pilots typically shed their spurs for flight.

By 1925, all of the army had adopted open-lapel uniform blouses, which meant that the fliers' uniforms no longer appeared distinctive. Airmen rejected the army's Sam Browne belt and adopted a simple leather belt. Later, when the rest of the army followed suit, the fliers began wearing a cloth belt. The visored cap worn by U.S. ARMY AIR CORPS and U.S. ARMY AIR FORCES officers was much floppier than that worn by regular army officers, and flying clothes—especially the A-2 leather flying jacket—were worn as much as possible even away from the flight line.

In January 1993, the USAF selected a new design for the Class A uniforms of officers and enlisted personnel. While the 1949 uniform had departed from the army look, the 1993 design moved even further from traditional military styling. The new design was uncluttered and shed many military adornments, including outer patch pockets and name tags. The longer cut of the lapels more closely resembled the civilian business suits worn by men as well as women. Even the fabric approached more closely to a high-grade civilian standard. Beginning in 1976, USAF uniform blouses and trousers had been made of 100 percent polyester; the new uniforms were a blend of polyester and wool. The only nod to tradition was a return to the inclusion of a silver star in the center of all enlisted chevrons, a feature that had been removed in the late 1970s.

During the era of the Vietnam War, USAF personnel found themselves increasingly assigned to combat ground duty that required appropriate battle dress. For the most part, army jungle uniforms were used, and it was not until 2003 that the USAF considered adopting its own battle dress uniform (BDU) or utility uniform. Inspired by the distinctive camouflage uniform adopted by the USMC early in the 21st century, the new USAF BDU is made of an advanced wash-and-wear fabric and incorporates a redesigned camouflage pattern that corresponds to the jobs airmen do in most situations that require a utility uniform. The pattern roughly recalls the "tiger-stripe" camouflage patterns the U.S. military used during the Vietnam War, but it incorporates the distinctive Air Force emblem embedded into a gray-green color scheme that promises to provide better camouflage.

Flight suits are, of course, an important aspect of the uniform of any nation's air arm. The World War I Army Air Service flier wore essentially a cavalry dress uniform. At higher altitudes, a long, fur-lined leather coat was added, as was a fur-lined leather helmet with tight-fitting goggles—essential in an open cockpit. World War II flying uniforms varied from simple, loose fatigue clothes for warm climates to fleece-lined leather flight jackets, insulated trousers, insulated boots, and leather balaclava-style helmets for high-altitude strategic bombing missions in unheated cabins. Many suits were electrically heated.

The jet age introduced radially redesigned flight suits that were designed to provide warmth as well as protection against blackouts during tight, high-speed turns, which create extraordinary high-G-force stresses on airmen. As early as 1941, Dr. Wilbur Franks, a Canadian researcher, developed an "anti-gravity" flight suit, which inflated strategically placed bladders to prevent blood from pooling in the pilot's extremities during high-G maneuvers. This helped to keep the brain supplied with sufficient blood to prevent loss of consciousness. The anti-gravity, or G-suit, concept was developed

extensively through many generations of flight suits to improve the mechanism as an aid to circulation in high-G environments. In addition to the G-suit, USAF pilots developed a forced-breathing technique called the anti-G straining maneuver. While executing high-G maneuvers, the pilot breathes rapidly, then holds his breath for several seconds while simultaneously tightening leg and stomach muscles. Although effective, the maneuver is quickly tiring. To decrease fatigue, researchers developed a technique called positive pressure breathing, which requires forcing pressurized air into the lungs through the pilot's face mask. The drawback of this technique is the possibility of damage to the lungs through overinflation. To counteract this, researchers introduced the Combat Edge System in the early 1990s. The system combines positive pressure breathing with a counterpressure vest fitted over the flight suit to protect the chest.

As of the early 21st century, the USAF was testing a new Advanced Technology Anti-G Suit, or Atags. The suit surrounds the legs and covers the entire lower body in one air-pumped garment. This more efficient flight suit, used in conjunction with the Combat Edge system, was expected to increase crew high-G endurance by some 350 percent. However, even more advanced research was being conducted with the so-called Libelle suit, under development by Life Support Systems, a Swiss company. This single-piece, full-body suit uses long tubes filled with fluid, not air, to combat high-G acceleration forces.

In addition to mechanisms necessary to counteract high-G forces, the modern USAF flight suit incorporates survival equipment, including a life vest and basic survival gear and an emergency radio and transponder beacon, to aid in air-sea rescue. The suits are fire resistant. Modern flight helmets are designed for comfort, maximum peripheral vision, and injury protection. They incorporate connections for advanced communication devices and for hookup of an oxygen mask. The modern flight suit is thoroughly utilitarian. Insignia and unit patches and emblems may be affixed to the suit by means of Velcro strips; however, it is the usual practice for pilots to remove all such distinguishing patches when flying combat missions, so that an enemy cannot readily identify a pilot's unit, if he is shot down.

United States Air Force Academy

On April 1, 1954, President Dwight D. Eisenhower authorized creation of the United States Air Force Academy, and in the summer of that year, SECRETARY OF THE AIR FORCE Harold Talbott selected a site near Colorado Springs, Colorado, for the academy's permanent residence. The first academy class entered interim facilities at Lowry AFB, Denver, in July 1955 while construction began. Occupancy by the cadet wing began in late August 1958.

The academy offers a four-year program of instruction and experience designed to provide cadets with the knowledge and character essential for leadership, and the motivation to serve as USAF career officers. Each cadet graduates with a bachelor of science degree and a commission as a second lieutenant in the USAF. The academy curriculum provides a general and professional foundation of a career USAF officer. Professionally oriented courses, including human physiology, computer science, economics, military history, astronautics, law, and political science address the special needs of future officers while the core curriculum includes courses in science, engineering, social sciences, and the humanities. About 60 percent of the cadets complete majors in science and engineering; the other 40 percent graduate in the social sciences and humanities.

Most of the academy's nearly 600 faculty members are USAF officers selected primarily from career-officer volunteers who have established outstanding records of performance and dedication. Each has at least a master's degree and more than 35 percent have doctorates. The academy's staff also includes several distinguished civilian professors and associate professors, and officers from other services are members of the faculty as well, as are a small number of officers from allied countries, who teach in the foreign language, history, and political science departments.

The academy's athletic program is designed to improve physical fitness, teach athletic skills, and develop leadership qualities. Cadets take at least three different physical education courses each year. Additionally, an aerospace-oriented military education, training, and leadership program begins with basic cadet training and continues throughout the four years. Seniors are responsible for the leadership of the cadet wing, while juniors and sophomores perform lower-level leadership and instructional tasks.

The academy offers courses in flying, navigation, soaring, and parachuting, building from basic skills to instructor duties. Cadets may fly light aircraft with the cadet aviation club. Those not qualified for flight training must enroll in a basic aviation course. Astronomy and advanced navigation courses also are available. Students bound for pilot training enroll in the pilot indoctrination course and fly the T-3 Firefly.

Cadets are required to complete two training periods per summer. Combat survival training is a required three-week program during cadets' second summer. For the other second-summer training period, cadets have options such as working with young airmen in an operational unit at a USAF installation, airborne training, soaring, or basic free-fall parachute training. During their last two summers, all cadets are offered leadership training as supervisors or instructors in summer programs, such as basic cadet training, survival training, and soaring.

Enrollment in the USAF Academy is by nomination, which may be obtained through a congressional sponsor or by meeting eligibility criteria in other categories of competition established by law. Women entered the academy on June 28, 1976, as members of the class of 1980.

Early in 2003, the academy was rocked by a widespread rape scandal. By March, 23 women—13 former cadets and 10 who were enrolled at the time—brought charges that male cadets had sexually assaulted them, and they accused academy officials of not only failing to investigate the incidents they reported but also actively discouraging such charges of sexual misconduct or rape. When some women nevertheless lodged charges, they suffered retaliation in the form of disciplinary action or unfavorable reports from superiors.

The sexual assault scandal was investigated by the office of the SECRETARY OF THE AIR FORCE and, independently, in January 2004, by the U.S. Senate's Armed Services Committee. Criminal investigations were also conducted, and, as of late 2004, several cadets had been indicted on rape or sexual assault charges; one, Darwin M. Paredesillescas, pleaded guilty to rape on July 26, 2004.

On March 25, 2004, U.S. Air Force secretary James G. Roche and U.S. Air Force Chief of Staff general John P. Jumper announced the transfer to other duties of the academy superintendent, General John R. Dallger, his second-in-command, Brigadier General S. Taco Gilbert III, the vice commandant, Colonel Robert D. Eskridge, and the commandant of cadet training, Colonel Laurie S. Slavec. The academy established a zero-tolerance policy on sexual assault, instituted revised training for academy personnel and cadets, and provided protection for anyone who reports misconduct.

United States Air Force Battlestaff Training School

Under direction of the AIR WARFARE CENTER (AWFC) the Battlestaff Training School develops and conducts command, control, communications, computers, and intelligence exercises. The school is located near Eglin AFB, Florida.

United States Air Force Chaplain Service

The USAF Chaplain Service is headquartered at Maxwell AFB, Alabama, and includes chaplains ordained in the Catholic, Protestant, Orthodox, Jewish, and Islamic faiths. Officer chaplains are assisted by enlisted specialists.

United States Air Force Museum (USAFM)

USAFM is the world's largest and oldest military aviation museum. It was opened in 1923 at McCook Field, Ohio, then moved in 1927 to Wright Field, Ohio. The collection was put in storage during WORLD WAR II, and the museum reopened at Wright-Patterson AFB, Ohio, in 1954.

Its mission is to portray the history and traditions of the USAF through specialized displays and exhibition of historical items, including more than 300 aircraft and missiles. More than 500,000 visitors tour the museum each year.

In addition to the museum itself, the USAF Museum manages the worldwide USAF Museum System (USAFMS) and it is responsible for all USAF historical property.

The USAF Museum is open seven days a week from 9 A.M. to 5 P.M., closed on Thanksgiving Day, Christmas Day, and New Year's Day only. It is located at historic Wright Field, Wright-Patterson AFB, six miles northeast of Dayton, Ohio.

United States Air Force NCO PME Graduate Ribbon   See DECORATIONS AND MEDALS.

United States Air Force School of Aerospace Medicine

Located at Brooks AFB, Texas, the USAF School of Aerospace Medicine is under the direction of the AIR FORCE SPACE COMMAND (AFSPC) and is the center for aeromedical education, training, and consultation in direct support of USAF, Department of Defense, and international aerospace operations. The school provides peacetime and contingency support in hyperbarics, human performance, clinical and dental investigations, environmental health, expeditionary medical support, and aeromedical evacuation. It trains 6,000 students annually, including physicians and nurses as well as other biomedical and biophysiological military and civilian professionals. See AVIATION MEDICINE for historical background and antecedent organizations.

United States Air Forces in Europe (USAFE)

USAFE conducts, controls, and coordinates offensive and defensive air operations in the European theater in an area of responsibility extending from the United Kingdom to Pakistan. USAFE operates as a component of the U.S. European Command, a unified command of the U.S. armed services. USAFE is a MAJCOM under supervision of the CHIEF OF STAFF, USAF, and the USAFE commander also serves as the commander of NATO's Allied Forces.

USAFE is headquartered at Ramstein AB, Germany.

"United States Air Force Song"

Also familiarly known as "Off We Go, Into the Wild Blue Yonder," the "United States Air Force Song" was originally called "The Army Air Corps Song" and was composed in 1939 in response to a $1,000 prize offered by *Liberty* magazine. The composer, Robert Crawford, was a civilian pilot and professional singer (known as "The Flying Baritone"), who, at the behest of the U.S. ARMY AIR CORPS, performed his composition nationally. The song was modified as "The Army Air Forces Song" and as "The United States Air Force Song." The song is copyrighted.

United States Air Forces Southern Command

In 1940, U.S. military aviation in the Panama Canal Zone was expanded, and the Panama Canal Air Force became a MAJCOM. In August 1941, it was redesignated the Caribbean Air Force, then the SIXTH AIR FORCE in 1942. In July 1946, the unit was redesignated Caribbean Air Command and, in July 1963, the U.S. Air Forces Southern Command. Inactivated in 1976, the unit's resources and mission were transferred to the TACTICAL AIR COMMAND (TAC). In turn, TAC created the 830th Air Division to handle the mission of the former Caribbean Air Command. The 830th Air Division was assigned to the TWELFTH AIR FORCE in 1990.

United States Air Force Special Operations School

Reporting directly to AIR FORCE SPECIAL OPERA-TIONS COMMAND (AFSOC), the Special Operations School educates U.S. military and other personnel

in the mission and functions of special operations in the evolving world threat. As the primary support unit of the USAF component of U.S. Special Operations Command and component of the Joint Special Operations Forces Institute, the school provides joint education to 8,000 students annually.

The school's antecedent organization, the U.S. Air Force Special Air Warfare School, was activated at Hurlburt Field (see Hurlburt AFB) in April 1967 and was redesignated the U.S. Air Force Special Operations School the following year. On June 1, 1987, the school was assigned to U.S. Special Operations Command as an organizational element of TWENTY-THIRD AIR FORCE. Courses offered include:

- Crisis Response Senior Seminar
- Latin America Orientation Courses
- Revolutionary Warfare Course
- Special Operations Liaison Element Staff Officer Course
- Dynamics of International Terrorism
- Responsible Officer's Course/Force Protection II
- Commander's Responsibilities and Awareness Course/Force Protection III
- Introduction to Special Operations
- Middle East Orientation Course
- Russia, Central Europe and Central Asia Orientation Course
- Special Operations in the 21st Century Seminar
- Asian-Pacific Orientation Course
- Joint Special Operations Staff Officer Course
- Sub-Saharan Africa Orientation Course
- Civil-Military Strategy for Internal Development Course
- Joint Special Operations Planning Workshop
- Cross-Cultural Communications Course
- Joint Psychological Operations Course
- Joint Special Operations Intermediate Seminar
- Joint Senior Psychological Operations Course

United States Air Force Test Pilot School

Located at Edwards Air Force Base, California, the United States Air Force Test Pilot School trains air force TEST PILOTS to impart the scientific and engineering knowledge, critical and reasoned judgment, and managerial skills required to test sophisticated modern aircraft. The school also provides training in precision handling of aircraft as well as systematic training in gathering and interpreting flight data.

The origin of the school dates to 1914, when the army set up its first dedicated aeronautical research and development establishment at North Island, San Diego. During WORLD WAR I, this function was transferred to McCook Field at Dayton, Ohio, which included a sophisticated aviation engineering laboratory. During the 1920s, the facilities were again moved, to nearby Wright Field, but most of the nation's basic flight research was shifted to the civilian National Advisory Committee for Aeronautics (NACA). Indeed, during the 1920s and early 1930s, aviation companies contracting with the army were encouraged to conduct their own flight tests and verification. By 1934, the army ceased developing its own aircraft, but established a small Flight Test Section to verify performance of aircraft under contract. The training of these early test pilots was entirely informal until the exigencies of World War II called for greater professionalism among test pilots and engineers. At Wright Field, Colonel Ernest K. Warburton, chief of the field's Flight Section, studied the British example. The Royal Air Force (RAF) had established its Empire Test Pilots' School at Boscombe Down, U.K., and Warburton adopted many of its procedures and standards. Ultimately, this resulted in a Flight Test Training Unit established on September 9, 1944 under the command of Major Ralph C. Hoewing.

The school, established at Ohio's Vandalia Municipal Airport (now the Dayton International Airport), was initially staffed by three or four instructors, who set up a formal three-month long curriculum stressing performance flight test theory and piloting techniques.

In the meantime, Colonel Albert Boyd had become chief of the Flight Test Division. He personally chose a staff of test pilots and assigned them to the Flight Test Division's Accelerated Service Test Section. Those who survived Boyd's scrutiny were given formal classroom training.

After World War II, Boyd's program moved to Muroc Air Force Base, California, and became the Flight Performance School, then, in 1951, the Air Materiel Command Experimental Test Pilot School. At this same time, Muroc was renamed Edwards Air Force Base. Before the year ended, the school was again renamed and became the Air Research and Development Command (ARDC) Experimental Test Pilot School. In 1952, it reverted to the less cumbersome U.S. Air Force Experimental Flight Test Pilot School. The school was very demanding. Not only did candidates have to be outstanding pilots, they had to be capable of excelling in course work that included flight mechanics, differential calculus, and supersonic aerodynamics.

The school emerged as the premier institution of its kind in the world and was renamed the United States Air Force Flight Test Pilot School on June 9, 1955. During the 1950s, its cutting-edge focus came to encompass space projects, including, most famously, work with the X-15 rocket plane. Ultimately, the school became the air force training ground for its astronauts, and on October 12, 1961, the school was redesignated the U.S. Air Force Aerospace Research Pilot School (ARPS). All U.S. military pilots wishing to qualify as astronauts were now sent here. Curriculum was expanded to include thermodynamics, bioastronautics, and Newtonian mechanics and occupied an entire year.

In 1972, the school shifted its focus from space and spaceflight training, once again becoming the United States Air Force Test Pilot School, with an emphasis on advanced classroom training, especially in the use of computers in the testing mission.

United States Central Command Air Forces (CENTAF)

CENTAF—U.S. Central Command Air Forces—is headquartered at Shaw AFB, South Carolina, and is charged with planning for and executing contingency operations ranging from humanitarian airlift to integration of multinational forces into coherent air operations in support of a major theater war. CENTAF is capable of deploying tactical aircraft and carrying out strategic reconnaissance and intelligence collection. CENTAF orchestrates the multinational Operation Southern Watch, through Joint Task Force–Southwest Asia.

CENTAF's tactical mission includes antiarmor capabilities to create a credible deterrence in the Middle East. If this deterrence fails, CENTAF's mission is to gain and maintain air superiority as a first step toward victory in a major theater war.

United States Strategic Air Forces (USSTAF)

USSTAF was established on February 4, 1944, as successor to the U.S. Strategic Air Forces in Europe (USSAFE)—not to be confused with UNITED STATES AIR FORCES IN EUROPE (USAFE)—that had been established in November 1943 to oversee and coordinate operations of the EIGHTH AIR FORCE and the FIFTEENTH AIR FORCE. Headquarters was at Bushey Park, near London. USSTAF was responsible for planning missions, selecting targets, setting the length of combat crew operational tours, and managing the movement of personnel between 8AF and 15AF.

U.S. Army Air Corps (USAAC)

With the U.S. ARMY AIR SERVICE (USAAS) and U.S. ARMY AIR FORCES (USAAF), the USAAC is one of the three major antecedent organizations of the USAF. It was established on July 2, 1926, by the AIR CORPS ACT OF 1926 to improve and expand the nation's air arm, the U.S. Army Air Service, which it replaced. Most significantly, unlike the USAAS, the USAAC had its own assistant secretary of war for air and air sections in the General Staff, together with a five-year plan for expansion. F. Trubee Davison was appointed as assistant secretary, serving until 1932. President Franklin D. Roosevelt never appointed a successor.

As originally established, the USAAC had five agencies: Training Center, for flight training; Technical School; Balloon and Airship School; Tactical School; and Materiel Division (which included an Engineering School, Depots, Procurement Planning Representatives, and Plant Representatives). In 1926, USAAC had 919 officers, 8,725 enlisted men, and 1,254 airplanes. On the eve of WORLD WAR II, it had 23,455 enlisted men, and when the war in Europe began, it rapidly expanded to more than 150,000 men in 1941, when it was replaced by the USAAF. In 1939, the USAAC had an inventory of 2,177 planes, a small number, although most were relatively modern.

In addition to managing men and materiel, USAAC made strides in developing air power strategy and doctrine, and it was as USAAC that the nation's air arm began to expand into a large modern air force capable of fighting a world war. USAAC also took a critical step to-ward operational independence with the creation in 1935 of GENERAL HEADQUARTERS AIR FORCE (GHQ Air Force), which centralized organization and, by 1939, was transferred from control by the army chief of staff to the chief of the Air Corps.

In June 1941, the USAAC became the USAAF.

U.S. Army Air Forces (USAAF)

With the U.S. ARMY AIR SERVICE (USAAS) and U.S. ARMY AIR CORPS (USAAC), USAAF is one of the three major antecedent organizations of the USAF.

As Nazi aggression increased after the Munich Conference of 1938 and culminated in the outbreak of WORLD WAR II in Europe in September 1939, the U.S. Congress, although generally isolationist, appropriated funds to expand the USAAC in anticipation of U.S. entry into the war. Between 1940 and 1941, USAAC tripled in size, and, seeing in the German *Blitzkrieg* of Europe the tremendous importance of air power, USAAC planners anticipated creating an air arm that would eventually number 2,165,000 men. An organization of this magnitude required a new status. Therefore, on

June 20, 1941, Army Regulation 95-5 created the USAAF, which would take its place alongside the army's three other major divisions: Army Ground Forces, Army Service Forces, and Defense and Theater Commands.

Internally the USAAF was divided into Combat Command, successor to GENERAL HEADQUARTERS AIR FORCE (GHQ Air Force), which would conduct air operations, and the Air Corps (AC), which encompassed two subcommands: Materiel, and Training and Operations. In turn, Training and Operations had four subordinate organizations—Technical Schools, Southwest Training, Gulf Training, and Southeast Training—designed to build a credible air force as quickly as possible.

The six-month-old USAAF had had precious little time for training before the attack on Pearl Harbor, December 7, 1941, thrust the United States into World War II. In its first year, USAAF quintupled to 764,000, and in its second year tripled this number. By 1944, it reached a staggering 2,372,292 —31 percent of U.S. Army strength—which would be the all-time high for the USAAF as well as the USAF. By the middle of 1944, the USAAF inventory boasted 78,757 aircraft, of which 445 were very heavy bombers and 11,720 were heavy bombers.

By 1944, the USAAF was organized into 10 major commands in the continental United States: Training, I Troop Carrier, Air Transport, Materiel, Air Service, and Proving Ground Commands, in addition to the FIRST AIR FORCE, SECOND AIR FORCE, THIRD AIR FORCE, and FOURTH AIR FORCE. There were also eight USAAF agencies: AAF Board, Tactical and Redistribution Centers, Army Airways Communications System and Weather Wings, School of Aviation Medicine, First Motion Picture Unit, and Aeronautical Chart Plant. Overseas organizations used air forces subordinate to theater of operations command.

In Europe, the USAAF conducted STRATEGIC BOMBING against the German aircraft industry, although, by June 1944, much of the USAAF effort was diverted to tactical operations in support of the Allies' Normandy invasion "Operation Overlord." Overlapping with invasion duty was a strategic campaign against the German oil industry,

beginning in May, and then an attack on the German transportation system, beginning early in 1945.

In the Pacific theater, the USAAF began a strategic bombing campaign against Japan from bases in the Marianas beginning in October 1944. By August 1945, bombing combined with a submarine blockade had reduced Japanese production by 75 percent, and the USAAF and the U.S. Navy believed the war against Japan could be ended without a land invasion. The U.S. Army disagreed, but the dropping of atomic bombs on Hiroshima (August 6, 1945) and Nagasaki (August 9, 1945) rendered the argument moot as Japan suddenly surrendered.

Recruiting poster for the Army Air Service   *(Library of Congress)*

USAAF forces rapidly demobilized after the war. Only two forces remained outside the continental United States, in occupied Germany and Japan. By May 1947, the USAAF mustered only 303,000 men and 25,000 aircraft. Counterpointed to this, however, was the restructuring of USAAF as an independent air arm, the USAF, which was created on September 18, 1947, pursuant to the NATIONAL SECURITY ACT OF 1947 and EXECUTIVE ORDER 9877.

U.S. Army Air Service (USAAS)

With the U.S. ARMY AIR CORPS (USAAC) and the U.S. ARMY AIR FORCES (USAAF) the USAAS was one of the three major antecedent organizations of the USAF.

On May 21, 1918, by executive order, President Woodrow Wilson transferred military aviation from the U.S. Army Signal Corps and created the USAAS, directly under the secretary of war. As originally conceived, the USAAS consisted of two agencies, the Bureau of Aircraft Production and the Division of Military Aeronautics. On August 27, Wilson assigned a new assistant secretary of war, John D. Ryan, as director of the USAAS. Wilson's wartime actions were confirmed by Congress after the war by the National Defense Act of l920, which officially made the USAAS an arm under the army.

During WORLD WAR I, the USAAS totalled 190,000 men. By June 1919, this number had been slashed to 27,000. Procurement of aircraft and other equipment stopped, and much was sold as surplus. In 1920, the now-diminutive organization was divided into four principal subsections: Administrative, Information, Training and Operations, and Supply. The USAAS had two wings, divided into seven groups and 27 squadrons, plus 42 companies for lighter-than-air aviation. Flight training, which had been suspended with demobilization, recommenced in January 1920, as did other aircrew, technical, and professional training. Procurement also resumed to a limited degree, but the service remained very small, mustering between 9,000 and 11,600 men during 1920–26. In 1924, the USAAS inventory consisted of 1,364 aircraft, of which only 754 were in commission. A large proportion of the inventory, 457 aircraft, were observation craft—only 78 were fighters and 59 bombers. In addition, the USAAS counted eight attack aircraft. Morale during this period was understandably low, and air power advocates, most notably Major General WILLIAM MITCHELL, vigorously campaigned for more and better aircraft (more fighters and bombers, fewer observation craft) and greater status within the army—or even independence from it. Ultimately, this activity resulted in the AIR CORPS ACT OF 1926, which replaced the USAAS on July 2, 1926, with the USAAC.

V

Vance AFB, Oklahoma   See AIR FORCE BASES.

Vandenberg AFB, California   See AIR FORCE BASES.

Vandenberg, Hoyt Sanford (1899–1954)
U.S. Air Force general and Chief of Staff

One of the principal architects of the USAF, Hoyt Vandenberg was born in Milwaukee, Wisconsin, and graduated from the U.S. Military Academy (West Point) in 1923. After graduation, he attended flying school at Brooks Field (Brooks AFB) and Kelly Field (Kelly AFB), both in Texas. After qualification as a pilot, he was assigned to the 3rd Attack Group in 1924, and, in 1927, he became a flight instructor at the Air Corps Primary Flying School, March Field (March AFB), California. Promoted to 1st lieutenant in August 1928, Vandenberg joined the 6th Pursuit Squadron at Wheeler Field, Hawaii, in May 1929. In November of that year, he was named to command of the squadron, then returned to the mainland in September 1931 as an instructor at Randolph Field (Randolph AFB), Texas.

Vandenberg attended the Air Corps Tactical School, from which he graduated in 1935. From there, he continued on to the Command and General Staff School at Fort Leavenworth, Kansas, graduating in 1936. He returned to the Air Corps

Tactical School as an instructor. After graduating from the Army War College in 1939, Vandenberg was assigned to the war plans division of Headquarters, U.S. Army Air Corps, Lieutenant General HENRY HARLEY ARNOLD. Promoted to major in July 1941, lieutenant colonel in November, and colonel on January 27, 1942, Vandenberg became opera-

Hoyt S. Vandenberg   *(U.S. Air Force)*

tions and training officer in the Air Staff, as well as chief of staff of the TWELFTH AIR FORCE under Lieutenant General JAMES H. DOOLITTLE. In this assignment, he played a major role in planning the American air component of the invasion of Operation Torch, the invasion of North Africa, during November 1942. After the success of this mission, Vandenberg was promoted to brigadier general in December.

In March 1943, Vandenberg was named chief of staff of the Northwest Africa Strategic Air Force. With his men, he flew many missions over Tunisia, Sicily, Sardinia, and southern Italy from March through August, when he was recalled to Washington as deputy chief of the Air Staff. In September 1943, Vandenberg was named to a delegation sent to the Soviet Union to arrange bases for shuttle-bombing missions against eastern European targets. After successfully negotiating the use of the bases, he returned to Air Corps Headquarters in Washington, where he formulated plans for the air component of the Normandy ("D-day") invasion.

Vandenberg was promoted to major general in March 1944 and was assigned to General Dwight D. Eisenhower's staff as deputy to Britain's Air Vice-Marshal Sir Trafford Leigh-Mallory, who was commander of the Allied Expeditionary Air Force. After the success of the Normandy invasion, Vandenberg was assigned to command the NINTH AIR FORCE, which provided extensive air support for Lieutenant General Omar N. Bradley's Twelfth Army Group, which swept across Europe. Promoted to lieutenant general in March, Vandenberg returned to Washington after V-E Day and, in July 1945, was named assistant chief of staff for operations for the Army Air Forces. After V-J Day, he became chief of the army general staff's Intelligence Division in January 1946. In June, he was made director of the Central Intelligence Group—precursor to the CIA.

In September 1947, Vandenberg returned to military aviation as vice chief of staff of the newly independent USAF. In July 1948, he succeeded GENERAL CARL A. SPAATZ as Air Force Chief of Staff, a position in which he served during the early years of the cold war. It was Vandenberg who was responsible for planning and directing the execution of the BERLIN AIRLIFT from June 1948 to May 1949. He also directed air operations during the KOREAN WAR, from June 1950 to July 1953. Stricken with cancer, Vandenberg retired from the USAF in June 1953 and died the following year.

Vandenberg brilliantly executed the mission of ground support in WORLD WAR II and, during the cold war, he was an effective champion of the development of the USAF as the nation's chief strategic deterrent force.

Vietnam War

Origins of the War

During the 19th century, France had established colonial hegemony in Laos, Cambodia, and Vietnam. At the beginning of WORLD WAR II, after France capitulated to Germany in 1940, the Japanese allowed French colonial officials nominal authority while actually assuming de facto control of these areas themselves. In 1945, with the liberation of France, the Japanese seized full control, eliminating the French police agencies and other armed authorities that had long kept in check indigenous nationalist groups seeking independence. In Vietnam, the largest and most powerful of these groups was the Viet Minh, which, under the leadership of Ho Chi Minh, launched a guerrilla war against the Japanese forces of occupation and soon took control of the nation's northern regions. In this, Ho Chi Minh was aided by U.S. Office of Strategic Services (OSS) military teams.

After the war in Europe had ended, Allied forces turned their attention to Vietnam (and the rest of Southeast Asia), a theater they had largely neglected during most of the Pacific war. Nationalist Chinese troops moved into the Tonkin provinces of northern Vietnam, and the British, anxious to restore France to the status of a world power in order to help counter the Soviet Union's rapidly expanding postwar sphere of influence, secured southern Vietnam for the reentry of the French, who ruthlessly suppressed all agitation for independence in that region. The French began talks with Ho Chi Minh, now firmly established in the north, but these quickly proved fruitless, and a state of chronic guerrilla conflict developed.

The conflict escalated during 1946, when Nationalist Chinese forces, who had occupied the northern part of the country, were voluntarily replaced there by the French military. Although Nationalist Chinese leader Chiang Kai-shek (Jiang Jieshi) harbored no love for French imperialism, in battling Mao Zedong's communist forces, he feared a communist takeover in Vietnam and preferred French control of the region. In November, fire was exchanged between a French patrol boat and Vietnamese militia in Haiphong harbor. The French retaliated by bombarding Haiphong, killing some 6,000 civilians and prompting Ho Chi Minh to break off all talks with the French, retreat with his government into the hill country of Tonkin, and conduct an all-out guerrilla war against the French.

Many in the United States strongly sympathized with Ho Chi Minh's nationalism. President Harry S. Truman, like President Roosevelt before him, was an anti-imperialist. But he also felt that an independent Vietnam would likely become a communist Vietnam. Still, Truman urged the French to reach a political solution in Vietnam and barred direct export of war materiel to French forces there—though he vacillated to the important extent of refusing to bar arms shipments to France itself, which, of course, was free to transship the materiel to its troops in Vietnam.

U.S. Involvement Begins

The fall of China to communism in 1949, together with the intensification of the cold war in Europe by the end of the decade, including the induction of much of eastern Europe into the Soviet camp, compelled the United States to accept French authority in Vietnam, no matter how distasteful. Moreover, if the newly formed North Atlantic Treaty Organization (NATO) were to succeed as a force against communism in Europe, the full support of France was required. Its military resources drained by the fierce guerrilla warfare in Vietnam, France was hardly in a position to offer the full

degree of support. Finally, on February 7, 1950, the United States recognized Vietnam as it was constituted by the French under their puppet, the former emperor Bao Dai. Within less than two weeks, the French requested U.S. economic and military aid, threatening to abandon the nation to Ho Chi Minh if the aid were not forthcoming. Some $75 million was appropriated immediately. Shortly afterward, on June 25, 1950, communist forces from North Korea invaded South Korea. Truman responded by stepping up aid to the French in Vietnam, sending eight C-47 transports directly to Saigon.

Flown into Vietnam by USAF pilots, these eight aircraft were the first aviation aid the United States furnished in the region. On August 3, 1950, the first contingent of U.S. military advisers—the U.S. Military Assistance Advisory Group (MAAG)—arrived in Saigon. Air assistance operations were at first directed by the air attaché in Saigon, then, on November 8, they came under the direction of the Air Force Section of MAAG–Indochina. At this point, the mission of the American advisers was primarily to supply aircraft and materiel to the French and, secondarily, to work with the French forces to improve their military capabilities. The least important aspect of the mission was to develop indigenous Vietnamese armed forces.

By 1952, the United States was financing one-third of the French military effort in Vietnam, yet it was becoming apparent that the French, though they were enjoying moderate success against the insurgents, were losing heart. It was at this juncture, on January 4, 1953, that the first sizable contingent of USAF personnel (other than those attached to MAAG) was deployed to Vietnam. This group included a substantial complement of enlisted USAF technicians, mainly to handle supply and the maintenance of aircraft. The contingent remained in Vietnam until August 14, 1952, when they were relieved by French forces.

In April 1953, the Viet Minh staged a major offensive in western Tonkin, advancing into Laos and menacing Thailand. The French requested the loan of C-119 transports to AIRLIFT heavy equipment into Laos. President Eisenhower, wary of committing USAF crews to a combat mission, ordered military crews to fly the aircraft to Nha Trang, where nonmilitary contract pilots took them over for the flight to Cat Bi Airfield near Haiphong. Enlisted ground personnel were dispatched to Cat Bi from the 24th Air Depot Wing to carry out maintenance and supply functions, and then accompanied the aircraft north to Gia Lam Airfield near Hanoi. The detachment withdrew in July, after completing their mission.

General Henri-Eugène Navarre, France's new commander in charge of operations in Vietnam, presented a plan to defeat the Viet Minh by luring them into open battle and reducing them to a low level of guerrilla warfare that could be contained by indigenous Vietnamese troops. Additional cargo planes were loaned to the French, and, in the fall of 1953, Navarre began operations on the strategically located plain of Dien Bien Phu in northwest Tonkin, near Laos. French paratroopers fortified an airstrip there beginning on November 20, and, on December 5, the U.S. FAR EAST AIR FORCES (FEAF) flew more C-119 transports to Cat Bi, from which civilian contract pilots or French personnel would fly them into the combat area. Ground personnel from the 483rd Troop Carrier Wing, the 8081st Aerial Resupply Unit, and a provisional maintenance squadron of the Far East Air Logistics Force were stationed at Cat Bi to service the aircraft.

American military officials and the Eisenhower administration were becoming increasingly anxious, however, noting that the Viet Minh were menacing Hanoi and Haiphong—from which Navarre had drawn forces to bolster Dien Bien Phu—and that the Viet Minh were also massing around Dien Bien Phu. President Eisenhower authorized increased military aid—short of committing American personnel to combat—and B-26s and RB-26s were dispatched on loan to the French. However, French air units were seriously undermanned, and the fateful decision was made on January 31, 1954, to dispatch some 300 airmen to service aircraft at Tourane and at the Do Son Airfield near Haiphong. This, the first substantial commitment of U.S. airmen—indeed, of U.S. military personnel—to the war in Vietnam, was highly classified. Addressing the American public, President Eisenhower described the forces he was committing as "some airplane mechanics . . . who would not get touched by combat."

Despite American logistical support, it became apparent day by day that the French situation at Dien Bien Phu was hopeless as the defensive perimeter steadily contracted around the enclave. President Eisenhower contemplated direct U.S. military intervention, principally in the form of air support, but decided not to act in the absence of approval from the British and a demonstration of a French willingness to train and employ indigenous troops and ultimately to grant Vietnam its independence. On April 7, 1954, President Eisenhower presented to the American press a rationale for fighting communism in Vietnam. "You have a row of dominoes set up," he explained, "you knock over the first one, and what will happen to the last one is the certainty it will go over very quickly." Yet American military experts were not sanguine about the prospect of committing U.S. combat forces in the region, concluding that French colonialism had alienated the indigenous people, who lacked the will to fight Ho Chi Minh's forces. Moreover, logistics in Southeast Asia generally were nightmarish, presenting support problems of gargantuan proportions. Finally, it was feared that commencing a war in Vietnam would mean beginning a war with Red China—under the worst conditions imaginable. On May 7, 1954, Diem Bien Phu fell to the forces of Ho Chi Minh. Dien Bien Phu was followed by additional Viet Minh victories, and, in July, at the conference table in Geneva, the French and the Viet Minh agreed to divide Vietnam along the 17th parallel and concluded an armistice.

In accordance with the terms of the armistice, the USAF evacuated its personnel from Vietnam and assisted in the medical evacuation of wounded French troops. Ho Chi Minh felt confident that the reunification plebiscite mandated by the armistice and scheduled for July 1956 would result in a communist victory. The United States, in the meantime, worked with French and South Vietnamese authorities to create a stable government and build an effective South Vietnamese military. The United States also sponsored the creation of the Southeast Asia Treaty Organization (SEATO) as a shield against communist aggression and Washington proposed building up the MAAG staff in Saigon to accommodate its increased advisory role. However, the international commission charged with enforcing the Geneva armistice refused to approve the buildup. When 350 men were authorized as a "Temporary Equipment Recovery Mission," ostensibly assigned to inventory and remove surplus equipment, MAAG appropriated them as logistical advisers, and they became (despite the international commission) the Combat Arms Training and Organization Division of MAAG. With the French now withdrawing, these men formed the nucleus from which U.S. involvement in Vietnam would expand.

When South Vietnam refused to conduct the reunification plebiscite mandated by the Geneva agreement, American officials braced for an anticipated invasion from the north. It failed to materialize, and President Eisenhower decided to commit the United States to a long-term advisory role, intending to accomplish what the French had not—the creation of an effective indigenous Vietnamese military. Nevertheless, North Vietnamese insurgency into the south increased during the closing years of the decade, and, in September 1959, the Vietcong—South Vietnamese communists—commenced guerrilla warfare by ambushing two South Vietnamese army companies in the Plain of Reeds southwest of Saigon. In 1960, the United States expanded its MAAG advisers to 685 men, including Special Forces teams assigned to train Vietnamese rangers. Despite these efforts, relations between the South Vietnamese civil government and disaffected elements of the military became strained to the point of an attempted coup against President Ngo Dinh Diem on November 11, 1960. Compounding this crisis was the situation in Vietnam's neighbor, Laos, the government of which was being challenged by military forces of the pro-communist Pathet Lao.

When President John F. Kennedy took office in January 1961, the number of Vietcong insurgents in South Vietnam had swelled to some 14,000. They waged a combination guerrilla war and campaign of terror and assassination, successfully targeting thousands of civil officials, government workers, and police officers. On April 29, 1961, President Kennedy authorized an additional 100 advisers, the establishment of a combat development and test center in Vietnam, increased economic aid, and other measures. On May 11, Kennedy committed 400 U.S. Special Forces troops to raise and train a force of irregulars in areas controlled by the Vietcong, particularly along the border.

U.S. Air Force Presence

The first USAF personnel to arrive in Vietnam on a permanent duty status were the 67 men assigned to a mobile combat reporting post, essentially a radar installation, which was secretly airlifted to Vietnam during September 26–October 3, 1961. After it was installed at Tan Son Nhut on October 5, 314 additional personnel were eventually assigned to the unit. These officers and airmen created the nucleus of what would become a massive and highly sophisticated tactical air control system. Within a short time, the USAF also assigned photo reconnaissance personnel to the region, and, on October 11, 1961, President Kennedy ordered the first combat detachment to Vietnam. Officially called the 4400 Combat Crew Training Squadron, this elite force of 124 officers and 228 airmen equipped with 16 C-47s, eight B-26s, and eight T-28s was nicknamed JUNGLE JIM and code named Farm Gate. This was an "air commando" organization, and the officers as well as airmen were chosen for their physical and emotional hardiness, their combat skill, and their sense of adventure.

The first air force contingent soon found themselves at the mercy of an ambiguous sense of mission. They were trained as a combat unit, yet were officially expected only to train Vietnamese forces. Nevertheless, they were briefed for combat. In fact, the group did train Vietnamese crews and performed difficult and frustrating aerial reconnaissance missions. Flying actual combat strikes was another matter, and, on December 26, 1961, word came from the highest level of command that the unit was to conduct combat missions only when the Vietnamese air force could not. Restrictions and mixed signals concerning their mission undermined the morale of Farm Gate. The situation would prove prophetic of the tenor of the entire war.

In October 1961, President Kennedy dispatched General Maxwell Taylor and Walt Rostow to survey the situation in Vietnam and advise him as to whether to continue the U.S. advisory role there or to commit to a direct combat function. Taylor and Rostow advised continuing USAF reconnaissance flights, setting up a tactical air-ground system, which included training functions, and giving Farm Gate a freer hand, but not committing substantial U.S. combat forces. Kennedy's approval of these recommendations on November 3, 1961, marked a shift from a purely advisory role for the United States to what was described as a "limited partnership and working collaboration." The flow of aid and materiel increased dramatically, so that by June 30, 1962, there were 6,419 Americans in South Vietnam. Even as these forces were building, President Kennedy reported to the press and public that no U.S. combat forces were in Vietnam. However, he admitted, the "training units" present there were authorized to return fire if fired upon. From this point through 1968, American involvement in the Vietnam War rapidly escalated.

Escalation, 1962–1964

Beginning in January 1962, the USAF executed an airlift operation dubbed Mule Train, transporting quantities of cargo and personnel into Vietnam. Shortly after this, the USAF launched Operation Ranch Hand, an early experiment in spraying chemical defoliants to reduce cover and concealment available to the Vietcong. On February 2, 1962, a C-123 training for this mission crashed, probably the result of ground fire or sabotage. The three crewmen killed were the first USAF fatalities in South Vietnam.

By June 1963, 16,652 American military personnel—including 4,790 USAF officers and airmen—were stationed in Vietnam, and Farm Gate, still the nucleus of the USAF presence there, officially became the 1st Air Commando Squadron. At this time, the 33rd and 34th Tactical Groups came into being as well at Tan Son Nhut. The 33rd included the 33rd Air Base Squadron and the 33rd Consolidated Aircraft Maintenance Squadron. The 34th Tactical Group, based at Bien Hoa, likewise included maintenance and support squadrons, all staffed largely by enlisted airmen. Other support units, including Mule Train, were reorganized and enlarged as troop carrier squadrons. Yet, during 1963, Vietcong attacks increased and, in the Mekong Delta, the Vietcong escalated the war from guerrilla engagements to full-scale field operations. By the end of the year, the Vietcong were clearly defeating the forces of South Vietnam, the administration of President Ngo Dinh Diem was rapidly losing support, and friction between the Diem government and the United States was intensifying. On September 2, 1963, President Kennedy declared in a television address to the American public that the Diem government was out of touch with the Vietnamese people and that the war could be won only if it had popular support. The seeds of dissent were also present in the United States, as many objected to America's increasing involvement in a distant war to support an unpopular and repressive regime. On November 1, 1963, elements of the Vietnamese army staged a coup against Diem, who was assassinated the following day. A military junta set up a provisional government, which the United States recognized on November 8. Taking advantage of the confusing situation, the Vietcong stepped up their attacks, and the USAF heightened its response to them.

Gulf of Tonkin Incident, 1964

In the midst of the deteriorating situation in Vietnam, on November 22, 1963, President John F. Kennedy was assassinated, and Vice President

The Vietnam War saw the introduction of the gunship, modified C-47s and C-130s, capable of pouring concentrated fire onto ground positions. Pictured is an AC-130.   *(U.S. Air Force)*

Lyndon Johnson took office. General CURTIS LEMAY and the Joint Chiefs of Staff advised the new president to expand the war with quick, decisive action against North Vietnam, including the bombing of Hanoi. Secretary of Defense Robert McNamara favored a more conservative approach, confining operations principally to South Vietnam, but relaxing the rules for air engagement within South Vietnam and thereby expanding the role of USAF personnel working with Vietnamese crews. A short time later, however, when Hanoi responded negatively to American peace feelers, Secretary McNamara called for the formulation of an air strike plan against North Vietnam. Formulated in the summer of 1964, the plan was held in abeyance, but the situation in Vietnam took a dramatic turn on August 7, 1964, when the U.S. Senate passed the so-called Gulf of Tonkin Resolution after the U.S. destroyer *Maddox,* conducting electronic espionage in international waters in the Gulf of Tonkin, was reported fired upon on two separate occasions (the second time in company with the *C.*

Turner Joy) by North Vietnamese torpedo boats. The Senate resolution gave the president almost unlimited authority to expand the war as he saw fit. (It was subsequently discovered that the second attack was a phantom and did not actually occur.)

It was during this period that USAF personnel were successfully improvising the tactical weapons that the hitherto strategically oriented air arm lacked. C-47 and, later, C-130, aircraft were modified as gunships, firing 7.62-mm Gatling guns from side cargo doors. Infrared reconnaissance techniques were also being developed, and defoliation and crop destruction operations were stepped up.

Airmen were increasingly called upon to augment Vietnamese forces to maintain interior security and provide perimeter defense for major air bases. On November 1, 1964, Vietcong forces penetrated the perimeter of the Bien Hoa air base, killing four USAF personnel and wounding 72 in addition to destroying or damaging a number of aircraft and buildings. Although the Joint Chiefs recommended severe reprisals against North Vietnam, President Johnson, on the eve of election, bided his time. Following his victory, however, Johnson authorized a program of restricted air strikes on infiltration targets in Laos (Operation Barrel Roll). When a 300-pound charge exploded in the Brink Hotel, bachelor officers' quarters for U.S. advisers, killing two Americans and injuring 64 others in addition to 43 Vietnamese, the Joint Chiefs again urged immediate reprisals. President Johnson demurred. A few days later, on December 27, Vietcong raided the hamlet of Binh Gia, then, on December 31, surrounded the U.S. 4th Marine Battalion, which had marched to Binh Gia's relief, inflicting heavy casualties. This action, combined with the Brink Hotel explosion, prompted Ambassador Maxwell Taylor, who had earlier argued for restraint, to recommend immediate air action against North Vietnam. Then, on February 7, Vietcong mortar squads and demolition teams attacked U.S. advisory forces and Camp Holloway, headquarters of the U.S. Army 52nd Aviation Battalion, near Pleiku, killing nine Americans and wounding 108. In response, the USAF launched Operation Flaming Dart against a Vietcong military barracks near Dong Hoi. A Vietcong counterstrike came on the tenth against a U.S.-ARVN barracks at Qui Nhon, killing 23 airmen and seven Vietnamese troops. This was followed by a U.S. response the next day. These exchanges marked the beginning of a long offensive escalation.

Rapid Escalation, 1965–1969

The air strikes against North Vietnam soon became known by the code name Rolling Thunder and began on March 2, 1965, continuing through May 11, when they were suspended while the United States sought peace talks. Rolling Thunder resumed on May 18 and continued through 1968. In May 1965, 10,000 USAF personnel were serving in Vietnam. By year's end, that number grew to 21,000 operating from eight major bases. By 1968, 58,000 USAF personnel were stationed "in country."

Aside from combat, the most formidable problems airmen met were logistical. Heavy tropical rainfall during the monsoon season made runway construction extremely difficult, and the dry season brought its own problems as sand under temporary aluminum taxiways and runways caused them to shift, buckle, and dip. By the end of 1966, Air Force "Prime Beef" (BEEF: Base Engineering Emergency Force) construction teams were working feverishly at Tan Son Nhut, Bien Hoa, Da Nang, Nha Trang, Pleiku, and Binh Thuy, building aircraft revetments, barracks, Quonset huts, aprons, guard towers, and adequate plumbing and electrical facilities. "Red Horse" (Rapid Engineering and Heavy Operational Repair Squadron, Engineering) engineering squadrons provided more long-range services.

By 1967, the USAF introduced a host of innovations and refinements in communication, aircraft, and munitions in an effort to find technological solutions to the daunting problems of providing air support to ground forces fighting a guerrilla war along a highly fluid front and often in impenetrable jungle terrain.

Ground commanders made ever greater demands on air support. Air traffic control over Southeast Asia became a major priority. Sorties by Strategic Air Command (SAC) B-52s—operations collectively code named "Arc Light"—numbered 1,562 in 1965, 5,217 in 1966, and 9,686 in 1967. Total tactical sorties for all USAF aircraft numbered 672,935 in 1967. In one operation alone, Junction City, which targeted the northern part of Tay Ninh Province along the Cambodian border and spanned February 22 to May 14, 1967, 5,002 tactical air sorties delivered to targets 7,430 tons of munitions, and 126 B-52 sorties delivered an additional 537 tons. Airlift sorties for this operation, transporting cargo and personnel, totaled 2,057. Control and coordination was provided both from ground radar sites and from airborne strike control aircraft such as the EC-121. At the height of the air war, Tan Son Nhut AB became the busiest air facility in the world.

Tet Offensive, 1968

The new year, ushering out 1968, in Vietnam began with the massive Tet offensive, in which North Vietnamese forces attacked major cities and military bases from Quang Tri and Khe Sanh near the demilitarized zone (DMZ) in the northern region of South Vietnam to Quang Long near the country's southern tip. Airmen had to defend Tan Son Nhut Air Base. Up north, near the demilitarized zone (DMZ), the U.S. Marine outpost at Khe Sanh was cut off by Vietcong beginning on January 30 and held under heavy siege until mid-March. In defense of Khe Sanh, B-52s and fighter bombers flew over 24,400 sorties, dropping 100,000 tons of ordnance, and airlift operations kept the isolated marines supplied. Weather conditions were so poor, that, for the first time in airlift history, crews dropped supplies under instrument flying conditions.

"Vietnamization" Period, 1969–1972

In January 1969, shortly after taking office, President Richard M. Nixon announced as one of the primary goals of his administration an end to U.S. combat involvement in Southeast Asia. "Vietnamization"—turning the war over to South Vietnamese forces—became a top priority, and the joint SEVENTH AIR FORCE—USAF Advisory Group Ad Hoc Committee was established in South Vietnam to aid in planning, implementing, and expediting the Vietnamization process. USAF officers and airmen trained Vietnamese operational and training crews in security, fire protection, weather, communications, electronics, air traffic control, and civil engineering.

During 1970–72, the Vietnamese air force was greatly expanded and reorganized, and, by 1971, the VNAF was flying more combat sorties than the USAF, which also transferred an increasing number of aircraft to Vietnamese control. By the end of 1971 the VNAF held sole responsibility for direct air support centers at Pleiku, Bien Hoa, and Da Nang. At the end of 1972, the Vietnamese air force had grown to 42,000 officers and enlisted men (with an additional 10,000 in training) and was equipped with 2,000 aircraft of 22 types, making it the fourth largest air force in the world, behind the People's Republic of China, the United States, and the Soviet Union.

Paris Peace Talks

In May 1969, the withdrawal of U.S. Army ground units from Vietnam began in earnest. USAF air support units lingered. In 1972, taking advantage of the reduced American ground presence, communist forces of the National Liberation Front crossed the DMZ and seized a South Vietnamese province. President Nixon ordered the mining of harbors of Haiphong and other North Vietnamese ports, and peace talks between the United States and North Vietnam, which had been conducted sporadically since 1968, broke down entirely in December. Nixon then ordered 11 days of intensive "Christmas bombing" of North Vietnamese cities. This operation was carried out by B-52s out of Anderson AFB on Guam and was dubbed "Linebacker II"—though many who served on the mission referred to it as the "Eleven-Day War."

Linebacker II, conducted from December 18 to December 29, followed Linebacker I, a campaign of B-52 interdiction bombing in North Vietnam during the spring, summer, and fall of 1972. Linebacker I, in turn, had followed the sustained program air interdiction over North Vietnam conducted from 1965 to 1968 and known as Rolling Thunder. The Linebacker II operation was far more concentrated and intensive than the earlier sustained operations and was intended to force the North Vietnamese back to the conference table at Paris. During the 11 days of Linebacker II, the B-52s flew 729 sorties against 34 targets in North Vietnam above the 20th parallel. Linebacker II broke the deadlock of mid-December, and the North Vietnamese resumed negotiations on January 8, 1973. A cease-fire agreement was hammered out by January 28.

This final major USAF mission was a success, but the cease-fire it produced did not bring an end to the fighting. Nevertheless, the United States continued to withdraw from Vietnam. On January 27, Secretary of Defense Melvin Laird announced an end to the military draft, and, on March 29, the last U.S. troops departed the country, leaving behind some 8,500 U.S. civilian "technicians." On June 13, a new cease-fire agreement among the United

States, South Vietnam, North Vietnam, and the Vietcong was drawn up to end cease-fire violations. Nevertheless, from 1973 to 1975, fighting continued. In January 1975, communist forces captured the province of Phuoc Binh, then launched a major offensive in the central highlands during March. South Vietnamese forces withdrew from parts of the northwest and central highlands, and, on March 25, 1975, the old imperial capital of Hue fell. In April, Da Nang and Qui Nhon followed, and, after a fierce battle, the South Vietnamese gave up Kuon Loc on April 22. A day earlier, President Nguyen Van Thieu resigned and was briefly replaced by Tran Van Huong, whom the communists found unacceptable for negotiations. Lieutenant General Duong Van Minh became South Vietnam's last president and surrendered to the forces of North Vietnam on April 30. North and South Vietnam were officially unified under a Communist regime on July 2, 1976. The war was over.

W

Weighted Airman Promotion System (WAPS)

WAPS is the primary program used to select airmen for promotion to staff sergeant, technical sergeant, and master sergeant. Six weighted factors are used to score candidates for promotion:

1. Specialty Knowledge Test (SKT) for the applicable career field
2. Promotion Fitness Examination (PFE), a test of general USAF knowledge
3. Time in service (TIS) credit
4. Time in grade (TIG) credit
5. Credit for decorations awarded
6. Average numerical score for ratings received on performance reports

Promotion is based on WAPS and USAF vacancies in the applicable grade within the career field specialty.

Western Air Defense Force

Established in 1949 at Hamilton AFB, California, this named air force was assigned to CONTINENTAL AIR COMMAND (CONAC) and was charged with the air defense of the western continental United States. Reassigned to AIR DEFENSE COMMAND in 1951, it was discontinued in 1960.

Whiteman AFB, Missouri   See AIR FORCE BASES.

wing (organizational unit)   See ORGANIZATION, USAF.

Women Airforce Service Pilots (WASP)

Acting on an earlier suggestion by famed aviator JACQUELINE COCHRAN, Lieutenant General HENRY HARLEY ARNOLD, Chief of Staff of the U.S. ARMY AIR FORCES, authorized on October 7, 1942, a training program for 500 women ferry pilots, which became the Women Airforce Service Pilots (WASP) on August 5, 1943. It was the *second* USAAF women's auxiliary force, after the WOMEN'S AUXILIARY FERRYING SQUADRON (WAFS), which had been authorized in September 1942. Whereas the WAFS recruited only pilots with at least 500 flying hours' experience, of which at least 50 hours had to be in aircraft rated at 200 horsepower or more, WASP requirements were much lower. Admission to the first WASP training class, which graduated in November 1942, required 200 hours; the second class (December 1941), 100 hours; the third class (January 1943), 75 hours; and all subsequent classes required only 35 hours' flying time as a prerequisite for enrollment. There was no horsepower requirement at all; however, it should be noted that the USAAF had *no* flying-time prerequisite for male pilot cadets. Originally, only women between the ages of 21 and 35 were enrolled in the WASP. Beginning in August 1943, the age requirement was lowered to 18 $^1/_2$. In the segregated WORLD WAR II USAAF, only white women were accepted for service.

In August 1943, all women pilots serving with the USAAF became members of WASP, and the WAFS, therefore, ceased to exist. During its period of operation, from 1942 until it was deactivated in December 1944, WASP attracted 25,000 applicants, of whom 1,857 were accepted for training and 1,074 graduated. WASP pilots delivered a very wide range of planes from manufacturers to air base destinations in the continental United States, including training aircraft, transports, attack aircraft, and bombers. In addition to performing ferrying service, WASPs also flight tested some production (not prototype) aircraft, and, in a pinch, made repairs on the aircraft they delivered. Flying military aircraft is always hazardous and is

even more dangerous with new aircraft just off the assembly line; 38 WASP pilots were killed in the line of duty.

Altogether, WASPs flew some 75 million miles, with each pilot averaging 14 flying hours each month. For this, they were paid significantly less than their male counterparts. Whereas a male second lieutenant was paid $291 per month, a first lieutenant $330, and a captain $396, a WASP received $250 per month. Even less equitable were the differences between the compensation provided the male USAAF cadet and the WASP trainee. Male cadets were transported to flight school at no expense, whereas WASPs had to pay their own way. If a male cadet washed out of the program, he was assigned to other duty; a WASP paid her own way home. Men were furnished their

These three female pilots leaving their ship at the four engine school at Lockbourne are members of a group of WASPs who have been trained to ferry the B-17 Flying Fortresses.   *(U.S. Air Force)*

room and board, but WASPs generally paid $1.65 a day for food and lodging. Male cadets were automatically furnished with a $10,000 G.I. insurance policy; not only did WASPs receive no insurance from the government, private insurers generally canceled whatever policies they might have carried. The WASP program did, however, contribute to an emergency fund. Uniforms were furnished free to all servicemen, whereas a WASP was required to pay more than $100 for hers. The army furnished full medical care for servicemen, but—at least initially—each WASP was responsible for her own medical care. Even in death, the unequal treatment continued. Fallen servicemen received a military funeral, including a military escort home, and the family of the airman was entitled to display a Gold Star. The government provided $200 for funeral expenses and a pine box for WASPs killed in the line of duty, but no military funeral or escort was provided, and the American flag could not be used on the coffin. Families were not authorized to display a Gold Star.

The WASP program was deactivated in December 1944, and the former WASP pilots were denied all veteran's benefits. Over the years, the women appealed to the U.S. government for recognition as veterans, but it was not until 1978 that Congress acted, at last recognizing those who served as veterans entitled to full benefits.

See also LOVE, NANCY HARKNESS; WOMEN IN THE AIR FORCE.

Women in the Air Force (WAF)

The Women's Army Corps (WAC) was created when President Franklin D. Roosevelt signed a bill on July 1, 1943. By January 1945, 42,181 WAC members served with the U.S. ARMY AIR FORCES, all in noncombat roles. It was not until after WORLD WAR II, when President Harry S. Truman signed the Women's Armed Services Integration Act on June 12, 1948, that women were permitted to join the newly created USAF as members of WAF, the first director of which was Geraldine Pratt May.

WAF members received the same training as male enlisted USAF members. Although women served in most enlisted roles, none performed flying duties, except for flight nurses. In 1958, restrictions were introduced barring women from service in intelligence, information, weather, certain maintenance specialties, and control tower operations. By 1965, almost 70 percent of WAF members served in clerical and administrative roles and 23 percent in medical fields. Women officers also held mainly desk jobs. On November 8, 1967, President Lyndon B. Johnson signed Public Law 90-130, which removed most restrictions for women officers. In June 1976, WAF ceased to exist, and women were fully integrated into the USAF.

Women's Auxiliary Ferrying Squadron (WAFS)

NANCY HARKNESS LOVE was one of two prominent female aviators of the 1930s who proposed the use of women in noncombat flying roles. But whereas JACQUELINE COCHRAN proposed training women as pilots, Love wanted to recruit women who already held commercial pilot's licenses, had 500 hours of flying time logged, and were rated to fly 200 horsepower craft. At first, Major General HENRY HARLEY ARNOLD, chief of the U.S. ARMY AIR FORCES, rejected Love's proposal, but, in September 1942, he approved the creation of a women's ferrying squadron. The WAFS was founded the same month.

Although the WAFS was established as the Second Ferrying Group, New Castle Army Air Base, near Wilmington, Delaware, with Love as its director, the organization was never formally activated as a USAAF squadron and was really a civil auxiliary. By the beginning of 1943, there were only 23 WAFS performing ferry duties, albeit performing them with a high degree of proficiency. Arnold decided to authorize a training school at Avenger Field, Sweetwater, Texas, and the WAFS were merged with the new women pilots. In August 1943, all women pilots serving

Mrs. Betty Gillies was the first woman pilot to be "flight checked" and accepted by the Women's Auxiliary Ferrying Squadron.   *(U.S. Air Force)*

with the USAAF became WOMEN AIRFORCE SERVICE PILOTS (WASP).

World War I

Background

World War I began among the nations of Europe at the end of July 1914. Under President Woodrow Wilson, the United States struggled to remain neutral as the war, on its principal front—the western front in France and Belgium—ground on with great destructiveness but little discernible progress. On May 7, 1915, German U-boats torpedoed and sank the British steamer *Lusitania,* with the loss of 1,198 lives, including 124 Americans. More sinkings followed, also with loss of American lives, and evidence of German espionage and sabotage in the United States came to light, most infamously with the Zimmermann Telegram of January 19, 1917, a coded message sent by Germany's foreign secretary, Alfred Zimmermann, to the German ambassador in Mexico, proposing a Mexican-German alliance against the United States through which Mexico might regain territory it had lost in the Mexican-American War of 1846–48. The revelation of the Zimmermann Telegram, on March 1, came only one month after Germany had resumed unrestricted submarine warfare against all Atlantic shipping. On February 3, 1917, the USS *Housatonic* was sunk without warning, and the United States severed diplomatic relations with Germany. On April 2, 1917, President Wilson asked Congress for a declaration of war, which was delivered on April 6, 1917.

Unpreparedness

The United States entered the war at what was a low point for the Allies, who reeled under a series of German offensives and who had just suffered the loss of Russia, which, after the revolutions of 1917, had made a "separate peace" with Germany, thereby releasing massive numbers of German troops, who had been committed to the eastern front, for service on the western front. For the French and English, the prospect of fresh troops from America was a brilliant ray of hope. However, the United States, staunchly isolationist since the end of the Spanish-American War in 1898, was ill prepared to fight in 1917. At the time of the war declaration, the U.S. Army numbered only about 200,000 men.

As modest as the U.S. Army was at the beginning of America's involvement in the war, the AVIATION SECTION, U.S. ARMY SIGNAL CORPS, was downright minuscule, in April 1917 consisting of 131 officers (almost all of them pilots or pilots-in-training) and 1,087 enlisted men. As General John J. Pershing, commander of the American Expeditionary Force (AEF) recorded in his diary, of this number, only 35 could fly and, "with the exception of five or six officers, none of them could have met the requirement of modern battle conditions." The Aviation Section's inventory of airplanes numbered fewer than 250, all of which were so obsolescent that, by European standards, they were fit to serve only as trainers—and primary trainers at that. The mainstay of army aviation at the time of America's entry into the war were Curtiss aircraft, chiefly the famed "Jenny," the JN-3, and the R-2. In terms of the prevailing European state of the art, the Aviation Section had no fighters or bombers.

Congress had turned a blind eye to preparedness during the European phase of the war and had consistently declined to appropriate significant funds for military aviation. Nor did the army formulate plans for building an air force. The small corps of American military pilots available in the spring of 1917 had received personalized rather than standardized flight training and no training at all in combat flying. Brigadier General BENJAMIN FOULOIS and others quickly inspected the Canadian flight training system in April 1917 and, under the direction of Hiram Bingham, a Yale professor now serving in the U.S. Army Signal Corps, inaugurated ground schools for flight cadets at a half-dozen major American universities. For those who made the cut, ground school was followed by primary flight training in the United States, then advanced training overseas.

Changing Role of U.S. Military Aviation

On entering the war, the U.S. Army planned to raise a force of a million men, with aviation playing (in the words of the original mobilization plan) "a relatively insignificant part." But France and Great Britain pressed for a major American air program, and French premier Alexandre Ribot cabled President Wilson on May 26, 1917, proposing a gargantuan U.S. "flying corps" consisting of 4,500 aircraft, 5,000 pilots, and 50,000 mechanics. With unbounded faith in America's industrial might, Ribot proposed the production of no fewer than 16,500 planes during the first six months of 1918. The month before, on April 12, 1917, the newly formed National Advisory Committee for Aeronautics had recommended a program for producing 3,700 aircraft in *all* of 1918, working up to 6,000 in 1919, and 10,000 in 1920. Even these more realistic goals must be regarded as extravagantly optimistic for a U.S. aircraft industry that had produced fewer than 1,000 aircraft from the Wright brothers' "Flyer" of 1903 through 1916. Early in June 1917, the U.S. Department of War proposed to turn out 22,625 airplanes, 44,000 engines, and the equivalent of another 17,600 airplanes in spare parts—all by the end of 1918. Congress immediately appropriated $640 million for "aeronautics," the greatest sum ever appropriated for a single purpose in U.S. history up to that time. In a single stroke, air power had advanced in American military thinking from a virtual nonpriority to the chief means of winning the war in Europe, and, in August, the Aviation Section finalized a plan for creating 345 combat squadrons (up from the *single* squadron it could field as of April 1917), plus 45 construction companies, 81 supply squadrons, 11 repair squadrons, and 26 BALLOON companies; 263 of the combat squadrons were to be deployed in Europe by June 30, 1918.

The reality was that the United States concentrated on building training aircraft. Pursuit planes and bombers were purchased from the French and manufactured in France from raw materials supplied by the United States. Some 6,000 French-made craft and 8,500 engines were to be delivered by July 1, 1918. American manufacturers did produce about 3,000 De Havilland 4 (DH-4) two-seater reconnaissance bombers, under license from the British firm. Other U.S. firms produced far lesser numbers of the Handley-Page and the Italian Caproni bombers. Only one American design, the twin-engine Martin MB-1 bomber, was developed during World War I, but it did not enter production until after the war. American engineers did make one original and very valuable contribution to World War I aeronautical development, the 8-cylinder and 12-cylinder Liberty engines, but the fact was that the Aviation Section and, subsequently, the U.S. ARMY AIR SERVICE flew exclusively foreign-built or foreign-designed aircraft, except in primary flight training (see AIRCRAFT, WORLD WAR I).

Toul

The Aviation Section and the USAAS flew for only seven months of World War I, from April to

November 1918. Prior to this period, U.S. aero squadrons struggled with strategic, training, and supply issues. However, as early as 1915, Americans had been flying in the European war, both with the French and the British—though it was the American-manned LAFAYETTE ESCADRILLE of France that earned the most enduring fame. In February 1918, the Lafayette Escadrille became the basis of the 103rd Pursuit Squadron, but remained attached to the French army because no other U.S. squadrons were yet ready for action. The 1st Aero Squadron was the first American air unit, under American control, to reach France, arriving on September 3, 1917.

Trained by the French as an observation squadron, the 1st would participate in a concentration of American forces in the Toul sector, the eastern end of the front that extended from the English Channel coast to Switzerland. However, the first American air units actually to reach Toul were the 95th Pursuit Squadron, in February, followed by the 94th on March 5. Both of these units were equipped with French Nieuport fighters, but they lacked the machine guns for them. This notwithstanding, the units began flying patrols, unarmed, on March 15. Nor did the arrival of the machine guns solve all of the American fliers' problems. The pilots of the 95th had never received gunnery training and had to be sent to French gunnery school before they could take to the air in active combat. The pilots of the 94th did have the requisite training and, therefore, as the famed "Hat-in-the-Ring" squadron, became the first American air unit to fight at the front, commencing operations on April 3, 1918. On the following day, the 1st Aero Squadron arrived in Toul. Its pilots flew two-place Spad reconnaissance missions beginning on April 15, the day after two pilots from the 94th—Lieutenants Alan F. Winslow and Douglas Campbell—scored the first two kills for their squadron.

The Toul buildup continued in May with the arrival of two more squadrons, which, with the 1st, formed the 1st Corps Observation Group, operating under French tactical control. In the meantime, the 94th and 95th pursuit squadrons were merged as the 1st Pursuit Group. On June 12, the 96th Bombardment Squadron, equipped with French Bréguets, began bombing raids on railroad yards at Dommary.

Château-Thierry

At the end of June, the 1st Pursuit Group and the 1st Corps Observation Group joined some French units as the First Brigade, under the command of Colonel WILLIAM MITCHELL, at Château-Thierry, which was taking the brunt of the great offensive the Germans had begun in March. The aircraft assigned to the Americans were greatly outclassed by the newest German Fokkers, and the German pilots outmatched the less-experienced Americans. Nevertheless, the First Brigade succeeded in carrying out its primary mission, which was reconnaissance, and even participated with a force of British bombers in a successful assault on the important German supply base at Fère-en-Tardenois.

Saint-Mihiel

Reinforced by fresh American troops, the Allies, in September 1918, launched a major offensive against the infamous "Saint-Mihiel salient," a strong German incursion into the French lines that had endured since the beginning of the war. Mitchell had combat command of what now totalled 49 squadrons of the USAAS, First Army, of which only half were American. Mitchell also commanded more than 40 additional French squadrons of a French aerial division and had secured the cooperation of nine British bombardment squadrons. Mitchell massed his forces—some 1,500 aircraft—in what he correctly called the "largest aggregation of air forces that had ever been engaged in one operation on the Western Front at any time during the entire progress of the war." They opposed approximately 300 German aircraft defending the Saint-Mihiel salient. The assault on the salient began on September 12, 1918, but bad weather kept most of the aircraft grounded until the 14th and 15th. During these two days, Mitchell unleashed some 500 observation and pursuit planes in support of the ground forces while using the balance of his aircraft—about a thousand ships—to strike behind German lines, disrupting communication and supply lines and strafing advancing columns of reinforcements. The air campaign was a success, keeping the Germans on the defensive and forcing them to fight well behind their own lines.

Meuse-Argonne

The offensive against German positions at Meuse-Argonne was launched on September 26, and, while Mitchell had fewer planes to deploy, he had a greater proportion of Americans: U.S. pilots flew 600 out of 800 craft. He used his forces to disrupt the Germans' rear in order to keep them on the defensive and deflect attack from American ground troops. For the first time, Americans were involved in large-scale bombing missions. On October 9, 200 Allied bombers were escorted by 100 pursuit aircraft and 50 three-seater planes in a raid behind the lines on a position where German forces were massing for a counterattack. The bombers were met by heavy fighter resistance, but nevertheless delivered some 30 tons of bombs onto critical targets. This final air campaign of World War I was the greatest Allied air success of the war.

World War II: North African and European theaters

For a brief discussion of the origins of World War II, see WORLD WAR II: PACIFIC AND ASIAN THEATERS.

The December 7, 1941, surprise attack on Pearl Harbor elicited an outcry for immediate vengeance against Japan, but, on December 22, 1941, British prime minister Winston Churchill met in Washington with President Franklin D. Roosevelt to formulate Anglo-American strategy for the war. It was decided to concentrate first on Nazi Germany, while fighting essentially a holding action against the Japanese in the Pacific.

First U.S. Army Air Force Contingents

Despite a military buildup that had begun in anticipation of American entry into the war, the U.S. ARMY AIR FORCES were short of aircraft, personnel,

and supplies. The first contingent of 1,800 personnel departed for Liverpool on April 27, 1942, and the first airplanes, 18 B-17s, began reaching England on July 1. By the end of August, 386 planes (119 B-17s, 164 P-38s, and 103 C-47s) had crossed the North Atlantic.

On July 4, 1942, the 15th Bomb Squadron became the first USAAF unit to go operational. Six 15th Bomb Squadron crews accompanied six British crews on a low-level attack against enemy airfields in Holland. A little more than a month later, on August 17, 1942, the 97th Bomb Group made the first U.S. heavy bomber raid. A dozen B-17s, escorted by RAF Spitfires, attacked the Sotteville railroad yards at Rouen, France, while six B-17s made a diversionary sweep along the French coast. An increasing number of U.S. missions were flown through early October, before the pace slackened as USAAF units prepared for Operation Torch, the Allied invasion of North Africa.

North African Campaign

Largely at the urging of the British, Allied planners decided to make their first offensive move against what Adolf Hitler called "Fortress Europe" via Italy, which Winston Churchill dubbed the "soft underbelly" of Europe. This, it was argued, would relieve some of the pressure on the Russians in the east and allow them to begin to assume the offensive. Once pressure was applied to the Axis forces from the east and south, a major Allied invasion could be launched from the west.

The first step in invading southern Europe would be the defeat of the Germans and Italians in North Africa. But during the spring of 1942, the German Afrika Korps, under the command of the notorious "Desert Fox," Field Marshal Erwin Rommel, had pushed the British back and had advanced across North Africa to El Alamein, deep inside Egypt. The British asked for USAAF assistance. American aircraft attacked Axis airfields and supply, munitions, and fuel dumps, as well as harbors and shipping. These attacks disrupted logistics sufficiently to force the Afrika Korps to retreat west on October 23, 1942. RAF and USAAF units quickly occupied the airfields abandoned by the Axis, and by the end of January 1943, German and Italian forces had been pushed back more than 1,000 miles to the Tunisian frontier.

During this period, on November 8, 1942, with the Afrika Korps in retreat, the Allies invaded French West Africa in Operation Torch. This pinched Axis forces between Allied armies to the east and west. In response, Germany and Italy flew forces into Tunis and Bizerte from Sicily, and over the next six months, these reinforced units battled the Allies on the frontiers of Tunisia.

The USAAF worked in concert with the RAF, hurling fighters, medium bombers, and heavy bombers (the B-17 and B-24) against ports, ship convoys, and supply depots, as well as in CLOSE AIR SUPPORT missions. On April 5, 1943, USAAF fighters concentrated attacks on the German airlift from Italy to Tunisia. By nightfall, the USAAF had shot down 201 enemy airplanes. By early May, combined USAAF and RAF forces had achieved air supremacy. Almost immediately afterward, German resistance on the ground folded, and, on May 10, 1943, the 15th Panzer Division surrendered, bringing an end to the Axis presence in North Africa.

Invasion of Sicily and Italy

Pantelleria and Lampedusa are Italian islands in the Mediterranean Sea between North Africa and Sicily. Pantelleria in particular was very well fortified and had to be taken in order to proceed with the invasion of Sicily from North Africa. Because the topography of Pantelleria made amphibious assault impractical, USAAF aircraft began, on May 18, 1943, almost daily bombardment in concert with naval bombardment. Allied forces began landing on the island on June 11, and, thanks to the air action, met with no resistance.

As Pantelleria surrendered, the USAAF sent B-25s, B-26s, A-20s, and A-36 dive bombers as well as British-made Wellington bombers against Lampedusa. The attack extended over June 11 and 12, and was followed by the dropping of surrender leaflets. Lampedusa was in Allied control by June 13, and

Allied aircraft were based at Pantelleria and Lampedusa to support the invasion of Sicily, which began with a day and night bombing raid on July 10, followed by an airdrop of glider troops and paratroops—the first large-scale Allied airborne operation of the war. This aerial assault was in turn followed by amphibious landings under close air support over the next two months. As Allied forces were built up on the island, German and Italian defenders withdrew.

By mid-July, the Allies had achieved air superiority over Sicily and, on July 19, the USAAF began air operations over mainland Italy with an air raid against Rome. Italian authorities surrendered on September 3, 1943. German occupying forces, however, continued to resist, and, for the Allies, the Italian campaign would be one of the most bitter, frustrating, and costly of the war.

The Ploeşti Raid

Even as the invasion of Sicily was under way, USAAF commanders decided to stage a daring strategic raid against the target identified as supplying some 60 percent of Germany's crude oil: the Ploeşti oil fields of Romania.

The raid was launched on August 1, 1943, using USAAF B-24 Liberators based in Libya. The target was a thousand miles away and was known to be very heavily defended. The bombers hit dense cloud cover over Bulgaria, which broke up the tight formations so important to defending against fighters. Worse, German radar tracked the incoming bombers, and the Ploeşti defense forces were ready for the attack.

The B-24s braved intense antiaircraft fire and fighter sorties, inflicting substantial, but not decisive, damage on Ploeşti. The cost, however, was great. Of the 177 planes and 1,726 men who took off from Libya, 54 planes—with 532 men—were lost.

The Daylight Bombing Campaign

Although the Allied strategy of invasion via the "soft underbelly" of Europe restricted ground action to Italy, air operations from England, by the

A Consolidated B-24F Liberator of the 98th Bomb Group, IX Bomber Command, pulls away from the target in the low-level bombing attack against oil refineries at Ploesti, Romania, on August 1, 1943. *(San Diego Aerospace Museum)*

USAAF and the RAF, continued during the winter of 1942–43. During this period, the primary targets were Nazi submarine pens on the French coast. These proved difficult to penetrate, however, because they were built of heavily reinforced concrete.

USAAF planners advocated daylight precision bombing, whereas RAF commanders considered this too hazardous and favored saturation bombing by night. Thus the two services worked in conjunction: The USAAF units that had begun arriving in England in the spring of 1942 (and that would be officially designated the EIGHTH AIR FORCE in February 1944) conducted daylight raids, while the RAF bombed at night. The problem was that low-level precision bombing by day brought terrible losses from antiaircraft fire. In December 1942, for example, USAAF losses were a staggering 8.8 percent.

The Schweinfurt Raid

For the USAAF, the crisis came during the second week of October 1943. On October 9, 352 bombers flew along the Baltic Sea north of Germany to hit targets in Poland and East Prussia. The massive raid produced devastating results on the ground, but at a loss of 8 percent of the bombers committed. On October 10, Münster was targeted. Of 236 bombers launched, 30 were lost.

With these losses looming in the background, a major raid was launched against the ball-bearing industries at Schweinfurt, Germany. The idea behind strategic bombing (see BOMBING, STRATEGIC) is to attack a nation's very ability to make war, and Allied planners reasoned that, without ball bearings, nothing mechanical could operate. Reduce the supply of ball bearings, and every war industry and instrument of war would suffer.

The raid was launched on October 14, 1943. As soon as the relatively short-range P-47 fighter escorts turned back at the German border to return to England, the bombers were set upon by Luftwaffe fighters. The surviving B-17s dropped their bombs on target, but they were again attacked on the return trip. Of 251 B-17s launched, 60 were shot down and another 138 damaged. Between October 9 and October 14, 148 USAAF heavy bombers had been lost.

It was clear that the Luftwaffe had regained air superiority over Germany, and the USAAF refrained from making deep clear-weather penetrations into Germany for the rest of 1943. Other targets were hit, but USAAF commanders decided to hold off on long-distance raids until P-38 Lightning and P-51 Mustang fighter escorts, capable of long range, arrived in England.

The Air Offensive Resumes

In January 1944, now equipped with long-range escort aircraft, the USAAF was prepared to recommence the strategic bombing of Germany. The first objective was the German aircraft industry. Once that was crippled, the ability to produce interceptors would be greatly reduced, and air superiority over Germany could be regained. Broader strategic targets could be attacked.

Despite USAAF crew and aircraft readiness, bad weather over England delayed major operations until February 20, 1944, when, at last, over 1,000 heavy bombers, with massive fighter escorts, struck a dozen aircraft factories in Germany. Over the next week—February 20–25, known in USAAF lore as the "Big Week"—raids were launched from England and Italy, the USAAF going by day, the RAF by night. By this time, USAAF heavy bombers were equipped with radar for bombing through clouds, and poor weather over the target seldom forced the USAAF to change to a secondary target.

In all, 3,300 bombers flew from England and 500 from Italy. Of the British-based bombers, 137 were lost; 89 of the Italian-based force also failed to return. In human terms, 2,600 U.S. personnel were killed, wounded, or missing as a result of the Big Week, but the raids destroyed 75 percent of the buildings attacked, greatly crippling the German aircraft industry. Moreover, some 600 Luftwaffe planes were shot down in what amounted to the greatest air battle in history.

Raids on Berlin

Berlin was among the first targets chosen after Big Week. Bombing the capital of Germany not only targeted an important industrial site but also one that the Luftwaffe would act to defend at all costs—and the Allies intended that those costs would be high.

The first attack, launched on March 4, 1944, was disappointing, because, due to bad weather, only 29 bombers reached Berlin. On March 6, however, 660 USAAF heavy bombers attacked Berlin and, as expected, were met by massive opposition. Of the 660 bombers flown, 69 were lost, together with 11 fighter escorts; however, USAAF pilots shot down 179 Luftwaffe aircraft—and caused extensive damage to Berlin. On March 8, 462 bombers, heavily escorted by 174 P-51s, bombed the Erkner ball bearing factory. The Luftwaffe, flying to the defense, suffered severe losses.

Preparation for D-day

During the early spring, Italian-based fighters and bombers of the FIFTEENTH AIR FORCE began target-

ing shipping, railroads, and highways with the objective of severely compromising the German transportation network to expedite the Allied ground advance on Rome.

While the 15AF tackled this mission, British-based 8AF planes concentrated on V-1 launch sites on the coasts of France and Belgium and also attacked Luftwaffe airfields and coastal defenses. The 8AF then turned to a campaign against the transportation network in northwestern France, hitting railroad yards and bridges there and also in Belgium. The objective was to reduce German ability to reinforce Normandy, the landing site for the planned amphibious invasion of France. The campaign proved highly successful. Prior to D-day, all 12 railroad and 14 highway bridges across the Seine River from Paris to Le Havre had been destroyed.

As D-day drew near, USAAF reconnaissance aircraft flew many sorties to obtain detailed photographs of German beach defenses. Some flights were made as low as 15 feet. Then, in the days immediately preceding the June 6, 1944, landings, 1,083 B-17s and B-24s dropped 3,000 tons of bombs on German defenses. This initial assault was followed by sorties by medium bombers and fighter bombers, which attacked targets further to the rear.

The Shuttle Raids

While strategic bombing was stepped up in western Europe, U.S. commanders persuaded the Soviet Union's Joseph Stalin to allow USAAF heavy bombers to fly "shuttle" missions to Russia in order to bomb eastern Germany and the Balkans without having to fly all the way back to England and Italy. USAAF crews and aircraft were stationed at three airfields near Kiev in the Ukraine.

The first shuttle raid took off from Italy on June 2. On June 6, a raid was launched from the Ukraine against a target in Romania. On June 11, the planes returned to Italy, bombing another Romanian target on the way. More shuttle missions followed through September 13, 1944, by which time the eastern front had advanced so far west that the Soviet bases were no longer needed.

The Normandy Invasion

Not only was air power essential in the preparation for the invasion of France, the invasion itself, on June 6, 1944, began from the air. USAAF C-47s carried paratroops and towed gliders, in the biggest airdrop in history: 17,000 men. Despite heavy antiaircraft fire and poor visibility, most of the transports and gliders reached their landing areas—although many paratroopers and gliders came down well outside their intended drop zones. Some historians believe this accidental scattering of the airborne troops actually contributed to the success of the invasion by confusing the enemy.

Throughout the Normandy landings, USAAF and RAF aircraft flew close air support (the British-based NINTH AIR FORCE was chiefly responsible for tactical action) before returning primarily to the strategic bombing mission. By the autumn of 1944, German oil production, a prime target of the strategic campaign, had been seriously curtailed—but at the cost of 922 bombers and 674 fighters during the summer of 1944.

Battle of Arnhem

USAAF units balanced the demands of the strategic mission with the tactical requirements of supporting the breakout from the Normandy beachheads and the advance across France. By the late summer of 1944, Allied troops had reached the border of Germany and Holland, and it was decided to attempt a breakthrough in southeastern Holland toward the Ruhr, a great German industrial region.

Operation Market Garden began on September 17, 1944, with a paratroop and glider drop behind German lines, with American, British, and Polish soldiers participating in landings at Eindhoven, Nijmegen, and Arnhem. The effectiveness of the German response had been badly underestimated. Powerful counterattacks were launched, especially against the British at Arnhem, and poor weather delayed aerial resupply and reinforcement. On September 23, the British withdrew from Arnhem.

Battle of the Bulge

While the advance in the north had been stopped at Arnhem, elsewhere Allied troops tore across France and into Germany. However, beginning on December 16, 1944, the Allies were met with a new crisis, as the Germans threw everything they had into a massive counteroffensive in the Ardennes, with the object of breaking through the Allied lines to Antwerp.

Withdrawing before the German onslaught, American commanders rushed the 101st Airborne to hold the strategically positioned village of Bastogne, Belgium. The paratroopers did just that, fighting a desperate holding action over Christmas while enveloped by German forces. Extremely adverse weather grounded Allied airpower, but, once the weather lifted, the USAAF (chiefly 9AF) and RAF prevailed against the now greatly outnumbered Luftwaffe. By the end of January 1945, the Allies had reclaimed most of the territory that had been lost in the counteroffensive, and, in February, the Allies approached the Rhine River, crossing at Remagen on March 7.

The Drive through Germany

North of Remagen, more Allied troops crossed the Rhine at Wesel during the night of March 23–24. On the morning of the 24th, the crossing was supported by an aerial invasion of more than 2,800 U.S. and British gliders and paratroop transports. By this point, most of the great strategic targets in Germany had been destroyed, and the USAAF turned to strafing and low-level bombing of targets of opportunity, in addition to providing close air support for the ongoing advance.

Although the Luftwaffe had begun to use its most advanced aircraft, early jet fighters, there were too few available to have much effect. In the final advance through Germany, the Allied air forces enjoyed air supremacy.

Toward V-E Day

During April 1945, Germany was being overrun from the west and the east. The last USAAF mission against an industrial target took place on April

25, with the bombing of the Skoda armament works at Pilsen, Czechoslovakia. After this, much of the USAAF's work consisted of missions of aid and mercy, air dropping food to civilians in northern Italy and the Netherlands, and evacuating liberated prisoners of war.

On May 2, German forces in Italy and southern and western Austria surrendered, and, on May 7, Germany surrendered unconditionally.

While no one would dispute the importance of air power in World War II, many military thinkers and historians have debated the effectiveness of strategic bombing. Certainly, the air war was costly to prosecute. The USAAF lost 27,694 aircraft in the war (from all causes), including 8,314 heavy bombers, 1,623 medium and light bombers, and 8,481 fighters. Personnel casualties totaled 91,105, including 34,362 killed, 13,708 wounded, and 43,035 missing, captured, or interned.

V-E Day meant an end to the war in Europe. The war in the Pacific continued, and many USAAF personnel and airplanes were transferred to the other theater; see WORLD WAR II: PACIFIC AND ASIAN THEATERS.

World War II: Pacific and Asian theaters

For a discussion of the war in North Africa and Europe, see WORLD WAR II: NORTH AFRICAN AND EUROPEAN THEATERS.

Origins of the War

The Treaty of Versailles, which ended WORLD WAR I, was so harshly punitive against Germany that the nation, already reeling economically from the war, was saddled with crippling reparations, humiliatingly compelled to admit guilt for having caused the war, and limited to a skeleton army of 100,000 men. Combined with the great worldwide depression of the 1930s, Germany's economic hardships and collective national disgrace wrought by the terms of the treaty pushed the nation over the brink of desperation. Threatened, too, by the effects of communist revolution in nearby Russia, the German people looked for a leader who prom-

ised not only immediate salvation but also a return to greatness. That man appeared to be Adolf Hitler, who rose through the 1920s and 1930s to become absolute dictator of Germany. He embarked on a program of rearmament and territorial expansion, in which the war-weary democracies of Europe, primarily France and Britain, acquiesced. On March 7, 1936, German armies violated the Treaty of Versailles by occupying the demilitarized Rhineland. The democracies did not respond. On July 11, 1936, Italy, under the fascist dictatorship of Benito Mussolini, agreed with Hitler that Austria should be deemed "a German state," and, on November 1, Italy and Germany concluded the Rome-Berlin Axis, which was followed on November 25 by the German-Japanese Anti-Comintern Pact—an alliance ostensibly against communism, but, in fact, an alliance of general military cooperation. Thus, Germany, Italy, and Japan, all militaristic states at this point in history, became allies in the Rome-Berlin-Tokyo Axis.

On March 13, 1938, having secured the blessing of Mussolini, Hitler invaded Austria and annexed it to Germany. This put Germany in position to make its next move, into Czechoslovakia. British prime minister Neville Chamberlain, seeking to avoid a new world war by a policy of "active appeasement," agreed, in the Munich conference of September 29–30, 1938, to Germany's annexation of the Czechoslovakian Sudetenland. Hitler promised an end to expansion, only to seize the rest of Czechoslovakia by occupying Prague on March 16, 1939. On August 23, 1939, Hitler signed a "Non-Aggression Pact" with his great ideological rival, Soviet premier Joseph Stalin, which gave him leave to invade Poland. That invasion came on September 1, 1939. The democracies could not overlook this act of aggression, and World War II commenced.

In the Pacific, in the meantime, Japan intensified its policy of expansion, which had begun early in the century. In the 1930s, Japan invaded China and annexed Manchuria (calling it Manchukuo). With the formation of the Rome-Berlin-Tokyo Axis, the administration of U.S. president Franklin Roosevelt introduced economic sanctions against

Japan in an effort to curb its expansionism and to pressure it to withdraw from China. FDR saw these sanctions as an alternative to war, but, in fact, Japan took them as a provocation. In the face of a U.S. embargo, Japan could not long continue the war against China. Rather than withdraw from China, the militarists who now controlled the Japanese government decided not only to risk war with the United States but also to move so aggressively throughout the Pacific that America would be overwhelmed into helplessness.

America Enters the War

At 7:55 on Sunday morning, December 7, 1941, a Japanese force of 183 carrier-based aircraft attacked without warning U.S. military and naval facilities at and around Pearl Harbor, Hawaii. The first assault was over in 30 minutes. A second wave of 170 planes launched an hour-long attack. The result was devastating: 2,343 U.S. service personnel killed, 960 missing, and 1,272 wounded; 151 planes were destroyed on the ground, and all eight great battleships at anchor in Pearl Harbor were either sunk or damaged.

While the attack was a tactical triumph for the Japanese, it was a strategic disaster, because it instantly mobilized a hitherto reluctant United States to war. The declaration came on December 8. Germany and Italy, bound by treaty with Japan, declared war on the United States on December 11, and the United States declared against them in turn.

Fall of the Philippines

After Pearl Harbor, the Japanese offensive moved swiftly. The Philippine Islands, at the time a U.S. territory, were attacked from the air on December 8, 1941, and invaded on the 9th. Overwhelmed, U.S. and Filipino forces made a fighting withdrawal to the peninsula of Bataan and to Corregidor Island in Manila Bay. Bataan fell on April 9, 1942; Corregidor, surrounded, held out until May 6, 1942.

U.S. ARMY AIR FORCES aircraft in the Philippines then consisted of only 72 P-40Es, 52 obsolescent P-

35As, and 12 obsolete P-26s. More than half the USAAF force was lost on the ground and in aerial combat. Many USAAF ground personnel were hurriedly transferred to army combat units and were ultimately captured or killed on Bataan or Corregidor. Others withdrew to the southernmost island of Mindanao along with a handful of B-17s. Those bombers that survived the initial attacks were soon withdrawn to Australia, evacuating as many men as they could carry. Many more, however, were left behind. On June 9, the last American and Filipino holdouts surrendered.

Action in Java

Simultaneously with the assault on the Philippines, the Japanese attacked the Netherlands East Indies. The USAAF attempted to assist the Dutch by bombing targets on the Malay Peninsula eastward to the Celebes Islands. The effort was small and inadequate, and, by early March, Java was evacuated. Except for the portion of New Guinea around Port Moresby, the Japanese now occupied territory from the eastern border of India, across the islands of the Southwest Pacific, to the northern doorstep of Australia.

The Doolittle Raid

U.S. military planners understood that, given time, American industrial and military forces would become a formidable and eventually overwhelming presence. However, since December 7, 1941, the United States had suffered one humiliating defeat after another and had fought a desperately defensive war. USAAF Lieutenant Colonel JAMES HAROLD DOOLITTLE and others formulated a morale-boosting offensive action, a bold air raid against Tokyo to be carried out by 16 B-25 Mitchell bombers launched from the aircraft carrier *Hornet*.

The planes were launched on April 18, 1942. Because the flotilla had been sighted by the Japanese, the aircraft took off not 450 to 650 miles from Japan, as planned, but 800 miles out, making it extremely difficult for the pilots to reach friendly airstrips in China after the raid. All 16 bombers did reach the Japanese islands, and they dropped their bombs on oil stores, factory areas, and military installations.

In strictly military terms, the damage inflicted by 16 medium bombers was minor. But it thrilled Americans, and it stunned the Japanese, who were forced to transfer back to the home islands fighter units that otherwise could have been used against the Allies. Incredibly, most of the Doolittle aircrews survived and eventually made their way back to U.S. military control. Doolittle himself went on to higher command.

Coral Sea, Midway, and New Guinea

Seeking to complete its conquest of New Guinea, Japanese invasion forces sailed to Tulagi and Port Moresby, New Guinea, in May 1942. Tulagi fell without opposition, but the larger Japanese force sailing to New Guinea was intercepted on May 7 by naval aircraft launched from *Lexington* and *York-town*. The main phase of the Battle of the Coral Sea began on May 8 and was entirely a duel between carrier-launched aircraft. U.S. aircraft damaged the carrier *Shokaku*, but 33 out of 82 of the attacking planes were lost. The Japanese sank the *Lexington*, a destroyer, and a tanker, losing 43 of 69 aircraft in the attack. The Battle of the Coral Sea was thus a Japanese tactical victory, but a strategic defeat; although U.S. losses were heavier, the Japanese advance had been stopped, Port Moresby saved, and the Japanese fleet driven out of the Coral Sea.

The next Japanese objective was Midway Island, which would provide a critical airbase to whichever side held it. Japanese admiral Isoruko Yamamoto sent a diversionary force to the Aleutian Islands, while Admiral Chuichi Nagumo, who had led the Pearl Harbor attack, took a four-carrier strike force followed by an invasion fleet—some 88 ships in all—to Midway. His American opponent, Admiral Chester A. Nimitz, having anticipated such an attack, brought together two task forces east of Midway, designated Number 16 (under Admiral Raymond Spruance) and Number 18 (under Admiral Frank Fletcher). The task forces included the carriers *Enterprise*, *Hornet*, and *Yorktown*, in addition to land-based U.S. Marine and USAAF aircraft

on Midway itself. The Midway-based planes attacked elements of the Japanese fleet on June 3, but inflicted little damage. On June 4, 108 Japanese aircraft struck Midway, destroying 15 of 25 U.S. Marine aircraft. U.S. Navy torpedo bombers twice attacked the Japanese fleet, but without success. A third attack, by Midway-based USAAF B-17 bombers, also failed to damage or sink any of the enemy carriers. A navy torpedo bomber attack, in which 35 of the 41 aircraft engaged were lost, also inflicted little damage, but it did open the way for a massive attack by 54 dive bombers from *Enterprise* and *Yorktown*, which sunk three Japanese aircraft carriers. The fourth Japanese carrier, *Hiryu*, was sunk in a separate attack later in the day—although not before *Hiryu*'s planes had delivered a fatal blow against the *Yorktown*.

Japanese forces began withdrawing on June 5, 1942, and Midway was the hard-fought turning point of the Pacific war. From this point forward, the United States would take a relentlessly offensive posture in the Pacific.

Guadalcanal and the Solomons

After the Midway battle, the Japanese moved into the lower Solomon Islands and, on Guadalcanal, rushed to complete an airfield, which would give them a base from which to attack the lifeline between Hawaii and Australia. USAAF B-17s performed reconnaissance that enabled U.S. Marines to make a surprise landing on Guadalcanal on August 7, 1942. In coordination with the navy and the marines, the USAAF successfully held the island.

Guadalcanal became a base from which U.S. forces conducted offensive operations in the Solomons, the campaign culminating in the November 1, 1943, marine landing on Bougainville.

It was during the Solomons campaign that, acting on intercepted and decoded Japanese radio traffic, P-38 pilots of the THIRTEENTH AIR FORCE intercepted and shot down an airplane transporting Admiral Yamamoto. The loss of Japan's most important naval strategist was a terrible blow to the Imperial Navy.

Aleutian Campaign

During the Midway campaign, as mentioned, the Japanese staged a diversionary strike far to the north, against the Aleutian Islands of Alaska. In June 1942, the enemy bombed Dutch Harbor in the Aleutian chain and landed troops on Kiska and Attu islands. Despite severe weather, the ELEVENTH AIR FORCE operated continuously against the enemy. In a six-month period, 13AF lost 72 planes —nine in combat, the others to the weather.

In May 1943, U.S. forces captured Attu, and on July 10 the USAAF set up a base on this forbidding island from which raids were staged against the Japanese-held Kuriles. When U.S. troops invaded Kiska on August 15, they found the enemy already evacuated.

Central Pacific Action

From the beginning of the war through the Battle of Midway, the role of the SEVENTH AIR FORCE, based in Hawaii, had been primarily defensive. After Midway, the Japanese made little attempt to advance in this theater. However, by late 1943, 7AF aircraft were being used to soften up islands scheduled for amphibious assault. The 7AF also flew missions to neutralize enemy forces on islands that were being bypassed by Allied forces as part of the "island-hopping" strategy that proved so effective in the Gilberts and Marshalls. The aircrews of 7AF often flew missions against targets more than a thousand miles away, and navigation over vast expanses of ocean became a high-risk proposition.

Gilbert and Marshall Islands

Each island wrested from the Japanese became a potential airbase. B-24s of the 7AF used Ellice Island as a refueling stop en route to bomb Tarawa and Nauru (in the Gilbert group) during April 1943. In November, after aerial bombardment by USAAF B-24s and carrier-based naval aircraft, Tarawa and Makin were invaded by the U.S. Army. Once these islands were secured, USAAF planes were transferred to bases in the Gilberts to support amphibious assaults in the Marshalls, and, by the

end of February 1944, those islands were in Allied hands. Among the Marshalls were Kwajalein and Eniwetok, which provided bases from which to attack and invade the Marianas, which, in turn, would furnish bases needed for operations by B-29 Superfortresses. These aircraft, the biggest bombers of the war, had the range to deliver huge bomb loads onto the Japanese home islands.

Triumph in New Guinea

While the campaign was ongoing in the Gilberts and Marshalls, the Thirteenth Air Force, based in New Guinea, flew to the Admiralty Islands to join the 7AF and naval units in neutralizing the Carolines, islands that were slated to be "hopped over." During these operations, General Douglas MacArthur's Southwest Pacific forces advanced west along the northern New Guinea coast. To protect this advance, it was necessary to attack Rabaul, a major Japanese base on New Britain Island. Therefore, in October 1943, 5AF and 13AF bombers pounded New Britain almost daily.

By the summer of 1944, the Allies had completed their advance along the northern New Guinea coast. This left many thousands of Japanese troops behind in the Solomons, on New Guinea, and elsewhere—completely cut off.

Philippines Campaign

General Douglas MacArthur was determined to redeem the famous pledge he had made when, in the face of Japanese invasion, he was forced to flee the Philippines: "I shall return."

Prior to the campaign to retake the Philippines, USAAF bombers hit petroleum facilities in the Netherlands East Indies. Next, Allied forces invaded the Palau Islands and Morotai, acquiring airfields from which targets in the Philippines could be struck, beginning in August 1944.

American forces landed on Leyte on October 20, 1944, and, a week later, 34 P-38s landed there, becoming the first USAAF aircraft in the Philippines since early 1942.

It was, however, during the desperate Battle of Leyte Gulf that Japan unleashed its latest air weapon: the Kamikaze suicide pilots, who transformed their airplanes into human-guided missiles. Nevertheless, by December 31, 1944, USAAF and U.S. Marine pilots shot down more than 356 Japanese planes—with the loss of only 23 U.S. fighters.

U.S. troops landed on Mindoro on December 15, 1944, and on January 9, 1945, Americans invaded Luzon, with USAAF aircraft operating freely, having won air supremacy. Explicitly targeted was Japanese shipping in the South China Sea and enemy forces in Formosa.

The culmination of the Philippine campaign was the recapture of Corregidor. The first U.S. troops were airdropped on February 16, 1945, by USAAF transports. Within two weeks, the Japanese had been defeated and, by June, most of the Philippines had been liberated.

Action in the Marianas

Just prior to the Allied assault on the Philippines, naval forces under Admiral Chester Nimitz in the central Pacific attacked the Marianas beyond Truk and the Carolines to secure bases for B-29s. Saipan was invaded on June 15, 1944, and, within a week, the airfield there had been captured. USAAF fighters moved onto the field to provide air cover for the island and to support amphibious assaults against Guam and Tinian, which were invaded on July 21 and 24. By mid-August, both Guam and Tinian were securely in U.S. hands, and major airbases were built to support the B-29s for operations against the Japanese homeland. The bombers began arriving in October and November.

Operations in China

While U.S. and other Allied forces were largely deployed in the central Pacific and southern Pacific areas, the China-Burma-India (CBI) theater was chronically undermanned and undersupplied. Very early in the war the AMERICAN VOLUNTEER GROUP, the celebrated "Flying Tigers," were the only U.S. presence in the theater—a mere 43 P-40B fighters manned by 84 former military pilots. In its brief career, spanning December 1941 to July 1942, the Flying Tigers destroyed 296 Japanese aircraft in China and Burma. (Some recent historians believe their number is somewhat inflated.)

The USAAF arrived in the CBI in July 1942. The Flying Tigers were dissolved, and some pilots joined their commander, CLAIRE CHENNAULT in a regular army unit called the China Air Task Force, which evolved into the FOURTEENTH AIR FORCE. The 14AF and its associated ground forces were supplied via "the Hump," the extraordinarily hazardous 500-mile air route from India to China over the Himalayas.

Despite chronic shortages, 14AF pilots destroyed or damaged more than 4,000 Japanese aircraft and sank in excess of 1 million tons of shipping. On land, 14AF planes interdicted rail and road transport.

Burma Operations

For most of the war, Allied operations on the Asian mainland were focused on holding the enemy while the principal offensive effort was directed elsewhere. By the middle of May 1942, the Japanese had taken all of Burma and had cut the Burma Road into China. The TENTH AIR FORCE, equipped with a handful of B-17s and LB-30s (export version of the B-24), was unable to stop the Japanese advance, and, in June, the 10AF's bombers were transferred to Africa to bolster defenses there.

Only as the Allies in CBI gradually received reinforcements did the British Royal Air Force (RAF) and 10AF begin to gain air superiority over the Japanese in Burma. Once this had been achieved, medium bombers and fighter bombers targeted enemy river traffic, bridges, and railroads.

In March 1944, Allied troop carrier units and a USAAF air commando group used gliders and C-47s to land and drop far behind enemy lines some 9,000 British "Chindit" raiders commanded by Major General Orde Wingate. These raiders struck enemy communications and supply routes. USAAF airdrops also sustained the U.S. guerrillas of Brigadier General Frank D. Merrill ("Merrill's Marauders") in a northern Burma campaign that reopened the Burma Road to China by January

1945. The 10AF and RAF also supported the capture of Mandalay in March 1945 and Rangoon in May, driving the remnants of the Japanese forces out of Burma.

Strategic Bombing of the Japanese Homeland

Major General CURTIS EMERSON LEMAY took command of the 21st Bomber Command on January 20, 1945 and, on February 3, conducted a high-altitude incendiary raid against the important industrial city of Kobe. Based on the results of the Kobe raid, LeMay decided to increase the effectiveness of raids against Japanese cities by changing from high-altitude, daylight precision bombing with high-explosive bombs to low-altitude night missions using incendiary bombs. His first major target was Tokyo, which 334 B-29s struck from only 5,000 to 9,000 feet on the night of March 9-10. The raid created firestorms that destroyed almost 16 square miles of the city. Tokyo was the first of many massive raids against the cities and industrial centers of Japan.

Iwo Jima Campaign

Iwo Jima is a sterile volcanic island halfway between Saipan and Japan. Uninviting, it was nevertheless of great strategic importance because it presented an obstacle to B-29 formations flying to Japan, and it was used as a staging area for Japanese strikes against B-29 bases in the Marianas. It also threatened air-sea rescue operations along the B-29 flight routes. If Iwo Jima could be captured, not only would these obstacles be removed, but the island could be used as a crucially important emergency landing field for B-29s and a base from which short-range USAAF fighters could escort the B-29s to Japan.

The campaign to take the island began with weeks of USAAF and naval aerial bombardment as well as shelling. With the island softened up, U.S. Marines landed on February 19, 1945. Despite the long preparation, the Japanese defended the island fanatically through late March. Once secured, Iwo Jima did provide landing facilities that ultimately

saved the lives of some 24,000 B-29 crew members, and the island also served as a P-51 base.

Okinawa Campaign

The ongoing B-29 incendiary bombing against Japan was interrupted during April and May 1945 as USAAF B-29s were diverted to attack airfields and aircraft plants and to mine Japanese waters in preparation for the invasion of Okinawa, largest of the Ryukyu Islands. Five days after the U.S. landings on Okinawa (April 1), the Japanese launched a massive aerial counterattack, including more than 350 Kamikaze sorties. In response, on April 8, the USAAF targeted the Kamikaze bases in Japan—to no avail, however, as the Kamikaze attacks approached 1,900 by June 22, resulting in the loss of 25 ships. Nevertheless, early in May, the USAAF moved P-51 fighters onto Okinawa airfields to provide more adequate aerial defense. Deemed secure on July 2, Okinawa became a base for 7AF medium bombers and fighters, close enough to attack the home islands.

Hiroshima and Nagasaki

As devastating as the unremitting incendiary raids against Japan had become, it was apparent that the nation intended to fight to the death. Air power alone seemed unable to achieve victory, and Allied planners prepared for a massive invasion that would dwarf the Normandy landings in Europe and that would cost perhaps a million Allied lives.

Unknown to all but the highest-placed government and military officials, the United States had been developing nuclear weapons since early in the war. Two bombs were ready for use, and, at 8:15 A.M. on August 6, 1945, the B-29 *Enola Gay*, based on Tinian, released a single atomic bomb over the city of Hiroshima, a virgin target. As planned, the weapon detonated at about 2,000 feet, instantly destroying most of the city. Called on to surrender, the Japanese government refused, and, on August 9, another B-29, *Bock's Car*, released an atomic bomb over Nagasaki at 10:58 A.M. The results were similarly devastating.

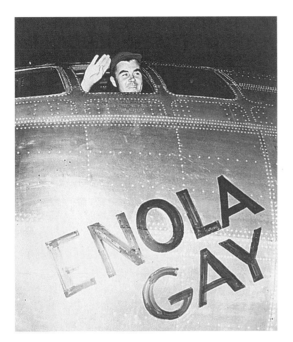

Colonel Paul Tibbetts, pilot, waves from the cockpit of the *Enola Gay* before taking off to drop the first atomic bomb on Hiroshima, Japan.   *(U.S. Air Force)*

On August 10, the Japanese government announced its willingness to accept most of the peace terms set forth by the Allies in the Potsdam Declaration. Negotiations faltered, and conventional bombing was resumed. The last USAAF raid was carried out on August 14, 1945, just before President Truman announced Japan's unconditional surrender. The Pacific War—and, with it, World War II—was over.

Wright-Patterson AFB, Ohio   See AIR FORCE BASES.

Y

Yeager, Charles E. "Chuck" (1923–)
World War II ace and test pilot

Yeager was the first human being to fly faster than the speed of sound, exceeding Mach 1 in the Bell X-1 aircraft on October 14, 1947.

Born in Myra, West Virginia, Yeager enlisted in the U.S. ARMY AIR FORCES in 1941. He worked as an aircraft mechanic before enrolling in flight training in 1942. Late in 1943, Yeager flew F-51 Mustangs for the 363rd Fighter Squadron, based in England.

Captain Charles E. Yeager is shown here standing in front of the Air Force's Bell-built X-1 supersonic research aircraft. *(U.S. Air Force)*

Shot down over France in March 1944, he successfully evaded capture and returned to the 363rd. Credited with 13 victories, Yeager ended the war as an ace.

Following WORLD WAR II, in 1945, Yeager became a TEST PILOT at the Fighter Test Branch, Wright Field, Ohio. His performance as a test pilot earned him selection as pilot of the Bell X-1, built expressly to investigate supersonic flight. Yeager was assigned to Edwards AFB, California, and, after flying the X-1 there, he continued to test every new experimental and prototype aircraft in the USAF inventory. In December 1953, he flew an X-1A to Mach 2.44. Although he nearly lost control of the aircraft due to high-speed instability (inertial coupling), his record-breaking achievement earned him the 1953 Harmon Trophy.

Yeager left Edwards in 1954 and was given command of operational units in Europe and California through 1961, when he was named to command the USAF Test Pilot School at Edwards. In 1966, he assumed command of the 405th Fighter Wing, stationed at Clark AB, Philippines, and, between 1966 and 1967, he flew 127 sorties in the VIETNAM WAR. Leaving the 405th in 1967, Yeager was given a number of command assignments and was ultimately named director of the AIR FORCE INSPECTION AND SAFETY CENTER. He served in this post from 1973 to 1975, when he retired.

Yokota AB, Japan   See AIR FORCE BASES.

Z

Zulu, or Zulu time

Greenwich Mean Time; always used in conjunction with 24-hour military time, for example 1300 Zulu. In written communication, "Zulu" is designated as Z, for example: 1300Z.

U.S. Air Force Abbreviations and Acronyms

★

AAC Alaskan Air Command
AAFAC Army Air Forces Antisubmarine Command
AB Air Base
ACC Air Combat Command
ADC Aerospace Defense Command
AEDC Arnold Engineering Development Center
AETC Air Education and Training Command
AF Air Force Association
AFAA Air Force Audit Agency
AFAMS Air Force Agency for Modeling and Simulation
AFB Air Force Base
AFBCA Air Force Base Conversion Agency
AFC Air Force Council
AFCAA Air Force Cost Analysis Agency
AFCC Air Force Combat Command; also, Air Force Communications Command
AFCCC Air Force Combat Climatology Center
AFCCCA Air Force Command, Control, Communications, and Computer Agency
AFCEE Air Force Center for Environmental Excellence
AFCERT Air Force Computer Emergency Response Team
AFCESA Air Force Civil Engineer Support Agency
AFCOMS Air Force Commissary Service
AFCQMI Air Force Center for Quality and Management Innovation
AFCSTC Air Force Cost Center
AFDC Air Force Doctrine Center
AFDD Air Force Doctrine Document
AFDTC Air Force Development Test Center
AFESC Air Force Engineering and Services Center
AFFMA Air Force Frequency Management Agency
AFFSA Air Force Flight Standards Agency
AFFTC Air Force Flight Test Center
AFHRA Air Force Historical Research Agency
AFHSO Air Force History Support Office
AFI Air Force Instruction
AFIA Air Force Inspection Agency; also Air Force Intelligence Agency
AFISC Air Force Inspection and Safety Center
AFIT Air Force Institute of Technology
AFIWC Air Force Information Warfare Center
AFLC Air Force Logistics Command
AFLMA Air Force Logistics Management Agency
AFLSC Air Force Legal Services Center
AFMC Air Force Materiel Command
AFMEA Air Force Management Engineering Agency
AFMIA Air Force Manpower and Innovation Agency
AFMOA Air Force Medical Operations Agency
AFMPC Air Force Military and Personnel Center

AFMSA   Air Force Medical Support Agency

AFNEWS   Air Force News Agency

AFNSEP   Air Force National Security Emergency Preparedness

AFOMS   Air Force Office of Medical Support

AFOSI   Air Force Office of Special Investigations

AFPC   Air Force Personnel Center

AFPCA   Air Force Pentagon Communications Agency

AFOSP   Air Force Office of Security Police

AFOG   Air Force Operations Group

AFOSR   Air Force Office of Scientific Research

AFOTEC   Air Force Operational Test and Evaluation Center

AFPC   Air Force Personnel Center

AFPD   Air Force Policy Document

AFPEO   Air Force Program Executive Office

AFPOA   Air Force Personnel Operations Agency

AFR   Air Force Reserve

AFRBA   Air Force Review Boards Agency

AFRC   Air Force Reserve Command

AFREA   Air Force Real Estate Agency

AFRL   Air Force Research Laboratory

AFROTC   Air Force Reserve Officer Training Corps

AFS   Air Force Specialty, or Air Force Station

AFSAA   Air Force Studies and Analyses Agency

AFSAB   Air Force Scientific Advisory Board

AFSC   Air Force Specialty Code; also Air Force Safety Center; also Air Force Systems Command

AFSOC   Air Force Special Operations Command

AFSPA   Air Force Security Police Agency

AFSPACECOM   Air Force Space Command

AFSVA   Air Force Services Agency

AFTAC   Air Force Technical Applications Center

AFWA   Air Force Weather Agency

AIA   Air Intelligence Agency

ALS   Airman Leadership School

AMC   Air Mobility Command

ANG   Air National Guard

ARPC   Air Reserve Personnel Center

AU   Air University

AVG   American Volunteer Group

AWACS   Airborne Warning and Control System

AWC   Air War College

AWFC   Air Warfare Center

AWS   Air Weather Service

BMT   Basic Military Training

C³I   Command, Control, Communications, and Intelligence

C⁴   Command, Control, Communications, and Computer Systems

C⁴I   Command, Control, Communications, and Intelligence

CAP   Civil Air Patrol

CAS   Close Air Support

CCAF   Community College of the Air Force

CCT   Combat Control Team

CENTAF   U.S. Central Command Air Forces

CINC   Commander in Chief

CMSAF   Chief Master Sergeant of the Air Force

COMPUSEC   Computer Security

COMSEC   Communications Security

CONAC   Continental Air Command

CONUS   Continental United States

DOD   Department of Defense

DRU   Direct Reporting Unit

EW   Electronic Warfare

FLY TAF   Flying Training Air Force

FOA   Field Operating Agency

HAF   Headquarters Air Force

IAAFA   Inter-American Air Forces Academy

ICBM   Intercontinental Ballistic Missile

IRBM   Intermediate Range Ballistic Missile

JADF   Japan Air Defense Force

JSF   Joint Strike Fighter

JSTARS   Joint Surveillance Target Attack Radar System

MAJCOM   Major Command

MAC   Military Airlift Command

MATS   Military Air Transport Service

MPF   Military Personnel Flight

MWR   Morale, Welfare, and Recreation

NAF   Numbered Air Force

NCO   Noncommissioned Officer

NCOIC   Noncommissioned Officer in Charge

NORAD   North American Aerospace Defense Command

OJT   On-the-Job Training

OTS   [Air Force] Officer Training School
PACAF   Pacific Air Forces
PME   Professional Military Education
QAF   Quality Air Force
SAC   Strategic Air Command
SDI   Strategic Defense Initiative
SEI   Special Experience Identifier
SERE   Survival, Evasion, Resistance, and Escape
SOA   Separate Operating Agency
SP   Security Police
SWC   Special Weapons Command
TAC   Tactical Air Command
TACP   Tactical Air Control Party
TECH TAF   Technical Training Air Force

USAAC   United States Army Air Corps
USAAF   United States Army Air Force
USAAS   United States Army Air Service
USAF   United States Air Force
USAFE   United States Air Forces in Europe
USAFM   United States Air Force Museum
USAFSC   United States Air Forces Southern Command
USSTAF   United States Strategic Air Forces
WAF   Women in the Air Force
WAFS   Women's Auxiliary Ferrying Squadron
WAPS   Weighted Airman Promotion System
WASP   Women Airforce Service Pilots

Bibliography
UNITED STATES AIR FORCE

★

GENERAL WORKS

Aldebol, Anthony. *Army Air Force and United States Air Force: Decorations, Medals, Ribbons, Badges and Insignia.* Fountain Inn, S.C.: Medals of America Press, 2003.

Anderton, David A. *Strategic Air Command: Two-thirds of the Triad.* London: Allan, 1975.

Angelucci, Enzo. *Encyclopedia of Military Aircraft: 1914 to the Present* London: Book Sales, 2001.

Bacevich, A. J. *The Pentomic Era: The U.S. Army between Korea and Vietnam.* Washington, D.C.: Office of Air Force History, 1986.

Barnaby, Frank. *The Automated Battlefield.* New York: Free Press, 1986.

Betts, Richard K. *Cruise Missiles: Technology, Strategy, Politics.* Washington, D.C.: Brookings Institution, 1982.

Bond, Charles, and Terry Anderson. *A Flying Tiger's Diary.* College Station: Texas A&M Press, 1984.

Bowers, Ray L. *The Air Force in Southeast Asia: Tactical Airlift.* Washington, D.C.: Office of Air Force History, 1983.

Bowman, Martin. *The USAF: 1947–1999.* Newbury Park, Calif.: Haynes, 2000.

Bright, Charles D., ed. *Historical Dictionary of the U.S. Air Force.* Westport, Conn.: Greenwood Press, 1992.

Byrd, Martha. *Chennault: Giving Wings to the Tiger.* Tuscaloosa: University of Alabama Press, 1987.

Campbell, Christopher. *Air Warfare: The Fourth Generation.* New York: Arco, 1984.

Chandler, Charles deForest, and Frank P. Lahm. *How Our Army Grew Wings: Airmen and Aircraft before 1914.* New York: Ronald Press, 1943.

Chinnery, Philip D. *Air Commando: Fifty Years of the USAF Air Commando and Special Operations Forces, 1944–1994.* New York: St. Martin's Press, 1997.

Clark, Jerome. *The Emergence of a Phenomenon: UFOs from the Beginning through 1959.* Detroit: Omnigraphics, 1992.

Coffey, Thomas M. *HAP: The Story of the U.S. Air Force and the Man Who Built It—General H. "Hap" Arnold.* New York: Viking, 1982.

———. *Iron Eagle: The Turbulent Life of General Curtis LeMay.* New York: Crown, 1986.

Cole, John H., and Michael F. Monaghan. *Top Cover for America: The Air Force in Alaska, 1920–1983.* Anchorage, Alaska: Anchorage Chapter-Air Force Association; Missoula, Mont.: Pictorial Histories Pub. Co., 1984.

Copp, DeWitt S. *A Few Great Captains: The Men and Events That Shaped the Development of U.S. Air Power.* Garden City, N.Y.: Doubleday, 1980.

Crouch, Tom D. *The Bishop's Boys: A Life of Wilbur and Orville Wright.* New York: Norton, 1989.

Dalfiume, Richard M. *Desegregation of the U.S. Armed Forces: Fighting on Two Fronts, 1939–1953.* Columbia: University of Missouri Press, 1969.

Davis, Burke. *The Billy Mitchell Affair.* New York: Random House, 1967.

Davis, Reed E. *From Aviation Section Signal Corps to United States Air Force.* New York: Vantage, 1984.

Doolittle, James H. (with Carroll V. Glines). *I Could Never Be So Lucky Again*. Reprint ed. New York: Ballantine, 2001.

Dorr, Robert F. *Fighters of the United States Air Force*. New York: Crown, 1990.

———. *Korean War Aces: Aircraft of the Aces*. London: Osprey, 1995.

Drendel, Lou. *Aircraft of the Vietnam War*. Ipswich, UK: Aero, 1980.

Farr, Finis. *Rickenbacker's Luck: An American Life*. Boston: Houghton Mifflin, 1979.

Flammer, Philip. *The Vivid Air: The Lafayette Escadrille*. Athens: University of Georgia Press, 1981.

Ford, Daniel. *Flying Tigers: Claire Chennault and the American Volunteer Group*. Washington, D.C.: Smithsonian Institution Press, 1991.

Foulois, Benjamin D., and Carroll V. Glines. *From the Wright Brothers to the Astronauts: The Memoirs of Major General Benjamin D. Foulois*. New York: McGraw-Hill, 1968.

Francis, Charles E. *The Tuskegee Airmen: The Men Who Changed a Nation*. Boston: Branden, 1997.

Frater, Michael, and Michael Ryan. *Electronic Warfare for the Digitized Battlefield*. Boston: Artech House, 2001.

Freeman, Roger A. *The Mighty Eighth: Units, Men, and Machines*. London: Macdonald and Co., 1970.

Frisbee, John L. *Makers of the United States Air Force*. Washington, D.C.: Office of Air Force History, 1987.

Futrell, Robert F., Riley Sunderland, and Martin Blumenson. *The Air Force in Southeast Asia: The Advisory Years, to 1965*. Washington, D.C.: Office of Air Force History, 1980.

Getz, C. W. "Bill," ed. *The Wild Blue Yonder: Songs of the Air Force*, vol. 1. Burlingame, Calif.: Redwood Press, 1981.

Glines, Carroll V. *The Compact History of the United States Air Force*. New York: Hawthorne Books, 1963.

Goodall, James C. *America's Stealth Fighters and Bombers*. Osceola, Wisc.: Motorbooks International, 1992.

Gordon, Michael R., and Bernard E. Trainor. *The Generals' War: The Inside Story of the Conflict in the Gulf*. Boston: Little, Brown, 1995.

Gorn, Michael H. *Vulcan's Forge: The Making of an Air Force Command for Weapons Acquisition, 1950–1986*. Andrews AFB, Md.: Office of History, Headquarters, Air Force Systems Command, 1986.

Gray, Colin S. *Missiles for the Nineties: ICBMs and Strategic Policy*. Denver: Westview, 1984.

Gregory, Shaun R. *Nuclear Command and Control in NATO: Nuclear Weapons Operations and the Strategy of Flexible Response*. London: Palgrave Macmillan, 1996.

Gropman, Alan L. *The Air Force Integrates, 1945–1964*. Washington, D.C.: Office of Air Force History, 1978.

Gross, Charles J. *The Air National Guard: A Short History*. Washington, D.C.: National Guard Bureau Historical Services Division, 1994.

Gunston, Bill, and Peter Gilchrist. *Jet Bombers: From the Messerschmidt Me 262 to the Stealth B-2*. Osceola, Wisc.: Motorbooks International, 1993.

Hallion, Richard P. *Strike from the Sky: The History of Battlefield Air Attack, 1911–1945*. Washington, D.C.: Smithsonian Institution Press, 1989.

———. *Test Pilots: The Frontiersmen of Flight*. Washington, D.C.: Smithsonian Institution Press, 1988.

Haydock, Michael D. *City Under Siege: The Berlin Blockade and Airlift, 1948–1949*. New York: Brassey's, 2000.

Heflin, Woodford A., ed. *The United States Air Force Dictionary*. Princeton, N.J.: Van Nostrand, 1956.

Hiscock, Melvyn. *Classic Aircraft of World War I*. London: Osprey, 1994.

Holder, Bill. *Planes of the Presidents: An Illustrated History of Air Force One*. Atglen, Pa.: Schiffer, 2000.

Holman, Lynn M., and Thomas Reilly. *Black Knights: The Story of the Tuskegee Airmen*. Gretna, La.: Pelican, 2001.

Holoway, John B. *Red Tails Black Wings: The Men of America's Black Air Force*. Las Cruces, N.M.: Yucca Tree Press, 2000.

Holsinger, Paul, and Mary Anne Schofield, eds. *Visions of War: World War II in Popular Literature and Culture* (1992).

Hudson, James J. *Hostile Skies: A Combat History of the American Air Service in World War I*. Syracuse, N.Y.: Syracuse University Press, 1968.

Hurley, Alfred F. *Billy Mitchell: Crusader for Air Power.* Bloomington: Indiana University Press, 1975.

Jackson, Robert. *Air War over Korea.* London: Allan, 1973.

———. *High Cold War: Strategic Air Reconnaissance and the Electronic Intelligence War.* Newbury Park, Calif.: Haynes, 1998.

Kenney, George C. *Dick Bong: Ace of Aces.* New York: Duell, Sloan and Pearce, 1960.

Lashmar, Paul. *Spy Flights in the Cold War.* Annapolis, Md.: U.S. Naval Institute Press, 1998.

Leyden, Andrew, ed. *Gulf War Debriefing Book: An After Action Report.* Grants Pass, Ore.: Hellgate Press, 1997.

Littauer, Raphael, and Norman Uphoff, eds. *The Air War in Indochina.* Revised ed. Boston: Beacon Press, 1972.

Lloyd, Alwyn T. *A Cold War Legacy: A Tribute to Strategic Air Command, 1946–1992.* Missoula, Mont.: Pictorial Histories, 2000.

Maurer, Maurer. *Air Force Combat Units of World War II.* Washington, D.C.: Office of Air Force History, 1983.

McDaid, Hugh, and David Oliver. *Smart Weapons.* New York: Barnes & Noble, 2001.

McGuire, Nina. *Jacqueline Cochran: America's Fearless Aviator.* Lake Buena Vista, Fla.: Tailored Tours Publications, 1997.

Meilinger, Phillip S. *Hoyt S. Vandenberg: The Life of a General.* Bloomington: Indiana University Press, 1989.

Mets, David R. *Master of Air Power: General Carl A. Spaatz.* Novato, Calif.: Presidio, 1988.

Miller, Charles E. *Airlift Doctrine.* Maxwell Air Force Base, Ala.: Air University Press, 1988.

Mondey, David. *American Aircraft of World War II.* London: Book Sales, 2002.

Mzorek, Donald J. *Air Power and the Ground War in Vietnam.* Washington, D.C.: Office of Air Force History, 1988.

Neufeld, Jacob. *Ballistic Missiles in the United States Air Force, 1945–1960.* Washington, D.C.: Office of Air Force History, 1990.

O'Leary, Michael. *High Viz: U.S. Cold War Aircraft.* London: Osprey, 1995.

Osur, Alan M. *Blacks in the Army Air Forces during World War II.* Washington, D.C.: Office of Air Force History, 1977.

Parrish, Thomas. *Berlin in the Balance, 1945–1949: The Blockade, the Airlift, the First Major Battle of the Cold War.* New York: Perseus, 1999.

Robinson, Douglas. *The Dangerous Sky: A History of Aviation Medicine.* Seattle: University of Washington Press, 1973.

Ross, Stewart Halsey. *Strategic Bombing by the United States in World War II: The Myths and the Facts.* Jefferson, N.C.: McFarland, 2002.

Rottman, Gordon. *U.S. Army Air Force Uniforms.* London: Osprey, 1998.

Shaw, Robert L. *Fighter Combat: Tactics and Maneuvering.* Annapolis, Md.: Naval Institute Press, 1985.

Smythe, Donald. *Punitive Expedition: Pershing's Pursuit of Villa, 1916–1917. Bloomington: Indiana University Press, 1985.*

Snyder, Thomas S., ed. *The Air Force Communications Command 1938–1986: An Illustrated History.* Washington, D.C.: U.S. Government Printing Office, 1986.

Stout, Joseph A. *Border Conflict: Villistas, Carrancistas and the Punitive Expedition.* Fort Worth: Texas Christian University Press, 1999.

Straubel, James H. *Crusade for Air Power: The Story of the Air Force Association.* Washington, D.C.: Aerospace Education Foundation, 1982.

Sullivan, George. *Famous Air Force Fighters.* New York: Dodd, Mead, 1985.

Taylor, Michael J. H., *Jane's Encyclopedia of Aviation.* New York: Crescent, 1989.

Thayer, Lucien. *America's First Eagles: The Official History of the U.S. Army Air Service.* Reprint ed. San Jose, Calif.: R.J. Bender Pub.; Mesa, Ariz.: Champlin Fighter Museum Press, 1983.

Tilford, Earl H., Jr. *Setup: What the Air Force Did to Vietnam and Why.* Honolulu: University Press of the Pacific, 1991.

Valey, Wayne A. *Airman's Guide.* 4th ed. Mechanicsburg, Pa.: Stackpole, 1997.

Yenne, Bill. *The History of the US Air Force.* New York: Crown, 1984.

MISCELLANEOUS

Basic Aerospace Doctrine of the United States Air Force, Air Force Manual 1-1. Washington, D.C.: Department of the Air Force, 1984.

USAF Fact Sheet. "Air Force Bands," at http://www.af.mil/news/factsheets/Air_Force_Bands.html

USAF Fact Sheet. "Air Force Center for Environmental Excellence," at http://www.af.mil/news/factsheets/Air_Force_Center_for_Environm.html

USAF Fact Sheet. "Air Force Civil Engineer Support Agency," at http://www.af.mil/news/factsheets/Air_Force_Civil_Engineer_Supp.html

USAF Fact Sheet. "Air Force Doctrine Center," available at http://www.af.mil/news/factsheets/Air_Force_Doctrine_Center_.html

U.S. Air Force. Air Force Information Warfare Center Public Web, at http://afiwcweb.lackland.af.mil/

USAF Fact Sheet. "Air Force Inspection Agency," at http://www.af.mil/news/factsheets/Air_Force_Inspection_Agency.html

Suggested reading: USAF Fact Sheet. "Air Force News Agency," available at http://www.af.mil/news/factsheets/Air_Force_News_Agency.html

U.S. Air Force. *USAF Scientific Advisory Board Charter,* at www.odam.osd.mil/omp/pdf/439.pdf

U.S. Air Force. "Air Warfare Center," at http://www.nellis.af.mil/units/awfc/

U.S. Air Force. "Organization and Lineage: Numbered Air Forces," www.au.af.mil/au/afhra/org11.htm

U.S. Air Force. "USAF Fact Sheet: Organization of the U.S. Air Force," www.af.mil/news/factsheets/usaf.html

USAF Fact Sheet. "Air Force Recruiting Service," at http://www.af.mil/news/factsheets/Air_Force_Recruiting_Service.html

USAF Fact Sheet. "Thunderbirds," at http://www.af.mil/news/factsheets/Thunderbirds.html

Air Force News Service. "Air Force Unveils New Uniform," at http://usmilitary.about.com/cs/airforce/a/newafuniform.htm

Tuskegee Airmen, Incorporated. "Who Were the Tuskegee Airmen in World War II?" at www.tuskegeeairmen.org/MainFrameset.htm

Index

Page numbers in **boldface** indicate primary discussions. Page numbers in *italic* indicate illustrations.

A

A-1 Skyraider 16
A-7 Corsair II 16
A-10 Thunderbolt II 4–5, *33*, 160
A-12 Shrike 10
A-20 Havoc 24
AAFAC (Army Air Forces Antisubmarine Command) **83**
abbreviations and acronyms 223–225
ACC. *See* Alaskan Air Command
ACC (Air Combat Command) **2–3**
ace 93–95, 166
ACM (AGM-129A Advanced Cruise Missile) 147
ADC (Aerospace Defense Command) **1**
ADM-20 Quail missile 146
ADM (air decoy missile) 146
AEDC (Arnold Engineering Development Center) **85**
AEF. *See* AmericanExpeditionary Force
Aerial Achievement Medal 105
Aeronautical Division, U.S. Army Signal Corps **1**, 98–99, 123, 139
Aerospace Defense Command (ADC) **1**
AETC. *See* Air Education and Training Command
AFAA (Air Force Audit Agency) **30**
AFA (Air Force Association) **30**
AFAMS (Air Force Agency for Modeling and Simulation) **30**
AFBCA (Air Force Base Conversion Agency) **32**
AFCAA (Air Force Cost Analysis Agency) **55**
AFC (Air Force Council) **55**
AFCC. *See* Air Force Combat Command
AFCC (Air Force Communications Command) **54**
AFCCC (Air Force Combat Climatology Center) **54**
AFCCCA (Air Force Command, Control Communications, and Computer Agency) **54**

AFCEE (Air Force Center for Environmental Excellence) **52–53**
AFCERT (Air Force Computer Emergency Response Team) **54**
AFCESA (Air Force Civil Engineer Support Agency) **53–54**
AFCOMS (Air Force Commissary Service) **54**
AFCQMI (Air Force Center for Quality and Management Innovation) **53**
AFCSTC (Air Force Cost Center) **55**
AFDC (Air Force Doctrine Center) **56–57**
AFDTC (Air Force Development Test Center) **56**
AFESC (Air Force Engineering and Services Center) **57**
AFFMA (Air Force Frequency Management Agency) **57**
AFFSA (Air Force Flight Standards Agency) **57**
AFFTC (Air Force Flight Test Center) **57**
Afghanistan 5, 16, 125
AFHF (Air Force Historical Foundation) **58**
AFHRA (Air Force Historical Research Agency) **58**
AFHSO (Air Force History Support Office) **58**
AFIA (Air Force Inspection Agency) **58–59**
AFIA (Force Intelligence Agency) **59–60**
AFISC (Air Force Inspection and Safety Center) **59**
AFIT (Air Force Institute Technology) **59**
AFIWC (Air Force Information Warfare Center) **58**
AFLC (Air Force Logistics Command) **60**
AFLMA (Air Force Logistics Management Agency) **60**

AFLSA (Air Force Legal Services Agency) **60**
AFMC (Air Force Materiel Command) **60**
AFMEA (Air Force Management Engineering Agency) **60**
AFMIA (Air Force Manpower and Innovation Agency) **60**
AFMOA (Air Force Medical Operations Agency) **61**
AFMSA (Air Force Medical Support Agency) **61**
AFNEWS (Air Force News Agency) **61–62**
AFNSEP (Air Force National Security Emergency Preparedness) **61**
AFNWCA (Air Force Nuclear Weapons and Counterproliferation Agency) **62**
AFOG (Air Force Operations Group) **65**
AFOMS (Air Force Office of Medical Support) **62–63**
AFOSI (Air Force Office of Special Investigations) **63–64**
AFOSP (Air Force Office of Security Police) **63**
AFOSR (Air Force Office of Scientific Research) **63**
AFOTEC (Air Force Operational Test and Evaluation Center) **65**
AFPC (Air Force Personnel Center) **66**
AFPCA (Air Force Pentagon Communications Agency) **66**
AFPEO (Air Force Program Executive Office) **66**
AFPOA (Air Force Personnel Operations Agency) **66**
AFR. *See* Air Force Reserve
AFRBA (Air Force Review Boards Agency) **70**
AFRC (Air Force Reserve Command) **69**
AFREA (Air Force Real Estate Agency) **66**

World War II: Pacific/Asian
theaters 213–214
Roosevelt, Theodore 123
Ross, Mac *179*
Rostow, Walt 197
ROTC (Reserve Officers Training Corps)
140. *See also* Air Force Reserve Officer
Training Corps
Royal Air Force (RAF) 208–212, 217,
218
Russia 205, 211, 213. *See also* cold war;
Soviet Union
Russian Revolution 213
Ryan, John D. 191

S

SAB (Air Force Scientific Advisory
Board) **71**
Sabre Jet (film) 115
SAC. *See* Strategic Air Command
Saint-Mihiel 149, 207–208
Salmson 2A-2 23
SALT I 173
San Juan Hill, Battle of 90
saturation bombing 210
Saudi Arabia 158
Schriever AFB, Colorado 48
Schwarzkopf, H. Norman 158
Schweinfurt raid 210
Scott, Frank S. 48
Scott, Winfield 89
Scott AFB, Illinois 48, 77, 143
Scud missile 159
SDI. *See* Strategic Defense Initiative
SEATO. *See* Southeast Asia Treaty
Organization
Second Air Force (2AF) 131, **168**
second lieutenant (rank/grade) 164
secretary of the Air Force **168**
segregation 1, 180
SEIs (Special Experience Identifiers)
172
Selected Reserve 68
Selfridge, Thomas E. 91, **168**
Selfridge Air Base, Michigan 179
Sembach AB, Germany 49
senior master sergeant (rank/grade) 164
September 11, 2001 terrorist attacks 125
SERE (Survival, Evasion, Resistance, and
Escape) **174**
sergeant/senior airman (rank/grade)
165
service associations **169**
Seventeenth Air Force (17AF) **169**
17th parallel 195
Seventh Air Force (7AF) **169–170**, 200,
216
Seversky Aircraft 11

sexual assault scandal 185–186
Seymour Johnson AFB, North Carolina
49, 152
Shafter, William R. 90
Shaw, Ervin D. 49
Shaw AFB, South Carolina 49
Shell Oil 110
Shemya AFB, Alaska 49–50
Shenandoah (dirigible) 150
Sheppard, Morris E. 50
Sheppard AFB, Texas 50
Sherburne, John H. 87
shuttle raids (WWII) 140, 211
Sicily 153, 209
Signal Corps 90, 98, 109, 166, 191
Sijan, Lance P. 108
Sikorsky 10, 15, 22
Sino-Japanese War 81
Sixteenth Air Force (16AF) **170**
Sixth Air Force (6AF) **170**
67th Intelligence Wing 75
Skybolt (GAM-87A) missile 145
Slavec, Laurie S. 186
SM-75 Thor Missile. *See* Thor Missile
Small Arms Expert Marksmanship
Ribbon 108
smart weapons 174
Smith, Joseph 92
snafu 118
Snark (SM-62) missile 145
Soesterberg AB, Netherlands 50
Solomon Islands 215
SOS 118
Southeast Asia Treaty Organization
(SEATO) 20, 196
Soviet Union 91–93, 133, 173, 193, 211.
See also cold war
Spaatz, Carl A. ("Tooey") 166, *171*,
171–172
space doctrine 30, **172**
Spad XIII 23, 139, 207
Spangdahlem AB, Germany 50
Spanish-American War 90, 119, 123,
149
Spanish language instruction 126–127
Special Experience Identifiers (SEIs)
172
Special Operations Forces 73, 160
Special Weapons Command (SWC) **172**
Springs, Elliott White 141
Sputnik I 63
squadron 156
SR-71 "Blackbird" *9,* 9–10, 125
SRAM (AGM-69 Short-Range Attack
Missile) 146
staff sergeant (rank/grade) 165
Stalin, Josef 133, 211, 213
Standby Reserve 68
START II treaty 127, 145

Star Wars. *See* Strategic Defense
Initiative
stealth aircraft 5–6, *172,* **172–173**
Stearman Aircraft Company 12
Stilwell, Joseph Warren 100
Strategic Air Command (film) 115
Strategic Air Command (SAC) **173**
B-70 Valkyrie 5
C-135 Stratolifter 6
8AF 111–112
15AF 114
history/overview of USAF 124
IRBM 128
Curtis LeMay 141
16AF 170
Vietnam War 199
Strategic Defense Initiative (SDI, "Star
Wars") 63, **173–174**
Stratemeyer, George E. 134, 137
Sudentenland 213
supersonic flight 101, 102
surface-to-air missiles 132
surgical bombing 159, **174**
Survival, Evasion, Resistance, and Escape
(SERE) **174**
SWC (Special Weapons Command) **172**
Sweet Vietnam (Richard Parque) 142
Symington, W. Stuart 154, *171*

T

T-6 Texan 29
T-28 Trojan 16
T-37 Tweet 21, *22*
T-38 Talon 21–22, *29,* 178
T-39 Sabreliner 22
TAC. *See* Tactical Air Command
TACP (Tactical Air Control Party) **175**
Tactical Air Command (TAC) 152, **175**
Tactical Air Control Party (TACP) **175**
Talbott, Harold 185
Taylor, Maxwell 197, 199
technical sergeant (rank/grade)
164–165
Technical Training Air Force (TECH
TAF) **175**
TECH TAF (Technical Training Air
Force) **175**
Tenth Air Force (10AF) **175–176**, 217,
218
Terry, Roger "Bill" 180
test facilities 85
test pilots 95, 101–102, 142, **176,**
187–188
Tet offensive 199–200
Texas Instruments 146
Thailand 169, 177, 194
Thieu, Nguyen Van 201
Third Air Force (3AF) **176–177**